THE GREAT HISTORIES

A series under the general editorship of

Hugh R. Trevor-Roper,

REGIUS PROFESSOR OF MODERN HISTORY, OXFORD UNIVERSITY

JOSEPHUS: THE JEWISH WAR

and

Other Selections

THE GREAT HISTORIES *Series*

HERODOTUS, *edited by W. G. Forrest.*

THUCYDIDES, *edited by P. A. Brunt.*

POLYBIUS, *edited by E. Badian.*

JOSEPHUS, *edited by Moses I. Finley.*

TACITUS, *edited by Hugh Lloyd-Jones.*

PROCOPIUS, *edited by Mrs. Averil Cameron.*

BEDE, *edited by James Campbell.*

AMMIANUS MARCELLINUS, *edited by Geoffrey de Ste. Croix.*

MACHIAVELLI, *edited by Myron P. Gilmore.*

GUICCIARDINI, *edited by J. R. Hale.*

SARPI, *edited by Peter Burke.*

VOLTAIRE, *edited by J. H. Brumfitt.*

GIBBON, *edited by Hugh R. Trevor-Roper.*

PRESCOTT, *edited by Roger Howell.*

MACAULAY, *edited by Hugh R. Trevor-Roper.*

BURCKHARDT, *edited by Alexander Dru.*

HENRY ADAMS, *edited by E. N. Saveth.*

JOSEPHUS, *Flavius*

THE JEWISH WAR
and Other Selections

Translated by H. St. J. Thackeray
and Ralph Marcus

Edited and Abridged
with an Introduction by

MOSES I. FINLEY

FELLOW OF JESUS COLLEGE
AND READER IN ANCIENT SOCIAL AND ECONOMIC HISTORY
UNIVERSITY OF CAMBRIDGE

TWAYNE PUBLISHERS, INC.
31 Union Square, N. Y. 3

The selections from *The Life, Against Apion, The Jewish Antiquities,*
and *The Jewish War* are from the Loeb Classical Library edition of
Josephus, translated by H. St. J. Thackeray and Ralph Marcus and
published by Harvard University Press. They are reprinted here
by permission of the publisher and the Loeb Classical Library.

Contents

CONTENTS

Introduction

JOSEPHUS' LIFE AND WORKS

If ever a man had greatness thrust upon him, that man was Joseph ben Matthias, who was born in Jerusalem in A.D. 37/38[1] into an aristocratic, priestly family, and who died about the year 100 as Flavius Josephus, a Roman citizen and protégé of the emperors Vespasian and Titus. He wrote four works in Greek and projected, but did not finish or publish, two others. The four which he completed were *The Jewish War*, the story of the revolt of the Jews against Roman rule in the years A.D. 66-70, at the beginning of which Josephus himself played a prominent part; *The Jewish Antiquities*, a long history starting from Adam and Eve; a very unbalanced *Autobiography*, which seems to have been first published as an appendix to a second edition of the *Antiquities;* and a lengthy apologetic tract, *Against Apion* (or *A Reply to Apion*).[2] The two which he projected were a brief history of the Jews after their defeat by the Romans and a great work in Jewish theology.

All four of Josephus' published works have survived in full, an uncommon fate among the writings of Græco-Roman antiquity, and one not shared by many far greater writers. Until the invention of printing in the fifteenth century, the survival of literature written in ancient Greek or Latin was normally possible only if manuscripts were copied and re-copied by hand in medieval European and Byzantine monasteries. This obvi-

---

[1] It is usually necessary to express ancient dates in this way when the month is unknown because the New Year in the various ancient calendars did not coincide with our January 1st.

[2] I shall use conventional Latin abbreviations for these works: BJ—*Jewish War;* A—*Antiquities;* V—*Autobiography;* Ap—*Against Apion.*

ously implied approval, or at least not severe disapproval, by devout Christians, who lacked the instinct to preserve solely for the sake of preservation. Two or three Latin translations were prepared in the fourth and fifth centuries, from one of which a Hebrew paraphrase was made, probably early in the eleventh century. *The Jewish War* was also translated into Old Slavonic in the Middle Ages, and that version, as we shall see, is of particular interest in connection with Josephus' references to Christianity. Nearer our own day, it was not long ago that a household in England was expected to possess at least two books, a Bible and a Josephus in the translation by William Whiston, published in 1737.

Altogether, this is a phenomenal record of success and longevity. What a pity it is, therefore, that everything we know about Josephus—every scrap—comes from himself, and what he tells us is neither very full nor very trustworthy. The main source is, of course, his *Autobiography,* which in some respects repeats a portion of *The Jewish War,* and which is supplemented, at least for an insight into his mentality, by the polemical *Against Apion.* Together these sources provide some basic facts about his life.

Josephus was given the training appropriate to his station, that of a future priest in a community which had a thin veneer of late Greek (or Hellenistic) culture in its upper classes. He was a child prodigy, or so he says: "When still a mere boy, about fourteen years old, . . . the chief priests and the leading men of the city used constantly to come to me for precise information on some particular in our ordinances" (V, 2).[3] At nineteen he opted for the Pharisees. He had three wives, at one time or another, and three sons. And that is all we know, apart from the fact that in 64 he went on a private mission to Rome to appeal to Nero on behalf of several fellow-countrymen threatened with "a slight and trifling charge," until the crucial years 66-67, when the Jewish authorities in Jerusalem sent him to Galilee

---

[3] For the subdivision of Josephus' works into books and sections, see p. xxxiii of the Introduction.

on an assignment which ended with his capture by the Romans at Jotapata. The rest of his life was spent in Rome under the protection and patronage of the emperors, and he devoted his time to his writing, with one important interlude—when he accompanied Titus to the siege of Jerusalem in 70 and made repeated efforts to persuade the Jews to surrender, all described in elaborate detail in his account of the war.

The odd thing about the *Autobiography* is its fantastic lack of proportion. Of its 76 sections, no less than 68 are devoted to the months in Galilee. And what makes that odder is the fact that Josephus had already told the story in *The Jewish War*. In the earlier work, the picture is of a country up in arms against the Romans, of acceptance of the situation by the Jerusalem authorities, who proceed to select generals for the various regions, among them Josephus to take charge in Galilee. In the *Autobiography*, however, everything is uncertain and fluid, and his initial role seems rather to be that of a pacifier: "Being informed, moreover, that the whole of Galilee had not yet revolted from Rome, and that a portion of it was still tranquil, they dispatched me with two other priests . . . to induce the disaffected to lay down their arms," the general policy being to "wait and see what action the Romans would take" (V, 7). In the end, and after being suspected of an intention to betray the country, Josephus was forced to commit himself to the war, chose to stand siege at Jotapata, and held out for 47 days.

The two statements are not wholly contradictory, but neither can they be reconciled; this is a fact not to be underestimated. Any historian has a right to make a mistake or to change his mind, but here we are faced with a problem of a different order. No man "forgets" why he was given a mission that marked the turning-point of his life. The reason why Josephus felt called upon to write his second account is stated clearly enough in section 65 of the *Autobiography*. Near the end of the century, another version of the war had been published, also in Greek and also by an upper-class Jew— Justus, a native of Tiberias in Galilee. This account was part of Justus' *Antiquities,* which began with Moses and ended with his own day. Unfortunately the book has not survived, and we are back to Josephus again, whose statements about Justus simply cannot be trusted. Josephus obviously won the argument, for Justus seems not to have been much read in subsequent centuries, judging from the paucity of quotations among later writers. He survived, it may be worth adding, at least until the ninth century, when he could still be read by Photius, the Byzantine *savant* and patron of learning who became Patriarch of Constantinople in 858. Photius made notes on his reading which he later published. Justus, he says, writes "with extreme conciseness; he merely runs through most of the bare essentials." And, he continues, "the history which he has written is for the most part, they say, pure invention, especially when he treats of the war between the Romans and the Jews and the capture of Jerusalem." Perhaps, but Photius wouldn't know, and he really did not claim to know, passing the responsibility for the negative judgment to others—"they say."

Two things, however, are fairly certain about Justus and his work. He and his pro-Roman family had not been among the rebels, and he charged Josephus with having been one of the instigators of the revolt. That hurt. Vespasian and Titus were dead by now, and Josephus could no longer feel quite secure. Hence the *Autobiography,* and hence its peculiar structure, as he strove to defend his life at the only point that mattered—the years 66 and 67—to offer his *Apologia pro vita sua* to the Romans. *Against Apion* was a defense of his ancestry and his faith (to which, in his way, he always remained loyal) against the accusations which were so common in his world. In the *Autobiography* he defended himself as an individual, on a political charge.

It is no use pretending that all this adds up to a pretty picture, either of the man or of the world in which he lived. Neither was pretty in many (perhaps in most) respects. To understand how Josephus got himself caught up in its nastier aspects, it is necessary to look at the history of Judæa and of its relations with Rome and the Roman Empire.

JUDAEA AND ROME

Judæa is an ill-defined region lying between the Dead Sea and the Mediterranean. The whole district of western Asia which we call Palestine, with its varied terrain of fertile land, mountain, and desert, had been the scene of perpetual migration, conquest, and conflict for thousands of years—and still is, for that matter, for much the same reasons. Its mixture of people was fantastic. So were its politics, for the land (and its location with respect to Arabia and Egypt to the south, Syria to the north, and the so-called Fertile Crescent to the east) lent itself to warring petty dynasts, loose tribal confederations, and incredibly large bands of nomads and outlaws in the deserts and mountains. All this is familiar enough from the Old Testament, and not too much was changed even when a great power tried to rule the country from outside. Before the Romans, the last such effort was made by the Græco-Oriental monarchy established in Syria and Babylon some time after the death of Alexander the Great, known as the Seleucid kingdom. For a period their control was fairly effective, aided by a newly developed Hellenizing faction within the Jewish upper class (what would be called an assimilationist party today). But about 166 B.C., King Antiochus IV Epiphanes and the Hellenizers blundered: they broke all precedent and tried to tamper with the religion, thereby inciting a nationalist revolt that was at once a war of independence and a resurgence of strict religious and cultural traditionalism. The rebellion was led by the Hasmonæan family, notably Mattathias and his son Judas, surnamed Maccabæus. After many vicissitudes it succeeded, thanks in part to a growing debility within the Seleucid monarchy.

Judæa under the Hasmonæans, who became autocratic (and increasingly unpopular) priest-kings, was independent once again, for the last time until the twentieth century, and it flourished materially. Neighboring territories were conquered, and some of them were forcibly converted to Judaism. One may properly speak of a Greater Judæa at the beginning of the first century B.C., but of a short-lived one. The inevitable internal conflicts, in which dynastic rivalries within the ruling family overlapped class and religious conflicts, opened the door to both strong and ambitious neighbors and to the far more powerful, though more distant, Roman state. The Romans had come into conflict with the Seleucids and other eastern rulers as far back as the beginning of the second century B.C. Now Roman armies were actively campaigning in the east to. meet the threat of Mithridates, king of Pontus' on the Black Sea (about whom more will be said later), and this time Rome proposed to settle the political situation in the area permanently, and on her own terms. In 63 B.C., Judæa fell to the Romans under Pompey, who preferred not to take over the country as a Roman province, but to establish a client-king, first stripping Greater Judæa of all but its really Jewish core (which included Galilee). Pompey's settlement failed to put an end to the feuding, as the various factions and dynasties took advantage of the civil war raging in Rome itself and now entering its final, most virulent phase. Pompey, Cæsar, Antony, and Augustus were all appealed to, allied with, and variously drawn into the Judæan picture. The winner in the end was Herod, an Idumæan (Edomite in the Biblical language), who became governor of Galilee in 47 B.C., at the age of twenty-five, and king of the Jews in 40.

Herod was a remarkable figure, thoroughly ruthless and odious. The mere fact that in the conditions of the age he could hold the throne from 40 to his death in 4 B.C. is proof enough, all the more so when it is remembered that he supported the losing side in the Roman civil war twice—first Cassius, one of Cæsar's assassins, then Marc Antony. His murders and executions cannot be counted. They included all surviving male Hasmonæans; his uncle Joseph (who was also his sister Salome's husband); his second wife, the Hasmonæan Mariamme I[4], and her mother; his two sons by her, Alexander and Aristobulus; another of Salome's husbands, named Costobar; and, five days before his own death, his eldest son, Antipater. His wealth, however, can be counted; Josephus gives it to us in detail. Obviously, Judæa could not have produced it all, not even under Herod's extortions. His interests and the territories under his control were far-flung, many of them not Jewish at all. This considerable extension of rule from Jerusalem under Herod cannot be called Greater Judæa (as under the Hasmonæans), for it was Herod's personal sovereignty which was involved, in the standard practice of the Greek East after Alexander the Great, and not an extension of the state of Judæa. Even within Judæa the nature of his rule is best exemplified by the vast palace-fortresses he constructed, both in Jerusalem and at Masada, which were carefully described by Josephus.

Was Herod a Jew? This is no frivolous question, and the answer "Yes," though technically correct, is insufficient. His immediate ancestors were among the forcible converts of the Hasmonæan period, and his enemies were quick to call him a Gentile. That was not really fair. He was apparently careful to obey the ritual requirements, once even calling off an important dynastic marriage he had arranged for Salome when the prospective husband refused to become converted and be circumcised. Because of the Second Commandment, he denied himself the standard Hellenistic privilege of putting his own portrait on his coins. He ate no pork. Beyond all this, he tried to aid the Jewish communities in lands outside his control. And he rebuilt the Temple on a scale and with a magnificence that would have made Solomon himself envious.

But the Gentile charge was not altogether ungrounded either. Herod secularized his government, divorcing the

---

[4] It is very hard to avoid confusion over names in this period because the royal and aristocratic families used a few, Hebrew and Greek, over and over. That is why I have sometimes resorted to the convention (in the text of Josephus as well) of employing Roman numerals for clarification.

throne from the high-priesthood, which he controlled
and manipulated at will. Some of his closest associates
and highest officials were not Jews, such as the historian Nicolaus, a Græco-Syrian from Damascus. In the
non-Jewish territories over which he ruled he was a
proper Hellenistic monarch, not a Jewish king, allowing statues of himself to be erected in public places,
fostering local cults and financing their temples. He
called his seaport Cæsarea and set up a temple to Rome
and Augustus there. He rebuilt Samaria and named it
Sebaste, which is Greek for Augusta. In Jerusalem itself he tried to introduce the most typical of all Roman
sports, the gladiatorial shows.

Culturally, at least, it was no longer so easy to de-
fine a Jew. Josephus was not exaggerating much when
he wrote, in the course of a long speech attributed to
Agrippa II, that "there is not a people in the world
which does not contain a portion of our race" (BJ, II,
xvi, 4). Many Jews had not returned from the Babylonian captivity, so that there was a large Jewish population east of the Euphrates River, well outside Roman
territory. There were Jews throughout Palestine and
Syria. There was a very large colony in Egypt, mostly
concentrated in Alexandria (though nothing like the
million asserted by the great Jewish philosopher of
Alexandria, Philo), and from there they spread west to
Cyrenaica (modern Libya). There were small communities in the cities of Asia Minor (modern Turkey) and
Greece, and in Rome itself Jews may have numbered
50,000 at this time, with no fewer than eleven different
synagogues or congregations that can be identified today.

It was in Egypt that the Pentateuch was translated
into Greek (the Septuagint) as early as the middle of
the third century B.C. The reason was quite simply that
the Jews of Egypt no longer knew enough Hebrew. Nor
did the Jews of Cyrene or Greece. In Rome, too, their
language was Greek, as is evidenced by hundreds of
tombstones, on which Hebrew or Aramaic appears only
four or five times, Latin more frequently but far less
often than Greek. And with language went other things,

especially among the intellectuals and the upper classes: the Greek gymnasium, Greek philosophy, Greek mistresses. On his mission to Rome in 64, Josephus was able to obtain the good offices of one Aliturus, "an actor who was a special favorite of Nero and of Jewish origin" (V, 3). But Judæa was different. There the Jews were not foreign elements within a foreign cultural and political complex; they were at home. There they could rule their lives according to their traditional laws, with their traditional ritual calendar, in their own language (which was now Aramaic rather than Hebrew), without having to accommodate themselves in any way to the dominant culture; without having to find a synthesis of their history with Greek history, of their religion with Greek philosophy, or of their daily practices with the requirements of Hellenistic rulers. They *could*, but not all would: the pull of the surrounding Hellenistic way of life was strong, and the upper classes of Judæa could not altogether resist. There had been trouble over this under Antiochus Epiphanes. Ironically, the later Hasmonæans again fell victim, and now there was Herod and his court.

It was this conflict which seems to lie behind the emergence of the "sects." Our chief witness is Josephus, who was writing too late to throw any light on their origins. But the plausible hypothesis has been put forward that the Pharisees arose as an opposition to the Hasmonean combination of the kingship with the high priesthood. At any rate, there is no doubt that the Sadducees were drawn from the court, the priesthood, and the landed magnates, and that they were the tolerant group, to put it most mildly, with respect to surface Hellenization (though there does not seem sufficient warrant for the later tradition that they had become irreligious and apostates). Against them, the Pharisees stood for strict interpretation of the law and the traditions. This position led them into opposition and conflict under the Hasmonæans; it was to bring the whole state tumbling down under the Romans.

After Herod's death, the Romans put up with a decade of mean and brutal squabbling among his heirs and then decided they had had enough. In A.D. 6, Judæa was incorporated into the Roman provincial system. The details of the reorganization are complicated and not very interesting. What really matters is that the growing lower-class rebelliousness, rooted in economic distress, now turned, perforce, against Rome, and acquired a nationalist character. But it did not lose its religious sectarianism in the process, and the triple combination created a unique situation for Rome. Dislike and even hatred of Roman rule in the eastern half of the Empire were widespread, but impotent. Only when a remarkable character like Mithridates came marching out of the east did the full measure of that feeling break onto the surface: at his order 80,000 Romans and Italians in the east had been massacred by the local populations in the year 88 B.C. The Romans had eventually defeated Mithridates, and no other province thereafter gave them so much trouble, in proportion to its negligible size and resources, as Judæa. There, it would seem, every popular preacher was distrusted as a potential inciter of rebellion by the Roman and Jewish authorities alike, and for good reason. That is why the old and still continuing debate as to who was responsible for the indictment and condemnation of Jesus, the Sanhedrin or Pilate, is so irrelevant. On the correct attitude to be taken towards popular preachers, the Romans and the Jewish establishment were of one mind.

This political and social discontent culminated in the great revolt in Judæa in A.D. 66-70—the subject of Josephus' *Jewish War*. The impetus came from the lower classes, inspired by the Zealot sect, but in the end it was a national undertaking which cost the Roman legions great effort before they could suppress it. In 66, Nero put Vespasian, then a general, in charge of operations in Palestine. Then came Nero's suicide in 68, followed by a brief but very sharp struggle for power in Rome out of which Vespasian emerged as the successful contender in 69. Vespasian could therefore not remain in the field, and he turned the command over to his elder son Titus, who captured Jerusalem in 70. Titus, in his turn, became Roman emperor on his father's death in the year 79.

One need read only a few pages of Josephus to appreciate the unhappy state of mind that the revolt generated among many of his class. True, Josephus was a Pharisee, not a Sadducee, but a change had come over the sects. The Pharisees had more or less split into right and left wings. The former abandoned its political role and was content to differ from the Sadducees on certain doctrinal matters; the latter, the Zealots, became a truly revolutionary faction, with an apparently secret organization based partly on outlaw bands in the mountains and deserts, but with a considerable following in the cities as well. Josephus relentlessly and monotonously calls them "bandits" or "robbers." In a strict legal sense, some of them were, but his language is more than technical correctness; it reveals precisely how close to pure class war Judæa had now come. Josephus underplays and effectively conceals the *programmatic* side of the Zealots. Their "zeal for God and the Law" meant, for them, no ruler other than God. Roman rule they called enslavement, and the stress they placed on the tax-collector shows that there was more than just religious belief at stake. It was the Zealots who forced the revolt in 66, and something of their dedication (in which there was a strong Messianic streak) comes over even in Josephus' wholly hostile account—and in the fact that they fought the Romans to the death for four years, a small band holding out until 73 in the great fortress of Masada above the Dead Sea and then committing suicide. Two generations later, it may be added, Judæa tried once more, in the uprising of 132-135 led by Bar Kochba (or Bar Koseba).

It must be remembered that it was not only the Zealots who fought. They were the activists, but virtually everyone was drawn in, some through compulsion (this must be one element behind Josephus' picture of constant rioting, massacre, and near-civil war inside Jerusalem); some because they, too, hated Roman rule and Roman officials, although they would have bowed their heads and been content merely to grumble and plead, had it not been for the Zealots. After all, whatever the truth may be about the original purpose of Josephus' mission in Galilee, there can be no doubt that, when he was given no choice, he joined the rebels and led as good a resistance as he was capable of. There must have been many like him among all classes, and their reluctance to take up arms cannot be attributed solely to the "sectarian" conflicts. There was also the matter of fear or prudence, the conviction that Rome was too powerful, that the Jews must surely be defeated and brutally punished. This was the line Josephus took in all his writings, embellished by much hokum about God's punishment, and it is unnecessary to believe that he did so solely to repay his imperial patrons. His first version of *The Jewish War*, as he tells us at the beginning, was written in Aramaic for the benefit of both Jews and "barbarians" on the eastern confines of the Roman Empire. We can only guess at his motives for so doing, but it is not a bad guess that one of them was to demonstrate how even so massive a revolt, coming under unusually propitious conditions, ended in total failure. He was reading to other peoples the lesson that prudence and safety come before honor and freedom. It is a lesson that has been read to the world on many subsequent occasions.

THE HISTORIAN

Josephus' historical writing consists of the two overlapping works, *The Jewish War* and *The Jewish Antiquities*. We know nothing whatever of the Aramaic version of *The Jewish War*. Although Josephus says he later decided to "translate" the work into Greek, that word was not intended to be taken literally. Quite apart from the opening reference to false accounts circulating in Greek that required correction, so much of the book we have is, in manner, tone, and content, a Hellenistic Greek work written directly for a Greek-speaking audience (and not, one must underscore, for Romans or Italians) that it could scarcely have been written that way in the Aramaic original for a Jewish-"barbarian" audience. The very title is revealing: "the *Jewish War*" is what the victors called it, not the conquered, who would certainly have resented the name. The thorough Greek-ness of the work is astonishing. When Josephus arrived in Rome after his capture, his knowledge of the Greek language and culture was surely very superficial, for he was a Palestinian Jew, not an Alexandrian. Although he had Greek assistants (to whom he makes but one passing reference in *Ap.* I, 9), they cannot be given the whole credit.[5] One must concede Josephus some warrant for his characteristic boast at the close of the *Antiquities*: "I make bold to say that no one else, whether Jew or alien, could with the best will in the world have produced a work of such accuracy as this for Greek readers. For my countrymen admit that I am easily preeminent among them in the lore of my native land; and I have moreover striven to acquaint myself with Greek literature and am proficient in the grammar. . . ."

So successful were Josephus and his assistants that modern scholars have been unable to find a trace of Semitism to mar the purity of the language. More than that, Josephus wrote not in the common literary language of the Hellenistic Age, of which the Greek New Testament is the best known example, but in the revived classical Greek of Athens that had become the fashion in his day. The Byzantine patriarch Photius may not have been a great literary critic, but his summary judgment is not without interest: "Josephus has great purity in his language, . . . with an agreeable clarity. He is persuasive and full of grace in his speeches; when he has occasion to make use of his eloquence for antithetical arguments, he is adroit and fertile in argument on both sides. . . . He excels in the art of expressing passion in language, and he is a master in heightening the emotions and then lowering them."

Some of these judgments may not strike the modern reader as the highest possible praise of an historian,

---

[5] There is disagreement among scholars on the precise contribution of these assistants.

or even as praise at all, but they must be viewed within the context of Hellenistic historiography, which had developed its own traditions and conventions. A historian was expected to provide both pleasure and moral instruction. He had to be able to maintain a continuous narrative which would be exciting and bring out the exploits and the characters of individual actors. Then, to clarify the issues, he was expected to compose long speeches for the protagonists; sometimes a single speech, such as that of a commander to his troops, and sometimes antithetical speeches in which two men summed up for the reader the arguments on both sides (whether or not to surrender, for example). He was expected to arouse pity and horror, and to do so with a skilled technique, heightening the tensions at the right moment, relaxing them at other times so that the effects would be most striking at the appropriate points in the tale. These are the things Photius expected of an historian in antiquity, and he was right to rank Josephus very high on his performance.

Equally conventional was the opening of *The Jewish War,* with its justification of the author's choice of subject and its sweeping criticisms of predecessors in the field. The all-out violence of Josephus' attack on Justus of Tiberias was no fiercer than that of Polybius, the greatest of the Hellenistic historians, writing in the middle of the second century B.C., against the historians Timæus and Phylarchus. Conventionally, too, Josephus did not plunge immediately into the war and its direct causes, but went back to the Maccabean revolt, bridging to his subject from that point.

The Greeks had had a long tradition of systematic historical writing—they invented it, in fact. Eventually, other peoples followed: the Egyptians, the Babylonians, the Romans; each adding its own national history—and glorifying it—to the stock of universal history. With the Jews the position was different, because they already had all they needed to know about their own past in the Pentateuch and the later historical books of the Old Testament. What they did not have, and on the whole did not want, was a continuous *historical* account available to their Greek-speaking neighbors, which would place their past in the framework of world history. It was this which Josephus supplied, and it is ironic that it was in his longer, inferior work, the *Antiquities*, that he was genuinely original—in conception if not in performance—rather than in *The Jewish War*. A start of a sort had been made by Nicolaus of Damascus, Herod's court philosopher and historian, who compiled a vast universal history in 144 books from the mythological period of the Assyrians, Babylonians, Lydians, Greeks and Romans, all synchronized, down to the death of Herod and who, it is worth noting, also wrote an *Autobiography* which became attached to his *History*. Nicolaus was very important for Josephus as a source of information about Herod, but he was not the model for the *Antiquities*. That function was performed by another eastern Greek, Dionysius of Halicarnassus in Asia Minor, a professional littérateur who lived in Rome from 30 B.C. on, where he was very influential in literary circles. In 7 B.C., Dionysius published his *Antiquities of the Romans* in Greek in 20 books, and it is no coincidence that Josephus' *Antiquities* is divided into precisely the same number of books.

Unlike Dionysius, of course, Josephus was faced with the need to be an apologist as well as an historian. It was one thing to tell the story that explained how the Romans came to rule the world; it was another matter when the subject of the history was an alien, misunderstood, and in many quarters disliked and reviled nation. One should not underestimate the boldness and difficulty of this self-imposed assignment.[6] Where was he to get his information? Down to the Maccabees he had the Bible, and on Herod he had Nicolaus of Damascus. For the Roman period of rule he was able to consult Roman official documents, including the *commentarii* of Vespasian and Titus (a kind of log kept by commanders, the most famous example being Cæsar's *Commentaries*). But for the rest, on the two centuries

---

6 The suggestion occasionally made that there were actual predecessors of Josephus, anonymous authors of lost works of which no trace remains, may be rejected out of hand.

preceding the Hasmoneans, for which there was little
Biblical authority, or on the years following the death
of Herod, after Nicolaus left off, he had no proper
sources. And, as is evident from the *Antiquities* (and
from those portions of *The Jewish War* which cover the
same ground), he could not really cope until he reached
the period when his own personal experiences provided
a new core for the story. That helps explain why the
Antiquities is a badly balanced work, very lengthy (and
often long-winded) when he could follow a pre-existing
authority, choppy to the point of triviality and unintel-
ligibility when he was on his own.

In part this is not a matter for criticism. Josephus
and his assistants took a long time over the *Antiquities*.
They lived in an age when facilities for research were
very sparse. If the Epaphroditus who became Josephus'
patron after Titus' death was the learned Greek gram-
marian of that name, reputed to have assembled in
Rome an astonishing private library numbering 30,000
books, then Josephus was better off for books than most
of his contemporaries. Nevertheless, there is little reason to believe that books existed which might have enabled him to close the gaps in the narrative, no matter
how energetic and thorough his reading. And, it must be
said, we do not really know whom and how much he
did read, for the ancients did not have the modern habit
of citing authorities regularly.

This much can be said on Josephus' behalf. However,
there is another side: that he was an incomplete and very
uncritical historian, even by ancient standards. He
could not have been expected to treat the Biblical narrative as anything but the sacred and literal truth—
that we must accept. But he was not required to follow
everything else he read slavishly, as he tended to do in
large blocks, except, as in the case of Justus, when he
had personal reasons to produce his own, competing version. For example, the picture he draws of Herod in
The Jewish War and the *Antiquities* is blatantly inconsistent, made up in unequal parts of toadying adulation,
copied more or less straight out of Nicolaus, and the
hostile tradition that lived on among the people in his

own Jerusalem. Josephus simply salted one view into a narrative based on the other, producing not a balance but an incoherence. He made a similarly awkward combination in *A, XI, viii* (not reproduced in the present volume) in order not merely to tell a long, wholly fictitious tale, full of anachronisms, about a visit to Jerusalem by Alexander the Great, but also to make Alexander out to be a great friend of the Jews and to create one more opportunity to impugn the hated Samaritans.[7] A good story was a good story, especially when it served apologetic ends, and no other criterion mattered.

There were times, too, when political and apologetic considerations recommended certain omissions. Thus, his account of Daniel's interpretation of Nebuchadnezzar's dream runs like this (*A, X, x, 4*); " '. . . but their empire will be destroyed by another king from the west, clad in bronze, and this power will be ended by still another, like iron, that will have dominion for ever through its iron nature,' which, he said, is harder than that of gold or silver or bronze. And Daniel also revealed to the king the meaning of the stone, but I have not thought it proper to relate this, since I am expected to write of what is past and done and not of what is to be. . . ." What Josephus omitted was the detail that the fourth kingdom was of "iron mixed with miry clay"; what he did not think it proper to relate at all was that "in the days of those kings shall the God of heaven set up a kingdom, which shall never be destroyed; . . . but it shall break in pieces and consume all these kingdoms, and it shall stand for ever" (*Daniel* 2:44). The reason for these omissions is very simple: current Jewish interpretation was that the fourth kingdom was Rome, which would be overthrown at the coming of the Messiah.

Josephus was clearly in a difficult position, and one must sympathize with his reticence on this particular prophecy. How Josephus retells the Bible is an interest-

---

7 The details of these Alexander legends in Josephus and Rabbinic writings are assembled and discussed by Ralph Marcus in an Appendix, in Volume VI of the Loeb Classical Library edition.

ing subject in itself, apart from these few tendentious twists. Any reader will quickly notice that whereas on the whole the narrative is faithful to the original, there are innumerable small divergences: omissions, additions, and variations.[8] Some are perhaps Josephus' own, either mistakes or personal interpretations, especially his passion for etymologies, which are almost invariably wrong, and often wildly so (in common with most ancient etymologists). Others arise from the fact that although he used a Hebrew or Aramaic Bible for the Pentateuch, Joshua, Judges, and perhaps Ruth, he relied chiefly on a Greek text for the remainder. Most numerous of all, however, and most important, are the variants which reflect the supporting legends and the interpretations of the Biblical material that were circulating in his own day. Many can be paralleled in Rabbinic sources, and they were obviously common coin.

The level of Biblical interpretation in Josephus is a low one. For all his claims to profound learning, he was no theologian, but a ritualist. He seems to have read a bit of Philo, the Jewish philosopher of Alexandria, but neither understood him nor sympathized with his serious efforts to give Judaism a Greek philosophical underpinning. His identification of the Pharisees with Stoicism (V, 2) and of the Essenes with the Pythagoreans (A, XV, x, 4) reveals both ignorance of and indifference to philosophy: that was merely an easy, though wholly inaccurate, way of trying to communicate with a Greek audience. For Josephus, religion was all on the surface —no doubt an attitude nurtured within the aristocratic priestly class in Jerusalem from which he stemmed— and it had better be kept that way. One accepted the omnipotence, ubiquity, and justice of God; one accepted all His works and revelations; one performed the requisite rites; one did not probe too hard. It was the letter of the law which was insisted upon; anything else invited turbulence, challenge to authority, and rebellion—witness the Zealots. It is not by oversight that

---

[8] The Loeb Classical Library edition of the *Antiquities* notes them with great regularity.

one finds no trace of Messianic hope or promise in Josephus, widespread though we know it to have been in the Judæa of his day.

These things are informative not only about Josephus himself but also about certain sectors in his society. They are, so to speak, Josephus' unconscious contribution to history. But what one wants to know, above all, is how much trust to put in his account of the Jewish War, its origins and conduct on both sides. That is what gives him his importance. And it must be said at once that any judgment is unavoidably and deeply subjective, based on little more than personal impressions from reading Josephus, for the absence of external controls over his history is to all intents and purposes total. Roman writers, such as Tacitus and Suetonius, merely confirm that there was a great and stubborn rebellion, that it was finally put down by Titus in the year 70 after a siege of Jerusalem (on which Tacitus has two or three pages), and that the participants were cruelly punished. A few pages will hold all that information, perhaps one or two more for independent evidence from later Jewish sources. The Dead Sea scrolls, much as they may add to our knowledge of religious thinking and movements of the period, have not contributed anything to the problem with which we are concerned. Nor has archæology, in any significant way, although there is some promise in the present excavation of Masada, and there is always a hope of unexpected discoveries such as the sensational ones a few years ago concerning the revolt led by Bar Kochba.

In what follows, therefore, I shall use the first person in order to underscore the subjective, personal nature of the position expressed. I think it is not unfair to begin by repeating and extending the argument for lack of confidence in Josephus as a man, as a moral being. His inconsistency about his mission in Galilee has already been noted. His tireless and insufferable boasting is also relevant, and one example will suffice of the hundreds which are available: "The affection and loyalty towards me of the people of Galilee were such that, when their cities were taken by storm and their wives and children enslaved, their lamentations over their own calamities were not so deep as their concern for my safety" (V, 16). To be sure, no one can prove that this is an untrue statement; just as no one can prove that Josephus was not the most learned Jew of his generation (revealing his superiority by the age of fourteen); that he was not an incomparable military strategist; that he was not a magnificent and persuasive orator who always succeeded in talking vast mobs out of some foolhardy or vicious action into which they were being stampeded by unprincipled demagogues and bandits; or that God did not regularly come to his rescue in shipwrecks, battles, and lynch-parties.

Anyone who chooses to believe all this, even with the traditional "grain of salt," must in all conscience come to terms with the most embarrassing single chapter in the whole of Josephus' writings: the final scene of the siege of Jotapata (BJ, III, viii). The Romans had finally seized the town, and Josephus was in hiding in a cave with "forty persons of distinction." There was a Roman search party out, for their general, the future emperor Vespasian, "considered that the issue of the war depended largely on his [Josephus'] capture." On the third day they were betrayed, and Vespasian sent emissaries requesting Josephus to surrender on a pledge of safe-conduct. Josephus hesitated until "suddenly there came back into his mind those nightly dreams, in which God had foretold to him the impending fate of the Jews and the destinies of the Roman sovereigns." He then agreed, whereupon his comrades threatened to kill him as a traitor and demanded that they all commit suicide. He tried reasoning with them, with no success. "In his straits, his resource did not forsake him. Trusting to God's protection, he put his life to the hazard," and proposed the alternative that they kill each other, drawing lots for turns. The men agreed. "Each man thus selected presented his throat to his neighbor, in the assurance that his general was forthwith to share his fate; for sweeter to them than life was the thought of death with Josephus. He, however (should one say by fortune or by the providence of God?), was left alone with one other: and, anxious neither to be condemned by the lot nor, should he be left to the last, to stain his hand with the blood·of a fellowcountryman, he persuaded this man also, under a pledge, to remain alive. Having thus survived both the war with the Romans and that with his own friends, Josephus was brought . . . into Vespasian's presence."

I have no idea what actually happened in the cave. Nor has anyone else. But I have no doubt whatever that a man who could write that chapter—and it does not matter whether one reads "should one say by fortune or by the providence of God?" or prefers the Slavonic alternative, "he counted the numbers with cunning and thereby misled them all"—has abandoned all claim to credibility. Naturally, I mean not that everything Josephus says is untrue, but that nothing he says can be accepted at face value.

There are also, I think, certain fairly clear distinctions to be drawn. It is generally agreed, for example, that the rhetorical speech against suicide in general, which Josephus quotes himself as having made in the cave, would have been neither attempted nor tolerated under such conditions. That is fair enough, for it was the recognized convention that the historian should compose fine speeches, and no contemporary reader was expected to take them as anything but free compositions. At best, they may have expressed ideas appropriate to the speaker and the occasion. This rule applies to all the numerous speeches in Josephus, and we are left where we started, with the open question whether the sentiments, at least, are accurately reflected. Was Titus, we must ask, as eager as he is made out to be to protect the Jewish sanctuary and Jewish lives? I do not believe we know.

In particular, speeches were employed to reveal motives, and that is precisely the subject on which distrust of Josephus seems to me most legitimate. The example of the Zealots, to whom he allows only the basest of instincts and aims, can be repeated without end. Josephus will not allow his opponents any virtue whatever. They are not only wrong in their ideas and policies, they are crooked in their methods, dishonest in their statements, evil beyond measure. Everything that is done on the other side 'is conspiracy, and that, to my mind, is the hallmark of a bad judge and a worse critic. We have had enough experience in our own time with the conspiracy-theory in politics. Invariably, it is a device for whipping up fear and prejudice, for preventing rational discussion, for denying the opposition any hearing. As a matter of odds, it is simply not possible that every opponent of Josephus was a black conspirator. And if that is conceded, then it must also be granted that we have little basis for drawing distinctions among the black portraits. We cannot even be sure about John of Gischala, the arch-devil of them all. Lack of confidence in Josephus unfortunately does not give us the right simply to turn all his portraits upside down, converting his devils into angels and vice versa. It allows in most instances no more than a "don't know."

There is, of course, a vast area in which Josephus had no stake, so to speak—the geographical descriptions, the innumerable details about civil and military life, the battles, and the bald narrative. These were matters on which he had both intimate personal knowledge and the advantage of his reading in the documents, and our judgment of their veracity is very different from what I have been saying about aims and motives. The geography and the detailed description of the buildings in and around Jerusalem can, unlike most of the rest, be checked on the spot. They have been, to Josephus' credit. The crusaders were right to use the old Latin translation of *The Jewish War* as a kind of guidebook to the Holy Land. Much of the narrative probably stands up, too, although certain aspects are suspicious. Titus, in particular, is altogether too much a fairy prince, as he invariably appears at the critical spot at the right moment, always takes the greatest risks, always escapes flying arrows and spears and mass onslaughts, always talks like Sir Galahad. The actual battle-scenes are set-pieces, on a pattern that goes back at least to Polybius. Besiegers and besieged outmaneuver each other in turn, with standard devices; stratagems follow upon feats of wild heroism; discipline and panic alternate; starvation sets in; and so on and so on. It is all very exciting and pitiable, but it probably bears no more relation to what actually went on than most descriptions of battles, an· cient or modern.

JOSEPHUS AND CHRISTIANITY

Finally, there is the special problem of Josephus and the Christians, about which many more words have been wasted in futile controversy than the subject warrants. There are exactly three references to anything Christian in the Greek text, all in the *Antiquities*:

XVIII, iii, 3: "Now about this time arises Jesus, a wise man, if indeed he should be called a man. For he was a doer of marvellous deeds, a teacher of men who received the truth with pleasure; and he won over to himself many Jews and many also of the Greeks. He was the Christ. And when, on the indictment of the principal men among us, Pilate had sentenced him to the cross, those who had loved him at first did not cease; for he appeared to them on the third day alive again, the divine prophets having foretold these and ten thousand other wonderful things concerning him. And even now the race of Christians, named after him, is not extinct."

XVIII, v, 2: "Some of the Jews, however, regarded the destruction of the army of Herod [Antipas, the Tetrarch] as the work of God, who thus exacted very righteous retribution for John surnamed the Baptist. For Herod had slain John—a good man who bade the Jews to cultivate virtue by justice towards each other and piety towards God and to come to baptism; for immersion, he said, would only appear acceptable to God if practiced, not as an expiation for specific offences, but for the purification of the body, when the soul had already been thoroughly cleansed by righteousness. Now when men flocked to him . . . Herod feared that the powerful influence which he exercised over men's minds might lead to some form of revolt, for they seemed ready to do anything on his advice. To forestall and kill him seemed far better than a belated repentance when plunged in the turmoil of an insurrection."

XX, ix, 1: The high priest Ananus "summoned the court of the Sanhedrin, brought before it the brother of Jesus who was called Christ (James was his name) and certain others, and, after accusing them of transgressing the law, delivered them up to be stoned."

There is nothing surprising in Josephus' lack of interest in Christianity, even to the extent of not mentioning the Neronic persecution of 64, the year of his first visit to Rome. It is only from hindsight that the new religion acquires such importance as to create the illusion that it must already have earned the serious attention of a Jewish historian writing towards the end of the first century. We have the authority of Photius that Justus of Tiberias "makes not the slightest reference to the birth of Christ nor to the events in which he was involved nor to the miracles he accomplished." And Josephus, we remember, was persistently silent about, and hostile to, all Messianic ideas. On the other hand, it is equally puzzling why anyone should have thought the casual references in Josephus important, as so many commentators have. They contribute nothing to our knowledge unless one needs persuading that there was a John the Baptist, that there was a Jesus Christ (who had a brother named James), and that they were executed. Finally, it is not possible that Josephus wrote the first, at least, of the three passages as it stands in the manuscripts. He was a pious, practicing Jew to the end of his days, with no taste for miracle-workers or popular preachers. One may guess what, if anything, stood in place of this passage originally, who altered it, when, and from what motives. And there have been learned and ingenious guesses by the score, but whatever the truth about them, they pertain to another subject, not to Josephus himself or to his work as an historian.

A further complication arose with the discovery of the Old Slavonic version of *The Jewish War,* of which some 17 different manuscripts are now known. It differs in many details from the Greek text, nowhere more startlingly than on the subject of John the Baptist and Jesus, about whom there are longer passages (in which, curiously, their names do not appear). These are made up in equal parts of what now stands in the Greek Josephus, of familiar Christian traditions, and of some quite remarkable nonsense. The passages are too long to quote in full,[9] and I shall limit myself to one revealing bit: "It was at that time that a man appeared—if 'man' is the right word—who had all the attributes of a man but seemed to be something greater. His actions certainly were superhuman, for he worked such wonderful and amazing miracles that I for one cannot regard him as a man; yet in view of his likeness to ourselves I cannot regard him as an angel either. Everything that some hidden power enabled him to do he did by an authoritative word." This sort of thing raises very interesting, but at present insoluble, problems, and again they are problems belonging primarily to another subject, in this instance the early Slavonic church.

EPILOGUE

It is not at all easy to sum Josephus up. The fact that he is virtually our sole source of information about an interesting and important period—or rather, situation—in ancient history is a reason for exasperation, not an excuse for accepting his account as more or less true just because we have no other. That he was widely used as an authority by Christian writers in the next few centuries also proves nothing, although it helps explain much about the thinking of the later centuries. Once it is agreed, as it is by every competent student, that there are serious internal discrepancies, not to mention dishonesty, in crucial places in the story, a pall of doubt and distrust falls on the whole, and most of the time we lack adequate tests with which to distinguish the

___

[9] All the passages are conveniently set out in an Appendix to the Penguin translation of *The Jewish War*, by G. A. Williamson, who belongs to the very small minority that believes Josephus did write them.

more from the less probable with any degree of certainty.

Yet, to leave it at that would not be right. Dislike of an author as a person, no matter how extreme, need not carry over to his work, at least not in the same measure. The history of literature is filled with important and pleasurable works written by men who themselves were not pleasant to contemplate. *The Jewish War,* the non-Biblical portions of the *Antiquities,* and the *Reply to Apion* all repay reading. Josephus was a good writer, sometimes almost a great one, after all. Even if his books are judged most harshly as accurate historical writing, they remain valid as testimonies. In the first place, they reveal the image that the official and aristocratic Romans and a sector of the Jewish world, too, wished to present to their contemporaries (and to posterity, insofar as that mattered to them) of themselves and their relations with each other. Second, Josephus has surely captured the tensions, the brutality, the religious fanaticism, and the intense horror of the war —he has that right even when his "facts" are most fictitious and distorted. For obvious reasons, that particular struggle retains an interest, nearly two thousand years later, unique among the many wars fought by and against the Romans. And so Josephus had greatness thrust upon him.

TEXT, TRANSLATION, AND BIBLIOGRAPHY

The best Greek text of the complete works of Josephus (first published in Basel in 1544) as well as the only reliable, copiously annotated English translation will be found in the Loeb Classical Library edition, begun in 1926 by H. St. J. Thackeray, continued by Ralph Marcus, and then by Allen Wikgren. This edition, of which the ninth and final volume, including the last three books of the *Antiquities* and a general index, is still to come (edited by C. H. Feldman), also provides full bibliographies, maps, and genealogical charts. Another translation of *The Jewish War* alone, by G. A. Williamson, is available in the Penguin series (1959).

The Loeb publishers, the Harvard University Press, have kindly given permission to use that translation and to reproduce two of the maps. In a very few cases I have presumed to make slight changes, preferring an alternative reading or rendition of a word or phrase. I have also abandoned their practice of transcribing rather literally into English Josephus' Greek forms of familiar Biblical names and have instead used the forms to which English readers of the Bible are accustomed (though I have not done this systematically for the minor figures). Occasionally, I have inserted a date or an identification of a person or an explanatory phrase, always in square brackets to make it clear that something has been added to the actual text of Josephus. The few subtitles are all mine.

I have selected something from each of the four works, presented in a logical order and not in the actual order of their composition or publication. The bulk comes from *The Jewish War*, in long, continuous sections giving the reader not only a full picture of how Josephus unfolds his narrative but also a fairly complete account of the most important events. From the *Autobiography* and *Against Apion* I have chosen only brief extracts in which Josephus explains his aims and methods; from the *Antiquities*, three sections illustrating, with familiar material, how Josephus retells the Biblical stories.[10] Deletions within an extract are indicated by ellipsis, and their length is approximately revealed by the section numbers. Josephus himself divided his works into "books," and modern editors have made further subdivisions into "chapters" and "sections," numbered here by small Roman and Arabic numerals, respectively. References to individual passages are given in this way, since page references would vary with each edition or translation.[11]

[10] The extract from Book X of the *Antiquities* is translated by Professor Marcus; all the rest in this volume by Dr. Thackeray.

[11] There exists another reference system for Josephus, which I have not used, eliminating the "chapters" and establishing very small "sections" numbered continuously within each "Book."

The basic study of Josephus in English remains that of H. St. J. Thackeray, *Josephus the Man and Historian* (1929). The recently published popular account by G. A. Williamson, *The World of Josephus* (1964), also has merit, although note must be taken of the author's insufficient mastery of the scholarly work on some of the most difficult questions. On special topics, A. H. M. Jones, *The Herods of Judæa* (1938), and Victor Tcherikover, *Hellenistic Civilization and the Jews* (1959), are invaluable. Mention should also be made of the novel, *Josephus*, by Lion Feuchtwanger, first published in English in 1932.

For helpful suggestions, I am indebted to the general editor of this series, Professor Hugh Trevor-Roper, and to Professors A. H. M. Jones of the University of Cambridge and A. D. Momigliano of London University.

M. I. FINLEY
July 20, 1964

CHRONOLOGICAL TABLE

81 Death of Titus, succeeded by his brother Domitian.

93/94 FIRST EDITION OF JOSEPHUS' *ANTIQUI-TIES.*

c. 100 DEATH OF JOSEPHUS.

132–135 Jewish revolt led by Bar Kochba.

(*Note:* The date of publication of the *Reply to Apion* is unknown.)

The Life

Introduction

1. My family is no ignoble one, tracing its descent far back to priestly ancestors. Different races base their claim to nobility on various grounds; with us connection with the priesthood is the hallmark of an illustrious line. Not only, however, were my ancestors priests, but they belonged to the first of the twenty-four divisions— a peculiar distinction—and to the most eminent of its constituent clans. Moreover, on my mother's side I am of royal blood; for the Hasmonæans, from whom she sprang, for a very considerable period were kings, as well as high priests, of our nation. I will give the pedigree. My great-grandfather's grandfather was Simon surnamed Psellus. He was a contemporary of the high priest Hyrcanus, the first of the name to hold that office, previously held by his father Simon. Simon Psellus had nine children, one of whom, Matthias, known as the son of Ephæus, married the daughter of Jonathan the high-priest, who was the first of the Hasmonæans to attain the high-priesthood, and brother of Simon who also held that office. Matthias, in the first year of the reign of Hyrcanus, had a son Matthias, surnamed Curtus; who, in the ninth year of the reign of Alexandra, begot Joseph, and he, in the tenth year of the reign of Archelaus, Matthias, to whom I was born in the year in which Gaius Cæsar became Emperor.* I have three sons: Hyrcanus, the eldest, born in the fourth, Justus in the seventh, and Agrippa in the ninth year of the reign of Vespasian Cæsar. With such a pedigree, which I cite as I find it recorded in the public registers, I can take leave of the would-be detractors of my family.

2. Distinguished as he was by his noble birth, my

---

* Commonly known as Caligula. The year is A.D. 37/8.

3

father Matthias was even more esteemed for his upright character, being among the most notable men in Jerusalem, our greatest city. Brought up with Matthias, my own brother by both parents, I made great progress in my education, gaining a reputation for an excellent memory and understanding. While still a mere boy, about fourteen years old, I won universal applause for my love of letters; insomuch that the chief priests and the leading men of the city used constantly to come to me for precise information on some particular in our ordinances.

At about the age of sixteen I determined to gain personal experience of the several sects into which our nation is divided. These, as I have frequently mentioned, are three in number—the first that of the Pharisees, the second that of the Sadducees, and the third that of the Essenes. I thought that, after a thorough investigation, I should be in a position to select the best. So I submitted myself to hard training and laborious exercises and passed through the three courses. Not content, however, with the experience thus gained, on hearing of one named Bannus, who dwelt in the wilderness, wearing only such clothing as trees provided, feeding on such things as grew of themselves, and using frequent ablutions of cold water, by day and night, for purity's sake, I became his devoted disciple. With him I lived for three years and, having accomplished my purpose, returned to the city. Being now in my nineteenth year I began to govern my life by the rules of the Pharisees, a sect having points of resemblance to that which the Greeks call the Stoic school.

3. Soon after I had completed my twenty-sixth year, it fell to my lot to go up to Rome for the reason which I will proceed to relate. At the time when Felix was procurator of Judæa, certain priests of my acquaintance, very excellent men, were on a slight and trifling charge sent by him in bonds to Rome to render an account to [Nero] Cæsar. I was anxious to discover some means of delivering these men, more especially as I learnt that, even in affliction, they had not forgotten the pious practices of religion, and supported themselves on figs

4

and nuts. I reached Rome after being in great jeopardy at sea. For our ship foundered in the midst of the Adriatic Sea, and our company of some six hundred souls had to swim all that night. About daybreak, through God's good providence, we sighted a ship of Cyrene, and I and certain others, about eighty in all, outstripped the others and were taken on board. Landing safely at Dicæarchia, which the Italians call Puteoli, I formed a friendship with Aliturus, an actor who was a special favorite of Nero and of Jewish origin. Through him I was introduced to Poppæa, Cæsar's consort, and took the earliest opportunity of soliciting her aid to secure the liberation of the priests. Having, besides this favor, received large gifts from Poppæa, I returned to my own country.

4. There I found revolutionary movements already on foot and widespread elation at the prospect of revolt from Rome. I accordingly endeavored to repress these promoters of sedition and to bring them over to another frame of mind. 1 urged them to picture to themselves the nation on which they were about to make war and to remember that they were inferior to the Romans, not only in military skill, but in good fortune; and I warned them not recklessly and with such utter madness to expose their country, their families and themselves to the direst perils. With such words I earnestly and insistently sought to dissuade them from their purpose, foreseeing that the end of the war would be most disastrous for us. But my efforts were unavailing; the madness of these desperate men was far too strong for me. . . .

Polemic against the Historian Justus

65. Having reached this point in my narrative, I propose to address a few words to Justus [of Tiberias], who has produced his own account of these affairs, and to others who, while professing to write history, care little for truth, and, either from spite or partiality, have no scruples about falsehood. The procedure of such persons resembles indeed that of forgers of contracts, but,

5

having no corresponding penalty to fear, they can afford to disdain veracity. Justus, for instance, having taken it upon himself to record the history of this war, has, in order to gain credit for industrious research, not only maligned me, but even failed to tell the truth about his native place. Being therefore now compelled to defend myself against these false allegations, I shall allude to matters about which I have hitherto kept silent. My omission to make such a statement at an earlier date should not occasion surprise. For, while veracity is incumbent upon a historian, he is none the less at liberty to refrain from harsh scrutiny of the misdeeds of individuals, not from any partiality for the offenders, but because of his own moderation.

How, then, Justus—if I may address him as though he were present—how, most clever of historians, as you boast yourself to be, can I and the Galilæans be held responsible for the insurrection of your native city against the Romans and against the king, seeing that, before I was elected by the general assembly at Jerusalem to the command of Galilee, you and all the citizens of Tiberias had not only resorted to arms, but were actually at war with the towns of the Syrian Decapolis? It was you who burnt their villages, and your domestic fell in the engagement on that occasion. This is no unsupported assertion of my own. The facts are recorded in the *Commentaries* of the Emperor Vespasian,* which further relate how insistently the inhabitants of Decapolis pressed Vespasian, when at Ptolemais, to punish you as the culprit. And punished you would have been under his orders, had not [the client] King Agrippa [II of Galilee], though empowered to put you to death, at the urgent entreaty of his sister Berenice, commuted the death penalty to a long term of imprisonment. Moreover, your subsequent public life is a sure index of character and proves that it was you who caused the revolt of your native city from Rome. Proofs of these statements I shall adduce presently.

* A sort of official journal, never published in the strict sense and now wholly lost.

6

I have, however, a few words which I would address,
on your account, to the other inhabitants of Tiberias,
in order to demonstrate to future readers of these histories that you and your fellow-citizens were friendly
neither to the Romans nor to the king. Of the cities of
Galilee the largest are Sepphoris and Tiberias—your native Tiberias, Justus. Now, Sepphoris, situated in the
heart of Galilee, surrounded by numerous villages, and
in a position, without any difficulty, had she been so inclined, to make a bold stand against the Romans, nevertheless decided to remain loyal to her masters, excluded
me from the town, and forbade any of her citizens to
take service with the Jews. Moreover, in order to secure
themselves against me, they inveigled me into fortifying the city with walls, and then voluntarily admitted a
garrison provided by Cestius Gallus, commander-in-chief
of the Roman legions in Syria; flouting me at a time
when I exercised great power and was universally held
in awe. Again, when Jerusalem, our capital, was besieged, and the Temple, which was common to us all,
was in danger of falling into the enemy's hands, they
sent no assistance, wishing to avoid all suspicion of having borne arms against the Romans.

Your native city, Justus, on the contrary, situated on
the lake of Gennesaret, and distant from Hippos thirty
furlongs, from Gadara sixty, and from Scythopolis, which
was under the king's jurisdiction, one hundred and twenty, with no Jewish city in the vicinity, might easily, had
it so desired, have kept faith with the Romans. You
were a populous community and well supplied with
arms. But, you maintain, it was I who was responsible
for your revolt at that time. Well, who was responsible,
Justus, later on? For you are aware that before the
siege of Jerusalem I was taken prisoner by the Romans,
that Jotapata and many other fortresses had been carried by storm, and that a large number of Galilæans had
fallen in battle. That was the proper occasion for you,
when you had nothing whatever to fear from me, to
abandon hostilities and to convince the king and the
Romans that it was not your own free will but compulsion which drove you into war against them. Instead,

you waited until Vespasian arrived in person, with his whole army, beneath your walls; and then, at last in alarm, you did lay down your arms. But your city would undoubtedly have been taken by storm, had not Vespasian yielded to the king's intercession to condone your folly.

The responsibility therefore rests not with me, but with you Tiberians, and your passion for war. Have you forgotten how, often as I had you in my power, I put not one of you to death? Whereas you in your party quarrels, not from any loyalty to the Romans and the king, but of your own malice, slew one hundred and eighty-five of your fellow-citizens at the time when I was besieged in Jotapata by the Romans. Again, were there not two thousand Tiberians found at the siege of Jerusalem, of whom some fell and others were taken prisoners?

But you, Justus, will urge that you at least were no enemy [of Rome], because in those early days you sought refuge with the king. I reply that it was fear of me which drove you to do so. I too, then, you assert, was a knave. Well, how do you account for your treatment by King Agrippa, to whom you owed your life, when condemned to death by Vespasian, and all that wealth which he lavished upon you? Why did he subsequently twice put you in irons and as often command you to quit the country, and once order you to execution, when he spared your life only at the earnest entreaty of his sister Berenice? And when, after all your knavish tricks, he had appointed you his private secretary, he detected you once more in fraudulent practices and banished you from his sight. But I forbear to scrutinize these matters too closely.

I cannot, however, but wonder at your impudence in daring to assert that your narrative is to be preferred to that of all who have written on this subject, when you neither knew what happened in Galilee—for you were then at Berytus with the king—nor acquainted yourself with all that the Romans endured or inflicted upon us at the siege of Jotapata; nor was it in your power to ascertain the part which I myself played in the siege, since all possible informants perished in that conflict. Perhaps, however, you will say that you have accurately narrated the events which took place at Jerusalem. How, pray, can that be, seeing that neither were you a combatant nor had you perused the *Commentaries* of [Titus] Cæsar, as is abundantly proved by your contradictory account? But, if you are so confident that your history excels all others, why did you not publish it in the lifetime of the Emperors Vespasian and Titus, who conducted the war, and while King Agrippa and all his family, persons thoroughly conversant with Hellenic culture, were still among us? You had it written twenty years ago, and might then have obtained the evidence of eyewitnesses to your accuracy. But not until now, when those persons are no longer with us and you think you cannot be confuted, have you ventured to publish it.

I had no such apprehensions concerning my work. No; I presented the volumes to the emperors themselves, when the events had hardly passed out of sight, conscious as I was that I had preserved the true story. I expected to receive testimony to my accuracy, and was not disappointed. To many others also I immediately presented my *History*, some of whom had taken part in the war, such as King Agrippa and certain of his relatives. Indeed, so anxious was the Emperor Titus that my volumes should be the sole authority from which the world should learn the facts, that he affixed his own signature to them and gave orders for their publication; while King Agrippa wrote sixty-two letters testifying to the truth of the record. Two of these I subjoin, from which you may, if you will, learn the nature of his communications:

"King Agrippa to dearest Josephus, greeting. I have perused the book with the greatest pleasure. You seem to me to have written with much greater care and accuracy than any who have dealt with the subject. Send me the remaining volumes. Farewell."

"King Agrippa to dearest Josephus, greeting. From what you have written you appear to stand

9

in no need of instruction, to enable us all to learn [everything from you] from the beginning. But when you meet me, I will myself by word of mouth inform you of much that is not generally known."

And, on the completion of my *History*, not in flattery, which was contrary to his nature, nor yet, as *you* no doubt will say, in irony, for he was far above such malignity, but in all sincerity, he, in common with all readers of my volumes, bore witness to their accuracy. But here let me close this digression on Justus which he has forced upon me. . . .

Josephus and Rome

75. After the siege of Jotapata [in A.D. 67] I was in the hands of the Romans and was kept under guard, while receiving every attention. Vespasian showed in many ways the honor in which he held me, and it was by his command that I married one of the women taken captive at Cæsarea, a virgin and a native of that place. She did not, however, remain long with me, for she left me on my obtaining my release and accompanying Vespasian to Alexandria. There I married again. From Alexandria I was sent with Titus to the siege of Jerusalem, where my life was frequently in danger, both from the Jews, who were eager to get me into their hands, to gratify their revenge, and from the Romans, who attributed every reverse to some treachery on my part, and were constantly and clamorously demanding of the Emperor that he should punish me as their betrayer. Titus Cæsar, however, knowing well the varying fortunes of war, repressed by his silence the soldiers' outbursts against me.

Again, when at last Jerusalem was on the point of being carried by assault, Titus Cæsar repeatedly urged me to take whatever I would from the wreck of my country, stating that I had his permission. And I, now that my native place had fallen, having nothing more precious to take and preserve as a solace for my personal misfortunes, made request to Titus for the freedom of some of my countrymen; I also received by his gracious favor a gift of sacred books. Not long after I made petition for my brother and fifty friends, and my request was granted. Again, by permission of Titus, I entered the Temple, where a great multitude of captive women and children had been imprisoned, and liberated all the friends and acquaintances whom I recognized, in number about a hundred and ninety; I took no ransom for their release and restored them to their former fortune. Once more, when I was sent by Titus Cæsar with Cerealius and a thousand horse to a village called Tekoa, to prospect whether it was a suitable place for an entrenched camp, and on my return saw many prisoners who had been crucified, and recognized three of my acquaintances among them, I was cut to the heart and came and told Titus with tears what I had seen. He gave orders immediately that they should be taken down and receive the most careful treatment. Two of them died in the physicians' hands; the third survived.

76. When Titus had quelled the disturbances in Judæa, conjecturing that the lands which I held at Jerusalem would be unprofitable to me because a Roman garrison was to be quartered there, he gave me another parcel of ground in the plain. On his departure for Rome, he took me with him on board, treating me with every mark of respect. On our arrival in Rome I met with great consideration from Vespasian. He gave me a lodging in the house which he had occupied before he became Emperor; he honored me with Roman citizenship; and he assigned me a pension. He continued to honor me up to the time of his departure from this life, without any abatement in his kindness towards me.

My privileged position excited envy and thereby exposed me to danger. A certain Jew, named Jonathan, who had promoted an insurrection in Cyrene, occasioning the destruction of two thousand of the natives whom he had induced to join him, on being sent in chains by the governor of the district to the Emperor asserted that I had provided him with arms and money. Undeceived by this mendacious statement, Vespasian condemned him to death, and he was delivered over to

11

execution. Subsequently, numerous accusations against me were fabricated by persons who envied me my good fortune; but, by the providence of God, I came safe through all. Vespasian also presented me with a considerable tract of land in Judæa.

At this period I divorced my wife, being displeased at her behavior. She had borne me three children, of whom two died; one, whom I named Hyrcanus, is still alive. Afterwards I married a woman of Jewish extraction who had settled in Crete. She came of very distinguished parents, indeed the most notable people in that country. In character she surpassed many of her sex, as her subsequent life showed. By her I had two sons, Justus the elder, and then Simonides, surnamed Agrippa. Such is my domestic history.

The treatment which I received from the Emperors continued unaltered. On Vespasian's decease [in A.D. 79] Titus, who succeeded to the empire, showed the same esteem for me as did his father, and never credited the accusations to which I was constantly subjected. Domitian succeeded Titus [two years later] and added to my honors. He punished my Jewish accusers, and for a similar offense gave orders for the chastisement of a slave, a eunuch and my son's tutor. He also exempted my property in Judæa from taxation—a mark of the highest honor to the privileged individual. Moreover, Domitia, Cæsar's wife, never ceased conferring favors upon me.

Such are the events of my whole life; from them let others judge as they will of my character.

Having now, most excellent Epaphroditus, rendered you a complete account of our antiquities,* I shall here for the present conclude my narrative.

---

* The *Life*, in its final edition, was an appendix to the *Antiquities*.

Against Apion

BOOK I

Introduction

1. In my history of our antiquities, most excellent
Epaphroditus, I have, I think, made sufficiently clear
to any who may peruse that work the extreme antiquity
of our Jewish race, the purity of the original stock, and
the manner in which it established itself in the country which we occupy today. That history embraces a
period of five thousand years, and was written by me in
Greek on the basis of our sacred books. Since, however,
I observe that a considerable number of persons, influenced by the malicious calumnies of certain individuals, discredit the statements in my history concerning
our antiquity, and adduce as proof of the comparative
modernity of our race the fact that it has not been
thought worthy of mention by the best known Greek
historians, I consider it my duty to devote a brief
treatise to all these points in order at once to convict
our detractors of malignity and deliberate falsehood, to
correct the ignorance of others, and to instruct all who
desire to know the truth concerning the antiquity of
our race. As witnesses to my statements I propose to
call the writers who, in the estimation of the Greeks,
are the most trustworthy authorities on antiquity as a
whole. The authors of scurrilous and mendacious statements about us will be shown to be confuted by themselves. I shall further endeavor to set out the various
reasons which explain why our nation is mentioned by
a few only of the Greek historians; at the same time I
shall bring those authors who have not neglected our
history to the notice of any who either are, or feign to
be, ignorant of them.

2. My first thought is one of intense astonishment
at the current opinion that, in the study of primeval
history, the Greeks alone deserve serious attention, that

15

the truth should be sought from them, and that neither we nor any others in the world are to be trusted. In my view the very reverse of this is the case, if, that is to say, we are not to take idle prejudices as our guide, but to extract the truth from the facts themselves. For in the Greek world everything will be found to be modern and dating, so to speak, from yesterday or the day before: I refer to the foundation of their cities, the invention of the arts, and the compilation of a code of laws; but the most recent, or nearly the most recent, of all their attainments is care in historical composition. On the contrary, as is admitted even by themselves, the Egyptians, the Chaldæans, and the Phœnicians—for the moment I omit to add our nation to the list—possess a very ancient and permanent record of the past. For all these nations inhabit countries which are least exposed to the ravages of the atmosphere, and they have been very careful to let none of the events in their history be forgotten, but always to have them enshrined in official records written by their greatest sages.

The land of Greece, on the contrary, has experienced countless catastrophes that have obliterated the memory of the past; and as one civilization succeeded another, the men of each epoch believed that the world began with them. They were late in learning the alphabet and found the lesson difficult; for those who would assign the earliest date to its use pride themselves on having learnt it from the Phœnicians and Cadmus. Even of that date no record, preserved either in temples or on public monuments, could now be produced, seeing that it is a highly controversial and disputed question whether even those who took part in the Trojan War so many years later made use of letters, and the true and prevalent view is rather that they were ignorant of the present-day mode of writing. Throughout the whole range of Greek literature no undisputed work is found more ancient than the poetry of Homer. His date, however, is clearly later than the Trojan War; and even he, they say, did not leave his poems in writing. At first transmitted by memory, the scattered songs were not united until later; to which circumstance the numerous inconsistencies of the work are attributable.

Again, the Greeks who, [first] essayed to write history, such as Cadmus of Miletus and Acusilaus of Argos and any later writers who are mentioned, lived but a short time before the Persian invasion of Greece. Once more, the first Greek philosophers to treat of celestial and divine subjects, such as Pherecydes of Syros, Pythagoras, and Thales were, as the world unanimously admits, in their scanty productions the disciples of the Egyptians and Chaldæans. These are the writings which the Greeks regard as the oldest of all, and they are sceptical even about their authenticity.

3. Surely, then, it is absurd that the Greeks should be so conceited as to think themselves the sole possessors of a knowledge of antiquity and the only accurate reporters of its history. Anyone can easily discover from the historians themselves that their writings have no basis of sure knowledge, but merely present the facts as conjectured by individual authors. More often than not they confute each other in their works, not hesitating to give the most contradictory accounts of the same events. It would be superfluous for me to point out to readers better informed than myself what discrepancies there are between Hellanicus and Acusilaus on the genealogies, how often Acusilaus corrects Hesiod, how the mendacity of Hellanicus in most of his statements is exposed by Ephorus, that of Ephorus by Timæus, that of Timæus by later writers, and that of Herodotus by everybody. Even on Sicilian history Timæus did not condescend to agree with Antiochus, Philistus, or Callias; there is similar divergence on Attic affairs between the authors of the "Atthides" and on Argive affairs between the historians of Argos. What need, however, to speak of the histories of individual states and matters of minor importance, when contradictory accounts of the Persian invasion and the events which accompanied it have been given by writers of the first rank? On many points even Thucydides is accused of error by some critics, notwithstanding his reputation for writing the most accurate history of his time.

4. For such inconsistency many other causes might possibly be found if one cared to look for them; for my part, I attach the greatest weight to the two which I proceed to mention. I will begin with that which I regard as the more fundamental. The main responsibility for the errors of later historians who aspired to write on antiquity and for the license granted to their mendacity rests with the original neglect of the Greeks to keep official records of current events. This neglect was not confined to the lesser Greek states. Even among the Athenians, who are reputed to be indigenous and devoted to learning, we find that nothing of the kind existed, and their most ancient public records are said to be the laws on homicide drafted for them by Draco [in 621 B.C.], a man who lived only a little before the tyranny of Pisistratus. Of the Arcadians and their vaunted antiquity it is unnecessary to speak, since even at a still later date they had hardly learnt the alphabet.

5. It is, then, this lack of any basis of documentary evidence, which would have served at once to instruct the eager learner and to confute the liar, that accounts in the main for the inconsistencies among different historians. But a second reason must be added. Those who rushed into writing were concerned not so much to discover the truth, notwithstanding the profession which always comes readily to their pen, as to display their literary ability; and their choice of a subject was determined by the prospect which it offered them of outshining their rivals. Some turned to mythology, others sought popularity by encomiums upon cities or monarchs; others, again, set out to criticize the facts or the historians as the road to a reputation. In short, their invariable method is the very reverse of historical. For the proof of historical veracity is universal agreement in the description, oral or written, of the same events. On the contrary, each of these writers, in giving his divergent account of the same incidents, hoped thereby to be thought the most veracious of all. While, then, for eloquence and literary ability we must yield the palm to the Greek historians, we have no reason to do so for veracity in the history of antiquity, least of all where the

particular history of each separate foreign nation is concerned.

6. Of the care bestowed by the Egyptians and Babylonians on their chronicles from the remotest ages; and how the charge and exposition of these were entrusted, in the former country to the priests, in the latter to the Chaldæans; and how, among the nations in touch with the Greeks, it was the Phœnicians who made the largest use of writing, both for the ordinary affairs of life and for the commemoration of public events; of all this I think I need say nothing, as the facts are universally admitted. But that our forefathers took no less, not to say even greater, care than the nations I have mentioned in the keeping of their records—a task which they assigned to their chief priests and prophets—and that down to our own times these records have been, and if I may venture to say so, will continue to be, preserved with scrupulous accuracy, I will now endeavor briefly to demonstrate.

7. Not only did our ancestors in the first instance set over this business men of the highest character, devoted to the service of God, but they took precautions to ensure that the priests' lineage should be kept unadulterated and pure. A member of the priestly order must, to beget a family, marry a woman of his own race, without regard to her wealth or other distinctions; but he must investigate her pedigree, obtaining the genealogy from the archives and producing a number of witnesses. And this practice of ours is not confined to the home country of Judæa, but wherever there is a Jewish colony; there too a strict account is kept by the priests of their marriages—I allude to the Jews in Egypt and Babylon and other parts of the world in which any of the priestly order are living in dispersion. A statement is drawn up by them and sent to Jerusalem, showing the names of the bride and her father and more remote ancestors, together with the names of the witnesses. In the not infrequent event of war, for instance when our country was invaded by Antiochus Epiphanes, by Pompey the Great, by Quintilius Varus, and above all in our own times, the surviving priests compile fresh

records from the archives; they also pass scrutiny upon the remaining women, and disallow marriage with any who have been taken captive, suspecting them of having had frequent intercourse with foreigners. But the most convincing proof of our accuracy in this matter is that our records contain the names of our high priests, with the succession from father to son for the last two thousand years. And whoever violates any of the above rules is forbidden to minister at the altars or to take any other part in divine worship.

It therefore naturally, or rather necessarily, follows (seeing that with us it is not open to everybody to write the records, and that there is no discrepancy in what is written; seeing that, on the contrary, the prophets alone had this privilege, obtaining their knowledge of the most remote and ancient history through the inspiration which they owed to God and committing to writing a clear account of the events of their own time, just as they occurred)—it follows, I say, that (8) we do not possess myriads of inconsistent books, conflicting with each other. Our books, those which are justly accredited, are but two and twenty, and contain the record of all time.

Of these, five are the books of Moses, comprising the laws and the traditional history from the birth of man down to the death of the lawgiver. This period falls only a little short of three thousand years. From the death of Moses until Artaxerxes [I], who succeeded Xerxes as king of Persia, the prophets subsequent to Moses wrote the history of the events of their own times in thirteen books. The remaining four books contain hymns to God and precepts for the conduct of human life.

From Artaxerxes to our own time the complete history has been written, but has not been deemed worthy of equal credit with the earlier records because of the failure of the exact succession of the prophets.

We have given practical proof of our reverence for our own Scriptures. For, although such long ages have now passed, no one has ventured either to add, or to remove, or to alter a syllable; and it is an instinct with every Jew, from the day of his birth, to regard them as the decrees of God, to abide by them, and, if need be, cheerfully to die for them. Time and again ere now the sight has been witnessed of prisoners enduring tortures and death in every form in the theatres, rather than utter a single word against the laws and the allied documents.

What Greek would endure as much for the same cause? Even to save the entire collection of his nation's writings from destruction he would not face the smallest personal injury. For to the Greeks they are mere stories improvised according to the fancy of their authors; and in this estimate, even of the older historians, they are quite justified when they see some of their own contemporaries venturing to describe events in which they bore no part, without taking the trouble to seek information from those who know the facts. We have actually had so-called histories even of our recent war published by persons who never visited the sites nor were anywhere near the actions described, but, having put together a few hearsay reports, have, with the gross impudence of drunken revellers, miscalled their productions by the name of history.

9. I, on the contrary, have written a veracious account, at once comprehensive and detailed, of the war, having been present in person at all the events. I was in command of those whom we call Galilæans, so long as resistance was possible; after my capture I was a prisoner in the Roman camp. Vespasian and Titus, keeping me under surveillance, required my constant attendance upon them, at first in chains. Subsequently I was liberated and sent from Alexandria with Titus to the siege of Jerusalem. During that time no incident escaped my knowledge. I kept a careful record of all that went on under my eyes in the Roman camp and was alone in a position to understand the information brought by deserters. Then, in the leisure which Rome afforded me, with all my materials in readiness, and with the aid of some assistants for the sake of the Greek, at last I committed to writing my narrative of the events. So confident was I of its veracity that I presumed to take as my witnesses, before all others, the commanders-in-

chief in the war, Vespasian and Titus. They were the first to whom I presented my volumes, copies being afterwards given to many Romans who had taken part in the campaign. Others I sold to a large number of my compatriots, persons well versed in Greek learning, among whom were Julius Archelaus, the most venerable Herod, and the most admirable King Agrippa [II] himself. All these bore testimony to my scrupulous safeguarding of the truth, and they were not the men to conceal their sentiments or keep silence had I, through ignorance or partiality, distorted or omitted any of the facts.

10. Nevertheless, certain despicable persons have essayed to malign my history, taking it for a prize composition such as is set to boys at school. What an extraordinary accusation and calumny! Surely they ought to recognize that it is the duty of one who promises to present his readers with actual facts first to obtain an exact knowledge of them himself, either through having been in close touch with the events, or by inquiry from those who knew them. That duty I consider myself to have amply fulfilled in both my works. In my *Antiquities*, as I said, I have given a translation of our sacred books; being a priest and of priestly ancestry, I am well versed in the philosophy of those writings. My qualification as historian of the war was that I had been an actor in many, and an eyewitness of most, of the events; in short, nothing whatever was said or done of which I was ignorant. Surely, then, one cannot but regard as audacious the attempt of these critics to challenge my veracity. Even if, as they assert, they have read the *Commentaries* of the imperial commanders, they at any rate had no first-hand acquaintance with our position in the opposite camp. . . .

The Jewish Antiquities

BOOK I

Introduction

Proem 1. Those who essay to write histories are actuated, I observe, not by one and the same aim, but by many widely different motives. Some, eager to display their literary skill and to win the fame therefrom expected, rush into this department of letters; others, to gratify the persons to whom the record happens to relate, have undertaken the requisite labor even though beyond their power; others again have been constrained by the mere stress of events in which they themselves took part, to set these out in a comprehensive narrative; while many have been induced by prevailing ignorance of important affairs of general utility to publish a history of them for the public benefit. Of the aforesaid motives the two last apply to myself. For, having known by experience the war which we Jews waged against the Romans, the incidents in its course, and its issue, I was constrained to narrate it in detail in order to refute those who in their writings were doing outrage to the truth.

2. And now I have undertaken this present work in the belief that the whole Greek-speaking world will find it worthy of attention; for it will embrace our entire ancient history and political constitution, translated from the Hebrew records. I had indeed ere now, when writing the history of the war, already contemplated describing the origin of the Jews, the fortunes that befell them, the great lawgiver under whom they were trained in piety and the exercise of the other virtues, and all those wars waged by them through long ages before this last in which they were involuntarily engaged against the

25

Romans. However, since the compass of such a theme was excessive, I made the [*Jewish*] *War* into a separate volume, with its own beginning and end, thus duly proportioning my work. Nevertheless, as time went on, as is wont to happen to those who design to attack large tasks, there was hesitation and delay on my part in rendering so vast a subject into a foreign and unfamiliar tongue. However, there were certain persons curious about the history who urged me to pursue it, and above all Epaphroditus, a man devoted to every form of learning, but specially interested in the experiences of history, conversant as he himself has been with large affairs and varying turns of fortune, through all which he has displayed a wonderful force of character and an attachment to virtue that nothing could deflect. Yielding, then, to the persuasions of one who is ever an enthusiastic supporter of persons with ability to produce some useful or beautiful work, and ashamed of myself that I should be thought to prefer sloth to the effort of this noblest of enterprises, I was encouraged to greater ardor. Besides these motives, there were two further considerations to which I had given serious thought, namely, whether our ancestors, on the one hand, were willing to communicate such information, and whether any of the Greeks, on the other, had been curious to learn our history.

3. I found then that Ptolemy II [Philadelphus, who reigned 283-246 B.C.], that king who was so deeply interested in learning and such a collector of books, was particularly anxious to have our Law and the political constitution based thereon translated into Greek; while, on the other side, Eleazar, who yielded in virtue to none of our high priests, did not scruple to grant the monarch the enjoyment of a benefit, which he would certainly have refused had it not been our traditional custom to make nothing of what is good into a secret. Accordingly, I thought that it became me also both to imitate the high priest's magnanimity and to assume that there are still today many lovers of learning like the king. For even he failed to obtain all our records; only

the portion containing the Law was delivered to him by those who were sent to Alexandria to interpret it.*

The things narrated in the Sacred Scriptures are, however, innumerable, seeing that they embrace the history of five thousand years and recount all sorts of surprising reverses, many fortunes of war, heroic exploits of generals, and political revolutions. But, speaking generally, the main lesson to be learnt from this history by any who care to peruse it is that men who conform to the will of God, and do not venture to transgress laws that have been excellently laid down, prosper in all things beyond belief, and for their reward are offered by God felicity; whereas, in proportion as they depart from the strict observance of these laws, things (else) practicable become impracticable, and whatever imaginary good thing they strive to do ends in irretrievable disasters. At the outset, then, I entreat those who will read these volumes to fix their thoughts on God and to test whether our lawgiver has had a worthy conception of His nature and has always assigned to Him such actions as befit His power, keeping his words concerning Him pure of that unseemly mythology current among others; albeit that, in dealing with ages so long and so remote, he would have had ample license to invent fictions. For he was born two thousand years ago, to which ancient date the poets never ventured to refer even the birth of their gods, much less the actions or the laws of mortals. The precise details of our Scripture records will, then, be set forth each in its place as my narrative proceeds, that being the procedure that I have promised to follow throughout this work, neither adding nor omitting anything.

4. But, since well-nigh everything herein related is dependent on the wisdom of our lawgiver Moses, I must first speak briefly of him, lest any of my readers should ask how it is that so much of my work, which professes

* In this brief allusion to the Septuagint—the Greek translation of the Pentateuch (the traditional account of its origin being repeated at length in Book XII)—Josephus neglects to mention that the rest of the Old Testament was also translated at a later date, and that he himself drew freely on those books.

to treat of laws and historical facts, is devoted to natural philosophy. Be it known, then, that that sage deemed it above all necessary, for one who would order his own life aright and also legislate for others, first to study the nature of God, and then, having contemplated His works with the eye of reason, to imitate so far as possible that best of all models and endeavor to follow it. For neither could the lawgiver himself, without this vision, ever attain to a right mind, nor would anything that he should write in regard to virtue avail with his readers, unless before all else they were taught that God, as the universal Father and Lord who beholds all things, grants to such as follow Him a life of bliss, but involves in dire calamities those who step outside the path of virtue.

Such, then, being the lesson which Moses desired to instil into his fellow-citizens, he did not, when framing his laws, begin with contracts and the mutual rights of man, as others have done: No, he led their thoughts up to God and the construction of the world; he convinced them that of all God's works upon earth we men are the fairest; and when once he had won their obedience to the dictates of piety, he had no further difficulty in persuading them of all the rest. Other legislators, in fact, following fables, have in their writings imputed to the gods the disgraceful errors of men and thus furnished the wicked with a powerful excuse; our legislator, on the contrary, having shown that God possesses the very perfection of virtue, thought that men should strive to participate in it, and inexorably punished those who did not hold with or believe in these doctrines.

I therefore entreat my readers to examine my work from this point of view, for, studying it in this spirit, nothing will appear to them unreasonable, nothing incongruous with the majesty of God and His love for man. Everything, indeed, is here set forth in keeping with the nature of the universe—some things the lawgiver shrewdly veils in enigmas, others he sets forth in solemn allegory; but wherever straightforward speech is expedient, there he makes his meaning absolutely plain. Should any further desire to consider the reasons for every article in our creed, he would find the inquiry profound and highly philosophical; that subject for the moment I defer, but if God grants me time I shall endeavor to write upon it after completing the present work. I shall now accordingly turn to the narrative of events, first mentioning what Moses has said concerning the creation of the world, as I find it recorded in the sacred books. His account is as follows.

Genesis

i. 1. In the beginning God founded the heaven and the earth. The earth had not come into sight, but was hidden in thick darkness, and a breath from above sped over it, when God commanded that there should be light. It came, and surveying the whole of matter He divided the light from the darkness, calling the latter night and the former day, and naming the dawn of the light and its cessation morning and evening. This then should be the first day, but Moses spoke of it as "one" day; I could explain why he did so now, but having promised to render an account of the causes of everything in a special work, I defer till then the explanation of this point also. After this, on the second day, He set the heaven above the universe, when He was pleased to sever this from the rest and to assign it a place apart, congealing ice about it and withal rendering it moist and rainy, to give the benefit of the dews in a manner congenial to the earth. On the third day he established the earth, pouring around it the sea; and on the self-same day plants and seeds sprang forthwith from the soil. On the fourth He adorned the heaven with sun and moon and the other stars, prescribing their motions and courses to indicate the revolutions of the seasons. The fifth day He let loose, in the deep and in the air, the creatures that swim or fly, linking them in partnership and union to generate and to increase and multiply their kind. The sixth day He created the race of four-footed creatures, making them male and female; on this day also He formed man. Thus, so Moses tells us, the world and everything in it was made in six days in all; and on the seventh God rested and had respite from His labors, for which reason we also pass this day in repose from toil and call it the Sabbath, a word which in the Hebrew language means "rest."

2. And here, after [recording] the seventh day, Moses begins to interpret nature, writing on the formation of man in these terms: "God fashioned man by taking dust from the earth and instilled into him spirit and soul." Now this man was called Adam, which in Hebrew signifies "red," because he was made from the red earth kneaded together; for such is the color of the true virgin soil. And God brought before Adam the living creatures after their kinds, exhibiting both male and female, and gave them the names by which they are still called to this day. Then seeing Adam to be without female partner and consort (for indeed there was none), and looking with astonishment at the other creatures who had their mates, He extracted one of his ribs while he slept and from it formed woman; and when she was brought to him Adam recognized that she was made from himself. In the Hebrew tongue woman is called *isshah;* but the name of that first woman was Eve, which signifies "mother of all (living)."

3. Moses further states that God planted a park eastward, abounding in all manner of plants, among them being the tree of life and another of the wisdom by which might be distinguished what was good and what evil; and into this garden he brought Adam and his wife and bade them tend the plants. Now this garden is watered by a single river whose stream encircles all the earth and is parted into four branches. Of these Phison (a name meaning "multitude") runs towards India and falls into the sea, being called by the Greeks Ganges; Euphrates and Tigris end in the Erythræan Sea . . . ; lastly Geon, which flows through Egypt, means "that which wells up to us from the opposite world," and by Greeks is called the Nile.

4. Now God bade Adam and his wife partake of the rest of the plants, but to abstain from the tree of wisdom, forewarning them that if they touched it, it would prove their destruction. At that epoch all the creatures

spoke a common tongue, and the serpent, living in the company of Adam and his wife, grew jealous of the blessings which he supposed were destined for them if they obeyed God's behests, and, believing that disobedience would bring trouble upon them, he maliciously persuaded the woman to taste of the tree of wisdom, telling her that in it resided the power of distinguishing good and evil, possessing which they would lead a blissful existence, no whit behind that of a god. By these means he misled the woman to scorn the commandment of God: she tasted of the tree, was pleased with the food, and persuaded Adam also to partake of it.

And now they became aware that they were naked, and ashamed of such exposure to the light of day, bethought them of a covering, for the tree served to quicken their intelligence. So they covered themselves with fig-leaves, and thus screening their genitals, believed themselves the happier for having found what they lacked before. But when God entered the garden, Adam, who ere then was wont to resort to His company, being conscious of his crime, withdrew; and God, met by action so strange, asked for what reason he who once took delight in His company now shunned and avoided it. But when he spoke not a word, conscious of having transgressed the divine command, God said, "Nay, I had decreed for thee to live a life of bliss, unmolested by all ill, with no care to fret thy souls. All things that contribute to enjoyment and pleasure were, through my providence, to spring up for thee spontaneously, without toil or distress of thine; blessed with these gifts, old age would not soon have overtaken thee, and thy life would have been long. But now thou hast flouted this my purpose by disobeying my commands; for it is through no virtue that thou keepest silence, but through an evil conscience."

Adam then began to make excuse for his sin and besought God not to be wroth with him, laying the blame for the deed upon the woman and saying that it was her deception that had caused him to sin; while she, in her turn, accused the serpent. Thereupon God imposed punishment on Adam for yielding to a woman's counsel,

31

telling him that the earth would no more produce anything of herself, but, in return for toil and grinding
labor, would but afford some of her fruits and refuse
others. Eve He punished by child-birth and its attendant
pains, because she had deluded Adam, even as the serpent had beguiled her, and so brought calamity upon
him. He moreover deprived the serpent of speech, indignant at his malignity to Adam; He also put poison
beneath his tongue, destining him to be the enemy of
men and admonishing them to strike their blows upon
his head, because it was therein that man's danger lay,
and there too that his adversaries could most easily inflict a mortal blow. He further bereft him of feet and
made him crawl and wriggle along the ground. Having
imposed these penalties upon them, God removed Adam
and Eve from the garden to another place.

ii. 1. Two male children were born to them; the
first was called Cain, whose name being interpreted
means "acquisition," and the second Abel, meaning
"nothing." They also had daughters. Now the brothers
took pleasure in different pursuits. Abel, the younger,
had respect for righteousness and, believing that God
was with him in all his actions, paid heed to virtue; he
led the life of a shepherd. Cain, on the contrary, was
thoroughly depraved and had an eye only to gain; he
was the first to think of ploughing the soil, and he slew
his brother for the following reason. The brothers having
decided to sacrifice to God, Cain brought the fruits of
the tilled earth and of the trees, Abel came with milk
and the firstlings of his flocks. This was the offering
which found more favor with God, Who is honored by
things that grow spontaneously and in accordance with
natural laws, and not by the products forced from nature by the ingenuity of grasping man. Thereupon Cain,
incensed at God's preference for Abel, slew his brother
and hid his corpse, thinking to escape detection. But
God, aware of the deed, came to Cain, and asked him
whither his brother had gone, since for many days He
had not seen him whom He had constantly before beheld in Cain's company. Cain, in embarrassment, having
nothing to reply to God, at first declared that he too was

perplexed at not seeing his brother, and then, enraged at the insistent pressure and strict inquiries of God, said that he was not his brother's guardian to keep watch over his person and his actions. Upon that word God now accused Cain of being his brother's murderer, saying, "I marvel that thou canst not tell what has become of a man whom thou thyself hast destroyed."

God, however, exempted him from the penalty merited by the murder, Cain having offered a sacrifice and therewith supplicated Him not to visit him too severely in His wrath; but He made him accursed and threatened to punish his posterity in the seventh generation, and expelled him from that land with his wife. But, when Cain feared that in his wanderings he would fall a prey to wild beasts and perish thus, God bade him have no melancholy foreboding from such cause: he would be in no danger from beasts, and might fare unafraid through every land. He then set a mark upon him, by which he should be recognized, and bade him depart.

2. After long travels, Cain settled with his wife in a place called Nais, where he made his abode and where children were born to him. His punishment, however, far from being taken as a warning, only served to increase his vice. He indulged in every bodily pleasure, even if it entailed outraging his companions; he increased his substance with wealth amassed by rapine and violence; he incited to luxury and pillage all whom he met, and became their instructor in wicked practices. He put an end to that simplicity in which men lived before by the invention of weights and measures: the guileless and generous existence which they had enjoyed in ignorance of these things he converted into a life of craftiness. He was the first to fix boundaries of land and to build a city, fortifying it with walls and constraining his clan to congregate in one place. This city he called Enocha after his eldest son Enoch.

Enoch had a son Jarad, of whom come Maruel, who begat Methusaleh, the father of Lamech, who had seventy-seven children by his two wives, Sella and Ada. Of these children, Jabal, son of Ada, erected tents and devoted himself to a pastoral life; Jubal, born of the same mother, studied music and invented harps and lutes; Tubal, one of the sons of the other wife, surpassing all men in strength, distinguished himself in the art of war, procuring also thereby the means for satisfying the pleasures of the body, and first invented the forging of metal. Lamech was also the father of a daughter named Noema; and because through his clear knowledge of divine things he saw that he was to pay the penalty for Cain's murder of his brother, he made this known to his wives. Thus, within Adam's lifetime, the descendants of Cain went to depths of depravity, and inheriting and imitating one another's vices, each ended worse than the last. They rushed incontinently into battle and plunged into brigandage; or if anyone was too timid for slaughter, he would display other forms of mad recklessness by insolence and greed.

3. Meanwhile Adam, the man first formed out of earth—for my narrative requires me to revert to him—after the slaughter of Abel and the consequent flight of his murderer Cain, longed for children, and was seized with a passionate desire to beget a family, when he had now completed 230 years of his life; he lived for 700 years more before he died. Many other children were born to him, and among them Seth. It would take me too long to speak of the rest, and I will only endeavor to narrate the story of the progeny of Seth. He, after being brought up and attaining to years of discretion, cultivated virtue, excelled in it himself, and left descendants who imitated his ways. These, being all of virtuous character, inhabited the same country without dissension and in prosperity, meeting with no untoward incident to the day of their death; they also discovered the science of the heavenly bodies and their orderly array. Moreover, to prevent their discoveries from being lost to mankind and perishing before they became known —Adam having predicted a destruction of the universe, at one time by a violent fire and at another by a mighty deluge of water—they erected two pillars, one of brick and the other of stone, and inscribed these discoveries on both, so that if the pillar of brick disappeared in the deluge, that of stone would remain to teach men what

was graven thereon and to inform them that they had also erected one of brick. It exists to this day in the land of Seiris.*

iii. 1. For seven generations these people continued to believe in God as Lord of the universe and to take virtue for their guide in everything; then, in course of time, they abandoned the customs of their fathers for a life of depravity. They no longer rendered to God His due honors, nor took account of justice towards men, but displayed by their actions a zeal for vice twofold greater than they had formerly shown for virtue, and thereby drew upon themselves the enmity of God. For many angels of God now consorted with women and begat sons who were overbearing and disdainful of every virtue, such confidence had they in their strength; in fact the deeds that tradition ascribes to them resemble the audacious exploits told by the Greeks of the giants. But Noah, indignant at their conduct and viewing their counsels with displeasure, urged them to come to a better frame of mind and amend their ways; but seeing that, far from yielding, they were completely enslaved to the pleasure of sin, he feared that they would murder him and with his wives and sons and his sons' wives quitted the country.

2. God loved Noah for his righteousness, but as for those men, He condemned not them alone for their wickedness, but resolved to destroy all mankind then existing and to create another race pure of vice, abridging their term of life from its former longevity to one hundred and twenty years. He therefore converted the dry land into sea. Thus were they all obliterated, while Noah alone was saved, God having put into his mind a device and means of salvation on this wise. He constructed an ark of four stories, three hundred cubits in length, fifty in breadth and thirty in depth, on which he embarked with his children, the mother of his children, and his sons' wives; not only furnishing it with all things requisite to supply their needs, but also taking

---

* Seiris is unidentified. It has been suggested that this story arose from some ancient monument with an inscription in a Hittite or some other unknown script.

with him creatures of every kind, male and female, to preserve their species, some among them being numbered by sevens. This ark had stout sides and roof so as not to be overwhelmed from any quarter and to defy the violence of the waters. Thus was Noah saved with his family. He was the tenth descendant of Adam, being son of Lamech. . . .

3. This catastrophe happened in the six hundredth year of Noah's rulership, in what was once the second month, called by the Macedonians Dius and by the Hebrews Marsuan, according to the arrangement of the calendar which they followed in Egypt. Moses, however, appointed Nisan, that is to say Xanthicus, as the first month for the festivals, because it was in this month that he brought the Hebrews out of Egypt; he also reckoned this month as the commencement of the year for everything relating to divine worship, but for selling and buying and other ordinary affairs he preserved the ancient order. It was, he tells us, on the seven and twentieth day of the said month that the deluge began. The time of this event was 2262 years after the birth of Adam, the first man; the date is recorded in the sacred books, it being the custom of that age to note with minute care the birth and death of the illustrious men. . . .

[*Josephus then shows how he came to the figure of 2262 years.*]

5. When God gave the signal and caused the rainfall to begin, the water poured down for forty entire days, insomuch that it rose to fifteen cubits above the surface of the earth. That was the reason why no more escaped, since they had no place of refuge. When the rain at length ceased, for 150 days the water scarcely began to sink, until at the opening of the seventh month, from the seventh day, it little by little subsided as the month drew to a close. Then the ark settled on a mountain-top in Armenia. Observing this, Noah opened the ark, and, seeing a little land surrounding it, with hopes now revived, remained where he was. But a few days later, the water continuing to sink, he let loose a

raven, to learn whether any other portion of the earth had emerged from the flood and would now make it safe to disembark; but the bird found the whole land inundated and returned to Noah. Seven days after, he sent forth a dove to explore the condition of the earth; it returned bearing the marks of clay and an olive-branch in its mouth. Noah, thus learning that the earth was delivered from the flood, waited yet seven days, and then let the animals out of the ark, went forth himself with his family, sacrificed to God, and feasted with his household. The Armenians call that spot the Landing-place, for it was there that the ark came safe to land, and they show the relics of it to this day.

6. This flood and the ark are mentioned by all who have written histories of the barbarians. Among these is Berosus the Chaldæan, who in his description of the events of the flood writes somewhere as follows: "It is said, moreover, that a portion of the vessel still survives in Armenia on the mountain of the Cordyæans, and that persons carry off pieces of the bitumen, which they use as talismans." These matters are also mentioned by Hieronymus the Egyptian, author of the ancient history of Phœnicia, by Mnaseas and by many others. Nicolaus of Damascus in his ninety-sixth book relates the story as follows: "There is above the country of Minyas in Armenia a great mountain called Baris, where, as the story goes, many refugees found safety at the time of the flood, and one man, transported upon an ark, grounded upon the summit, and relics of the timber were for long preserved; this might well be the same man of whom Moses, the Jewish legislator, wrote."*

---

* Nicolaus of Damascus, born about 64 B.C., wrote in his native Greek a vast *Universal History* from earliest times to the death of Herod the Great, whose close adviser he was. This work was one of Josephus' main sources.

BOOK·II

The Exodus

ix. 1. The Egyptians, being a voluptuous people and slack to labor, slaves to pleasure in general and to a love of lucre in particular, eventually became bitterly disposed towards the Hebrews through envy of their prosperity. For seeing that the race of the Israelites flourished and that their virtues and aptitude for labor had already gained them the distinction of abundant wealth, they believed that their growth in power was to their own detriment. Those benefits which they had received from Joseph being through lapse of time forgotten, and the kingdom having now passed to another dynasty, they grossly maltreated the Israelites and devised for them all manner of hardships. Thus they ordered them to divide the river into numerous canals, to build ramparts for the cities and dikes to hold the waters of the river and to prevent them from forming marshes when they overflowed its banks; and with the rearing of pyramid after pyramid they exhausted our race, which was thus apprenticed to all manner of crafts and became inured to toil. For full four hundred years they endured these hardships; it was indeed a contest between them, the Egyptians striving to kill off the Israelites with drudgery, and these ever to show themselves superior to their tasks.

2. While they were in this plight, a further incident had the effect of stimulating the Egyptians yet more to exterminate our race. One of the sacred scribes—persons with considerable skill in accurately predicting the future—announced to the king that there would be born to the Israelites at that time one who would abase the sovereignty of the Egyptians and exalt the Israelites, were he reared to manhood, and would surpass all men in virtue and win everlasting renown. Alarmed thereat,

38

the king, on this sage's advice, ordered that every male child born to the Israelites should be destroyed by being cast into the river, and that the labors of Hebrew women with child should be observed and watch kept for their delivery by the Egyptian midwives; for this office was, by his orders, to be performed by women who, as compatriots of the king, were not likely to transgress his will. Those who notwithstanding defied this decree, and ventured stealthily to save their offspring, he ordered to be put to death along with their progeny.

Terrible then was the calamity confronting the victims: not only were they to be bereft of their children, not only must the parents themselves be accessories to the destruction of their offspring, but the design of extinguishing their race by the massacre of the infants and their own approaching dissolution rendered their lot cruel and inconsolable. Such was their miserable situation; but no man can defeat the will of God, whatever countless devices he may contrive to that end. For this child, whose birth the sacred scribe had foretold, was reared, eluding the king's vigilance, and the prophet's words concerning all that was to be wrought through him proved true; and this is how it happened.

3. Amram, a Hebrew of noble birth, fearing that the whole race would be extinguished through lack of the succeeding generation, and seriously anxious on his own account because his wife was with child, was in grievous perplexity. He accordingly had recourse to prayer to God, beseeching Him to take some pity at length on men who had in no wise transgressed in their worship of Him, and to grant them deliverance from the tribulations of the present time and from the prospect of the extermination of their race. And God had compassion on him and, moved by his supplication, appeared to him in his sleep, exhorted him not to despair of the future, and told him that He had their piety in remembrance and would ever give them its due recompense, even as He had already granted their forefathers to grow from a few souls into so great a multitude. He recalled how Abraham, departing alone from Mesopotamia on his journey to Canaan, had in every way been blessed;

and above all how his wife, once barren, had thereafter, thanks to His will, been rendered fertile; how he had begotten sons and had bequeathed the land of Arabia to Ishmael and his descendants, Troglodytis to his children by Katura, and Canaan to Isaac.

"Aye," He said, "and all that prowess that he displayed in war under my auspices, ye would indeed be deemed impious not to hold in remembrance. Jacob too became famous even among an alien people for the height of that prosperity to which he attained in his lifetime and which he left to his children. With but seventy souls in all, he arrived in Egypt, and already ye are become upwards of six hundred thousand. And now be it known to you that I am watching over the common welfare of you all and thine own renown. This child, whose birth has filled the Egyptians with such dread that they have condemned to destruction all the offspring of the Israelites, shall indeed be thine; he shall escape those who are watching to destroy him, and, reared in marvellous wise, he shall deliver the Hebrew race from their bondage in Egypt, and be remembered, so long as the universe shall endure, not by Hebrews alone but even by alien nations; that favor do I bestow upon thee and upon thy posterity. Furthermore, he shall have a brother so blessed as to hold my priesthood, he and his descendants, throughout all ages."

4. These things revealed to him in vision, Amram on awaking disclosed to Jochebed, his wife; and their fears were only the more intensified by the prediction in the dream. For it was not merely for a child that they were anxious, but for that high felicity for which he was destined. However, their belief in the promises of God was confirmed by the manner of the woman's delivery, since she escaped the vigilance of the watch, thanks to the gentleness of her travail, which spared her any violent throes. For three months they reared the child in secret; and then Amram, fearing that he would be detected and, incurring the king's wrath, would perish himself along with the young child and thus bring God's promise to nought, resolved to commit the salvation and protection of the child to Him, rather than to trust

to the uncertain chance of concealment and thereby endanger not only the child, clandestinely reared, but himself also; assured that God would provide complete security that nothing should be falsified of that which He had spoken.

Having so determined, they constructed a basket of papyrus reeds, fashioned in the form of a cradle, spacious enough to give the infant ample room for repose. Then, having daubed it with bitumen, that substance serving to prevent the water from penetrating through the wicker-work, they placed the young child within, and launching it on the river, committed his salvation to God. The river received its charge and bore it on, while Miriam, the sister of the child, at her mother's bidding, kept pace with it along the bank to see whither the basket would go. Then once again did God plainly show that human intelligence is nothing worth, but that all that He wills to accomplish reaches its perfect end; and that they who, to save themselves, condemn others to destruction, utterly fail, whatever diligence they may employ; while those are saved by a miracle and attain success almost from the very jaws of disaster, who hazard all by divine decree. Even so did the fate that befell this child display the power of God.

5. The king had a daughter, Thermuthis. Playing by the river bank and spying the basket being borne down the stream, she sent off some swimmers with orders to bring that cot to her. When these returned from their errand with the cot, she, at sight of the little child, was enchanted at its size and beauty; for such was the tender care which God showed for Moses, that the very persons who by reason of his birth had decreed the destruction of all children of Hebrew parentage were made to condescend to nourish and tend him. And so Thermuthis ordered a woman to be brought to suckle the infant. But when instead of taking the breast, it spurned it, and then repeated this action with several women, Miriam, who had come upon the scene, apparently without design and from mere curiosity, said, "It is lost labor, my royal lady, to summon to feed the child these women who have no ties of kinship with it. Wert thou

now to have one of the Hebrew women fetched, maybe it would take the breast of one of its own race." Her advice seemed sound, and the princess bade her do this service herself and run for a foster-mother. Availing herself of such permission, the girl returned bringing the mother, whom no one knew. Thereupon the infant, gleefully as it were, fastened upon the breast, and by request of the princess, the mother was permanently entrusted with its nurture.

6. It was indeed from this very incident that the princess gave him the name recalling his immersion in the river, for the Egyptians call water *môu* and those who are saved *esês*; so they conferred on him this name compounded of both words. And all agree that in accordance with the prediction of God, for grandeur of intellect and contempt of toils he was the noblest Hebrew of them all. He was the seventh from Abraham, being the son of Amram, who was the son of Caath, whose father was Levi, the son of Jacob, who was the son of Isaac, the son of Abraham.

His growth in understanding was not in line with his growth in stature, but far outran the measure of his years. Its maturer excellence was displayed in his very games, and his actions then gave promise of the greater deeds to be wrought by him on reaching manhood. When he was three years old, God gave wondrous increase to his stature; and none was so indifferent to beauty as not, on seeing Moses, to be amazed at his comeliness. And it often happened that persons meeting him as he was borne along the highway turned, attracted by the child's appearance, and neglected their serious affairs to gaze at leisure upon him; indeed childish charm so perfect and pure as his held the beholders spellbound.

7. Such was the child whom Thermuthis adopted as her son, being blessed with no offspring of her own. Now one day she brought Moses to her father and showed him to him, and told him how she had been mindful for the succession, were it God's will to grant her no child of her own, by bringing up a boy of divine beauty and generous spirit, and by what a miracle she

had received him of the river's bounty, "and methought," she said, "to make him my child and heir to thy kingdom." With these words she laid the babe in her father's arms; and he took and clasped him affectionately to his breast, and to please his daughter, placed his diadem upon his head. But Moses tore it off and flung it to the ground, in mere childishness, and trampled it underfoot. This was taken as an omen of evil import to the kingdom.

At that spectacle the sacred scribe who had foretold that this child's birth would lead to the abasement of the Egyptian empire rushed forward to kill him with a fearful shout: "This," he cried, "O king, this is that child whom God declared that we must kill to allay our terrors; he bears out the prediction by that act of insulting thy dominion and trampling the diadem under foot. Kill him then, and at one stroke relieve the Egyptians of their fear of him and deprive the Hebrews of the courageous hopes that he inspires." But Thermuthis was too quick for him and snatched the child away; the king too delayed to slay him, from a hesitation induced by God, whose providence watched over Moses' life. He was accordingly educated with the utmost care, the Hebrews resting the highest hopes upon him for their future, while the Egyptians viewed his upbringing with misgiving. However, since even if the king slew him there was no one else in sight, whether relative by adoption or any other, in whom they could put more confidence to act in the interest of the Egyptians through his foreknowledge of the future,* they refrained from slaying him.

x. 1. Moses then, born and brought up in the manner already described, on coming of age gave the Egyptians signal proof of his merits, and that he was born for their humiliation and for the advancement of the Hebrews; here is the occasion which he seized. The Ethiopians, who are neighbors of the Egyptians, invaded their territory and pillaged their possessions; the Egyptians in indignation made a campaign against them to

---

* Translator's note: "Text corrupt and meaning obscure."

avenge the affront, and being beaten in battle, some fell and the rest ingloriously escaped to their own land by flight. But the Ethiopians followed in hot pursuit, and deeming it feebleness not to subdue the whole of Egypt, they assailed the country far and wide, and having tasted of its riches, refused to relinquish their hold. And since the neighboring districts exposed to their first incursions did not venture to oppose them, they advanced as far as Memphis and to the sea, none of the cities being able to withstand them.

Oppressed by this calamity, the Egyptians had recourse to oracles and divinations; and when counsel came to them from God to take the Hebrew for their ally, the king bade his daughter give up Moses to serve as his general. And she, after her father had sworn to do him no injury, surrendered him, judging that great benefit would come of such an alliance, while reproaching the knavish priests who, after having spoken of putting him to death as an enemy, were now not ashamed to crave his succor.

2. Moses, thus summoned both by Thermuthis and by the king, gladly accepted the task, to the delight of the sacred scribes of both nations; for the Egyptians hoped through his valor both to defeat their foes and at the same time to make away with Moses by guile, while the Hebrew hierarchy foresaw the possibility of escape from the Egyptians with Moses as their general. He thereupon, to surprise the enemy before they had even learned of his approach, mustered and marched off his army, taking the route not by way of the river but through the interior.

There he gave a wonderful proof of his sagacity. For the route is rendered difficult for a march by reason of a multitude of serpents, which the region produces in abundant varieties, insomuch that there are some found nowhere else and bred here alone, remarkable for their power, their malignity, and their strange aspect; and among them are some which are actually winged, so that they can attack one from their hiding-place in the ground or inflict unforeseen injury by rising into the air. Moses, then, to provide security and an innocuous pas-

sage for his troops, devised a marvelous stratagem: he
had baskets, resembling chests, made of the bark of
papyrus and took these with him full of ibises. Now
this animal is the serpents' deadliest enemy: they flee
before its onset and in making off are caught, just as
they are by stags, and swallowed up. The ibis is otherwise a tame creature and ferocious only to the serpent
tribe; but I refrain from further words on this subject,
for Greeks are not unacquainted with the nature of the
ibis. When, therefore, he entered the infested region,
he by means of these birds beat off the vermin, letting
them loose upon them and using these auxiliaries to
clear the ground.

Having thus accomplished the march, he came wholly
unexpected upon the Ethiopians; joined battle with
them and defeated them, crushing their cherished hopes
of mastering the Egyptians; and then proceeded to
attack and overthrow their cities, great carnage of the
Ethiopians ensuing. After tasting of this success which
Moses had brought them, the Egyptian army showed
such indefatigable energy that the Ethiopians were
menaced with servitude and complete extirpation. In
the end they were all driven into Saba, the capital of
the Ethiopian realm, . . . and were there besieged.
But the place offered extreme obstacles to a besieger,
for the Nile enclosed it in a circle, and other rivers, the
Astapus and the Astabaras, added to the difficulty of the
attack for any who attempted to cross the current. The
city which lies within in fact resembles an island:
strong walls encompass it, and as a bulwark against its
enemies it has the rivers, besides great dikes within
the ramparts to protect it from inundation when the
force of the swollen streams is unusually violent; and
it is these which made the capture of the town so
difficult, even to those who had crossed the rivers.

Moses, then, was chafing at the inaction of his army,
for the enemy would not venture upon an engagement,
when he met with the following adventure. Tharbis, the
daughter of the king of the Ethiopians, watching Moses
bringing his troops close beneath the ramparts and
fighting valiantly, marvelled at the ingenuity of his

maneuvers and, understanding that it was to him that the
Egyptians, who but now despaired of their independence,
owed all their success, and through him that the Ethiopians, so boastful of their feats against them, were
reduced to the last straits, fell madly in love with him;
and under the mastery of this passion she sent to him
the most trusty of her menials to make him an offer of
marriage. He accepted the proposal on condition that
she would surrender the town, pledged himself by oath
verily to take her to wife, and once master of the town,
not to violate the pact; whereupon action outstripped
parley. After chastisement of the Ethiopians, Moses rendered thanks to God, celebrated the nuptials, and led
the Egyptians back to their own land.

xi. 1. But the Egyptians, thus saved by Moses, conceived from their very deliverance a hatred for him
and thought good to pursue with greater ardor their
plots upon his life, suspecting that he would take advantage of his success to revolutionize Egypt, and suggested to the king that he should be put to death. He
on his own part was harboring thoughts of so doing,
alike from envy of Moses' generalship and from fear of
seeing himself abased, and so, when instigated by the
hierarchy, was prepared to lend a hand in the murder
of Moses. Their victim, however, informed betimes of
the plot, secretly escaped, and since the roads were
guarded, directed his flight across the desert to where
he had no fear of being caught by his foes; he left
without provisions, proudly confident of his powers of
endurance. On reaching the town of Midian, situated
by the Red Sea and named after one of Abraham's sons
by Katura, he sat down on the brink of a well and
there rested after his toil and hardships at midday, not
far from the town. Here he was destined to play a part,
arising out of the customs of the inhabitants, which
exhibited his merits and proved the opening of better
fortune.

2. For, those regions being scant of water, the shepherds used to make a first claim on the wells for fear
that, the water being exhausted by others beforehand,
there should be nothing for their flocks to drink. Now

there came to this well seven sisters, virgin daughters of Raguel, a priest held in high veneration by the people of the country. They were in charge of their father's flocks, for this function is customarily undertaken by women also among the Troglodytes, and arriving first, they drew from the well sufficient water for their flocks into troughs constructed to receive it. But when shepherds, appearing, set upon the young women in order to appropriate the water for themselves, Moses, deeming it monstrous to overlook this injury to the girls and to suffer these men's violence to triumph over the maidens' rights, beat off the arrogant intruders and afforded the others opportune aid. And they, after this beneficent act, went to their father, and recounting the shepherds' insolence and the succor which the stranger had lent them, besought him not to let such charity go for nought or unrewarded.

The father commended his children for their zeal for their benefactor and bade them bring Moses to his presence to receive the gratitude that was his due. On his arrival, he told him of his daughters' testimony to the help which he had rendered, and expressing admiration for his gallantry, added that he had not bestowed this service upon those who had no sense of gratitude, but on persons well able to requite a favor, indeed to outdo by the amplitude of the reward the measure of the benefit. He therewith adopted him as his son, gave him one of his daughters in marriage, and appointed him keeper and master of his flocks, which formerly made up all the wealth of the barbarian races.

xii. 1. So Moses, having received these benefits from Jethroglæus—such was the surname of Raguel—abode there feeding the cattle. And some while afterward, he led the flocks to graze on the mount called Sinai—it is the highest of the mountains in this region and the best for pasturage, for it produces excellent turf, and owing to a belief that the Deity sojourned there, had not hitherto been cropped, the shepherds not venturing to invade it. Here it was that he witnessed an amazing prodigy: a fire was ablaze on a bramble-bush, yet had left its vesture of green and its bloom intact, nor had

47

one of its fruit-laden branches been consumed, albeit
the flame was great and exceeding fierce. Moses was
terrified at this strange spectacle, but was amazed yet
more when this fire found a tongue, called him by name,
and communed with him, signifying to him his hardi-
hood in venturing to approach a spot whither no man
had penetrated before by reason of its divinity, and
admonishing him to withdraw as far as might be from
the flame, to be content with what he, as a man of
virtue sprung from illustrious ancestors, had seen,
but to pry no further.

The voice furthermore predicted the glory and honor
that he would win from men, under God's auspices,
and bade him courageously return to Egypt, to act as
commander and leader of the Hebrew hosts, and to
deliver his kinsmen from the outrage that they there
endured. "For indeed," continued the voice, "they shall
inhabit this favored land wherein Abraham dwelt, the
forefather of your race, and shall enjoy all its blessings,
and it is thou, aye and thy sagacity, that shall conduct
them thither." Howbeit he charged him, after he had
brought the Hebrews out of Egypt, to come to that
spot and there offer sacrifices of thanksgiving. Such
were the divine oracles that issued from the fire.

2. Moses, in consternation at what he had seen and
much more at what he had heard, replied: "To mistrust,
O Lord, thy power, which I venerate myself and know
to have been manifested to my forefathers, were madness too gross, I trow, for my mind to conceive. Yet
am I at a loss to know how I, a mere commoner, blest
with no strength, could either find words to persuade
my people to quit that land that they now inhabit and
follow me to that whereunto I would lead them, or
even, should they be persuaded, how I should constrain
Pharaoh to permit the exodus of those to whose toils
and tasks his subjects look to swell their own prosperity."

3. But God exhorted him to have perfect confidence,
promising Himself to assist him, and when words were
needed, to lend persuasion, when action was called for,
to furnish strength; and He bade him cast his staff to
the ground and to have faith in His promises. Moses did

so, and, lo, there was a serpent crawling and coiling itself in spiral fashion and rearing its head as in defense against assailants; then once more it became a stick. Next He bade him put his right hand into his bosom; he obeyed and drew it forth white, of a color resembling chalk; then it resumed its ordinary aspect. Receiving a further command to take of the water of a neighboring brook and pour it on the ground, he beheld it turned to the color of blood. And while he marvelled at these wonders, God exhorted him to be of good courage, to be assured that His mighty aid would be ever with him, and to use miracles to convince all men (said He) "that thou art sent by me and doest all at my command. And I bid thee without more delay make speed to Egypt, pressing forward by night and day, and by no dallying to prolong the time for the Hebrews, now suffering in servitude."

4. Moses, unable to doubt the promises of the Deity, after having seen and heard such confirmation of them, prayed and entreated that he might be vouchsafed this power in Egypt; he also besought Him not to deny him the knowledge of His name, but, since he had been granted speech with Him and vision of Him, further to tell him how He should be addressed, so that, when sacrificing, he might invoke Him by name to be present at the sacred rites. Then God revealed to him His name, which ere then had not come to men's ears, and of which I am forbidden to speak. Moreover, Moses found those miracles at his service not on that occasion only, but at all times whensoever there was need of them; from all which tokens he came to trust more firmly in the oracle from the fire, to believe that God would be his gracious protector, and to hope to be able to deliver his people and to bring disaster upon the Egyptians.

xiii. 1. Accordingly, on learning that the king of Egypt, the Pharaoh under whom he had fled the country, was dead, he besought Raguel to permit him for the welfare of his countrymen to go to Egypt; and taking with him Zipporah his wife, daughter of Raguel, and the children whom he had by her, Gershom and Eliezer, he hastened thither. Of these two names, the one, Gershom, means in the Hebrew tongue that he had come to "a foreign land"; the other, Eliezer, that it was with the assistance of the God of his fathers that he had escaped from the Egyptians. On approaching the frontier he was met, at God's bidding, by his brother Aaron, to whom he revealed what had befallen him on the mount and the commandments of God. And they, as they proceeded on their way, were met by the most distinguished of the Hebrews, who had learned of his coming. Moses, failing to convince these by a mere description of the miracles, performed them before their eyes. Amazed at this astonishing spectacle, they took courage and were in hopes that all would go well, since God was caring for their safety.

2. Now that he was assured of the allegiance of the Hebrews, of their agreement to follow his orders, and of their love of liberty, Moses betook himself to the king, recently promoted to the throne, and represented to him what services he had rendered to the Egyptians when they were humiliated and their country was ravaged by the Ethiopians, giving him to know how he had commanded and labored and imperilled himself for the troops as for his own people, and how for these services he had received from them no due reward. Furthermore, what had befallen him on Mount Sinai, the utterances of God and the miraculous signs which He had shown him to inspire confidence in His injunctions, all this he rehearsed in detail and besought him by no incredulity to obstruct God's purpose.

3. When the king mocked, Moses caused him to see with his own eyes the signs that had been wrought on the mount of Sinai. But the king was wroth and dubbed him a criminal, who had once escaped from servitude in Egypt, and had now effected his return by fraud and was trying to impose on him by juggleries and magic. With these words he ordered the priests to give him an exhibition of the same spectacles, and show that the Egyptians were skilled in these arts also, and that Moses could not, by posing as the only expert and pretending that he owed his marvellous gifts to God, ex-

pect them, as simpletons, to believe him. The priests thereupon dropped their staves, which became pythons. But Moses, nothing daunted, said, "Indeed, O king, I too disdain not the cunning of the Egyptians, but I assert that the deeds wrought by me so far surpass their magic and their art as things divine are remote from what is human. And I will show that it is from no witchcraft or deception of true judgment, but from God's providence and power that my miracles proceed." With that he dropped his staff to earth, bidding it be transformed into a serpent. It obeyed and, making the circuit of the Egyptians' staves, which looked like pythons, devoured them until it had consumed them all; then it reverted to its own shape and was recovered by Moses.

4. Howbeit, the king was no more dumbfounded by this performance, but only indignant thereat, and telling Moses that it would profit him nothing to practice his cunning and craft upon the Egyptians, he ordered the overseer of the Hebrews to grant them no relaxation from their labors, but to subject them to hardships yet more oppressive than before. Accordingly that officer, who had heretofore provided them with straw for their brick-making, provided it no more, but constrained them in the daytime to toil at their tasks and at night to collect the straw. Their affliction being thus doubled, they held Moses to account for this increased severity of their labors and pains. But he, neither wavering before the king's threats, nor yielding to the recriminations of the Hebrews, steeled his soul against both and devoted all his efforts to procuring his people's liberty. So he went to the king and urged him to let the Hebrews go to Mount Sinai to sacrifice there to God, for so He had commanded, and in no wise to oppose His will, but to esteem His gracious favor above all else and permit them exit, lest haply, in hindering them, he should unwittingly have but himself to blame for suffering such a fate as was like to befall him who opposed the commands of God. For to them that rouse the divine ire, dread calamities arise from all around them: to them neither earth nor air is friendly, to them no progeny is born after nature's laws, but all things are hostile and

at enmity; and such trials, he affirmed, would the
Egyptians undergo and withal would see the people of
the Hebrews quit their country despite their will.

xiv. 1. But since the king disdained these words of
Moses and paid no more heed to them, dire plagues
descended upon the Egyptians. I shall recount them all,
first because no such plagues as the Egyptians then experienced ever befell any nation before, next from a desire to show that Moses in not one of his predictions to
them was mistaken, and further because it behooves
mankind to learn to restrict themselves to such action
as shall not offend the Deity nor provoke Him in wrath
to punish them for their iniquities.

To begin with, their river, at God's command, ran
with a blood-red stream, impossible to drink; other source
of water they had none, nor was it only the color which
rendered it so repugnant, but whoever sought to drink
of it was seized with tortures and excruciating pain.
Such were its effects upon the Egyptians, but for the
Hebrews it remained sweet and drinkable and suffered
no change from its natural state. Perplexed, therefore,
at this prodigy and apprehensive for the Egyptians, the
king permitted the Hebrews to depart; and then, when
the plague abated, he again changed his mind and denied them exit.

2. But God, seeing that the graceless king after deliverance from the calamity was no longer willing to be
wise, brought another plague upon the Egyptians. An
endless multitude of frogs now devoured their land,
while the river was full of them, insomuch that when
they delved they found their drinking-water befouled
with the juices of these creatures dying and putrefying
in it; the country was saturated with their horrible slime
as they bred and died; all articles of the household they
ruined, being found in their meat and drink and swarm-
ing over their beds; a stench, intolerable and foul, was
everywhere, of frogs dying, living, and dead. Seeing the
Egyptians harassed by these pests, the king bade Moses
be gone and the Hebrews with him, and no sooner had
he said this than the mass of frogs disappeared, and
land and river returned to their natural state. But

Pharaoh, on the instant that he was quit of this plague, forgot the reason of it and retained the Hebrews; and, as though desirous to learn, the nature of further inflictions, withdrew that permission to the followers of Moses to depart, which fear rather than wisdom had extorted from him.

3. Again therefore the Deity sent a fresh plague to punish him for his deceit. A vast multitude of lice broke out on the persons of the Egyptians, issuing from their bodies, whereby the miserable wretches miserably perished, neither lotions nor unguents availing them to destroy these vermin. Confounded by this scourge, dreading the destruction of his people, and withal reflecting on the ignominy of such an end, the king of Egypt was forced to listen to reason, though, in his depravity, still only in half measure; for he offered egress to the Hebrews themselves, and when thereupon the plague ceased, he required them to leave their wives and children behind as hostages for their return. Thus he did but exasperate God the more, in thinking to impose upon His providence, as though it were Moses and not He who was punishing Egypt on the Hebrews' behalf; for He now sent wild beasts of every species and kind, the like of which no man had ever encountered before, to infest their country, whereby the people perished and the land was deprived of the care of its laborers, while all that escaped their ravages was wasted by disease even though the men stood their ground.

4. Yet since even so Pharaoh would not yield to the will of God, but while permitting the wives to accompany their husbands, required the children to be left behind, the Deity lacked not the means to pursue and torment the sinner with divers chastisements yet mightier than those prevalent heretofore. For now their bodies were smitten with horrible ulcers, and their intestines wasted away, and the greater part of the Egyptians perished thus. But when even this plague failed to sober the king, hail, till then unknown to the climate of Egypt, nor yet like that which in other countries falls in winter, but hail larger than that known to the dwellers in northern, polar regions, descended when spring was at its prime

and beat down their crops. Thereafter a horde of locusts devoured whatever seed had not been ruined by the hail, thus literally destroying all hopes that the Egyptians may have cherished of a harvest from the soil.

5. The calamities already named might indeed have sufficed to recall to reason and a sense of his own interests a mere imbecile devoid of malice. But Pharaoh, less fool than knave, though alive to the cause of it all, was matching himself against God as a deliberate traitor to the cause of virtue. And now he ordered Moses to take off the Hebrews, women and children included, but to leave their livestock to the Egyptians, who had lost their own. Moses replied that this demand was inequitable, since they needed their cattle to offer sacrifices to God, and while time in consequence dragged on, dense darkness, without a particle of light, enveloped the Egyptians—darkness so thick that their eyes were blinded by it and their breath choked, and they either met with a miserable end or lived in terror of being swallowed up by the fog. This dispersed after three days and as many nights, and then, since Pharaoh was still impenitent regarding the departure of the Hebrews, Moses went to him and said: "How long wilt thou disobey the will of God? For the command is His, to let the Hebrews go; and by no other means can thy people be quit of these ills save by acting thus." Infuriated by this speech, the king threatened to behead him, should he ever again come and pester him on this matter. Moses replied that for his part he would speak thereon no more, but that it was the king himself, along with the chief of the Egyptians, who would implore the Hebrews to depart. And with those words he left him.

6. God, having revealed that by yet one more plague he would constrain the Egyptians to release the Hebrews, now bade Moses instruct the people to have ready a sacrifice, making preparations on the tenth of the month Xanthicus over against the fourteenth day (this is the month called by the Egyptians Pharmuthi, by the Hebrews Nisan, and by the Macedonians termed Xanthicus) and then to lead off the Hebrews, taking all their possessions with them. He accordingly had the Hebrews

ready betimes for departure, and ranging them in fraternities kept them assembled together; then when the fourteenth day was come the whole body, in readiness to start, sacrificed, purified the houses with the blood, using bunches of hyssop to sprinkle it, and after the repast burnt the remnants of the meat as persons on the eve of departure. Hence comes it that to this day we keep this sacrifice in the same customary manner, calling the feast *Pascha*, which signifies "passing over," because on that day God passed over our people when he smote the Egyptians with plague. For on that selfsame night, destruction visited the firstborn of Egypt, insomuch that multitudes of those whose dwellings surrounded the palace trooped to Pharaoh to urge him to let the Hebrews go. And he, summoning Moses, ordered him to depart, supposing that once his people were quit of the country, Egypt's sufferings would cease. They even honored the Hebrews with gifts, some to speed their departure, others from neighborly feelings towards old acquaintances.

xv. 1. So they departed, amid the lamentations and regrets of the Egyptians for having treated them so hardly. . . . Quitting the country by the shortest route they arrived on the third day at Beelsephon, a place beside the Red Sea. Being bereft of any sustenance from the barren soil, they kneaded flour, baked it with merely a slight heating, and subsisted on the bread so made. On this they lived for thirty days, for they could make what they had brought from Egypt last no longer, notwithstanding that they rationed the food, limiting the portions to bare needs without eating to satiety. Hence it is that in memory of that time of scarcity, we keep for eight days a feast called the feast of unleavened bread. To estimate the total number of emigrants, including women and children, was no easy task, but those of military age numbered about six hundred thousand.

2. They left Egypt in the month of Xanthicus, on the fifteenth by lunar reckoning, 430 years after the coming of our forefather Abraham to Canaan, Jacob's migration to Egypt having taken place 215 years later. Moses had already reached his eightieth year; his brother

55

Aaron was three years older. They were bringing with them the bones of Joseph in accordance with that patriarch's injunctions to his sons.

3. But the Egyptians repented of having let the Hebrews go, and their king being mortified at the thought that it was the jugglery of Moses that had brought this about, they resolved to set out after them. So with arms and full equipment they started in pursuit, determined to bring them back could they overtake them; for no longer (they deemed) were they accountable to God, now that these people had had their exodus, and they looked for an easy victory over unarmed folk exhausted by their march. Inquiring, therefore, on all hands which route the fugitives had taken, they vigorously pushed the pursuit, albeit the ground was difficult to traverse, not only for great armies, but even for a solitary traveller.

Now Moses had led the Hebrews out by this route in order that if the Egyptians changed their minds and wished to pursue them, they should be punished for this malicious breach of the pact; partly also on account of the Philistines, a people hostile in virtue of an ancient feud, from whom he wished at all costs to conceal his departure, for their country was coterminous with that of the Egyptians. That was why he did not conduct his people by the direct route to Palestine, but chose to accomplish a long and arduous march through the desert in order to invade Canaan. Furthermore, he was influenced by the behests of God, who had commanded him to lead His people to Mount Sinai, there to do Him sacrifice. However, the Egyptians, having overtaken the Hebrews, prepared for battle, and thanks to their multitudinous forces, cooped them into a narrow space: they were, in fact, being pursued by 600 chariots along with 50,000 horsemen and heavy infantry to the number of 200,000. Barring all routes by which they expected the Hebrews to attempt escape, they confined them between inaccessible cliffs and the sea; for it was the sea in which terminated a mountain whose rugged face was destitute of tracks and prohibitive for retreat. Accordingly, occupying the pass where the mountain abuts upon the sea, they blocked the passage of the Hebrews, pitching their camp at its mouth, to prevent their escape to the plain.

4. Thus, unable, for lack of supplies, to hold out in the manner of the beleaguered, seeing no opportunity for flight, and destitute of arms even should they decide to give battle, the Hebrews were left with no prospect but that of utter destruction, failing deliberate surrender to the Egyptians. And now they turned to accusing Moses, forgetful of all those miracles wrought by God in token of their liberation, insomuch that the words of the prophet, who cheered them and promised them salvation, were met with incredulity, and they wished to stone him and resolved to give themselves up to the Egyptians. Then there were the wailings and lamentations of women and children, with death before their eyes, hemmed in by mountains, sea, and enemy, and seeing nowhere from these any imaginable escape.

5. But Moses, for all that enragement of the multitude against him, relaxed not his forethought on their behalf, and proudly trusted in God, who, having done all that He had promised towards their deliverance, would not now suffer them to fall into their enemies' hands, whether for servitude or destruction. Standing up, then, in their midst, he said: "Were they but men who till now have happily directed your affairs, it were an injustice to doubt that even they would prove themselves alike in future; but to despair at this moment of the providence of God were an act of madness, seeing that from Him there has come to you everything that He promised to perform through me for your salvation and deliverance from bondage, though far beyond your expectations. Rather ought ye, in straits such as ye deem hopeless, to expect help from God, who has even now caused you to be compassed about on this difficult ground, to the end that, in extricating you from extremities, whence neither ye nor the enemy think ye can escape, He may display both His own power and His tender care for you. For it is not in trivial circumstances that the Deity lends His own aid to whom He favors, but where He sees men have lost all hope of

ameliorating their lot. Wherefore, have faith in such a defender, who has power alike to make the little great and to sentence such mighty hosts as these to impotence. Be not dismayed at the Egyptians' array, nor, because yonder sea and the mountains behind you offer no means of escape, for that reason despair of your salvation; for ye may see these hills leveled to a plain, should God so will, or land emerge from the deep."

xvi. 1. Having spoken thus far, he led them towards the sea under the eyes of the Egyptians; for these were in view but, exhausted with the fatigue of the pursuit, judged it well to defer battle until the morrow. Then, when he reached the shore, Moses took his staff and made supplication to God, invoking His alliance and aid in these words: "Thou thyself knowest full well that escape from our present plight passes alike the might and the wit of man; nay, if there be any means of salvation at all for this host which at thy will has left Egypt, thine it is to provide it. For our part, despairing of other hope or resource, we fling ourselves upon thy protection alone, and expectantly, if aught be forthcoming from thy providence of might to snatch us from the wrath of the Egyptians, we look to thee. May it come quickly, this aid that shall manifest to us thy power; raise the hearts of this people, whom hopelessness has sunk into the depths of woe, to serenity and confidence of salvation. Nor are these straits in which we find ourselves without thy domain; nay, thine is the sea, thine the mountain that encompasseth us: this then can open at thy command, or the deep become dry land, or we might e'en find escape through the air, should it please thine almighty power that after this manner we should be saved."

2. After this solemn appeal to God, he smote the sea with his staff. And at that stroke it recoiled and, retreating into itself, left bare the soil, affording passage and flight for the Hebrews. Moses, beholding this clear manifestation of God and the sea withdrawn from its own bed to give them place, set the first foot upon it and bade the Hebrews follow him and pursue their way by this God-sent road, rejoicing at the peril awaiting

their advancing foes and rendering thanks to God for the salvation thus miraculously brought by Him to light.

3. They, without more ado, sped forth with zest, assured of God's attendant presence; whereupon the Egyptians at first deemed them mad, thus rushing to a certain death, but when they saw them far advanced unscathed, unchecked by obstacle or discomfiture, they made speed to pursue them, imagining that the sea would remain motionless for them also, and with the cavalry leading they proceeded to descend. But the Hebrews, while their enemies were arming and wasting time over that, had outstripped them and emerged unharmed on the opposite shore; this, however, but stimulated the ardor of the Egyptians for the pursuit, in the belief that they too would suffer nothing. Little dreamed they that it was a road reserved for the Hebrews, no public highway, whereon they were setting foot, a road created solely for the salvation of those in jeopardy, not for the use of them that were bent upon their destruction. When, therefore, the entire army of the Egyptians was once within it, back poured the sea, enveloping and with swelling wind-swept billows descending upon the Egyptians: rain fell in torrents from heaven, crashing thunder accompanied the flash of lightning, aye, and thunderbolts were hurled. In short, there was not one of those destructive forces which in token of God's wrath combine to smite mankind that failed to assemble then; for withal a night of gloom and darkness overwhelmed them. Thus perished they to a man, without a single one remaining to return with tidings of the disaster to those whom they had left at home.

4. As for the Hebrews, they could scarce contain themselves for joy at this miraculous deliverance and the destruction of their foes, believing themselves assuredly at liberty, now that the tyrants that would have enslaved them had perished and that God had so manifestly befriended them. After having themselves thus escaped from peril and furthermore beheld their enemies punished in such wise as within men's memory no others had ever been before, they passed that whole

night in melody and mirth, Moses himself composing in hexameter verse a song to God to enshrine His praises and their thankfulness for His gracious favor.

5. For my part, I have recounted each detail here told just as I found it in the sacred books. Nor let anyone marvel at the astonishing nature of the narrative or ~ubt that it was given to men of old, innocent of crime, ~ a road of salvation through the sea itself, whether by ~~~ will of God or maybe by accident, seeing that the hosts of Alexander king of Macedon, men born but the other day, beheld the Pamphylian Sea retire before them, and when other road there was none, offer a passage through itself, what time it pleased God to overthrow the Persian empire; and on that all are agreed who have recorded Alexander's exploits. However, on these matters everyone is welcome to his own opinion.

6. On the morrow, the arms of the Egyptians having been carried up to the Hebrews' camp by the tide and the force of the wind setting in that direction, Moses, surmising that this too was due to the providence of God, to ensure that even in weapons they should not be wanting, collected them and, having accoutred the Hebrews therewith, led them forward for Mount Sinai, with intent there to sacrifice to God and to render Him the thank-offerings of the people for their deliverance, even as he had received commandment.

BOOK X

Daniel

x. 1. Then Nebuchadnezzar, the Babylonian king, took the Jewish youths of noblest birth and the relatives of their king Sacchias, who were remarkable for the vigor of their bodies and the comeliness of their features, and gave them over to tutors to be cared for by them, making some of them eunuchs; this same treatment he also gave to those taken in the flower of their age from among the other nations that he had subdued. And he supplied them with food from his own table and had them educated and taught the learning of both the natives and the Chaldæans. And these youths became proficient in the wisdom which he had ordered them to study; among them were four of the family of Sacchias, the first of whom was named Daniel; the second, Hananiah; the third, Mishael; and the fourth, Azariah. But the Babylonian king changed their names and commanded them to use others; and so they called Daniel Belteshazzar, Hananiah Shadrach, Mishael Meshach, and Azariah Abednego. And these youths, because of their surpassing natural gifts, their zeal in learning and their wisdom, made great progress, wherefore the king held them in esteem and continued to cherish them.

2. Now, as Daniel together with his relatives had resolved to live austerely and abstain from the dishes which came from the king's table and in general from all animal food, he went to Aschanes, the eunuch who had been entrusted with their care, and requested him to take the food brought to them from the king and consume it himself and give them pulse and dates for nourishment and whatever other kind of non-animal food he chose, for, he said, they were attracted to such a diet but felt distaste for any other. Aschanes then said that he was ready to comply with their request but

61

was somewhat afraid that they might be detected by the king through the leanness of their bodies and the alteration of their features—for, he said, their bodies and complexions would necessarily change with their diet—and they would be especially marked because of the healthy condition of the other youths and so would be the cause of his being placed in danger and punished.

Accordingly, as Aschanes was apprehensive about this matter, they persuaded him to give them these foods for ten days by way of trial and, if their bodily condition did not change, to continue in the same way, as no further harm would be likely to come to them; but if he saw that they were growing thin and were weaker than the others, he should put them back on their former diet. And not only did they not suffer from taking that kind of food but they were better nourished in body than the others, so that one supposed that those to whom the king's provisions were given were worse off, while Daniel and his friends were living in the greatest abundance and luxury; and so from that time on Aschanes without any qualms took for himself what the king regularly sent to the youths from his table day by day, and he supplied them with the foods mentioned above. Thus these youths, whose souls were in this way kept pure and fresh for learning and their bodies more vigorous for arduous labor—for they did not oppress and weigh down the former with a variety of food nor did they soften their bodies by the same means—readily mastered all the learning which was found among the Hebrews and the Chaldæans. In particular Daniel, who had already acquired sufficient skill in wisdom, devoted himself to the interpretation of dreams, and the Deity manifested Himself to him.

3. Two years after the sacking of Egypt, King Nebuchadnezzar had a wonderful dream, the outcome of which God Himself revealed to him in his sleep, but, when he arose from his bed, he forgot it; he therefore sent for the Chaldæans and the Magi and the soothsayers and told them he had had a certain dream and, informing them how he had happened to forget it, bade

them tell him both what the dream was and what its meaning might be. When they said that it was impossible for any man to discover this but promised that, if he would describe to them the appearance of the dream, they would tell him its meaning, he threatened them with death unless they told him what the dream was, and commanded that they should all be put to death when they confessed that they could not do as they were ordered.

Now, when Daniel heard that the king had commanded all the wise men to be killed and that among them he and his relatives were in danger, he went to Arioches, to whom was entrusted the command of the king's bodyguard, and asked him to let him know the reason why the king had commanded all the wise men and Chaldæans and Magi to be put to death; and, on learning about the dream and how, when they were ordered to relate it to the king who had forgotten it, they had made him angry by saying that they were unable to do so, he requested Arioches to go in to the king and ask him to give the Magi one night and to put off their execution only so long, for, he said, he hoped within that time to learn the dream by praying to God. Arioches, therefore, reported to the king this request of Daniel, and so he ordered the execution of the Magi to be put off until he should learn what Daniel had promised to disclose.

Then the youth returned to his house with his relatives and throughout the whole night besought God to enlighten him and to save the Magi and the Chaldæans, together with whom they too must perish from the king's wrath, by revealing and making clear to him the vision which the king had seen in his sleep on the preceding night and had forgotten. Thereupon God, taking pity on those who were in danger and at the same time admiring Daniel's wisdom, made known to him both the dream and its interpretation so that the king too might learn from him what it signified. When Daniel received this knowledge from God, he joyfully arose and told his brothers, and though they were already in despair of their lives and had their thoughts fixed on death, he aroused them to cheerfulness and to hope of life; then together with them he gave thanks to God who had taken pity on their youth, and when day came, he went to Arioches and asked him to lead him to the king, for, he said, he wished to reveal to him the dream which he said he had had on the night before the preceding one.

4. Then Daniel went in to the king and first begged that he might not be thought wiser than the others, that is, the Chaldæans and Magi, merely because, while no one of them had been able to find out what his dream was, he was about to tell him; for this was not due to his skill nor to his having through his own effort acquired a better understanding than they "but to God who took pity on us when we were in danger of death and, in answer to my prayer for my own life and the lives of my countrymen, has made clear to me both the dream and its interpretation. For no less than my sorrow for ourselves who had been condemned to death by you was my concern for your good name, seeing that you had unjustly ordered these men to be put to death, especially such fine and excellent men, on whom you had imposed a task which is by no means within the limits of human wisdom, and demanded of them something which only God can do.

"Now then, when you were anxious about who should rule the whole world after you, God wished to reveal to you in your sleep all those you are to reign and sent you the following dream. You seemed to see a great image standing up, of which the head was of gold, the shoulders and arms of silver, the belly and thighs of bronze and the legs and feet of iron. Then you saw a stone break off from a mountain and fall upon the image and overthrow it, breaking it to pieces and leaving not one part of it whole, so that the gold and silver and bronze and iron were made finer than flour, and when the wind blew strongly, they were caught up by its force and scattered abroad; but the stone grew so much larger that the whole earth seemed to be filled with it. This, then, is the dream which you saw; as for its interpretation, it is as follows. The head of gold rep-

resents you and the Babylonian kings who were before
you. The two hands and shoulders signify that your
empire will be brought to an end by two kings. But
their empire will be destroyed by another king from the
west, clad in bronze, and this power will be ended by
still another, like iron, that will have dominion for ever
through its iron nature," which, he said, is harder than
that of gold or silver or bronze. And Daniel also revealed
to the king the meaning of the stone, but I have not
thought it proper to relate this, since I am expected to
write of what is past and done and not of what is to
be. If, however, there is anyone who has so keen a
desire for exact information that he will not stop short
of inquiring more closely but wishes to learn about the
hidden things that are to come, let him take the trouble
to read the Book of Daniel, which he will find among
the sacred writings.

5. When King Nebuchadnezzar had heard these things
and recognized his dream, he was amazed at Daniel's
natural gifts, and falling on his face, hailed him in the
manner in which men worship God. He also commanded
that they should sacrifice to him as to a god, and not
only that, but he even gave him the name of his own
god and made him and his relatives governors of the
kingdom; but these, as it happened, fell into great danger from envy and jealousy when they offended the
king for the following reason. The king had an image
made of gold, sixty cubits high and six broad, and set
it up in the great plain of Babylon; and, when ready to
consecrate it, he summoned the chief men from all the
lands over which he ruled, having first commanded that
at the moment when they heard the trumpet sound
they should fall down and worship the image, and those
who would not do so he threatened to have thrown into
a fiery furnace.

Accordingly all who heard the trumpet sound worshipped the image, but it is said the relatives of Daniel
did not do so because they were unwilling to transgress
their fathers' laws. And so they were convicted and
straightway thrown into the fire, but were saved by
divine providence and miraculously escaped death, for

the fire did not touch them; and indeed it was, I believe, in consideration of their being thrown into it without having done any wrong that it did not touch them, and it was powerless to burn the youths when it held them, for God made their bodies too strong to be consumed by the fire. This proved to the king that they were righteous and dear to God, and so they continued thereafter to be held worthy by him of the highest honor.

6. A little while afterward the king again had another vision in his sleep, which was that he would fall from power and make his home with beasts, and after living in this way in the wilderness for seven years, would again recover his royal power. After beholding this dream, he again summoned the Magi and inquired of them about it and asked them to tell him what it signified. Now none of the others could discover the import of the dream or make it known to the king, but Daniel alone interpreted it, and as he foretold to him so it came to pass. For the king spent the forementioned period of time in the wilderness, none venturing to seize the government during these seven years. And, after praying to God that he might recover his kingdom, he was again restored to it. But let no one reproach me for recording in my work each of these events as I have found them in the ancient books, for at the very beginning of my history I safeguarded myself against those who might find something wanting in my narrative or find fault with it, and said that I was only translating the books of the Hebrews into the Greek tongue, promising to report their contents without adding anything of my own to the narrative or omitting anything therefrom.

xi. 1. Now King Nebuchadnezzar's life came to an end after a reign of forty-three years; he was a man of bold action and more fortunate than the kings before him. His deeds are also mentioned by Berosus in the third book of his *History of Chaldæa*. . . . [Megasthenes in his *History of India*] attempts to show that this king surpassed Heracles in bravery and in the greatness of his deeds, saying that he subdued the greater part of Libya and Iberia. And Diocles, as well, mentions this king in the second book of his *History of Persia;* and Philostratos in his *History of India and Phœnicia* writes that this king besieged Tyre for thirteen years at the time when Ithobalos was king of Tyre. This, then, is what has been written about this king by all the historians.

2. After the death of Nebuchadnezzar, his son Abilmathadachos, who took over the royal power, at once released Jechonias, the king of Jerusalem, from his chains and kept him as one of his closest friends, giving him many gifts and setting him above the kings in Babylonia. For his father had not kept faith with Jechonias when he voluntarily surrendered himself with his wives and children and all his relatives for the sake of his native city, that it might not be taken by siege and razed, as we have said before. When Abilmathadachos died after reigning eighteen years, his son Eglisaros took over the royal power and held it for forty years until the end of his life. After him the succession to the throne fell to his son Labosordachos and, after holding it nine months in all, he died; it then passed to Belshazzar, who was called Nabonidus by the Babylonians.

It was against him that Cyrus, king of Persia, and Darius, king of Media, took the field; and while he was being besieged in Babylon, there appeared to him a wonderful and portentous vision as he reclined at table, feasting and drinking in a great hall made for royal entertainments, with his concubines and friends, for, as it pleased him to do so, he ordered that there be brought from his own temple the vessels of God which Nebuchadnezzar had taken as spoil from Jerusalem, but instead of using them had deposited in his own temple. Belshazzar, however, went so far in his audacity as to use them, and while drinking and blaspheming God, he saw a hand coming out of the wall and writing certain syllables on [another] wall. Being troubled by this vision, he summoned the Magi and Chaldæans and all of that class who were in Babylonia and could interpret signs and dreams, in order that they might inform him what the writing meant. But, when the Magi were unable to read anything and said that they did not understand it, the king felt great anxiety and distress about the miraculous vision and made a proclamation throughout the entire country, promising to give to anyone who would make plain the writing and the meaning contained therein a necklace of linked gold, and purple dress to wear like the kings of Chaldæa, and the third part of his own realm. When this proclamation was made, the Magi gathered in still greater numbers and made still greater efforts to read the writing, but were no less at a loss than before.

Seeing the king despondent over this, his grandmother began to console him by saying that there was a certain captive from Judæa, a native of that country, who had been brought from there by Nebuchadnezzar when he sacked Jerusalem; his name was Daniel, and he was a wise man and skilful in discovering things beyond man's power and known only to God, and he had brought to light what King Nebuchadnezzar had tried to find, when no one else was able to tell him what he wanted to know. She therefore begged the king to send for him and inquire of him concerning the writing and so condemn the ignorance of those who could not read it, even though a dark outlook might be indicated by God.

3. On hearing this, Belshazzar called Daniel and, after telling him that he had learned of him and his wisdom and of the divine spirit that attended him, and how he alone was fully able to discover things which were not within the understanding of others, he asked him to tell him what the writing was and to explain its meaning, for, he said, if Daniel did this, he would give him purple to wear and put a chain of linked gold about his neck and give him a third of his realm as an honor and reward for his wisdom, so that through these he might become most illustrious to all who saw him and asked the reason why he had obtained them.

Then Daniel begged him to keep his presents—for, he said, that which was wise and divine could not be bought with gifts but freely benefited those who asked for help—and said that he would explain the writing to him. It signified that his life would come to an end because not even from the punishment which his an-

cestor had suffered for his insolence to God had he
learned to be pious and not to attempt things beyond
the natural power of man; on the contrary, though Nebuchadnezzar's way of living had been changed to that
of beasts because of his impieties, and only on obtaining [God's] mercy after many supplications and entreaties had he been restored to a human way of living
and to his kingdom, and had therefore until the day of
his death praised God as the possessor of all power and
the guardian of men, Belshazzar had forgotten these
things and had grievously blasphemed the Deity and
had allowed himself with his concubines to be served
from His vessels. Seeing these things, he said, God had
become wrathful with him and was making known beforehand through this writing to what an end he must
come.

Now the meaning of the letters was as follows. *"Mané:
this,"* he said, "would in the Greek tongue signify 'number'; that is to say, God has numbered the time of your
life and reign, and there still remains for you a brief
while. *Thekel:* this means 'weight'; for God has weighed
the time of your kingship and shows that it is already
declining. *Phares:* this means 'a break' in the Greek
tongue; accordingly He will break up your kingdom and
divide it between the Medes and the Persians."

4. When Daniel told the king that this was what
the writing on the wall signified, Belshazzar, as was
natural upon the revelation of such dread news, was
seized with grief and unhappiness. Nevertheless he did
not, on the ground that Daniel was a prophet of evil to
him, withhold from him the gifts he had promised, but
gave him all of them, reasoning, in the first place, that
the things for the prophesying of which they were to
be given were peculiar to himself and his destiny, and
in no way attributable to the one who had prophesied
them, and judging, in the second place, that they had
been promised to a man who was good and just, even
though the future should turn out to be dark for himself; this, then, was his decision. And not long afterwards both he and the city were captured when Cyrus,
the king of Persia, marched against it. For it was in the

time of Belshazzar that the capture of Babylon took place, in the seventeenth year of his reign.

Such, then, as we learn from history, was the end to which the descendants of King Nebuchadnezzar came. Now Darius, who with his relative Cyrus put an end to the Babylonian sovereignty, was in his sixty-second year when he took Babylon; he was a son of Astyages but was called by another name among the Greeks. And he took the prophet Daniel to his own palace in Media and kept him by his side, bestowing every honor on him. For Daniel was one of the three satraps whom he appointed over the three hundred and sixty satrapies; so many rulers did Darius create in each satrapy.*

5. And so Daniel, being held in such great honor and such dazzling favor by Darius and being the only one associated with him in all matters because he was believed to have the divine spirit in him, became a prey to envy, for men are jealous when they see others held by kings in greater honor than themselves. But, although those who were resentful of the esteem in which he was held by Darius sought some pretext for slander and accusation against him, he never gave them a single cause, for, being superior to considerations of money and scorning any kind of gain and thinking it most disgraceful to accept anything even if it were given for a proper cause, he did not let those who were envious of him find a single ground for complaint. Since these men, therefore, had nothing to bring against him before the king and so injure him in the king's esteem by their abuse and slander, they sought other means of getting him out of the way. Accordingly, when they saw Daniel praying to God three times a day, they realized that they had found a pretext for destroying him. And, going to Darius, they informed him that his satraps and governors had resolved to give the people a respite for thirty days during which no one should address a petition or prayer either to him or to their gods, and they

* The translator notes that the Greek text of this sentence is uncertain. All efforts to identify "Darius the Mede" have been unsuccessful, and there is a confusion with Darius I, King of Persia, and his organization of the Persian satrapy system.

had, moreover, decided that anyone who transgressed
this decree of theirs should be thrown into the lions'
den to perish.

6. Thereupon the king, who did not see through
their wicked scheme or suspect that they had framed
this measure against Daniel, said that he approved of
their decree, and undertaking to ratify their proposal,
issued an edict announcing to the people what had been
decreed by the satraps. Accordingly, while all the rest
of the people took care not to transgress these orders
and remained quiet, Daniel took no thought of them
whatever but, as his custom was, stood up and prayed
to God in the sight of all. Thereupon the satraps, being
presented with the opportunity to act against Daniel
which they had looked for, straightway went to the
king and accused Daniel of being the only one to transgress his orders. For, they said, though no one else
had dared to pray to the gods—and this not because of
impiety but in order to observe and preserve . . .* out
of envy. For, imagining that Darius might treat him
with greater favor than they had expected, so as readily
to pardon him even after he had shown contempt for
the king's orders, and for this very reason being envious of Daniel, they would not adopt a milder course,
but demanded that he be cast into the lions' den in
accordance with the law.

So Darius, hoping that the Deity would save Daniel
and that he would suffer no harm from the beasts, bade
him bear his fate with good courage. Then, when he
had been cast into the den, the king sealed the stone
that was placed over the entrance as a door, and withdrew; and he went without food or sleep the whole
night in his anxiety for Daniel. But, when day came, he
arose and went to the den, where he found the seal intact which he had left to mark the stone, and opening
it, he called to Daniel with a shout and asked whether
he was safe. Daniel, on hearing the king, said that he
had not been harmed, whereupon he ordered him to be
drawn up from the beasts' den.

---

* Translator's note: "The text is in disorder here."

Daniel's enemies, however, on seeing that he had suffered no harm, did not choose to believe that it was through the Deity and His providence that he had been saved, but held that the lions had been stuffed with food and therefore had not touched Daniel nor come near him, and so they told the king. But he, in his detestation of their wickedness, ordered a large quantity of meat to be thrown to the lions and, when they had eaten their fill, commanded Daniel's enemies to be cast into the den in order that he might discover whether the lions would refuse to come near them because of satiety. When the satraps were thrown to the beasts, it became evident to Darius that it was the Deity who had saved Daniel, for the lions spared no one of them but tore them all to pieces as though they were terribly famished and in need of food. And it was not, I think, the beasts' hunger that aroused them, for they had been satisfied a little while before with an abundance of meat, but the wickedness of the men—for this would be apparent even to irrational animals—which resulted in their being punished, as was the intention of God.

7. Now after those who had plotted against Daniel had perished in this manner, King Darius sent throughout the entire country, praising the God whom Daniel worshipped and saying that He alone was the true and Almighty God. He also showed Daniel extraordinarily high honor by designating him the first of his Friends. And Daniel, being now so renowned and distinguished because of his reputation as a man dear to God, built at Ecbatana in Media a fortress which was a very beautiful work and wonderfully made, and remains and is preserved to this day; it appears to those who view it to have been recently constructed and to have been completed on the very day on which the visitor sees it, so fresh and radiant is its beauty, which has in no way aged in this long period of time—for buildings suffer the same changes as men; they turn grey and lose their strength with the years, and their beauty fades. In this fortress they bury the kings of Media, Persia, and Parthia even now, and the person to whose care it is en-

trusted is a Jewish priest; this custom is observed to this very day.

Now it is fitting to relate certain things about this man [Daniel] which one may greatly wonder at hearing, namely that all things happened to him in a marvellously fortunate way as to one of the greatest prophets, and during his lifetime he received honor and esteem from kings and people, and since his death, his memory lives on eternally. For the books which he wrote and left behind are still read by us even now, and we are convinced by them that Daniel spoke with God, for he was not only wont to prophesy future things, as did the other prophets, but he also fixed the time at which these would come to pass. And whereas the other prophets foretold disasters and were for that reason in disfavor with kings and people, Daniel was a prophet of good tidings to them, so that through the auspiciousness of his predictions he attracted the goodwill of all, while from their realization he gained credit among the multitude for his truthfulness and at the same time won their esteem for his divine power.

And he left behind writings in which he has made plain to us the accuracy and faithfulness to truth of his prophecies. For he says that when he was in Susa, the metropolis of Persia, and went out into the plain with his companions, there was a sudden shaking and trembling of the earth, and he was left alone by his friends, who fled, and in confusion he fell on his face and his two hands, whereupon someone touched him and at the same time bade him arise and see what was to happen to his countrymen in the future after many generations. When he arose, there was shown to him, he reveals, a great ram with many horns growing out of him, the last of which was higher than the rest. Then he looked toward the west and beheld a goat borne through the air from that quarter, which rushed upon the ram, struck him twice with his horns, and hurling him to the ground, trampled on him. Thereupon he saw a very great horn sprouting up from the goat's forehead, and when this was broken off, four horns came up, facing each of the four winds. From these, he writes,

73

there arose another smaller horn, which God, Who revealed these things to him, told him would grow and make war on his nation, take their city by force, disrupt the temple service, and prevent the sacrifices from being offered for one thousand two hundred and ninety-six days.

This, Daniel writes, is what he saw in the plain of Susa, and he relates that God interpreted to him the form of the vision as follows. The ram, he declares, signified the kingdoms of the Medes and Persians, and the horns those who were to reign, the last horn signifying the last king, for this king would surpass all the others in wealth and glory. The goat, he said, indicated that there would be a certain king of the Greeks who would encounter the Persian king twice in battle and defeat him and take over all his empire. The great horn in the forehead of the goat indicated the first king, and the growing out of the four horns after the first horn fell out, and their facing each of the four quarters of the earth denoted the successors of the first king after his death, and the division of the kingdom among them; and that these, who were neither his sons nor his relatives, would rule the world for many years. And there would arise from their number a certain king who would make war on the Jewish nation and their laws, deprive them of the form of government based on these laws, spoil the temple, and prevent the sacrifices from being offered for three years. And these misfortunes our nation did in fact come to experience under Antiochus Epiphanes, just as Daniel many years before saw and wrote that they would happen. In the same manner Daniel also wrote about the empire of the Romans and that Jerusalem would be taken by them and the temple laid waste.

All these things, as God revealed them to him, he left behind in his writings, so that those who read them and observe how they have come to pass must wonder at Daniel's having been so honored by God and learn from these facts how mistaken are the Epicureans— who exclude Providence from human life and refuse to believe that God governs its affairs or that the universe is directed by a blessed and immortal Being to the end that the whole of it may endure, but say that the world runs by its own movement without knowing a guide or another's care. If it were leaderless in this fashion, it would be shattered through taking a blind course and so end in destruction, just as we see ships go down when they lose their helmsmen or chariots overturn when they have no drivers. It therefore seems to me, in view of the things foretold by Daniel, that they are very far from holding a true opinion who declare that God takes no thought for human affairs. For if it were the case that the world goes on by some automatism, we should not have seen all these things happen in accordance with his prophecy.

Now I have written about these matters as I have found them in my reading; if, however, anyone wishes to judge otherwise of them, I shall not object to his holding a different opinion.

The Jewish War

BOOK I

Introduction

1. The war of the Jews against the Romans—the greatest not only of the wars of our own time, but, so far as accounts have reached us, well nigh of all that ever broke out between cities or nations—has not lacked its historians. Of these, however, some, having taken no part in the action, have collected from hearsay casual and contradictory stories which they have then edited in a rhetorical style; while others, who witnessed the events, have, either from flattery of the Romans or from hatred of the Jews, misrepresented the facts, their writings exhibiting alternatively invective and encomium, but nowhere historical accuracy. In these circumstances, I—Josephus, son of Matthias, a Hebrew by race, a native of Jerusalem, and a priest; who at the opening of the war myself fought against the Romans and in the sequel was perforce an onlooker—propose to provide the subjects of the Roman Empire with a narrative of the facts, by translating into Greek the account which I previously composed in my vernacular tongue and sent to the barbarians in the interior.

2. I spoke of this upheaval as one of the greatest magnitude. The Romans had their own internal disorders. The Jewish revolutionary party, whose numbers and fortunes were at their zenith, seized the occasion of the turbulence of these times for insurrection. As a result of these vast disturbances the whole of the Eastern Empire was in the balance; the insurgents were fired with hopes of its acquisition, their opponents feared its loss. For the Jews hoped that all their fellow-countrymen beyond the Euphrates would join with them in revolt; while the Romans, on their side, were occupied with their neighbors the Gauls, and the Celts were in motion. Nero's death [in A.D. 68], moreover, brought uni-

79

versal confusion; many were induced by this opportunity to aspire to the sovereignty, and a change which might make their fortune was after the heart of the soldiery.

I thought it monstrous, therefore, to allow the truth in affairs of such moment to go astray, and that, while Parthians and Babylonians and the most remote tribes of Arabia with our countrymen beyond the Euphrates and the inhabitants of Adiabene were, through my assiduity, accurately acquainted with the origin of the war, the various phases of calamity through which it passed and its conclusion, the Greeks and such Romans as were not engaged in the contest should remain in ignorance of these matters, with flattering or fictitious narratives as their only guide.

3. Though the writers in question presume to give their works the title of histories, yet throughout them, apart from the utter lack of sound information, they seem, in my opinion, to miss their own mark. They desire to represent the Romans as a great nation, and yet they continually depreciate and disparage the actions of the Jews. But I fail to see how the conquerors of a puny people deserve to be accounted great. Again, these writers have respect neither for the long duration of the war, nor for the vast numbers of the Roman army that it engaged, nor for the prestige of the generals, who, after such herculean labors under the walls of Jerusalem, are, I suppose, of no repute in these writers' eyes, if their achievement is to be underestimated.

4. I have no intention of rivaling those who extol the Roman power by exaggerating the deeds of my compatriots. I shall faithfully recount the actions of both combatants; but in my reflections on the events I cannot conceal my private sentiments, nor refuse to give my personal sympathies scope to bewail my country's misfortunes. For, that it owed its ruin to civil strife, and that it was the Jewish tyrants who drew down upon the holy temple the unwilling hands of the Romans and the conflagration, is attested by Titus Cæsar himself, who sacked the city; throughout the war he commiserated the populace who were at the mercy of

the revolutionaries, and often of his own accord deferred the capture of the city, and by protracting the siege, gave the culprits time for repentance. Should, however, any critic censure me for my strictures upon the tyrants or their bands of marauders or for my lamentations over my country's misfortunes, I ask his indulgence for a compassion which falls outside an historian's province. For of all the cities under Roman rule it was the lot of ours to attain to the highest felicity and to fall to the lowest depths of calamity. Indeed, in my opinion, the misfortunes of all nations since the world began fall short of those of the Jews; and since the blame lay with no foreign nation, it was impossible to restrain one's grief. Should, however, any critic be too austere for pity, let him credit the history with the facts, the historian with the lamentations.

5. Yet I, on my side, might justly censure those erudite Greeks who, living in times of such stirring actions as by comparison reduce to insignificance the wars of antiquity, yet sit in judgment on these current events and revile those who make them their special study—authors whose principles they lack, even if they have the advantage of them in literary skill. For their own themes they take the Assyrian and Median empires, as if the narratives of the ancient historians were not fine enough. Yet, the truth is, these modern writers are their inferiors no less in literary power than in judgment. The ancient historians set themselves severally to write the history of their own times, a task in which their connection with the events added lucidity to their record; while mendacity brought an author into disgrace with readers who knew the facts. In fact, the work of committing to writing events which have not previously been recorded, and of commending to posterity the history of one's own time, is one which merits praise and acknowledgement. The industrious writer is not one who merely remodels the scheme and arrangement of another's work, but one who uses fresh materials and makes the framework of the history his own.

For myself, at a vast expenditure of money and pains, I, a foreigner, present to Greeks and Romans this memorial of great achievements. As for the native Greeks, where personal profit or a lawsuit is concerned, their mouths are at once agape and their tongues loosed; but in the matter of history, where veracity and laborious collection of the facts are essential, they are mute, leaving to inferior and ill-informed writers the task of describing the exploits of their rulers. Let us at least hold historical truth in honor, since by the Greeks it is disregarded.

6. To narrate the ancient history of the Jews, the origin of the nation and the circumstances of their migration from Egypt, the countries which they traversed in their wanderings, the extent of the territory which they subsequently occupied, and the incidents which led to their deportation, would, I considered, be not only here out of place, but superfluous; seeing that many Jews before me have accurately recorded the history of our ancestors, and that these records have been translated by certain Greeks into their native tongue without serious error. I shall therefore begin my work at the point where the historians of these events and our prophets conclude. Of the subsequent history, I shall describe the incidents of the war through which I lived with all the detail and elaboration at my command; for the events preceding my lifetime I shall be content with a brief summary.

7. I shall relate how Antiochus, surnamed Epiphanes, took Jerusalem by storm, and after holding it for three years and six months, was expelled from the country by the Hasmonæans; next how their descendants, in their quarrel for the throne, dragged the Romans and Pompey upon the scene; how Herod, son of Antipater, with the aid of Sossius, overthrew the Hasmonæan dynasty; of the revolt of the people, after Herod's death, when Augustus was Roman emperor and Quintilius Varus provincial governor; of the outbreak of war in the twelfth year of Nero's principate, the fate which befell Cestius, and the success which attended the Jewish arms in overrunning the country in the opening engagements.

8. Then I shall proceed to tell how they fortified the neighboring towns; how Nero, apprehensive for the Em-

pire in consequence of the reverses of Cestius, entrusted
the conduct of the war to Vespasian; of his invasion
of Jewish territory, accompanied by his elder son; of
the strength of the forces, Roman and auxiliary, with
which he penetrated into Galilee, and of the towns of
that province which he captured either by main force or
by negotiation. In this connection I shall describe the
admirable discipline of the Romans on active service
and the training of the legions; the extent and nature
of the two Galilees, the limits of Judæa, the special
features of the country, its lakes and springs. I shall
give a precise description of the sufferings of the prisoners taken in the several towns, from my own observa-
tion or personal share in them. For I shall conceal
nothing even of my own misfortunes, as I shall be addressing persons who are well aware of them.

9. I shall next relate how, at the moment when the
Jewish fortunes were on the decline, Nero's death occurred, and how Vespasian's advance upon Jerusalem
was diverted by the call to imperial dignity; the portents
of his elevation which he received, and the revolutions
which took place in Rome; his proclamation by his soldiers as Emperor against his will; the civil war which,
on his departure for Egypt to restore order to the realm,
broke out among the Jews, the rise of the tyrants to
power and their mutual feuds.

10. My narrative will proceed to tell of the second
invasion of our country by Titus, starting from Egypt;
how and where he mustered his forces, and their
strength; the condition to which civil war had reduced
the city on his arrival; his various assaults and the
series of earthworks which he constructed. Further, the
triple line of our walls and their dimensions; the defenses of the city and the plan of the temple and sanctuary, the measurements of these buildings and of the
altar being all precisely stated; certain festival customs,
the seven degrees of purity, the ministerial functions
of the priests, their vestments and those of the high
priest, with a description of the Holy of Holies. Nothing
shall be concealed, nothing added to facts which have
been brought to light.

11. I shall then describe the tyrants' brutal treatment of their fellow-countrymen and the clemency of the Romans towards an alien race, and how often Titus, in his anxiety to save the city and the temple, invited the rival parties to come to terms with him. I shall distinguish between the sufferings and calamities of the people, culminating in their defeat, as attributable respectively to the war, the sedition, and the famine. Nor shall I omit to record either the misfortunes of the deserters or the punishments inflicted on the prisoners; the burning of the Temple, contrary to Cæsar's wishes, and the number of the sacred treasures rescued from the flames; the taking of the whole city and the signs and portents that preceded it; the capture of the tyrants, the number of the prisoners and the destiny allotted to each; nor yet how the Romans crushed the last remnants of the war and demolished the local fortresses; how Titus paraded the whole country and restored order; and lastly his return to Italy and triumph.

12. All these topics I have comprised in seven books. While I have left no pretext for censure or accusation to persons who are cognizant of the facts and took part in the war, my work is written for lovers of the truth and not to gratify my readers. . . .

The First Roman Military Interventions: Pompey, Cæsar and Antony (63-42 B.C.)

[*While Pompey the Great was campaigning in the East, a struggle for the throne between two brothers, Hyrcanus II and Aristobulus II, gave him a welcome opportunity to intervene in Judæa. After various maneuvers, carried on in characteristically bad faith, Aristobulus withdrew to Jerusalem and prepared for war.*

vi. 6. Pompey, allowing him no time for these preparations, followed forthwith. A further impetus to his pace was given by the death of Mithridates [king of Pontus], news of which reached him near Jericho. (The soil here is the most fertile in Judæa and produces abundance of palms and balsam-trees; the stems of the latter are cut with sharp stones and the balsam is collected at the incisions, where it exudes drop by drop.) At this spot Pompey encamped for an evening only and at daybreak pressed on to Jerusalem. Terrified at his approach, Aristobulus went as a suppliant to meet him, and by the promise of money and of the surrender of himself and the city pacified Pompey's wrath. However, none of his undertakings was fulfilled; for when Gabinius was dispatched to take over the promised sum, the partisans of Aristobulus refused even to admit him to the city.

vii. 1. Indignant at this treatment, Pompey kept Aristobulus under arrest and, advancing to the city, carefully considered the best method of attack. He noted the solidity of the walls and the formidable task of their assault, the frightful ravine in front of them, and within the ravine the temple also so strongly fortified as to afford, after the capture of the town, a second line of defense to the enemy.

2. However, during the long period of indecision, sedition broke out within the walls; the partisans of Aristobulus insisting on a battle and the rescue of the king, while those of Hyrcanus were for opening the gates to Pompey. The numbers of the latter were increased by the fear which the spectacle of the perfect order of the Romans inspired. The party of Aristobulus, finding themselves beaten, retired into the temple, cut the bridge which connected it with the city, and prepared to hold out to the last. The others admitted the Romans to the city and delivered up the palace. Pompey sent a body of troops to occupy it under the command of Piso, one of his lieutenant-generals. That officer distributed sentries about the town and, failing to induce any of the refugees in the temple to listen to terms, prepared the surrounding ground for an assault. In this work the friends of Hyrcanus keenly assisted him with their advice and services.

3. Pompey himself was on the north side, engaged in banking up the fosse and the whole of the ravine with materials collected by the troops. The tremendous depth

to be filled, and the impediments of every sort to which the work was exposed by the Jews above, rendered this a difficult task. Indeed, the labors of the Romans would have been endless, had not Pompey taken advantage of the seventh day of the week, on which the Jews, from religious scruples, refrain from all manual work, and then proceeded to raise the earthworks, while forbidding his troops to engage in hostilities; for on the Sabbaths the Jews fight only in self-defense. The ravine once filled up, he erected lofty towers on the earthworks, brought up the battering engines which had been conveyed from Tyre, and tried their effect upon the walls; the catapults, meanwhile, beating off resistance from above. However, the towers, which in this sector were extraordinarily massive and beautiful, long resisted the blows.

4. While the Romans were undergoing these severe hardships, Pompey was filled with admiration for the invariable fortitude of the Jews, and in particular for the way in which they carried on their religious services uncurtailed, though enveloped in a hail of missiles. Just as if the city had been wrapt in profound peace, the daily sacrifices, the expiations and all the ceremonies of worship were scrupulously performed to the honor of God. At the very hour when the temple was taken, when they were being massacred about the altar, they never desisted from the religious rites for the day. It was the third month of the siege when, having with difficulty succeeded in overthrowing one of the towers, the Romans burst into the temple. The first to venture across the wall was Faustus Cornelius, son of Sulla; after him came two centurions, Furius and Fabius. Followed by their respective companies, they formed a ring round the court of the temple and slew their victims, some flying to the sanctuary, others offering a brief resistance.

5. Then it was that many of the priests, seeing the enemy advancing sword in hand, calmly continued their sacred ministrations, and were butchered in the act of pouring libations and burning incense; putting the worship of the Deity above their own preservation.

Most of the slain perished by the hands of their countrymen of the opposite faction; countless numbers flung
themselves over the precipices; some, driven mad by
their hopeless plight, set fire to the buildings around
the wall and were consumed in the flames. Of the Jews
twelve thousand perished; the losses of the Romans
in dead were trifling, in wounded considerable.

6. Of all the calamities of that time none so deeply
affected the nation as the exposure to alien eyes of the
Holy Place, hitherto screened from view. Pompey indeed,
along with his staff, penetrated to the sanctuary, entry
to which was permitted to none but the high priest,
and beheld what it contained: the candelabrum and
lamps, the table, the vessels for libation and censers,
all of solid gold, an accumulation of spices and the store
of sacred money amounting to two thousand talents.
However, he touched neither these nor any other of
the sacred treasures and, the very day after the capture
of the temple, gave orders to the custodians to cleanse
it and to resume the customary sacrifices. He reinstated
Hyrcanus as high priest, in return for his enthusiastic
support shown during the siege, particularly in detach-
ing from Aristobulus large numbers of the rural population who were anxious to join his standard. By these
methods, in which goodwill played a larger part than
terrorism, he, like the able general he was, conciliated
the people. Among the prisoners was the father-in-law of
Aristobulus, who was also his uncle. Those upon whom
lay the main responsibility for the war were executed.
Faustus and his brave companions in arms were presented with splendid rewards. The country and Jerusalem were laid under tribute.

7. Pompey, moreover, deprived the Jews of the cities
which they had conquered in Cœle-Syria, placing these
under the authority of a Roman governor appointed
for the purpose, and thus confined the nation within
its own boundaries. To gratify Demetrius, one of his
freedmen, a Gadarene, he rebuilt Gadara, which had
been destroyed by the Jews. He also liberated from their
rule all the towns in the interior which they had not
already razed to the ground, namely Hippos, Scythopolis,

Pella, Samaria, Jamnia, Marisa, Azotus, and Arethusa; likewise the maritime towns of Gaza, Joppa, Dora, and the city formerly called Strato's Tower, which afterwards, when reconstructed by King Herod with magnificent buildings, took the name of Cæsarea. All these towns he restored to their legitimate inhabitants and annexed to the province of Syria. That province, together with Judæa and the whole region extending as far as Egypt and the Euphrates, he entrusted, along with two legions, to the administration of Scaurus; and then set out in haste across Cilicia for Rome, taking with him his prisoners, Aristobulus and his family. That prince had two daughters and two sons. Of the latter, one, Alexander, made his escape on the journey; Antigonus, the younger, was conducted with his sisters to Rome. . . .

viii. 2. Alexander, son of Aristobulus, the one who escaped from Pompey, in course of time mustered a considerable force and caused Hyrcanus serious annoyance by his raids upon Judæa. Having already advanced to Jerusalem and had the audacity to begin rebuilding the wall which Pompey had destroyed, he would in all probability have soon deposed his rival, but for the arrival of Gabinius, who had been sent to Syria [in 57 B.C.] as successor to Scaurus. Gabinius, whose valor had been proved on many other occasions, now marched against Alexander. The latter, alarmed at his approach, raised the strength of his army to ten thousand foot and fifteen hundred horse, and fortified the strategic positions of Alexandreion, Hyrcania, and Machærus, adjacent to the Arabian mountains.

3. Gabinius sent Mark Antony ahead with a division of his army, following himself with the main body. Antipater's picked troops* and the rest of the Jewish contingent under the command of Malichus and Peitholaus joined forces with Antony's generals and proceeded against Alexander. Gabinius appeared before long

---

* Antipater, father of Herod the Great and most powerful of the supporters of Hyrcanus, had been introduced by Josephus earlier in the narrative (vi. 1) in these words: "An Idumæan by race, his ancestry, wealth, and other advantages put him in the front rank of his nation."

with the heavy infantry. Alexander, unable to withstand the combined forces of the enemy, retired, but when approaching Jerusalem was forced into an engagement. In this battle he lost six thousand of his men, three thousand killed, and as many prisoners. With the remnant of his army he fled to Alexandreion.

4. Gabinius, following him thither, found many of his men camping outside the walls. Before attacking them, he endeavored, by promise of pardon for past offenses, to bring them over to his side; but, on their proudly refusing all terms, he killed a large number of them and confined the remainder in the fortress. The honors of this combat went to the commanding officer, Mark Antony; his valor, displayed on every battlefield, was never so conspicuous as here. Leaving the reduction of the fort to his troops, Gabinius made a parade of the country, restoring order in the cities that had escaped devastation, and rebuilding those which he found in ruins. It was, for instance, by his orders that Scythopolis, Samaria, Anthedon, Apollonia, Jamnia, Raphia, Marisa, Adoreus, Gamala, Azotus, and many other towns were repeopled, colonists gladly flocking to each of them.

5. After supervising these arrangements, Gabinius returned to Alexandreion and pressed the siege so vigorously that Alexander, despairing of success, sent him a herald with a petition for pardon for his offenses and an offer to surrender the fortresses of Hyrcania and Machærus, still in his possession; subsequently he gave up Alexandreion as well. All these places Gabinius demolished, to prevent their serving as a base of operations for another war. He was instigated to take this step by Alexander's mother, who had come to propitiate him, in her concern for her husband [Aristobulus] and remaining children, then prisoners in Rome. After this Gabinius reinstated Hyrcanus in Jerusalem and committed to him the custody of the Temple. The civil administration he reconstituted under the form of an aristocracy. He divided the whole nation into five unions [or councils]; one of these he attached to Jerusalem, another to Gezer, the third had Amathus as its center

of government, the fourth was allotted to Jericho, the fifth to Sepphoris, a city of Galilee. The Jews welcomed their release from the rule of an individual and were from that time forward governed by an aristocracy.

6. They were soon, however, involved in fresh troubles through the escape of Aristobulus from Rome. Once more he succeeded in mustering a large body of Jews, some eager for revolution, others long since his devoted admirers. He began by seizing Alexandreion and attempting to restore the fortifications; but on hearing that Gabinius had dispatched an army against him, under the command of Sisenna, Antony, and Servianus, he retreated towards Machærus. Disencumbering himself of his rabble of inefficient followers, he retained only those who were armed, numbering eight thousand; among these was Peitholaus, the second in command at Jerusalem, who had deserted to him with a thousand men. The Romans pursued and an engagement took place. Aristobulus and his men for long held their ground, fighting valiantly, but were ultimately overpowered by the Romans. Five thousand fell; about two thousand took refuge on a hill; Aristobulus and the remaining thousand cut their way through the Roman lines and flung themselves into Machærus.

There, as he camped among the ruins on that first evening, the king entertained hopes of raising another army, given but a respite from war, and proceeded to erect some weak fortifications; but, when the Romans attacked the place, after holding out beyond his strength for two days, he was taken, and, with his son Antigonus, who had shared his flight from Rome, was conducted in chains to Gabinius, and by Gabinius was sent back once more to Rome. The Senate imprisoned the father, but allowed his children to return to Judæa, Gabinius having written to inform them that he had promised this favor to the wife of Aristobulus in return for the surrender of the fortresses.

7. An expedition against the Parthians, on which Gabinius had already started, was cut short by Ptolemy [Auletes], to effect whose restoration to Egypt the former returned from the banks of the Euphrates. For this

campaign Hyrcanus and Antipater put their services
entirely at his disposal. In addition to providing money,
arms, corn, and auxiliaries, Antipater further induced
the local Jewish guardians of the [Nile] Delta at Pelusium to let Gabinius through. His departure, however,
was the occasion for a general commotion in Syria; and
Alexander, son of Aristobulus, heading a new Jewish
revolt, collected a vast army and proceeded to massacre
all Romans in the country. Gabinius was alarmed. He
was already on the spot, news of the local disturbances
having hastened his return from Egypt. Sending Antipater in advance to address some of the rebels he
brought them over to reason. Alexander, however, had
still thirty thousand left and was burning for action.
Gabinius, accordingly, took the field, the Jews met him,
and a battle was fought near Mount Tabor, in which
they lost ten thousand men; the remainder fled and dispersed. Gabinius then proceeded to Jerusalem, where
he reorganized the government in accordance with Antipater's wishes. From there he marched against the
Nabatæans, whom he fought and defeated. . . .

8. The government of Syria now passed into the
hands of Crassus, who came to succeed Gabinius. To
provide for his expedition against the Parthians, Crassus
stripped the temple at Jerusalem of all its gold, his
plunder including the two thousand talents left un-
touched by Pompey. He then crossed the Euphrates and
perished with his whole army; but of those events this
is not the occasion to speak.

9. After the death of Crassus [in 53 B.C.] the Parthians rushed to cross the river into Syria, but were repulsed by Cassius, who had made his escape to that
province. Having secured Syria, he hastened towards
Judæa, capturing Tarichææ, where he reduced thirty
thousand Jews to slavery and put to death Peitholaus,
who was endeavoring to rally the partisans of Aristobulus. His execution was recommended by Antipater.
Antipater had married a lady named Cypros, of an
illustrious Arabian family, by whom he had four sons—
Phasael, Herod afterwards king, Joseph, and Pheroras—
and a daughter, Salome. He had, by kind offices and hos-

pitality, attached to himself persons of influence in every quarter; above all, through this matrimonial alliance, he had won the friendship of the king of Arabia, and it was to him that he entrusted his children when embarking on war with Aristobulus. Cassius, having bound over Alexander by treaty to keep the peace, returned to the Euphrates to prevent the Parthians from crossing it. Of these events we shall speak elsewhere.

ix. 1. When Pompey fled with the Senate across the Ionian Sea, [Julius] Cæsar, now master of Rome and the empire, set Aristobulus at liberty; and, putting two legions at his service, dispatched him in haste to Syria, hoping by this means to have no difficulty in bringing over both that province and Judæa with the surrounding country to his side. But the zeal of Aristobulus and the hopes of Cæsar were thwarted by malice. Poisoned by Pompey's friends, it was long before Aristobulus obtained even burial in his native land; the corpse lay preserved in honey until it was sent to the Jews by Antony for interment in the royal sepulchres.

2. His son Alexander also perished; under Pompey's orders, he was beheaded at Antioch by Scipio, after a trial in which he was accused of the injuries which he had caused to the Romans. Alexander's brother and sisters were taken under the roof of Ptolemy, son of Mennæus, prince of Chalcis in the Lebanon valley, who sent his son Philippion to Ascalon to fetch them. The latter succeeded in tearing Antigonus and his sisters from the arms of Aristobulus's widow and escorted them to his father. Becoming enamored of one of the princesses, the young man married her, but was subsequently slain by his father on account of this same Alexandra, whom Ptolemy, after murdering his son, married himself. His marriage made him a more attentive guardian to her brother and sister.

3. Antipater, on the death of Pompey, went over to his opponent and paid court to Cæsar. When Mithridates of Pergamum, with the army which he was leading to Egypt, was forbidden to pass the Pelusiac arm of the Nile and was held up at Ascalon, it was Antipater who induced his friends the Arabs to lend their assistance,

and himself brought up an army of three thousand Jewish infantry. It was he who roused in support of Mithridates persons so powerful in Syria as Ptolemy, in his Lebanon home, and Iamblichus, through whose influence the cities in those parts readily took their share in the war. Emboldened by the reinforcements which Antipater had brought him, Mithridates now marched on Pelusium, and being refused a passage, laid siege to the town. In the assault it was Antipater again who won the greatest distinction; for he made a breach in the portion of the wall which faced him and was the first to plunge into the place at the head of his troops.

4. Thus Pelusium was taken; but the conqueror's advance was again barred by the Egyptian Jews who occupied the district which took its name from Onias. Antipater, however, prevailed on them not only to refrain from opposition, but even to furnish supplies for the troops; with the result that no further resistance was encountered even at Memphis, whose inhabitants voluntarily joined Mithridates. The latter, having now rounded the Delta, gave battle to the rest of the Egyptians at a spot called "Jews' camp." In this engagement he, with the whole of his right wing, was in serious danger, when Antipater, victorious on the left where he was in command, wheeled round and came along the river bank to his rescue. Falling upon the Egyptians who were pursuing Mithridates he killed a large number of them and pushed his pursuit of the remainder so far that he captured their camp. He lost only eighty of his men; Mithridates in the rout had lost about eight hundred. Thus saved beyond all expectation, Mithridates bore to Cæsar's ears ungrudging witness of Antipater's prowess.

5. The praise bestowed by Cæsar at the time on the hero of the day and the hopes which it excited spurred Antipater to further ventures in his service. Showing himself on all occasions the most daring of fighters, and constantly wounded, he bore the marks of his valor on almost every part of his person. Later, when Cæsar had settled affairs in Egypt and returned to Syria, he conferred on Antipater the privilege of Roman citizenship

with exemption from taxes, and by other honors and marks of friendship made him an enviable man. It was to please him that Cæsar confirmed the appointment of Hyrcanus to the office of high priest.

x. 1. About this time Antigonus, son of Aristobulus, waited upon Cæsar and, contrary to his intentions, became the means of Antipater's further promotion. Antigonus ought to have confined himself to lamentation over his father's fate, believed to have been poisoned on account of his differences with Pompey, and to complaints of Scipio's cruelty to his brother, without mixing up with his plea for compassion any sentiments of jealousy. But, not content with that, he came forward and accused Hyrcanus and Antipater. They had, he said, in utter defiance of justice, banished him and his brothers and sisters from their native land altogether; they had, in their insolence, repeatedly done outrage to the nation; they had sent supports into Egypt, not from any goodwill to Cæsar, but from fear of the consequences of old quarrels and to obliterate the memory of their friendship for Pompey.

2. At these words Antipater stripped off his clothes and exposed his numerous scars. His loyalty to Cæsar needed, he said, no words from him; his body cried it aloud, were he to hold his peace. But the audacity of Antigonus astounded him. The son of an enemy of the Romans, son of a fugitive from Rome, one who inherited from his father a passion for revolution and sedition, presuming to accuse others in the presence of the Roman general and looking for favors when he ought to be thankful to be alive! Indeed (said Antipater), his present ambition for power was not due to indigence; he wanted it in order to sow sedition among the Jews and to employ his resources against those who had provided them.

3. After hearing both speakers, Cæsar pronounced Hyrcanus to be the more deserving claimant to the high priesthood, and left Antipater free choice of office. The latter, replying that it rested with him who conferred the honor to fix the measure of the honor, was then appointed procurator of all Judæa. He was further autho-

rized to rebuild the ruined walls of the metropolis. Orders were sent by Cæsar to Rome for these honors to be graven in the Capitol, as a memorial of his own justice and of Antipater's valor.

4. After escorting Cæsar across Syria, Antipater returned to Judæa. There his first act was to rebuild the wall of the capital which had been overthrown by Pompey. He then proceeded to traverse the country, quelling the local disturbances, and everywhere combining menaces with advice. Their support of Hyrcanus, he told them, would ensure them a prosperous and tranquil existence, in the enjoyment of their own possessions and of the peace of the realm. If, on the contrary, they put faith in the vain expectations raised by persons who for personal profit desired revolution, they would find in himself a master instead of a protector, in Hyrcanus a tyrant instead of a king, in the Romans and Cæsar enemies instead of rulers and friends; for they would never suffer their own nominee to be ousted from his office. But, while he spoke in this strain, he took the organization of the country into his own hands, finding Hyrcanus indolent and without the energy necessary to a king.* He further appointed his eldest son, Phasael, governor of Jerusalem and the environs; the second, Herod, he sent with equal authority to Galilee, though a mere lad.

5. Herod, energetic by nature, at once found material to test his metal. Discovering that Ezekias, a brigand-chief at the head of a large horde, was ravaging the district on the Syrian frontier, he caught him and put him and many of the brigands to death. This welcome achievement was immensely admired by the Syrians. Up and down the villages and in the towns the praises of Herod were sung, as the restorer of their peace and possessions. This exploit, moreover, brought him to the notice of Sextus Cæsar, a kinsman of the great Cæsar and governor of Syria. Phasael, on his side, with a generous emulation, vied with his brother's reputation; he

---

* Here and again later Josephus incorrectly calls Hyrcanus "king."

increased his popularity with the inhabitants of Jerusalem, and kept the city under control without any tact-
less abuse of authority. Antipater, in consequence, was
courted by the nation as if he were king and universally
honored as lord of the realm. Notwithstanding this, his
affection for Hyrcanus and his loyalty to him under-
went no change.

6. But it is impossible in prosperity to escape envy.
The young men's fame already caused Hyrcanus a secret
pang. He was vexed in particular by Herod's successes
and by the arrival of messenger after messenger with
news of each new honor that he had won. His resentment was further roused by a number of malicious persons at court, who had taken offense at the prudent behavior either of Antipater or of his sons. Hyrcanus, they
said, had abandoned to Antipater and his sons the direction of affairs, and rested content with the mere
title, without the authority, of a king. How long would
he be so mistaken as to rear kings to his own undoing?
No longer masquerading as procurators, they had now
openly declared themselves masters of the state, thrusting him aside; seeing that, without either oral or written instructions from Hyrcanus, Herod, in violation of
Jewish law, had put all this large number of people to
death. If he is not king but still a commoner, he ought
to appear in court and answer for his conduct to his
king and to his country's laws, which do not permit
anyone to be put to death without trial.

7. These words gradually inflamed Hyrcanus; until
at last, in an explosion of rage, he summoned Herod to
trial. Herod, on his father's advice, and with the confidence that his own conduct inspired, went up to the
capital, after posting garrisons throughout Galilee. He
went with a strong escort, calculated to avoid, on the
one hand, the appearance of wishing to depose Hyrcanus by bringing an overwhelming force, and, on the
other, the risk of falling, unprotected, a prey to envy.
Sextus Cæsar, however, fearing that the young man
might be isolated by his adversaries and meet with misfortune, sent express orders to Hyrcanus to clear Herod
of the charge of manslaughter. Hyrcanus, being inclined

to take that course on other grounds, for he loved Herod, acquitted him.

8. Herod, however, imagining that his escape was contrary to the king's wishes, retired to join Sextus at Damascus, and made ready to refuse compliance to a second summons. The knaves at court continued to exasperate Hyrcanus, saying that Herod had departed in anger and was prepared to attack him. The king believed them, but knew not what to do, seeing his adversary to be more than a match for himself. But when Sextus Cæsar proceeded to appoint Herod governor of Cœle-Syria and Samaria, and he was now doubly formidable owing to his popularity with the nation and his own power, Hyrcanus was reduced to consternation, expecting every moment to see him marching upon him at the head of an army.

9. Nor was he mistaken in his surmise. Herod, furious at the threat that this trial had held over him, collected an army and advanced upon Jerusalem to depose Hyrcanus. This object he would indeed have speedily achieved, had not his father and brother gone out in time to meet him and mollified his rage. They implored him to restrict his revenge to menaces and intimidation, and to spare the king under whom he had attained to such great power. Indignant as he might be at the summons to trial, he ought on the other hand to be thankful for his acquittal; after facing the black prospect of condemnation, he ought not to be ungrateful for escaping with his life. Moreover, if we are to believe that the fortunes of war are in the hands of God, the injustice of his present campaign ought to be taken into consideration. He should not, therefore, be altogether confident of success, when about to make war on his king and companion, frequently his benefactor, never his oppressor, save that, under the influence of evil counselors, he had menaced him with a mere shadow of injury. To this advice Herod yielded, thinking that he had satisfied his expectations for the future by this exhibition of his strength before the eyes of the nation.

10. Meanwhile, at Apamea, the Romans had trouble on their hands leading to civil war. Cæcilius Bassus, out

of devotion to Pompey, assassinated Sextus Cæsar and took command of his army; whereupon Cæsar's other generals, to avenge the murder, attacked Bassus with all their forces. Antipater, for the sake of his two friends, the deceased and the surviving Cæsar, sent them reinforcements under his sons. The war dragged on and Murcus arrived from Italy to succeed Antistius.

xi. 1. At this time the great war of the Romans broke out, arising out of the death of Cæsar, treacherously murdered by Cassius and Brutus after holding sovereign power for three years and seven months. This murder produced a tremendous upheaval; leading men split up into factions; each joined the party he considered would best serve his personal ambitions. Cassius, for his part, went to Syria to take command of the armies concentrated round Apamea. There he effected a reconciliation between Murcus and Bassus and the opposing legions, raised the siege of Apamea, and, putting himself at the head of the troops, went round the towns levying tribute and exacting sums which it was beyond their ability to pay.

2. The Jews received orders to contribute seven hundred talents. Antipater, alarmed at the threats of Cassius, to expedite payment distributed the task of collection between his sons and some of his acquaintance, including —so urgent was the necessity of the case—one of his enemies named Malichus. Herod was the first to bring his quota—the sum of one hundred talents—from Galilee, thereby appeasing Cassius and being regarded as one of his best friends. The rest Cassius abused for dilatoriness and then vented his wrath on the cities themselves. Gophna, Emmaus and two other places of less importance he reduced to servitude. He was proceeding so far as to put Malichus to death for tardiness in levying the tribute; but Antipater saved both his life and the other cities from destruction, by hastily propitiating Cassius with a gift of a hundred talents.

3. However, on the departure of Cassius, Malichus, far from remembering this service of Antipater, concocted a plot against the man who had often saved his life, impatient to remove one who was an obstacle to

his malpractices. Antipater, dreading the man's strength and cunning, crossed the Jordan to collect an army to defeat the conspiracy. Malichus, though detected, succeeded by effrontery in outwitting Antipater's sons; for Phasael, the warden of Jerusalem, and Herod, the custodian of the armory, cajoled by a multitude of excuses and oaths, consented to act as mediators with their father. Once again Antipater saved Malichus by his influence with Murcus, who when governor of Syria had determined to put him to death as a revolutionary.

4. When the young Cæsar* and Antony declared war on Cassius and Brutus, Cassius and Murcus levied an army in Syria, and, regarding Herod's future assistance as a great asset, appointed him then and there procurator of the whole of Syria, putting a force of horse and foot at his disposal; Cassius further promising on the termination of the war to make him king of Judæa. These powers and brilliant expectations of the son proved in the end the occasion of his father's destruction. For Malichus, taking alarm, bribed one of the royal butlers to serve poison to Antipater. Thus, a victim of the villainy of Malichus, Antipater expired after leaving the banquet—a man of great energy in the conduct of affairs, whose crowning merit was that he recovered and preserved the kingdom for Hyrcanus.

5. Malichus, being suspected of poisoning him, appeased the indignant populace by denial, and strengthened his position by mustering troops. For he never supposed that Herod would remain idle, and in fact the latter appeared forthwith at the head of an army to avenge his father. Phasael, however, advised his brother not to proceed to open vengeance on the scoundrel, for fear of exciting a popular riot. Herod, accordingly, for the moment accepted Malichus's defense and professed to clear him from suspicion. He then celebrated with splendid pomp the obsequies of his father.

6. Samaria being distracted by sedition, Herod betook himself thither, and after restoring order in the

---

* Julius Cæsar's nephew, Octavian, who took the name Augustus in 27 B.C. and was the first Roman emperor.

city, set out on the return journey to Jerusalem, then keeping festival, at the head of his troops. Instigated by Malichus, who was alarmed at his approach, Hyrcanus sent orders forbidding him to intrude aliens upon the country-folk during their period of purification. Herod, scorning the subterfuge and the man from whom the order came, entered by night. Malichus again waited on him and wept over Antipater's fate. Herod, scarce able to restrain his wrath, dissembled in his turn. At the same time he sent a letter to Cassius, deploring the murder of his father. Cassius, who had other grounds for hating Malichus, replied, "Have your revenge on the murderer," and gave secret orders to the tribunes under his command to lend Herod aid in a righteous deed.

7. When Cassius took Laodicea, and the grandees from all parts of the country flocked to him with gifts and crowns, Herod fixed on this as the moment for his revenge. Malichus had his suspicions, and on reaching Tyre resolved to effect the secret escape of his son, then a hostage in that city, while he made his own preparations to fly to Judæa. Desperation stimulated him to conceive yet grander schemes; he had dreams of raising a national revolt against the Romans, while Cassius was preoccupied with the war against Antony, of deposing Hyrcanus without difficulty, and of mounting the throne himself.

8. But Destiny derided his hopes. Herod, divining his intention, invited him and Hyrcanus to supper, and then dispatched one of his attendant menials to his house, ostensibly to prepare the banquet, in reality to instruct the tribunes to come out for the ambuscade. Remembering the orders of Cassius, they came out, sword in hand, to the sea-shore in front of the city, and there, surrounding Malichus, stabbed him through and through to death. Hyrcanus from sheer fright instantly swooned and fell; when brought, not without difficulty, to himself, he asked Herod by whom Malichus was killed. One of the tribunes replied, "By Cassius's orders." "Then," said Hyrcanus, "Cassius has saved both me and

my country, by destroying one who conspired against both." Whether he expressed his real opinion or from fear acquiesced in the deed, was uncertain. Be that as it may, thus was Herod avenged on Malichus.

xii. 1. The exit of Cassius from Syria was followed by a fresh outbreak at Jerusalem. A certain Helix, with a body of troops, attacked Phasael, wishing to punish Herod, through his brother, for the chastisement which he had inflicted on Malichus. Herod at the time was with Fabius the Roman general at Damascus, where, though impatient to lend his aid, he was detained by illness. Meanwhile Phasael, unassisted, defeated Helix and reproached Hyrcanus for ingratitude both in abetting the rebel and in allowing the brother of Malichus to take possession of the fortresses. Quite a large number of these had been taken, including Masada, the strongest of all.

2. But nothing could avail the captor against the might of Herod. Once restored to health, he recovered the other forts and ousted him from Masada, a suppliant for mercy. He likewise expelled from Galilee Marion, the despot of Tyre, already master of three of the strongholds. The Tyrians whom he took prisoners, he spared to a man; some he even sent away with presents, to procure for himself the favor of the citizens and for the tyrant their hatred. Marion owed his position to Cassius, who had cut up the whole of Syria into principalities. Hatred of Herod had led to his taking part in bringing back the exiled Antigonus, son of Aristobulus; and in this he was influenced still more by Fabius, whom Antigonus had induced by bribery to assist in his restoration. All the exile's expenses were met by his brother-in-law, Ptolemy.

3. These enemies were opposed by Herod at the entry to the territory of Judæa, where a battle took place in which he was victorious. Antigonus being banished from the country, Herod returned to Jerusalem, where his success won him all men's hearts. Even those who had hitherto stood aloof were now reconciled by his marriage into the family of Hyrcanus. His first wife was a

Jewess of some standing, named Doris, by whom he had a son, Antipater; but now he married* Mariamme, daughter of Alexander, the son of Aristobulus, and grand-daughter of Hyrcanus, and thus became kinsman of the king.

4. After the death of Cassius at Philippi, the victors departed, Cæsar going to Italy, Antony to Asia. Embassies from the various states waited upon Antony in Bithynia, and among them came the Jewish leaders, who accused Phasael and Herod of usurping the government and leaving to Hyrcanus merely titular honors. Herod thereupon appeared and by large bribes so wrought upon Antony that he refused his adversaries a hearing. So for the time being these enemies were dispersed.

5. But on a later occasion a hundred Jewish officials approached Antony, now a slave to his passion for Cleopatra, at Daphne beside Antioch, and putting forward the most eminent and eloquent of their number, laid accusations against the brothers. The defense was undertaken by Messala, Hyrcanus supporting him because of his marriage connection with Herod. After hearing both parties, Antony inquired of Hyrcanus who was the best qualified ruler. Hyrcanus pronouncing in favor of Herod and his brother, Antony was delighted, because he had formerly been their father's guest and had been hospitably entertained by Antipater when he accompanied Gabinius on his Judæan campaign. He, accordingly, created the brothers tetrarchs, entrusting to them the administration of the whole of Judæa.

6. The deputies giving vent to indignation, Antony arrested and imprisoned fifteen of them, and was even prepared to put them to death; the rest he ignominiously dismissed. His action intensified the agitation in Jerusalem. A second embassy, numbering this time a thousand, was sent to Tyre, where Antony had broken the journey to Jerusalem. To check the clamor of this party he dispatched the governor of Tyre, with orders

* From xiii. 7 and xvii. 8, however, it appears that they were only betrothed at this time and married in 37 B.C.

to chastise all whom he caught and to support the
authority of the tetrarchs whom he had appointed.

7. Before these orders were executed, Herod, accompanied by Hyrcanus, came out to the deputies on the
shore, and strongly recommended them not to bring
ruin upon themselves and war upon their country by
injudicious strife. His words only increasing their fury,
Antony ordered out troops, who killed or wounded a
large number; burial for the dead and medical attention for the wounded were granted by Hyrcanus. Those
who escaped were, even now, not silenced, and by the
disturbance which they created in the city so exasperated Antony that he put his prisoners to death.

xiii. 1. Two years later, Barzapharnes, the Parthian
satrap, with Pacorus, the [Parthian] king's son, occupied
Syria. Lysanias, who had inherited the principality
of his father Ptolemy, son of Mennæus, induced the
satrap, by the promise of a thousand talents and five
hundred women, to bring back Antigonus and raise him
to the throne, after deposing Hyrcanus. Lured by this
offer, Pacorus followed the coast route, directing Barzapharnes to advance through the interior. Of the
maritime towns, Tyre closed its gates to Pacorus; Ptolemais and Sidon admitted him. Entrusting a squadron of
horse to one of the royal cup-bearers who bore his own
name, the prince ordered him to proceed in advance
into Judæa, to reconnoiter the enemy's position and to
lend Antigonus such aid as he might require.

2. While these troops were raiding Carmel, Jews
flocked to Antigonus in large numbers and volunteered
for the invasion. These he sent forward with orders to
capture a place called Drymus. Here they came into
action, repulsed the enemy, rushed in pursuit to Jerusalem, and, with growing numbers, actually reached the
palace. They were met by Hyrcanus and Phasael with
a strong force, and a fierce battle ensued in the market-
place. The Herodian party routed their adversaries, shut
them up in the temple, and posted sixty men in the adjoining houses to keep guard over them. The section
of the populace that was in league against the brothers
attacked this garrison and burnt them to death, which

so enraged Herod that he turned his arms against the citizens and slew many of them. Every day small companies sallied out against each other, and slaughter was incessant.

3. When the feast called Pentecost came round, the whole neighborhood of the temple and the entire city were crowded with country-folk, for the most part in arms. Phasael defended the walls; Herod, with a small force, the palace. With this he descended upon the enemy's disordered ranks in the suburb, killed large numbers of them, put the rest to flight, and shut them up; some in the city, others in the temple, others in the entrenched camp outside the walls. Thereupon, Antigonus petitioned for the admission of Pacorus* as mediator. Phasael consented, and received into the city and offered hospitality to the Parthian, who, with five hundred horsemen, had come ostensibly to put an end to strife, in reality to support Antigonus. With this object, Pacorus insidiously induced Phasael to go on an embassy to Barzapharnes with a view to the cessation of hostilities. So, notwithstanding the strong dissuasion of Herod, who urged his brother to kill the schemer and not to abandon himself to his schemes, barbarians being (he said) by nature perfidious, Phasael left the city, accompanied by Hyrcanus. To allay suspicions, Pacorus left with Herod some of the cavalry called by the Parthians "Freemen"; with the remainder he escorted Phasael on his way.

4. On their arrival in Galilee they found the inhabitants in revolt and up in arms. The satrap, with whom they had an audience, was a very crafty individual who disguised his plot under a show of benevolence: he gave them presents, and then laid an ambush to catch them on their departure. They discovered the conspiracy at a maritime town named Ekdippa, where they halted. There they heard of the promise of the thousand talents, and that the five hundred women whom Antigonus had devoted to the Parthians included most of their own;

---

* Two men named Pacorus seem to be involved, this one not the king's son, but the cup-bearer mentioned a little earlier in the narrative.

that the barbarians invariably kept a watch upon them at night; and that they would long since have been arrested, had not the conspirators been waiting till Herod was caught at Jerusalem, fearing that the news of their capture would put him on his guard. This was now no mere idle gossip: for already they could see the sentries posted in the distance.

5. Phasael, however, notwithstanding the urgent exhortations to flee made to him by a certain Ophellius, who had learned the whole plan of the conspiracy from Saramalla, the wealthiest Syrian of his time, could not bring himself to desert Hyrcanus. Instead, he went to the satrap and frankly reproached him for the plot, and in particular for acting as he had done from mercenary motives; undertaking, for his part, to give him a larger sum for his life than Antigonus had promised for a kingdom. To this the Parthian made a wily reply, clearing himself of suspicion by protestations and oaths, and went off to join Pacorus. Immediately after, certain Parthians who had been left behind, with orders to do so, arrested Phasael and Hyrcanus, the prisoners cursing them bitterly for their perjury and breach of faith.

6. Meanwhile a plot to arrest Herod also was in progress, and the cup-bearer who had been sent to execute it was, in accordance with instructions, endeavoring to lure him to come outside the walls. Herod, however, having suspected the barbarians from the first, had now learned that letters informing him of the conspiracy had fallen into the enemy's hands. He, therefore, refused to come out, notwithstanding the highly plausible assertions of Pacorus that he ought to meet the bearers of the documents, which, he said, had neither been intercepted by his enemies, nor contained any mention of a plot but a full report of Phasael's proceedings. But Herod had already heard from another source of his brother's arrest. Moreover, Mariamme, the daughter of Hyrcanus, most sagacious of women, came and implored him not to venture out or trust himself to the barbarians, who were now openly planning his ruin.

7. While Pacorus and his accomplices were still de-

liberating by what stealthy means they might achieve their design, as it was impossible openly to triumph over so powerful an adversary, Herod forestalled them, and unobserved by his enemies, set out by night, with the nearest and dearest of his family, for Idumæa. The Parthians, discovering his flight, started in pursuit. Herod thereupon directed his mother and sisters, the young girl who was betrothed to him, with her mother, and his youngest brother to continue their journey, and then, aided by his attendants, secured their retreat, holding the barbarians at bay. In every encounter he slew large numbers of them, and then pressed on to the fortress of Masada.

8. But he found in this flight the Jews even more troublesome than the Parthians, for they perpetually harassed him, and at a distance of sixty furlongs from the city brought on a regular action which was prolonged for a considerable time. Here Herod eventually defeated them with great slaughter; and here subsequently, to commemorate his victory, he founded a city, adorned it with the most costly palaces, erected a citadel of commanding strength, and called it after his own name Herodion. Thenceforward the fugitive was joined daily by many others, and on reaching Rhesa in Idumæa was advised by his brother Joseph, who met him there, to disencumber himself of the bulk of his followers, Masada being unable to accommodate such a crowd, numbering upwards of nine thousand. Herod, acting on his advice, dispersed throughout Idumæa those who were more an encumbrance than an assistance, after supplying them with provisions, and retaining the most stalwart of them together with his cherished kinsfolk, reached the fortress in safety. Leaving there a guard of eight hundred to protect the women, with sufficient supplies to withstand a siege, he himself pushed on to Petra in Arabia.

9. In Jerusalem, meanwhile, the Parthians gave themselves up to pillage, breaking into the houses of the fugitives and into the palace; refraining only from the funds of Hyrcanus, which, however, amounted to no more than three hundred talents. Elsewhere they found

less than they had expected; for Herod, long since suspecting the barbarians of perfidy, had taken the precaution of removing the most precious of his treasures to Idumæa, and each of his friends had done likewise. After the pillage, the insolence of the Parthians proceeded to extremes. They let loose on the whole country the horrors of implacable war, laid the city of Marisa in ruins, and not content with raising Antigonus to the throne, delivered up to him Phasael and Hyrcanus in chains, for torture. Hyrcanus threw himself at the feet of Antigonus, who with his own teeth lacerated his suppliant's ears, in order to disqualify him for ever, under any change of circumstances, from resuming the high priesthood; since freedom from physical defect is essential to the holder of that office.

10. Phasael, on the other hand, courageously forestalled the king's malice by dashing his head upon a rock, being deprived of the use of hands or steel. Thus showing himself to be a true brother of Herod, and Hyrcanus the most ignoble of men, he died a hero's death—an end in keeping with his life's career. According to another account, Phasael recovered from his self-inflicted blow, and a physician sent by Antigonus, ostensibly to attend him, injected noxious drugs into the wound and so killed him. But whichever account be true, the initial act redounds to his glorious credit. It is said, moreover, that before he expired, being informed by a woman of Herod's escape, he exclaimed, "Now I shall depart happy, since I leave one behind me who will have vengeance on my foes."

11. Such was Phasael's end. The Parthians, though disappointed of their most coveted prize, the women, none the less installed Antigonus as master in Jerusalem, and carried off Hyrcanus a prisoner to Parthia.

xiv. 1. Herod, in the belief that his brother was still alive, was now accelerating his march to Arabia, hastening to obtain from its king the money by which alone he hoped to move the avaricious barbarians on behalf of Phasael. For, should the Arab prove unduly forgetful of the ties of friendship with his (Herod's) father and too mean to make him a present, he counted on borrowing from him the amount of the ransom and leaving in pledge the son of the prisoner whom he wished to redeem; for he had with him his nephew, a lad of seven years old. He was, moreover, prepared to give three hundred talents, offering as his sureties the Tyrians who had volunteered their services. Fate, however, proved to have outstripped his zeal: Phasael was dead and Herod's fraternal affection was all in vain. He found, too, that the Arabs were no longer his friends. For their king, Malchus, forwarded peremptory orders to him instantly to quit his territory, pretending to have received formal notice from the Parthians to expel Herod from Arabia. In reality, he was determined not to repay his debts to Antipater, nor to be forced by any sense of shame into making the slightest return, for all he had received from the father, to his children in their hour of need. His advisers in this shameless conduct were the most powerful men at his court, who like himself desired to embezzle the moneys entrusted to them by Antipater.

2. Herod, finding the Arabs hostile to him for the very reasons which had made him look for their warm friendship, gave the messengers the reply which his feelings dictated and turned back towards Egypt. The first evening, he encamped in one of the temples of the country, where he picked up those of his men who had been left in the rear. The next day he advanced to Rhinocorura, where he received the news of his brother's death. His load of anxiety thus replaced by as heavy a burden of grief, he resumed his march. The Arab king, now tardily repenting his conduct, dispatched messengers in haste to recall his insulted suitor; but Herod outstripped them, having already reached Pelusium. Here, being refused a passage by the fleet stationed in that port, he applied to the authorities, who, out of respect for his fame and rank, escorted him to Alexandria. On entering the city he had a magnificent reception from Cleopatra, who hoped to entrust him with the command of an expedition which she was preparing; but he eluded the queen's solicitations, and deterred

neither by the perils of mid-winter nor by the disturbances in Italy, set sail for Rome.

3. Nearly shipwrecked off Pamphylia, after throwing the bulk of the cargo overboard, he came safe to
Rhodes, which had suffered severely from the war with
Cassius. Here he was welcomed by his friends Ptolemy
and Sapphinius, and notwithstanding his lack of funds,
procured the construction of an immense trireme, which
carried him and his friends to Brundisium, whence he
sped to Rome. He waited first on Antony, as his father's
friend, and told him the story of his own and his
family's misfortunes, and how he had left his nearest
relatives besieged in a fortress and crossed the sea in
the depth of winter to implore his aid.

4. Antony was moved with compassion at his reverse
of fortune, and influenced by the recollection of Antipater's hospitality, but above all by the heroic qualities
of the man in front of him, determined then and there
to make him king of the Jews whom he had himself
previously appointed tetrarch. Besides admiration for
Herod, he had as strong an incentive in his aversion for
Antigonus, whom he regarded as a promoter of sedition
and an enemy of Rome. Cæsar proved a yet more ready
champion than Antony, as his memory recalled the part
which Antipater had borne with his own father in the
Egyptian campaigns, his hospitality and invariable
loyalty; while his eyes rested on Herod and read his
enterprising character. So he convened the Senate, to
which Messala, seconded by Atratinus, presented Herod
and dwelt on the services rendered by his father and
his own goodwill towards the Roman people; demonstrat-
ing at the same time that Antigonus was their enemy,
not only from the earlier quarrel which they had had
with him, but because he had also just been guilty of
contempt of Rome in accepting his crown from Parthian
hands. These words stirred the Senate, and when Antony came forward and said that with a view to the
war with Parthia it was expedient that Herod should be
king, the proposal was carried unanimously [in 40 B.C.].
The meeting was dissolved, and Antony and Cæsar left
the senate-house with Herod between them, preceded by

the consuls and the other magistrates, as they went to offer sacrifice and to lay up the decree in the Capitol. On this, the first day of his reign, Herod was given a banquet by Antony.

Herod the King: The Earlier Years

xv. 1. All this time Antigonus was besieging the occupants of Masada, who, though well supplied with all other necessaries, were in want of water. In these straits Joseph, Herod's brother, with two hundred of his men resolved to escape to Arabia, having heard that Malchus had repented of his criminal treatment of Herod. He was on the point of leaving the fortress, when on the very night fixed for his departure, rain fell in abundance; the reservoirs were replenished and Joseph saw no further need for flight. Instead, the garrison now began to sally out against the forces of Antigonus and partly in open combat, partly by ambuscades, destroyed a considerable number. They were not, however, uniformly successful, meeting with occasional reverses themselves and being forced to retire.

2. Meanwhile Ventidius, the Roman general dispatched from Syria to hold the Parthians in check, had in his pursuit of them advanced into Judæa, nominally to relieve Joseph and his friends, but in reality to extort money from Antigonus. He accordingly encamped in the immediate vicinity of Jerusalem, and after glutting his avarice, retired with the bulk of his troops; leaving, however, a detachment under the command of Silo, to prevent the detection of his mercenary proceedings which might ensue from the withdrawal of the entire force. Antigonus, on his side, hoping for renewed assistance from the Parthians, meanwhile paid court to Silo, as he had to Ventidius, to prevent any trouble from him before his expectations were realized.

3. But already Herod, having sailed from Italy to Ptolemais and collected a considerable army of foreign and native troops, was advancing through Galilee upon Antigonus. Ventidius and Silo, induced by Dellius, Antony's emissary, to assist in reinstating Herod, were co-

110

operating. But Ventidius was occupied in quelling local
disturbances arising out of the Parthian invasion, while
Silo, corrupted by the bribes of Antigonus, lingered in
Judæa. Herod, however, had no lack of support: new
recruits added daily to his strength as he advanced, and
with few exceptions, all Galilee went over to him. The
most urgent task ahead of him was Masada and, above
all, the liberation of his relatives from the siege. But
Joppa was a preliminary obstacle, for that town being
hostile had first to be reduced, in order that there
might be no stronghold left in enemy hands in his rear
when he marched against Jerusalem. Silo, glad of an
excuse for quitting Jerusalem, now proceeded to join
him, hotly pursued by the Jews. Herod with a small
party flew out upon them and soon routed them, rescu-
ing Silo, who was making but a poor defense.

4. Then, after taking Joppa, he hastened to Masada
to rescue his friends. The country-folk rallied to him,
some drawn by old affection for his father, others by his
own renown; some in return for benefits conferred by
both father and son, but the majority attracted by their
expectations from one whose claim to the throne seemed
assured; so that by now he had assembled a formidable
army. Antigonus sought to obstruct his advance by posting ambuscades in suitable passes, but caused little or
no injury to the enemy. Herod rescued his friends in
Masada without difficulty, recovered the fortress of
Rhesa, and then marched against Jerusalem; where he
was joined by Silo's troops and by many of the citizens,
who were alarmed at the strength of his army.

5. Having encamped on the west side of the town,
his forces were assailed by showers of arrows and javelins from the guards posted at that quarter, while others
sallying out in companies made attacks on his outposts.
At the outset, Herod ordered heralds to patrol the walls
and proclaim that he had come for the good of the
people and the salvation of the city, that he had no intention of punishing even avowed enemies and would
grant an amnesty to his bitterest foes. But when Antigonus issued counter-exhortations forbidding any to
listen to these proclamations or to go over to the enemy,

Herod at once gave his men permission to retaliate on their assailants on the ramparts, and with their missiles they soon drove them all out of the towers.

6. And now Silo's conduct betrayed his corruption. For he induced a large number of his soldiers to raise an outcry about a lack of supplies and to demand money for the purchase of provisions and to be marched to suitable winter quarters, as the troops of Antigonus had already completely cleared the neighborhood of the city and reduced it to a desert. He therefore broke up his camp and attempted to retire. Herod, however, interceded with first the officers of Silo's staff and then with the assembled troops, and besought them not to desert him, holding, as he did, a commission from Cæsar, Antony, and the senate; "for," said he, "this very day I will relieve your wants." After making this appeal he instantly set off in person into the country and brought back such an abundance of supplies as to cut away all Silo's excuses; while, to ensure that there should be no shortage in the immediate future, he instructed the inhabitants of the district of Samaria, that city having declared in his favor, to bring corn, wine, oil, and cattle down to Jericho.

Hearing of this, Antigonus issued orders throughout the country to hold up and waylay the convoys. Acting on these orders, large bodies of men in arms assembled above Jericho and took up positions on the hills, on the look-out for the conveyors of the supplies. Herod, however, was on the alert, and with ten cohorts, of which five were Roman, and five Jewish with mercenaries intermixed, and a small body of horse, proceeded to Jericho. He found the city deserted and the heights occupied by five hundred persons with their wives and children. These he made prisoners and then released, while the Romans fell upon and rifled the rest of the town, where they found the houses full of treasures of every sort. Leaving a garrison in Jericho, the king returned and dismissed his Roman army to winter quarters in the districts which had joined his standard, Idumæa, Galilee, and Samaria. Antigonus, on his side, to ingra-

tiate himself with Antony, induced Silo by a bribe to
billet a division of his troops in Lydia.

xvi. 1. While the Romans were thus living on the
fat of the land, at rest from arms, Herod, never idle,
occupied Idumæa with two thousand foot and four
hundred horse, which he sent thither under his brother
Joseph, to prevent any insurrection in favor of Antigonus. His own care was the removal of his mother
and other relations, whom he had rescued from Masada,
to Samaria; having safely installed them there, he set
out to reduce the remaining strongholds of Galilee and
to expel the garrisons of Antigonus.

2. He pushed on to Sepphoris through a very heavy
snowstorm and took possession of the city without a
contest, the garrison having fled before his assault.
Here, provisions being abundant, he refreshed his
troops, sorely tried by the tempest, and then started
on a campaign against the cave-dwelling brigands, who
were infesting a wide area and inflicting on the inhabitants evils no less than those of war. Having sent
in advance three battalions of infantry and a squadron
of cavalry to the village of Arbela, he joined them forty
days later with the rest of his army. Nothing daunted
by his approach, the enemy, who combined the experience of seasoned warriors with the daring of brigands,
went armed to meet him, and coming into action, routed
Herod's left wing with their right. Herod instantly wheeling round his troops from the right wing, where he was
in command, came to the relief, and not only checked
the flight of his own men, but falling upon their pur-
suers broke their charge, until, overpowered by his
frontal attacks, they in turn gave way.

3. Herod pursued them, with slaughter, to the Jordan
and destroyed large numbers of them; the rest fled
across the river and dispersed. Thus was Galilee purged
of its terrors, save for the remnant still lurking in the
caves, and their extirpation required time. So, before
proceeding further, Herod awarded to his soldiers the
fruits of their labors, distributing to each man a hundred and fifty drachmas of silver and to their officers
much larger sums, and then dismissed them to their

various winter quarters. He instructed Pheroras, his
youngest brother, to take charge of the commissariat
department and to fortify Alexandrion; both tasks received his brother's attention.

4. At this time Antony was residing in the neighborhood of Athens, and Silo and Herod were summoned
by Ventidius for the war with Parthia, being instructed
first to settle affairs in Judæa. Herod gladly dismissed
Silo to Ventidius, and set out himself on a campaign
against the bandits in the caves. These caves, opening on to mountain precipices, were inaccessible from
any quarter, except by some tortuous and extremely narrow paths leading up to them; the cliff in front of
them dropped sheer down into ravines far below, with
water-courses at the bottom. The king was, consequently, for long baffled by the impracticable nature of
the ground, but at length had recourse to a most hazardous scheme. By means of ropes he lowered the most
stalwart of his men in cradles and so gave them access
to the cavern-mouths; these then massacred the brigands
and their families, hurling in fire-brands upon those
who resisted. Anxious to save some of them, Herod, by
word of herald, summoned them to his presence. Not
one of them voluntarily surrendered, and of those taken
by force many preferred death to captivity.

It was then that one old man, the father of seven
children, being asked by them and their mother permission to leave under Herod's pledge, killed them in
the following manner. Ordering them to come forward
one by one, he stood at the entrance and slew each
son as he advanced. Herod, watching this spectacle from
a conspicuous spot, was profoundly affected and, extending his hand to the old man, implored him to spare
his children; but he, unmoved by any word of Herod,
and even upbraiding him as a low-born upstart, followed up the slaughter of his sons by that of his wife,
and, having flung their corpses down the precipice,
finally threw himself over after them.

5. Herod having thus mastered the caves and their
inhabitants—leaving behind him under the command
of Ptolemy a contingent sufficient, in his opinion, to

repress insurrection—returned towards Samaria, bringing to meet Antigonus a force of three thousand heavy
infantry and six hundred cavalry. Thereupon, emboldened by his departure, the usual promoters of disturbance in Galilee made a surprise attack on his general
Ptolemy and slew him, and proceeded to ravage the
country, finding refuge in the marshes and other places
difficult to search. Apprised of the revolt, Herod returned in haste to the relief, killed a large number of
the rebels, besieged and destroyed all their fortresses,
and imposed on the towns, as the penalty for their
defection, a fine of a hundred talents.

6. The Parthians having now [38 B.C.] at last been
expelled and Pacorus slain, Ventidius, under instructions from Antony, dispatched a thousand horse with
two legions to support Herod in opposing Antigonus,
the officer in command being Machæras. To this general Antigonus wrote, imploring him instead to come
to his own assistance, complaining bitterly of Herod's
high-handed and abusive treatment of the realm, and
adding a promise of money. Machæras, not being prepared for such contempt of his superior's orders, especially as Herod was offering him a larger sum, declined
the temptation to treason, but feigning amity, went
off to spy out the position of Antigonus, without listen-
ing to Herod, who tried to dissuade him. Antigonus,
divining his intention, refused him admittance to the
city, and repulsed him from the walls as an enemy;
until at length Machæras, for very shame, was forced
to retire to Emmaus and rejoin Herod. Infuriated by
his discomfiture, he killed all the Jews whom he met on
his march, not even sparing the Herodians, but treating
all alike as friends of Antigonus.

7. At this, Herod, in indignation, hastened to attack
Machæras as an enemy, but restraining his anger, set
out instead to lay before Antony an accusation of his
enormities. Machæras, reflecting on his errors, pursued
after the king and by dint of entreaties succeeded in
pacifying him. Herod, notwithstanding, continued his
march to join Antony; the receipt of intelligence that the
latter with a large army was assaulting Samosata, a

JOSEPHUS

strong city near the Euphrates, quickened his pace, as
he saw in this a favorable opportunity for displaying his
courage and strengthening his hold upon Antony's affection. His arrival, in fact, brought the siege to a conclusion. He killed numbers of the barbarians and secured booty in abundance, with the result that Antony,
who had long admired his valor, now held it in even
higher respect, and largely increased both his honors
and his high expectations of sovereignty; while King
Antiochus was compelled to surrender Samosata.

xvii. 1. Meanwhile Herod's cause had suffered a grave
reverse in Judæa. He had left his brother Joseph in
charge of the realm, with injunctions to take no action
against Antigonus until his return, because the previous
conduct of Machæras proved him to be an untrust-
worthy ally. No sooner, however, did Joseph hear that
his brother was at a safe distance, than, disregarding instructions, he marched towards Jericho with five cohorts sent to him by Machæras, with the object of carrying off the corn-crop in its midsummer prime. On the
way he was attacked by his adversaries on difficult
ground in the hills; after displaying great gallantry in
the battle he fell, and the whole Roman force was cut
to pieces. For the cohorts had been recently levied in
Syria and had no leavening of the so-called "veterans"
to support these raw recruits.

2. Not content with his victory, Antigonus was so
far carried away by rage as actually to do outrage to
Joseph's corpse. Being in possession of the bodies of the
slain, he had his head cut off, notwithstanding the ransom of fifty talents with which Pheroras, the brother of
the deceased, offered to redeem it. In Galilee this victory
of Antigonus led to so serious a revolution that his partisans dragged out of their houses the men of rank who
were in favor of Herod and drowned them in the lake.
There was defection also in many parts of Idumæa,
where Machæras was rebuilding the walls of a fortress
called Gittha. Of all this Herod as yet knew nothing.
For after the capture of Samosata, Antony had appointed Sossius governor of Syria, with orders to support Herod in opposing Antigonus, and had then taken

his departure for Egypt. Sossius, thereupon, sent on two legions into Judæa to assist Herod, and followed himself close behind with the rest of his troops.

3. But while Herod was at Daphne, near Antioch, he had a dream distinctly warning him of his brother's death, and springing in horror from his bed, was met by the messengers bringing news of the catastrophe. After brief lamentation for his loss, he deferred further mourning for another season and set out in haste to meet his foes. By forced marches he pushed on to Lebanon, where he received a reinforcement of eight hundred of the mountaineers and was joined by one of the Roman legions. With these allies, without waiting for daylight, he invaded Galilee; he was met by the enemy, but drove them back to the position which they had just left. He made repeated attacks upon their fortress, but before he could capture it was compelled by a terrific storm to encamp in the neighboring villages. A few days later he was joined by the second of Antony's legions, whereupon the enemy, alarmed at his strength, under cover of night evacuated their stronghold.

4. His subsequent march, accelerated by the desire for speedy vengeance on his brother's murderers, took him through Jericho. Here he had a providential and miraculous escape, the surprising nature of which won him the reputation of a special favorite of heaven. A large company of magistrates had dined with him that evening, and no sooner had the banquet ended and all the guests departed, than the building collapsed. Seeing in this an omen alike of perils and of preservation during the coming campaign, he at daybreak put his troops in motion. Some six thousand of the enemy rushed down from the hills and assailed his vanguard; they had not the courage to come to close quarters with the Romans, but pelted them from a distance with stones and darts, wounding many of them. On this occasion Herod himself, while riding along the lines, was struck by a javelin in the side.

5. Antigonus, wishing to create an impression of the superiority of his men, not only in enterprise but in numbers, dispatched an army to Samaria under one of

his comrades named Pappus, whose commission was to
oppose Machæras. Herod, meanwhile, ravaged the enemy's territory, subdued five small towns, slew two thousand of their inhabitants, set fire to the houses, and returned to his camp. His present headquarters were in
the neighborhood of a village called Cana.

6. Multitudes of Jews now joined him daily from
Jericho and elsewhere, some drawn by hatred of Antigonus, others by his own successes, the majority by a
blind love of change. Herod was burning for a fight,
and Pappus, undeterred either by the number or the
ardor of his adversaries, advanced with alacrity to meet
them. On coming into action the enemy made a brief
stand in other parts of the line; but Herod, with his
memories of his murdered brother, hazarding all to be
avenged on his murderers, quickly overcame the troops
in front of him, and then, successively directing his attacks upon any that still held together, routed the whole
body. A scene of carnage ensued, the enemy driven pell-
mell back into the village from which they had issued,
Herod pressing upon their rear and massacring untold
numbers. Rushing with his foes into the village, he found
every house packed with soldiers and the roofs thronged
with others who attacked him from above. After defeat-
ing his enemies in the open, he pulled the buildings to
pieces and dragged out those within. Many perished in
a mass under the roofs which he brought down upon
their heads, while those who escaped from beneath the
ruins were met by the soldiers with drawn swords, and
there was such a heap of corpses that the streets were
impassable to the victors. This blow was too much for
the enemy; those of them who rallied after the battle,
when they saw the village strewn with dead, dispersed
and fled. With the confidence of his victory, Herod
would instantly have marched upon Jerusalem, had he
not been detained by a storm of exceptional severity.
This accident impeded the completion of his success and
the defeat of Antigonus, who was by now meditating
the abandonment of the capital.

7. That evening, Herod, having dismissed his companions to refresh themselves after their fatigues, went

himself just as he was, yet hot from the fight, to take
a bath, like any common soldier, for only a single slave
attended him. Before he entered the bath-house, one of
the enemy ran out in front of him, sword in hand, then
a second and a third, followed by more. These were men
who had escaped from the combat and taken refuge,
fully armed, in the baths. There for a while they had
remained lurking and concealed; but when they saw the
king, they were panic-stricken and ran trembling past
him, unarmed though he was, and made for the exits.
By chance not a man was there to lay hands on them;
but Herod was content to have come off unscathed, and
so they all escaped.

8. On the following day he cut off the head of Pappus,
Antigonus's general, who had been killed in the combat,
and sent it to his brother Pheroras in retribution for the
murder of their brother; for it was Pappus who had slain
Joseph. When the tempest abated, he advanced upon
Jerusalem and marched his army up to the walls, it being now just three years since he had been proclaimed
king in Rome. He encamped opposite the Temple, for
from that quarter the city was open to attack and had
on a previous occasion been captured by Pompey. He
then appointed his army their several tasks, cut down
the trees in the suburbs, and gave orders to raise three
lines of earth-works and to erect towers upon them.
Leaving his most efficient lieutenants to superintend
these works, he went off himself to Samaria to fetch the
daughter of Alexander, son of Aristobulus, who, as we
have said, was betrothed to him. Thus, so contemptuous
was he already of the enemy, he made his wedding an
interlude of the siege.

9. After his marriage he returned with a larger force
to Jerusalem. Here too he was joined by Sossius with an
imposing army of horse and foot, which that general had
sent on ahead through the interior, while he himself
took the route by Phœnicia. The total strength of the
united armies amounted to eleven battalions of infantry
and six thousand cavalry, not including the Syrian auxiliaries, who formed no inconsiderable contingent. The
two generals encamped near the north wall: Herod with

the confidence inspired by the senatorial decrees, which had proclaimed him king; Sossius relying on Antony, who had dispatched the army under his command in support of Herod.

xviii. 1. Throughout the city the agitation of the Jewish populace showed itself in various forms. The feebler folk, congregating round the Temple, indulged in transports of frenzy and fabricated numerous oracular utterances to fit the crisis. The more daring went out in companies on marauding expeditions of all kinds, their main object being to seize all provisions in the neighborhood of the city and to leave no sustenance for horse or man. Of the military the more disciplined men were employed in repelling the besiegers, from their position on the ramparts beating off the excavators of the earth-works and constantly contriving some new means of parrying the enemy's engines; but it was above all in their mining operations that they showed their superiority.

2. To stop the raiders the king arranged ambuscades, by which he succeeded in checking their incursions; to meet the shortage of provisions he had supplies brought from a distance; while as for the combatants, the military experience of the Romans gave him the advantage over them, although their audacity knew no bounds. If they did not openly fling themselves against the Roman lines, to face certain death, they would through their underground passages appear suddenly in the enemy's midst; and before one portion of the wall was overthrown they were erecting another in its stead. In a word, neither in action nor ingenuity did they ever flag, fully resolving to hold out to the last. In fact, notwithstanding the strength of the beleaguering army, they sustained the siege into the fifth month; until some of Herod's picked men ventured to scale the wall and leapt into the city, followed by Sossius's centurions.

The environs of the Temple were first secured, and when the troops poured in, a scene of wholesale massacre ensued; for the Romans were infuriated by the length of the siege, and the Jews of Herod's army were determined to leave none of their opponents alive. Masses were butchered in the alleys, crowded together in the houses, and flying to the sanctuary. No quarter was given to infancy, to age, or to helpless womanhood. Nay, though the king sent messengers in every direction, entreating them to spare, none stayed his hand, but like madmen they wreaked their rage on all ages indiscriminately. In this scene Antigonus, regardless alike of his former fortune and that which now was his, came down from the castle and threw himself at the feet of Sossius. The latter, far from pitying his changed condition, burst into uncontrollable laughter and called him "Antigone." He did not, however, treat him as a woman and leave him at liberty: no, he was put in irons and kept under strict guard.

3. Now master of his enemies, Herod's next task was to gain the mastery over his foreign allies; for this crowd of aliens rushed to see the Temple and the holy contents of the sanctuary. The king expostulated, threatened, sometimes even had recourse to weapons to keep them back, deeming victory more grievous than defeat, if these people should set eyes on any objects not open to public view. Now too he put a stop to the pillage of the town, forcibly representing to Sossius that, if the Romans emptied the city of money and men, they would leave him king of a desert, and that he would count the empire of the world itself too dearly bought with the slaughter of so many citizens. Sossius replying that he was justified in permitting the soldiers to pillage in return for their labors in the siege, Herod promised to distribute rewards to each man out of his private resources. Having thus redeemed what remained of his country, he duly fulfilled his engagement, remunerating each soldier liberally, the officers in proportion, and Sossius himself with truly royal munificence; so that none went unprovided. Sossius, after dedicating to God a crown of gold, withdrew from Jerusalem, taking Antigonus in chains with him to Antony. This prisoner, to the last clinging with forlorn hope to life, fell beneath the axe, a fitting end to his ignominious career.

4. King Herod, discriminating between the two classes of the city population, by the award of honors attached more closely to himself those who had es-

poused his cause, while he exterminated the partisans of Antigonus. Finding his funds now reduced, he converted all the valuables in his possession into money, which he then transmitted to Antony and his staff. Yet even at this price he failed to secure for himself complete exemption from injury; for Antony, already demoralized by his love for Cleopatra, was becoming wholly enslaved to his passion, and Cleopatra, after killing off her own family, one after another, till not a single relative remained, was now thirsting for the blood of foreigners. Laying before Antony calumnious charges against high officials in Syria, she urged him to put them to death, in the belief that she would have no difficulty in appropriating their possessions; and now, her ambitions extending to Judæa and Arabia, she was secretly contriving the ruin of their respective kings, Herod and Malchus.

5. One part, at any rate, of her orders brought Antony to his sober senses: he held it sacrilege to take the lives of innocent men and kings of such eminence. But —what touched them more nearly—he threw over his friends. He cut off large tracts of their territory—including, in particular, the palm-grove of Jericho where the balsam grows—and presented them to Cleopatra, together with all the towns to the south of the river Eleutherus, Tyre and Sidon excepted. Now mistress of all this land, she escorted Antony, who was starting on a campaign against the Parthians, as far as the Euphrates, and then, by way of Apamea and Damascus, came into Judæa. There, by large bounties, Herod appeased her ill will and agreed to take on lease for an annual sum of two hundred talents the lands which had been detached from his realm. He then escorted her to Pelusium, treating her with every mark of respect. Not long after, Antony returned from Parthia, bringing as a present for Cleopatra his prisoner Artabazes, son of Tigranes; for upon her, together with the money and all the spoils of war, the Parthian* was instantly bestowed.

xix. 1. On the outbreak of the war of Actium Herod

* He was actually king of Armenia, not a Parthian.

prepared to join forces with Antony; for he was now rid of disturbances in Judæa and had captured the fortress of Hyrcania, hitherto held by the sister of Antigonus. The craft of Cleopatra, however, precluded him from sharing Antony's perils. For, as we have stated, she had designs on the kings, in pursuance of which she now induced Antony to entrust the war against the Arabs to Herod, hoping, if he were successful, to become mistress of Arabia, if unsuccessful, of Judæa, and by means of one of the two potentates to overthrow the other.

2. Her scheme, however, turned to Herod's advantage. For, beginning with raids upon the enemy's territory, he mustered a large body of cavalry, flung them at the foe in the neighborhood of Diospolis, and though he met with a stubborn resistance, defeated them. This defeat occasioned a great commotion among the Arabs, who assembled in vast numbers at Canatha in Cœle-Syria and there awaited the Jews. Herod, arriving with his troops, endeavored to conduct operations with due caution and ordered the camp to be fortified. His orders, however, were defied by the rank and file, who, flushed with their recent victory, rushed upon the Arabs. With their first charge they routed them and followed at their heels; but during the pursuit a snare was laid for Herod by Athenion, one of Cleopatra's generals, who had always been hostile to him, and now let loose upon him the natives of Canatha. Encouraged by their allies' attack, the Arabs faced about, and after uniting their forces on rocky and difficult ground, routed Herod's troops with immense slaughter. Those who escaped from the battle took refuge in Ormiza, where, however, the Arabs surrounded and captured their camp with all its defenders.

3. Shortly after this disaster Herod arrived with reinforcements, too late to be of use. This calamity was brought upon him by the insubordination of the divisional officers, for had they not precipitated an engagement, Athenion would have found no opportunity for a ruse. However, Herod subsequently avenged himself on the Arabs by constantly raiding their territory, so that they had frequent occasion to rue their single victory.

But while he was punishing his foes, he was visited by another calamity—an act of God which occurred in the seventh year of his reign, when the war of Actium was at its height. In the early spring an earthquake destroyed cattle innumerable and thirty thousand souls; but the, army, being quartered in the open, escaped injury. At the same moment the confidence of the Arabs rose, stimulated by rumor which always exaggerates the horrors of a tragedy. Imagining that the whole of Judæa was in ruins and that they had only to take possession of an abandoned country, they hastened to invade it, after massacring the envoys whom the Jews had sent to them. So dismayed were the people at this invasion, and so demoralized by the magnitude of these successive disasters, that Herod called them together and endeavored to rouse them to resistance by the following speech.

4. "This alarm which has now laid hold of you seems to me most unreasonable. To be disheartened by the visitations of heaven was natural; but to be similarly despondent at the attack of a human foe is unmanly. For my part, far from being intimidated by the enemy's invasion following the earthquake, I regard that catastrophe as a snare which God has laid to decoy the Arabs and deliver them up to our vengeance. It is not because they have confidence in their weapons or their might that they are here, but because they count on our accidental calamities. But hopes are fallacious which are dependent not on one's own strength, but on the misadventures of another.

"Moreover, with mankind fortune is never permanently either adverse or favorable; one sees her veering from one mood to the other. Of this you might find an illustration in your own experiences: conquerors in the first battle, you were then conquered by our enemies, who in all probability, expecting a victory, will now be defeated. For excessive confidence throws men off their guard, whereas fear teaches precaution; so that your very timidity is to me reassuring. When you displayed uncalled for temerity, and disdaining my advice, dashed out upon the foe, Athenion had his opportunity for a ruse; but now your hesitation and apparent despondency are to me a sure pledge of victory. Appropriate, however, as are such feelings before an impending battle, when once in action your spirits must be roused and you must teach these scoundrels that no disaster, whether inflicted by God or man, will ever reduce the valor of Jews, so long as they have breath in their bodies, and that not one of them will consent to see his property pass into the hands of an Arab, who has often so narrowly escaped becoming his prisoner.

"Do not let the convulsions of inanimate nature disturb you or imagine that the earthquake is a portent of a further disaster. These accidents to which the elements are subject have physical causes, and beyond the immediate injury inflicted bring no further consequences to mankind. A pestilence, a famine, subterranean commotions may possibly be preceded by some slighter premonition, but these catastrophes themselves are limited by their very magnitude to their instant effects. I ask you, can war, even if we are defeated, do us more harm than the earthquake?

"Our adversaries, on the other hand, have one grave portent of impending disaster in a recent incident, due neither to natural causes nor to the action of others. Contrary to the universal law of mankind they have brutally murdered our ambassadors; such are the garlanded victims which they have offered to God to obtain success! But they will not escape His mighty eye, His invincible right hand; and to us they will soon answer for their crimes if, with some vestige of the spirit of our fathers, we now arise to avenge this violation of treaties. Let us each go into action not to defend wife or children or country at stake, but to avenge our envoys. They will conduct the campaign better than we who are alive. I myself will bear the brunt of the battle, if I have you obedient at my back; for, be assured, your courage is irresistible, if you do not by some reckless action bring injury upon yourselves."

5. Having by this speech reanimated his army, Herod, observing their ardor, offered sacrifice to God, and then proceeded to cross the Jordan with his troops. Encamp-

ing in the neighborhood of Philadelphia, close to the enemy, and anxious to force on an engagement, he began skirmishing with them for the possession of a fort which lay between the opposing lines. The enemy on their side had sent forward a detachment to occupy this post; the party sent by the king promptly beat them off and secured the hill. Daily, Herod marched out his troops, formed them in battle array, and challenged the Arabs to combat. But when none came out to oppose him—for a dire consternation had seized them and, even more than the rank and file, their general Elthemus was paralyzed with fright—the king advanced and proceeded to tear up their palisades. Thereupon, impelled by necessity, the enemy at length emerged for action in disorder, infantry and cavalry intermingled. Superior in numbers to the Jews, they had less stomach for a fight, though despair of success rendered even them reckless.

6. Consequently, so long as they held out, their casualties were slight; but when they turned their backs multitudes were slain by the Jews, and many others were trodden to death by their own men. Five thousand fell in the rout; the rest of the crowd succeeded in forcing their way into their entrenched camp. There Herod surrounded and besieged them, and they must have succumbed to an assault, had not the failure of their water-supply and thirst precipitated their capitulation. The king treated their envoys with scorn, and although they offered a ransom of five hundred talents, only pressed his attack the harder. Parched with thirst, the Arabs came out in crowds and willingly surrendered to the Jews, so that in five days four thousand were made prisoners. On the sixth the remnant in desperation came forth to battle; these Herod engaged, killing some seven thousand more. Having, by this crushing blow, punished Arabia and broken the spirit of its people, he gained such a reputation with them that the nation chose him for its Protector.

xx. 1. But, this peril surmounted, Herod was instantly plunged into anxiety about the security of his position. He was Antony's friend, and Antony had been defeated [in 31 B.C.] by Cæsar at Actium. (In reality, he inspired more fear than he felt himself; for Cæsar considered his victory to be incomplete so long as Herod remained Antony's ally). The king, nevertheless, resolved to confront the danger, and having sailed to Rhodes where Cæsar was sojourning, presented himself before him without a diadem, a commoner in dress and demeanor, but with the proud spirit of a king. His speech was direct; he told the truth without reserve.

"Cæsar," he said, "I was made king by Antony, and I acknowledge that I have in all things devoted my services to him. Nor will I shrink from saying that, had not the Arabs detained me, you would assuredly have found me in arms inseparable from his side. I sent him, however, such auxiliary troops as I could and many thousand measures of corn; nor even after his defeat at Actium did I desert my benefactor. When no longer useful as an ally, I became his best counsellor; I told him the one remedy for his disasters—the death of Cleopatra. Would he but kill her, I promised him money, walls to protect him, an army, and myself as his brother to arms in the war against you. But his ears, it seems, were stopped by his infatuation for Cleopatra and by God who has granted you the mastery. I share Antony's defeat and with his downfall lay down my diadem. I am come to you resting my hope of safety upon my integrity, and presuming that the subject of inquiry will be not whose friend, but how loyal a friend, I have been."

2. To this Cæsar replied: "Nay, be assured of your safety, and reign henceforth more securely than before. So staunch a champion of the claims of friendship deserves to be ruler over many subjects. Endeavor to remain as loyal to those who have been more fortunate; since, for my part, I entertain the most brilliant hopes for your high spirit. Antony, however, did well in obeying Cleopatra's behests rather than yours; for through his folly we have gained you. But you have already, it seems, done me a service; for Quintus Didius writes to me that you have sent a force to assist him against the gladiators. I therefore now confirm your kingdom to you by decree; and hereafter I shall endeavor to confer

upon you some further benefit, that you may not feel the loss of Antony."

3. Having thus graciously addressed the king, he placed the diadem on his head, and publicly notified this award by a decree, in which he expressed his commendation of the honored man in ample and generous terms. Herod, after propitiating Cæsar with presents, then sought to obtain pardon for Alexas, one of Antony's friends, who had come to sue for mercy; but here Cæsar's resentment was too strong for him, and with many bitter complaints against Herod's client the emperor rejected his petition. Subsequently, when Cæsar passed through Syria on his way to Egypt, Herod entertained him for the first time with all the resources of his realm; he accompanied the emperor on horseback when he reviewed his troops at Ptolemais; he entertained him and all his friends at a banquet; and he followed this up by making ample provision for the good cheer of the rest of the army. Then, for the march to Pelusium across the arid desert, and likewise for the return, he took care to furnish the troops with abundance of water; in short, there were no necessaries which the army lacked.

The thought could not but occur both to Cæsar himself and to his soldiers that Herod's realm was far too restricted, in comparison with the services which he had rendered them. Accordingly, when Cæsar reached Egypt, after the death of Cleopatra and Antony, he not only conferred new honors upon him, but also annexed to his kingdom the territory which Cleopatra had appropriated, with the addition of Gadara, Hippos and Samaria and the maritime towns of Gaza, Anthedon, Joppa, and Strato's Tower. He further presented him, as a bodyguard, with four hundred Gauls who had formerly served Cleopatra in the same capacity. And nothing so strongly moved the emperor to this liberality as the generous spirit of him who was the object of it.

4. After the first period of the Actian era, Cæsar added to Herod's realm the country called Trachonitis, with the adjacent districts of Batanæa and Auranitis. The occasion of this grant was as follows. Zenodorus,

who had taken on lease the domain of Lysanias, was
perpetually setting the brigands of Trachonitis to molest
the inhabitants of Damascus. The latter fled for protection to Varro, the governor of Syria, and besought him
to report their sufferings to Cæsar. On learning the facts,
Cæsar sent back orders to exterminate the bandits. Varro, accordingly, led out his troops, cleared the district
of these pests, and deprived Zenodorus of his tenure.
This was the territory which Cæsar subsequently presented to Herod, to prevent it from again being used
by the brigands as a base for raids upon Damascus.
When, ten years after his first visit, Cæsar returned to
the province, he moreover gave Herod the position of
procurator of all Syria, for the [Roman] procurators
were forbidden to take any measures without his con-
currence. Finally, on the death of Zenodorus, he further
assigned to him all the territory between Trachonitis
and Galilee. But what Herod valued more than all these
privileges was that in Cæsar's affection he stood next
after Agrippa, in Agrippa's next after Cæsar. Thenceforth he advanced to the utmost prosperity; his noble
spirit rose to greater heights, and his lofty ambition
was mainly directed to works of piety.

Herod's Building Activities

xxi. 1. Thus, in the fifteenth year of his reign, he
restored the Temple, and by erecting new foundation-
walls, enlarged the surrounding area to double its former extent. The expenditure devoted to this work was
incalculable, its magnificence never surpassed; as evidence one would have pointed to the great colonnades
around the Temple courts and to the fortress which
dominated it on the north. The colonnades Herod reconstructed from the foundations; the fortress he restored at a lavish cost in a style no way inferior to that
of a palace, and called it Antonia in honor of Antony.
His own palace, which he erected in the upper city,
comprised two most spacious and beautiful buildings,
with which the Temple itself bore no comparison; these

he named after his friends, the one Cæsareum, the other Agrippeum.

2. He was not content, however, to commemorate his patrons' names by palaces only; his munificence extended to the creation of whole cities. In the district of Samaria he built a town enclosed within magnificent walls twenty furlongs in length, introduced into it six thousand colonists, and gave them allotments of highly productive land. In the center of this settlement he erected a massive temple, enclosed in ground, a furlong and a half in length, consecrated to [Augustus] Cæsar; while he named the town itself Sebaste. The inhabitants were given a privileged constitution.

3. When, later on, through Cæsar's bounty he received additional territory, Herod there too dedicated to him a temple of white marble near the sources of the Jordan, at a place called Paneion. At this spot a mountain rears its summit to an immense height aloft; at the base of the cliff is an opening into an overgrown cavern. Within this, plunging down to an immeasurable depth, is a yawning chasm, enclosing a volume of still water, the bottom of which no sounding-line has been found long enough to reach. Outside and from beneath the cavern well up the springs from which, as some think, the Jordan takes its rise; but we will tell the true story of this in the sequel.

4. At Jericho, again, between the fortress of Cypros and the former palace, the king constructed new buildings, finer and more commodious for the reception of guests, and named them after the same friends. In short, one can mention no suitable spot within his realm that he left destitute of some mark of homage to Cæsar. And then, after filling his own territory with temples, he let the memorials of his esteem overflow into the province and erected in numerous cities monuments to Cæsar.

5. His notice was attracted by a town on the coast called Strato's Tower, which, though then dilapidated, was from its advantageous situation suited for the exercise of his liberality. This he entirely rebuilt with white stone and adorned with the most magnificent palaces, displaying here, as nowhere else, the innate gran-

deur of his character. For the whole sea-board from Dora
to Joppa, midway between which the city lies, was without a harbor, so that vessels bound for Egypt along the
coast of Phœnicia had to ride at anchor in the open
when menaced by the south-west wind; for even a moderate breeze from this quarter dashes the waves to such
a height against the cliffs that their reflux spreads a
wild commotion far out to sea. However, by dint of expenditure and enterprise, the king triumphed over nature and constructed a harbor larger than the Piræus
[at Athens], including other deep roadsteads within its
recesses.

6. Notwithstanding the totally recalcitrant nature of
the site, he grappled with the difficulties so successfully
that the solidity of his masonry defied the sea, while its
beauty was such that it were as if no obstacle had
existed. Having determined upon the comparative size
of the harbor as we have stated, he had blocks of stone
let down into twenty fathoms of water, most of them
measuring fifty feet in length by nine in depth and ten
in breadth, some being even larger. Upon the submarine
foundation thus laid he constructed above the surface
a mole two hundred feet broad; of which one hundred
were built out to break the surge, whence this portion
was called the breakwater, while the remainder supported a stone wall encircling the harbor. From this wall
arose, at intervals, massive towers, the loftiest and most
magnificent of which was called Drusion after the step-
son of Cæsar.

7. Numerous inlets in the wall provided landing-
places for mariners putting in to harbor, while the
whole circular terrace fronting these channels served
as a broad promenade for disembarking passengers. The
entrance to the port faced northwards, because in these
latitudes the north wind is the most favorable of all. At
the harbor-mouth stood colossal statues, three on either
side, resting on columns; the columns on the left of
vessels entering port were supported by a massive tower,
those on the right by two upright blocks of stone clamped
together, whose height exceeded that of the tower on the
opposite side. Abutting on the harbor were houses, also

of white stone, and upon it converged the streets of the town, laid at equal distances apart. On an eminence facing the harbor-mouth stood Cæsar's temple, remarkable for its beauty and grand proportions; it contained a colossal statue of the emperor, not inferior to the Olympian Zeus, which served for its model, and another of Rome, rivalling that of Hera at Argos. The city Herod dedicated to the province, the harbor to navigators in these waters, to Cæsar the glory of this new foundation, to which he accordingly gave the name of Cæsarea.

8. The rest of the buildings—amphitheater, theater, public places—were constructed in a style worthy of the name which the city bore. He further instituted quinquennial games, likewise named after Cæsar, and inaugurated them himself, in the hundred and ninety-second Olympiad, offering prizes of the highest value. At these games not the victors only, but also those who obtained second and third places, participated in the royal bounty.

Another maritime town, which had been destroyed in war-time, namely Anthedon [near Gaza], he rebuilt and renamed Agrippium; and so great was his affection for this same friend Agrippa, that he engraved his name upon the gate which he erected in the Temple [at Jerusalem].

9. No man ever showed greater filial affection. As a memorial to his father he founded a city in the fairest plain in his realm, rich in rivers and trees, and named it Antipatris. Above Jericho he built the walls of a fortress, remarkable alike for solidity and beauty, which he dedicated to his mother under the name of Cypros. To his brother Phasael he erected the tower in Jerusalem called by his name, the appearance and splendid proportions of which we shall describe in the sequel. He also gave the name of Phasaelis to another city which he built in the valley to the north of Jericho.

10. But while he thus perpetuated the memory of his family and his friends, he did not neglect to leave memorials of himself. Thus he built a fortress in the hills on the Arabian frontier and called it after himself Herodium. An artificial rounded hill, sixty furlongs from

Jerusalem, was given the same name, but more elaborate embellishment. The crest he crowned with a ring of round towers; the enclosure was filled with gorgeous palaces, the magnificent appearance of which was not confined to the interior of the apartments, but outer walls, battlements, and roofs all had wealth lavished upon them in profusion. He had, at immense expense, an abundant supply of water brought into it from a distance, and provided an easy ascent by two hundred steps of the purest white marble; the mound, though entirely artificial, being of a considerable height. Around the base he erected other palaces for the accommodation of his furniture and his friends. Thus, in the amplitude of its resources this stronghold resembled a town, in its restricted area a simple palace.

11. After founding all these places, he proceeded to display his generosity to numerous cities outside his realm. Thus, he provided gymnasia for Tripolis, Damascus and Ptolemais, a wall for Byblus, halls, porticoes, temples, and market-places for Berytus and Tyre, theaters for Sidon and Damascus, an aqueduct for Laodicea on the sea, baths, sumptuous fountains and colonnades, admirable alike for their architecture and their proportions, for Ascalon; to other communities he dedicated groves and meadow-land. Many cities, as though they had been associated with his realm, received from him grants of land; others, like Cos, were endowed with revenues to maintain the annual office of gymnasiarch to perpetuity, to ensure that this honorable post should never lapse. Corn he supplied to all applicants; to the people of Rhodes he made contributions again and again for shipbuilding, and when their Pythian temple was burnt down he rebuilt it on a grander scale at his own expense. Need I allude to his donations to the people of Lycia or Samos, or to his liberality, extended to every district of Ionia, to meet its needs? Nay, are not Athenians and Lacedæmonians, the inhabitants of Nicopolis and of Pergamum in Mysia, laden with Herod's offerings? And that broad street in Syrian Antioch, once shunned on account of the mud—was it not he who paved its twenty fur-

longs with polished marble, and as a protection from the rain, adorned it with a colonnade of equal length?

12. In these cases, it may be said, the individual communities concerned were the sole beneficiaries; his bounty to the people of Elis, on the other hand, was a gift not only to Hellas at large but to the whole world, wherever the fame of the Olympic Games penetrates. For observing that these were declining for want of funds and that this solitary relic of ancient Greece was sinking into decay, he not only accepted the post of president for the quadrennial celebration which coincided with his visit on his voyage to Rome, but he endowed them for all time with revenues, which should preserve an unfading memory of his term as president. The enumeration of the debts and taxes discharged by himself would be endless; it was thus, for instance, that he lightened the burden of their annual taxes for the inhabitants of Phaselis, Balanea and various minor towns in Cilicia. Often, however, his noble generosity was thwarted by the fear of exciting either jealousy or the suspicion of entertaining some higher ambition, in conferring upon states greater benefits than they received from their own masters.

Herod's Last Years: Family Intrigues

13. Herod's genius was matched by his physical constitution. Always foremost in the chase, in which he distinguished himself above all by his skill in horsemanship, he on one occasion brought down forty wild beasts in a single day; for the country breeds boars and, in greater abundance, stags and wild asses. As a fighter he was irresistible; and at practice spectators were often struck with astonishment at the precision with which he threw the javelin and the unerring aim with which he bent the bow. But besides these pre-eminent gifts of soul and body, he was blessed by good fortune; he rarely met with a reverse in war, and when he did, this was due not to his own fault, but either to treachery or to the recklessness of his troops.

xxii. 1. But in revenge for his public prosperity, fortune visited Herod with troubles at home; his ill-fated career originated with a woman to whom he was passionately attached. For,' on ascending the throne, he had dismissed the wife whom he had taken when he was still a commoner, a native of Jerusalem named Doris, and married Mariamme, daughter of Alexander, the son of Aristobulus. It was she who brought into his house the discord that, beginning at an earlier date, was greatly aggravated after his return from Rome. For, in the first place, in the interests of his children by Mariamme, he banished from the capital the son whom he had had by Doris, namely Antipater, allowing him to visit it on the festivals only. Next he put to death, on suspicion of conspiracy, Hyrcanus, Mariamme's grandfather, who had come back from Parthia to Herod's court. Hyrcanus had been taken prisoner by Barzapharnes when the latter overran Syria, but had been liberated through the intercession of his compassionate countrymen living beyond the Euphrates. Had he but followed their advice not to cross the river to join Herod, he would have escaped his tragic fate; but the marriage of his grand-daughter lured him to his death. He came relying upon that and impelled by an ardent longing for his native land, and roused Herod's resentment not by making any claim to the throne, but because it actually belonged to him by right.

2. Herod had five children by Mariamme, two daughters and three sons. The youngest son died in the course of his training in Rome; to the two elder sons [Alexander and Aristobulus] he gave a princely education, both out of respect for their mother's illustrious parentage, and because they had been born after his accession to the throne. But a still stronger influence in their favor was Herod's passion for Mariamme, the consuming ardor of which increased from day to day, so that he was insensible to the troubles of which his beloved one was the cause; for Mariamme's hatred of him was as great as was his love for her. As the events of the past gave her just reason for aversion, and her husband's love enabled her to speak plainly, she openly upbraided him with the fate of her grandfather Hyrcanus and her

135

brother Jonathan. For Herod had not spared even this poor lad; [in 35 B.C.] he had bestowed upon him in his seventeenth year the office of high priest, and then immediately after conferring this honor had put him to death because, on the occasion of a festival, when the lad approached the altar clad in the priestly vestments, the multitude with one accord burst into tears. He was consequently sent by night to Jericho, and there, in accordance with instructions, plunged into a swimming-bath by the Gauls and drowned.*

3. It was on these grounds that Mariamme upbraided Herod, and then proceeded violently to abuse his mother and sister. He was paralyzed by his infatuation, but the women, seething with indignation, brought against her the charge which was bound in their opinion to touch Herod most nearly, that of adultery. Among much else which they invented to convince him, they accused Mariamme of having sent her portrait to Antony in Egypt and of carrying wantonness so far as to exhibit herself, though at a distance, to a man with a madness for her sex and powerful enough to resort to violence. This accusation struck Herod like a thunderbolt. His love intensified his jealousy; he reflected on Cleopatra's craft which had brought both King Lysanias [of Chalcis] and the Arab Malchus to their end; he was menaced, he reckoned, with the loss not merely of his consort but of his life.

4. So, being on the eve of departure from his realm, he entrusted his wife to Joseph, the husband of his sister Salome, a faithful friend whose loyalty was assured by this marriage connection, giving him private injunctions to kill her, should Antony kill him. Joseph, not with any malicious intention, but from a desire to convince her of the love which the king bore her, since even in death he could not bear to be separated from her, betrayed the secret. When Herod, on his return, in familiar intercourse was protesting with many oaths his affection for her and that he had never loved any other

---

* We have already been told, however, that Herod did not receive his guard of Gauls until after the death of Cleopatra in 30 B.C.

woman, "A fine exhibition you gave," she replied, "of your love for me by your orders to Joseph to put me to death!"

5. He was beside himself, the moment he heard the secret was out. Joseph, he exclaimed, would never have disclosed his orders had he not seduced her, and frenzied with passion, he leaped from the bed and paced the palace to and fro in his distraction. His sister Salome, seizing this opportunity to slander Mariamme, confirmed his suspicion of Joseph. Mad with sheer jealousy, he ordered that both should instantly be put to death. But remorse followed hard upon rage; his wrath subsided, his love revived. So consuming, indeed, was the flame of his passion that he believed she was not dead, and in his affliction would address her as though she were alive; until time taught him the reality of his loss, when his grief was as profound as the love which he bore her while she was alive.*

xxiii. 1. The sons inherited their mother's resentment, and reflecting on their father's abominable crimes, eyed him as an enemy, even in the early days of their education in Rome, and still more on their return to Judæa. The antagonism grew with their years, and when, on reaching an age to marry, one [Aristobulus] espoused the daughter of his aunt Salome, their mother's accuser, and the other [Alexander] the daughter of Archelaus, king of Cappadocia, their hatred found vent in open speech. Their rashness lent a handle to slanderers, and from this time certain persons threw out plainer hints to the king that both his sons were conspiring against him, and that the son-in-law of Archelaus, counting on his father-in-law's influence, was preparing to fly, in order to lay an accusation against his father before the emperor. Herod, drugged with these calumnies, recalled Antipater, his son by Doris, [in about 14 B.C.] to serve as a bulwark against his other sons, and began to honor him with every mark of his special esteem.

2. To the young men this new departure was intoler-

---

* Mariamme was put to death in about 29 B.C., her grandfather Hyrcanus perhaps a year earlier.

able. At the sight of the promotion of this son of a woman of no standing, they in their pride of birth could not restrain their indignation, and on every fresh occasion for annoyance openly displayed their wrath. The result was that while each succeeding day saw them in greater disfavor, Antipater was now gaining respect on his own merits. Showing remarkable adroitness in flattering his father, he concocted various calumnies upon his half-brothers, some of which he set in motion himself, while others were at his instigation circulated by his confidants, until he completely wrecked his brothers' prospects of the throne. For both in his father's will and by public acts he was now declared to be the heir. Thus, when he was sent on an embassy to [Augustus] Cæsar, he went as a prince, with the robes and all the ceremonial of royalty except the diadem. Eventually his influence was strong enough to bring back his mother to Mariamme's bed, and by employing against his brothers the two weapons of flattery and slander, he stealthily so wrought upon the king's mind as to make him even contemplate putting his sons to death.

3. One of them, at any rate, namely Alexander, was dragged by his father to Rome and there accused at Cæsar's tribunal of attempting to poison him. The young man, finding himself at last at liberty to vent his grievances and in the presence of a judge with far more experience than Antipater, more sagacity than Herod, modestly threw a veil over his father's faults, but forcibly exposed the calumnies directed against himself. He next proved that his brother, his partner in peril, was equally innocent, and then proceeded bitterly to complain of Antipater's villainy and of the ignominy to which he and his brother were exposed. He was assisted not only by a clear conscience but by his powerful oratory, for he was an extremely able speaker. Concluding with the remark that it was open to their father to put them to death, if he really believed the charge to be true, he reduced all his hearers to tears, and so deeply affected Cæsar that he acquitted the accused and brought Herod to a reconciliation on the spot. The conditions of the agreement were that the sons should render im-

plicit obedience to their father, and that he should be
at liberty to bequeath the kingdom to whom he would.

4. After this, the king left Rome on his homeward
journey, apparently dismissing his charges against his
sons, though not abandoning his suspicions. For he was
accompanied by Antipater, the cause of all this hatred,
who, however, was withheld by awe of the author of the
reconciliation from openly displaying his animosity.
Skirting the coast of Cilicia, Herod put in at Elæusa and
received friendly entertainment at the table of Archelaus, who congratulated him on his son-in-law's acquittal and was delighted at the reconciliation; for he had
previously written to his friends in Rome to assist Alexander on his trial. He accompanied his guests as far as
Zephyrion and made them presents amounting in value
to thirty talents.

5. On reaching Jerusalem, Herod assembled the people, presented to them his three sons, made his excuses
for his absence, and rendered profuse thanks to God,
and no less to Cæsar, who had re-established his disordered household and had given his sons a greater
boon than a kingdom, namely concord.

"The ties of that concord," he continued, "I shall bind
more closely myself; for Cæsar has appointed me lord
of the realm and arbiter of the succession, and I, in con-
sulting my own advantage, also repay my debt to him.
I now declare these my three sons kings, and I beseech
first God, and then you, to ratify my decision. They are
entitled to the succession, this one by his age, the others
by their noble birth; indeed the extent of my kingdom
would suffice for even a greater number. Those, therefore, whom Cæsar has united and their father now
nominates, do you uphold; let the honors you award
them be neither undeserved nor unequal, but propor-
tioned to the rank of each; for in paying deference to
any beyond the deserts of his age, you gratify him less
than you grieve the one whom you slight. I myself shall
select the advisers and attendants who are to consort
with each of my sons, and shall hold them responsible
for keeping the peace, being well aware that factions
and rivalries among princes are produced by the malign

influence of associates, while virtuous companions promote natural affection.

"I must require these persons, however, and not them only but also the officers of my army, for the present to rest their hopes on me alone; for it is not the kingdom, but the mere honors of royalty that I am now delivering over to my sons. They will enjoy the pleasures of power, as if actual rulers, but upon me, however unwilling, will fall the burden of office. Consider, each one of you, my age, my manner of life, my piety. I am not so old that my life may soon be past praying for, nor given over to the pleasures of luxury, which cut short the lives even of the young: I have served the Deity so faithfully that I may hope for the longest term of life. Whoever, then, pays court to my sons to bring about my downfall shall be punished by me for their sakes as well as my own. For it is not jealousy of my offspring which causes me to restrict the homage to be paid them; it is the knowledge that such flattering attentions foster recklessness in the young. If everyone who is brought into contact with my sons will but remember that if he acts honorably he will win his reward from me, whereas if he promotes discord his malicious conduct will bring him no benefit even from the object of his flattery, then I think that all will have my interests, in other words my sons' interests, at heart; for it is to their advantage that I should govern, and to mine that they should live in harmony.

"As for you, my good children, think first of the sacred ties of nature and the constancy of affection which she instills even into the beasts; think of Cæsar, who brought about our reconciliation; think, lastly, of me, who entreat you when I might command, and continue as brothers. I present you, from this moment, with the robes and retinue of royalty; and I pray God to uphold my decision, if you live in unity."

With these words he tenderly embraced each of his sons and then dismissed the multitude. Of these some joined in his prayer; while those who hankered for change pretended that they had not even heard him.

xxiv. 1. But the brothers on parting carried with

them discord in their hearts. They separated more suspicious of each other than before: Alexander and Aristobulus aggrieved at the confirmation of Antipater's right
of primogeniture, Antipater resenting the rank accorded
to his brothers, even though second to his own. The
latter, however, with the extreme subtlety of his character, knew how to hold his tongue and with much adroitness dissembled his hatred of his brothers; while they,
from their pride of birth, had all their thoughts upon
their lips. They were, moreover, beset by many persons
trying to excite them, while a still larger number insinuated themselves into their friendship to spy upon
them.

Every word spoken in Alexander's circle was instantly
in the possession of Antipater and passed from Antipater to Herod, with amplifications. The young man
could not make the simplest remark without becoming
incriminated, so distorted were his words for the purposes of slander; if he spoke with a little freedom, the
merest trifles were magnified into enormities. Antipater
was constantly setting his agents on to irritate him, in
order that his lies might have some basis of truth; and
if among the speeches reported one item was established,
that was sufficient warrant for the rest. His own friends
were all either of a very secretive nature or were induced by presents to divulge no secrets; so that Antipater's life might have been not incorrectly described as
a mystery of iniquity. Alexander's associates, on the
other hand, either by bribery or by that seductive flattery, which Antipater invariably found effective, had
been converted by the latter into traitors and detectives
to report all that was said or done by his brother. With
a careful eye to every detail in the staging of the play,
he would plan with consummate art the modes of bringing these calumnies to the ears of Herod, himself assuming the rôle of a devoted brother, and leaving that
of informer to others. Then, when any word was spoken
against Alexander, he would come forward and play his
part, and, beginning by ridiculing the allegation, would
afterwards quietly proceed to confirm it and so call
forth the king's indignation. Everything was interpreted

as a plot and made to produce the impression that Alexander was watching his opportunity to murder his father; and nothing lent more credit to these calumnies than Antipater's pleading in his brother's defense.

2. These insinuations exasperating Herod, his affection for the young princes diminished daily, while his regard for Antipater proportionately increased. The king's alienation from the lads was shared by people at court, some acting of their own accord, others under orders, such as Ptolemy, the most honored of his friends, the king's brothers and all his family. For Antipater was all-powerful, and—this was Alexander's bitterest blow—all-powerful too was Antipater's mother, who was in league with him against the two and harsher than a stepmother, with a hatred for these sons of a princess greater than for ordinary stepchildren. All persons, accordingly, now paid court to Antipater, because of the expectations which he inspired; everyone was further instigated to desert his rivals by the orders of the king, who had forbidden those highest in his favor to approach or pay any attention to Alexander or his brother. Herod's formidable influence extended, moreover, beyond his realm to his friends abroad; for no other sovereign had been empowered by Cæsar, as he had, to reclaim a fugitive subject even from a state outside his jurisdiction. The young men, meanwhile, as their father had never openly reproached them, were ignorant of these calumnies, and being consequently off their guard, laid themselves still more open to them; but little by little their eyes were opened by his coldness and increased asperity whenever anything annoyed him.

Antipater further roused against them the enmity of their uncle Pheroras and their aunt Salome, perpetually coaxing and working upon his aunt's feelings, as though she had been his wife. Salome's hostility was aggravated by Glaphyra, Alexander's wife, who boasted of her noble ancestry and claimed to be mistress of all the ladies at court because she was descended on her father's side from Temenus, on her mother's from Darius, son of Hystaspes. On the other hand, she was constantly taunting with their low birth Herod's sister and his wives, all

of whom had been chosen for their beauty and not for
their family. His wives were numerous, since polygamy
was permitted by Jewish custom and the king gladly
availed himself of the privilege. All these, on account
of Glaphyra's arrogance and abuse, hated Alexander.

3. Aristobulus himself alienated Salome, his own
mother-in-law, furious as she already was at Glaphyra's
scurrility, for he was continually upbraiding his wife for
her low origin, saying that he had married a woman of
the people, and his brother Alexander, a princess. Salome's daughter reported this, with tears, to her mother;
she added that Alexander and Aristobulus had threatened, when they came to the throne, to set the mothers
of their other brothers to work at the loom along with
the slave-girls, and to make the princes themselves village clerks, sarcastically referring to the careful education which they had received. At that Salome, unable
to control her indignation, reported the whole to Herod;
as she was accusing her own son-in-law, her evidence
carried very great weight. Another calumny came simultaneously to inflame the king's wrath. He was told that
the young princes had their mother's name perpetually
on their lips, cursing him while they bemoaned her,
and that when he distributed, as he often did, some of
Mariamme's apparel to his more recent wives, they
would threaten that they would ere long strip them of
these royal robes and clothe them in rags.

4. Herod, though he had learned through such reports to fear these high-spirited young men, did not
abandon hopes of their reformation. Just before setting
sail for Rome he sent for them, and delivered some curt
threats as sovereign, followed by a long paternal ad-
monition, exhorting them to love their brothers and
promising to pardon their past offenses if they would
amend their ways for the future. For their part, they
repudiated the charges, declaring that they were false,
and assured their father that their actions would vindi-
cate their statement; he ought, however, on his side to
stop the mouths of these tale-bearers by refusing so
readily to believe them; for there would never be want-

ing persons ready to calumniate them, so long as they found anyone to listen to them.

5. The father's heart was quickly reassured by their words; but if the youths thus dispelled their immediate anxiety, the thought of the future brought them new apprehensions, knowing, as they did, the hostility of Salome and their uncle Pheroras. Both were formidable and dangerous, but the more redoubtable was Pheroras, who shared with Herod all the honors of royalty, except the diadem. He had a private income of a hundred talents, exclusive of the revenue derived from the whole of the trans-Jordanic region, a gift from his brother, who had also, after requesting Cæsar's permission, appointed him tetrarch. Herod had conferred upon him the further honor of marrying one of the royal family, by uniting him to the sister of his own wife. On her death, he had pledged to him the eldest of his own daughters, with a dowry of three hundred talents; but Pheroras rejected the royal wedding to run after a slave-girl of whom he was enamored. Herod, indignant at this slight, married his daughter to one of his nephews, who was subsequently killed by the Parthians; his resentment, however, subsided ere long and he made allowance for his love-sick brother.

6. Long before, while the queen [Mariamme] was still alive, Pheroras had been accused of a plot to poison Herod; but at the period now reached, informers came forward in such numbers that Herod, though the most affectionate of brothers, was led to believe their statements and to take alarm. After putting many suspected persons to the torture he came last of all to the friends of Pheroras. None of these admitted outright that there was such a plot, though they said that Pheroras was preparing to fly to Parthia, carrying off his mistress with him, and that his accomplice in this design and partner in his intended flight was Costobarus, Salome's husband, to whom the king had given his sister, when her former husband was put to death on a charge of adultery. Even Salome herself did not escape calumny: she was accused by her brother Pheroras of signing a contract to marry Syllæus, the procurator of Obadas, king of

Arabia, and Herod's bitterest enemy. However, though convicted of this and of everything else of which she was accused by Pheroras, she was pardoned; while Pheroras himself was acquitted by the king of the charges against him.

7. The tempest lowering over Herod's house thus veered round to Alexander and burst in full force about his devoted head. There were three eunuchs who held a special place in the king's esteem, as is indicated by the services with which they were charged: one poured out his wine, another served him his supper, and the third put him to bed and slept in his chamber. Alexander by large presents corrupted these menials for criminal ends, on being informed of which the king submitted them to trial by torture. They at once confessed their relations with Alexander, and then went on to reveal the promises which had brought them about. Alexander, they said, had inveigled them by saying: "You ought not to place your hopes on Herod, a shameless old man who dyes his hair, unless this disguise has actually made you take him for a youngster; it is to me, Alexander, that you should look, to me, who am to inherit the throne, whether he will or no, and shall ere long be avenged on my enemies and bring fortune and bliss to my friends, and above all to you." They added that persons of rank secretly paid court to Alexander and that the generals and officers of the army had clandestine interviews with him.

8. These disclosures so terrified Herod that at the time he did not even dare to divulge them; but, sending out spies night and day, he scrutinized all that was done or said, and at once put to death any who fell under suspicion. The palace was given over to frightful anarchy. Everyone, to gratify some personal enmity or hatred, invented calumnies; many turned to base account against their adversaries the murderous mood of wrathful royalty. Lies found instant credit, but chastisement was even swifter than calumny: the accuser of a moment ago found himself accused and led off to death with him whose conviction he had obtained; for the grave peril to his life cut short the king's inquiries. He

145

grew so embittered that he had no gentle looks even for those who were not accused and treated his own friends with the utmost harshness: many of these he refused to admit to court, while those who were beyond the reach of his arm came under the lash of his tongue.

To add to Alexander's misfortunes, Antipater returned to the charge, and raising a band of kindred spirits, had recourse to every conceivable form of calumny. By his portentous fictions and fabrications the king was, in fact, reduced to such a state of alarm, that he fancied he saw Alexander coming upon him sword in hand. He, accordingly, had the prince suddenly arrested and imprisoned, and then proceeded to put his friends to the torture. Many died silent, without saying anything beyond what they knew; but some were driven by their sufferings to falsehood and declared that Alexander and his brother Aristobulus were conspiring against him and were watching for an opportunity to kill him, while out hunting, meaning then to escape to Rome. This statement, improbable as it was and invented off-hand under the pressure of torment, the king nevertheless found satisfaction in believing, consoling himself for having imprisoned his son with the thought that his action had been justified.

xxv. 1. Alexander, perceiving the impossibility of shaking his father's belief, resolved boldly to confront the perils that menaced him. He, therefore, composed four books directed against his enemies, in which he avowed the conspiracy, but denounced most of them as accomplices, above all Pheroras and Salome. The latter, he declared, had one night even forced her way into his chamber, and against his will, had sexual relations with him. These documents—a mass of shocking accusations incriminating persons of the highest rank—had passed into Herod's hands, when Archelaus, alarmed for his son-in-law and daughter, arrived in haste in Judæa. Coming with singular sagacity to their aid, he succeeded by stratagem in diverting the king's threats in another direction. For, the moment he met him, he exclaimed: "Where is my scoundrel of a son-in-law? Where shall I set eyes on the person of this parricide, that I may tear him in pieces with my own hands? My daughter, too, shall share the fate of her fine spouse; for even if she has had no part in his schemes, as the wife of such a miscreant she is polluted. But you too, the intended victim of the plot, astonish me by your forbearance, in leaving, as it seems, Alexander still alive! For my part, I hurried hither from Cappadocia expecting to find that the culprit had long since paid his penalty and to hold an inquiry with you upon my daughter, whom, out of regard for your exalted rank, I gave away to that wretch. But now I find we have to deliberate about the pair of them. If, then, the fondness of a father's heart unnerves you for punishing a rebellious son, let us each lend the other his hand, each take the other's place in visiting our wrath upon our children."

2. With this blustering oration he deluded Herod, notwithstanding the latter's attitude of defiance. Herod, at any rate, handed him for perusal the documents composed by Alexander and examined chapter after chapter with him, dwelling upon each. Archelaus, finding here an opportunity for furthering his ruse, little by little shifted the blame on to the persons whose names appeared in the volumes, particularly Pheroras. When he observed that he was gaining the king's confidence, he remarked: "We must be careful to see that all these villains have not been conspiring against this young man, and not the young man against you. For I can see no reason why he should have plunged into such heinous crime, when he already enjoyed the honors of royalty and expected to succeed to the throne, unless there were others seducing him and misguiding the tractable spirit of youth. Such persons, indeed, have been known to impose not only on the young, but on old men as well; by them the most illustrious houses and entire kingdoms have been overturned."

3. Herod assented to this speech; and for a while relaxed his wrath with Alexander and vented it upon Pheroras, as he was the main theme of the four documents. Pheroras, observing this quick change in the king's feelings and the paramount influence exercised on him by his friend Archelaus, despairing of saving himself

by honorable means sought protection in effrontery: he abandoned Alexander and threw himself on the mercy of Archelaus. The latter replied that he did not see how he could sue for pardon for a man involved in such grave charges, which clearly proved that he had plotted against the king and been the cause of the young prince's present misfortunes, unless he were prepared to renounce his villainy and his denials, to own up to the crimes of which he was accused, and to ask pardon of his brother, who indeed loved him; for that object, said Archelaus, he would render him every possible assistance.

4. Pheroras took his advice, and assuming an attitude calculated to arouse the deepest compassion, in black raiment and in tears, threw himself at Herod's feet and craved his pardon as he had often successfully done before. He confessed himself a polluted wretch, guilty of all that was laid to his charge, but deplored his mental derangement and madness, which he attributed to his passion for his wife. Archelaus, after thus inducing Pheroras to appear as his own accuser and to bear witness against himself, now proceeded to plead for him and sought to appease Herod's wrath, citing parallel cases in his own family history. He had himself, he said, suffered much worse injury from his brother, but had preferred the claims of natural affection to revenge; for in kingdoms, as in corpulent individuals, there was always some member becoming inflamed from the weight which it supported; yet what it needed was not amputation but some milder method of cure.

5. By many such representations Archelaus succeeded in soothing Herod's anger against Pheroras. He himself, however, affected to be still indignant with Alexander, protesting that he would divorce his daughter and carry her off with him, until he brought Herod round into the position of a suppliant on the young man's behalf and a suitor once more for the hand of Archelaus's daughter for his son. With an air of complete sincerity, Archelaus said that he had his permission to unite her to whom he would, save only Alexander; for his dearest desire was to maintain the marriage ties which linked

him to Herod. To this the king replied that Archelaus, by consenting not to break the marriage, would really be giving his son back to him, seeing that they already had children and that the young man was so deeply attached to his wife; if she remained with him, her very presence would make him ashamed of his errors, whereas, were she torn from him, he would be driven to utter desperation; for the domestic affections exercised a chastening and diverting influence on reckless characters. Archelaus was induced, not without difficulty, to assent, was reconciled to the youthful offender, and reconciled him to his father; he added, however, that it was absolutely essential that the latter should be sent to Rome for an interview with Cæsar, as he himself had forwarded a full report of the matter to the emperor.

6. Such was the end of the ruse by which Archelaus rescued his son-in-law. After the reconciliation the time was passed in festivity and interchange of courtesies. On his departure Herod presented him with seventy talents, a throne of gold set with precious stones, some eunuchs, and a concubine named Pannychis; he conferred other favors upon each of his friends, proportionate to their rank. Magnificent presents were, likewise, by order of royalty, made to Archelaus by all the high officials at court. Herod and his nobles then escorted him as far as Antioch.

xxvi. 1. Not long after, however, there arrived in Judæa a man whose influence far outmatched the artifices of Archelaus, and who not only broke up the reconciliation which the latter had negotiated in the interest of Alexander, but also proved the cause of that prince's ruin. He was a Lacedæmonian, named Eurycles, whose accursed visit to the realm arose from a craving for money, when Greece could no longer meet his extravagant requirements. He brought with him magnificent presents for Herod, as a bait to secure his quarry, and instantly found them returned with interest; but he accounted a pure and simple gift as nothing, if he failed to make merchandise out of the realm at the price of blood. So he proceeded to impose on the king by flattery, clever talk, and lying encomiums upon his merits. Quickly reading Herod's character and studying in all he said or did to please him, he was soon numbered among his principal friends; indeed the king and the whole court were delighted to show special honor to this Spartan, out of regard for his country.

2. When he had learned everything about the rottenness that was sapping the royal house, the quarrel between the brothers and their father's disposition towards each of them, Eurycles, although under a prior obligation to Antipater for the latter's hospitality, nevertheless feigned a friendship for Alexander, falsely claiming to be an old comrade of Archelaus. With this recommendation he was quickly received as a proved friend and was at once introduced by Alexander to his brother Aristobulus. Exploiting in turn all the various personages, he insinuated himself into favor with each by a different method; but he chiefly acted as a hireling of Antipater and a traitor to Alexander. To the former he represented how disgraceful it was that he, the eldest son, should overlook the intrigues of persons who had an eye upon his prospects; to Alexander, that he, the son of one princess and husband of another, should suffer the son of a woman of no station to succeed to the throne, especially when he had in Archelaus such powerful support behind him.

The fiction of his being a friend of Archelaus made the young prince regard him as a counselor to be trusted; and so, without any reserve, Alexander poured out to him his grievances against Antipater, adding that it would not be surprising if Herod, after murdering their mother, should rob him and his brother of her kingdom. Thereupon Eurycles pretended to pity and condole with him. He then inveigled Aristobulus into using similar language, and having implicated both brothers in complaints against their father, went off with these confidences to Antipater; with the addition of his own invention, that the brothers were plotting against him, watching their opportunity, and even then were almost upon him sword in hand. Richly rewarded for his intelligence, he proceeded to sing the praises of Antipater to his father. Finally, having undertaken at a price to bring about the death of Aristobulus and Alexander, he came to lay his indictment of them before their parent.

Visiting Herod, he declared that he came to bring him life in return for his benefactions to himself, the light of day in repayment for his hospitality. "For," he said, "a sword has long since been sharpened for your destruction and Alexander's right arm braced to wield it. It is I who have retarded the blow by pretending to assist him." Alexander, he continued, had said that Herod, not content with reigning himself over an empire which belonged to others, not content, after murdering their mother, with squandering her realm, was now proceeding to foist in a bastard as his successor and to offer their grandfather's kingdom to that pest, Antipater.

But he, Alexander [so Eurycles reported him], would avenge the spirits of Hyrcanus and Mariamme; for it would ill become him to inherit the throne from such a father without bloodshed. Then there were the constant daily provocations to which he was subjected, insomuch that he could not utter a single word which escaped calumny. Were allusion made to other persons' noble lineage, his father gratuitously insulted him by remarking, "Nobody is noble but Alexander here, who scorns his father for the baseness of his birth!" On the hunting-field, were he silent, he gave offense; did he express commendation, he was pronounced ironical to boot. On all occasions, in fact, he found his father implacable, reserving all his affection for Antipater. He would, therefore, willingly die if his enterprise miscarried. If, on the other hand, he struck the fatal blow, he had protectors to fall back upon: first Archelaus, his father-in-law, to whom he could easily make his escape; and then Cæsar, who to that very day was ignorant of Herod's true character. For he would not, as once before, stand before the emperor, overawed by his father's presence, nor would he confine his observations to his personal grievances. No; he would first proclaim to the world the sufferings of his nation, bled to death by

151

taxation, and then go on to describe the luxury and
malpractices on which the money obtained by its blood
was lavished, the characters of the men who had
grown rich at his and his brother's expense, and the
motives which had led to the favoritism shown to particular cities. There, too, he would bring up for inquiry
the fate of his great-grandfather and his mother, and
make public all the abominations of the reign. Under
such conditions he could not be condemned as a parricide.

3. Having delivered this monstrous tirade against Alexander, Eurycles proceeded to extol Antipater to the skies,
as the only son who had any filial affection, an affection which had so far enabled him to thwart the plot.
The king, who had scarcely recovered his composure
after previous shocks, burst into ungovernable fury.
Antipater, seizing this new opportunity, privily sent in
others to accuse his brothers of holding clandestine
interviews with Jucundus and Tyrannus, at one time
commanders of the king's cavalry, but now, owing to
some misdemeanors, degraded. This report brought Herod's indignation to a climax, and he instantly had the
two men put to the torture. They made no confession
of the crimes imputed to them; but a letter was produced, addressed by Alexander to the governor of
Alexandrion, requesting him to admit him and his brother Aristobulus to that fortress after they had slain
their father, and to grant them the use of the arms and
the other resources of the place. This letter Alexander
declared to be the handiwork of Diophantus, a secretary of the king, an audacious fellow who had a clever
knack of imitating any handwriting, and who, after
numerous forgeries, was eventually put to death for a
crime of that nature. Herod had the keeper of the fortress put to the torture, but from him too failed to elicit
anything bearing on the alleged facts.

4. Notwithstanding the weakness of the obtainable
evidence, Herod gave orders for a watch to be kept
on his sons, though still leaving them their liberty. As
for Eurycles, the bane of his house and stage-manager
of the whole abominable business, the king called him

his savior and benefactor, and presented him with fifty talents. That villain then, before the true story of the affair got abroad, made off to Cappadocia, where he extorted more money from Archelaus, having the impudence to assert that he had reconciled Herod to Alexander. Thence he crossed to Greece, where he employed the proceeds of his crimes on equally criminal objects. Twice arraigned before Cæsar for spreading sedition throughout Achæa and fleecing the cities of that province, he was condemned to exile. Thus did retribution overtake him for his betrayal of Alexander and Aristobulus.

5. As a contrast to the conduct of this Spartan, that of Euarestus to Cos may fitly be mentioned. The latter, who was one of Alexander's most intimate friends, paid a visit to Judæa at the same time as Eurycles, and on being questioned by the king upon the allegations made by his other guest, affirmed on oath that he had heard nothing of the kind from the young men. His testimony, however, was of no avail to the unfortunate wretches; for Herod had a ready ear only for slander, and all stood high in his favor who shared his credulity and his indignation.

xxvii. 1. A further stimulus to Herod's cruelty to his sons was given by Salome. For Aristobulus, wishing to involve her, who was at once his mother-in-law and aunt, in the perils threatening himself, sent her a warning to look to her own safety, as the king was prepared to kill her on the charge previously brought against her: namely that, in her anxiety to marry the Arab Syllæus, she had privately communicated to him the secrets of the king, whose enemy he was. This was, as it were, the final hurricane which submerged the tempest-tossed youths. For Salome ran off to the king and reported the warning which she had received. Herod, his patience exhausted, put both his sons in irons and in separate confinement; he then hastily dispatched Volumnius, the military tribune, and Olympus, one of his friends, with all the information in writing, to Cæsar. Taking ship to Rome they delivered the king's dispatches to the emperor, who, while deeply distressed for the young men,

153

did not think it right to deprive the father of his authority over his sons. He replied accordingly, leaving Herod complete liberty of action, but adding a recommendation to him to hold an inquiry into the plot before a joint council of his own relatives and the provincial governors; then, if his sons were convicted, to put them to death, but if they had merely meditated flight, to be content with a milder penalty.

2. Acting on this advice, Herod repaired to Berytus [probably in 7 or 6 B.C.], the place appointed by Cæsar, and there assembled the court. In accordance with written instructions received from Cæsar, the Roman officers presided, namely Saturninus and his legates, Pedanius and others; with them was associated Volumnius the procurator. Next came the king's relatives and friends, including Salome and Pheroras, and after these all the aristocracy of Syria, with the exception of King Archelaus; for, as Alexander's father-in-law, he was regarded by Herod with distrust. His sons were not produced by Herod in court—a very wise precaution, for he knew that their mere appearance would be sure to arouse compassion, while, if they were further permitted to speak, Alexander would have no difficulty in rebutting the charges. So they were detained in custody at Platana, a village in the territory of Sidon.

3. The king, on rising, nevertheless inveighed against them as though they had been present. His accusation of a plot was, for lack of proofs, weak; but he dwelt on the affronts, mockeries, insults, and offenses innumerable of which he had been the victim, and which, he declared to the court, were more cruel than death itself. After that, none contradicting him, he commiserated his hard fate that even in winning his case against his sons his triumph would be bitter and himself the loser, and then asked them all to express their opinions. Saturninus first delivered his opinion, which was to condemn the young men, but not to death; as the father of three children present in court, it would not be right for him, he said, to vote for the destruction of the children of another. His two legates voted in the same sense and their example was followed by some others. Volum-

nius was the first to pronounce a pitiless sentence; and all who followed him condemned the lads to death, some from flattery, others from hatred of Herod, none from indignation against the prisoners.

From that moment all Syria and Jewry were in suspense, anxiously awaiting the last act of the drama; yet none supposed that Herod would carry his cruelty to the length of murdering his children. He, meanwhile, dragged his sons to Tyre, and, taking ship thence to Cæsarea, pondered in his mind over the manner of their execution.

4. Now there was an old soldier in the king's army, named Tiro, whose son was on very intimate and friendly terms with Alexander, and who had a personal affection himself for the young princes. This man, in the excess of his indignation, lost his reason. At first he went about shouting that justice had been trampled under foot, truth was dead, the laws of nature confounded, the world full of iniquity, and whatever else his emotion suggested to one who was careless of his life. At length he boldly presented himself to the king and thus addressed him: "Most god-forsaken of men, that is my opinion of you, you who to the injury of your nearest and dearest trust the word of the basest of scoundrels, if it be true that Pheroras and Salome, whom you have so often sentenced to death, have now made you believe their slanders upon your children. They are cutting off your legitimate heirs, leaving you none but Antipater, choosing him for king as the most manageable in their leading-strings. But take care that the death of his brothers does not one day rouse against him the hatred of the army; for there is not a man there who does not pity the lads, and many of the officers are freely expressing their indignation." He forthwith named these malcontents; and they were promptly arrested by the king, together with Tiro and his son.

5. Thereupon, one of the court barbers, named Trypho, possessed by some strange frenzy, rushed forward and turned informer against himself. "Me too," he cried, "this Tiro tried to induce to cut your throat with my razor when in attendance upon you, promising me a

large reward from Alexander." On hearing this, Herod put Tiro, his son, and the barber under the torture, and when father and son denied all and the other would add nothing more, gave orders to rack Tiro still more severely. The son, thereupon, moved with compassion, promised to tell the king everything if he would spare him his father. Herod granting his request, he stated that his father, at the instigation of Alexander, intended to kill him. This statement, according to some, was a fabrication to end his father's sufferings, while others maintained that it was true.

6. Herod summoned a public assembly, formally accused the officers concerned and Tiro, and enlisted the aid of the populace to dispatch them; they and the barber were beaten to death on the spot with cudgels and stones. He then sent his sons to Sebaste, a town not far from Cæsarea, and ordered them to be strangled. The order was promptly executed, and direction was given to convey the bodies to the fortress of Alexandrion, for burial there with Alexander, their maternal grandfather. Such was the end of Alexander and Aristobulus.

xxviii. 1. Antipater, having now an indisputable claim to the succession, became an object of intolerable abhorrence to the nation; for all knew that it was he who had contrived all the calumnies against his brothers. He was, moreover, haunted with grave alarm at the sight of the children of his victims growing to maturity. For Alexander had by Glaphyra two sons: Tigranes and Alexander; and Aristobulus, by his marriage with Berenice, Salome's daughter, had three: Herod, Agrippa, and Aristobulus, besides two daughters, Herodias and Mariamme. After the execution of Alexander, Herod had sent back Glaphyra to Cappadocia with her dowry; Bernice, the widow of Aristobulus, he gave in marriage to Antipater's maternal uncle, this match being arranged by Antipater in order to conciliate his enemy Salome. Antipater further sought to ingratiate himself with Pheroras by presents and other attentions, and with Cæsar's friends by sending considerable sums to Rome. Saturninus and all his staff in Syria were glutted with his gifts. Yet the more he gave, the more he was hated, as it was felt that his bounties were not the outcome of generosity but extorted from him by fear. The result was that the recipients were no better disposed to him than before, while those whom he overlooked became more implacable enemies. The presents distributed, nevertheless, became daily more magnificent, when he saw the king, to the undoing of his own expectations, taking care of the orphans and showing his remorse for the murder of his sons by his compassion for their offspring.

2. For Herod, one day, assembled his relatives and friends, set the young children before them, and said, with tears in his eyes: "I have been bereaved by some evil genius of the fathers of these infants, but pity for the orphans and nature alike commend them to my care. If I have been the most unfortunate of fathers, I will try at any rate to prove myself a more considerate grandfather and to leave their tutelage, after my death, to those most dear to me. I affiance your daughter, Pheroras, to the elder of these brothers, Alexander's sons, in order that this alliance may make you his natural guardian. To your son, Antipater, I betroth the daughter of Aristobulus; so may you become a father to this orphan girl. Her sister [Herodias] my own Herod shall take, for on his mother's side he is grandson of a high priest. Let then effect be given to my wishes, and let no friend of mine frustrate them. And I pray God to bless these unions, to the benefit of my realm and of my descendants, and to look with serener eyes upon these children here than those with which He beheld their fathers."

3. Having thus spoken, he gave way to tears and joined the children's hands, and then fondly embracing one after the other, dismissed the assembly. At that Antipater's blood ran cold, and his chagrin was evident to all; for he imagined that the honor bestowed by his father on the orphans was his own ruin, and that his claims to the throne would be again endangered if Alexander's children were to have, in addition to the support of Archelaus, that of Pheroras, a tetrarch. He

reflected on the hatred which the nation bore him and their pity for the orphans, the enthusiasm which the Jews had shown for his brothers in their lifetime and their fond memory of them now that, in his interest, they were dead. He resolved accordingly at all costs to break off these betrothals.

4. Afraid of practising a ruse upon so harsh a father, whose suspicions were easily aroused, he boldly ventured into his presence and besought him outright not to deprive him of the honor which he had deigned to confer on him, nor to leave him the mere title of king while others enjoyed the power; for he would never be master of affairs should Alexander's son, with Archelaus as his grandfather, also have Pheroras as his father-in-law. He therefore earnestly entreated him, as the palace contained a numerous family, to modify these matrimonial arrangements. The king, in fact, had nine wives [besides the deceased Mariamme I] and issue by seven of them. Antipater himself was son of Doris; Herod [II] of Mariamme [II], the high priest's daughter; Antipas and Archelaus were sons of Malthace, the Samaritan; Olympias, a daughter by this last wife, had married Joseph, the king's nephew. By Cleopatra, a native of Jerusalem, he had Herod and Philip; by Pallas, Phasael. He had besides other daughters, Roxane and Salome, one by Phædra, the other by Elpis. Two of his wives, one a cousin, the other a niece, were childless. In addition there were two daughters by Mariamme [I], sisters of Alexander and Aristobulus. In view of this large family, Antipater begged for an alteration in the projected marriages.

5. The king, on discovering Antipater's attitude to the orphans, was highly indignant, and the thought crossed his mind—might not his murdered sons also have been the victims of this man's slanders? He, accordingly, at the moment replied in a long and angry speech, and dismissed Antipater from his presence. Subsequently, however, seduced by his flatteries, he made other arrangements, and gave the daughter of Aristobulus to Antipater himself, and the daughter of Pheroras to his son.

6. How powerful was the effect of Antipater's adulation on this occasion may be gauged from Salome's ill success in a similar suit. For, although she was Herod's sister and had recourse to the intercession of the [Roman] empress Livia to plead with him for permission to marry the Arab Syllæus, Herod swore that he would regard her as his bitterest enemy if she did not renounce this passion; and in the end, he married her, against her will, to one of his friends named Alexas, and one of her daughters to the son of Alexas, the other to Antipater's maternal uncle. Of his daughters by Mariamme, one was given to Antipater, his sister's son; the other to Phasæl, his brother's.

xxix. 1. Antipater, having cut off the orphans' expectations and arranged the marriages to his own advantage, regarded his prospects as securely anchored, and with assurance now added to villainy, became insufferable. For, unable to avert the hatred which he inspired in all, he sought security in intimidation. He was assisted by Pheroras, who looked on Antipater's claim to the throne as already assured. There was, moreover, a gang of women at court who created new disturbances. The wife of Pheroras, in league with her mother and sister and the mother of Antipater, displayed constant effrontery in the palace, and even ventured to insult two young daughters of the king. She became, in consequence, the object of Herod's special aversion; yet, notwithstanding the king's hatred, these women domineered over the rest. The sole opponent of their league was Salome, who reported it to the king as a conclave not conducive to the interests of his realm. Informed of this denunciation and of Herod's wrath, they abandoned their public meetings and all signs of friendly recognition, and on the contrary pretended to quarrel with one another in the king's hearing; Antipater joined in their dissimulation by taking offense, in public, at Pheroras. But they continued to hold clandestine meetings and nocturnal carousals, and the knowledge that they were watched only bound them closer together. Salome, however, was ignorant of none of their proceedings and reported everything to Herod.

2. The king was furiously indignant, particularly at the wife of Pheroras, the principal object of Salome's charges. He, accordingly, assembled a council of his friends and relations and accused the wretched woman of numerous misdeeds, among others of insulting his own daughters, of subsidizing the Pharisees to oppose him, and of alienating his brother, after bewitching him with drugs. In conclusion, he addressed Pheroras and told him that he must choose one or the other, either his brother or his wife. Pheroras replying that he would sooner part with his existence than with his wife, Herod, in perplexity, turned to Antipater and ordered him to have no further relations either with the wife of Pheroras, or with her husband, or with any of her set. Antipater, while not openly violating this injunction, continued secretly and at night to associate with them; but fearing the vigilance of Salome he contrived, with the help of friends in Italy, a visit to Rome. A letter arriving from them, suggesting that Antipater ought to be sent before long to Cæsar's court, Herod without a moment's delay sent him off with a brilliant retinue, a large sum of money and his will, in which Antipater was named as heir to the throne, and Herod, the king's son by Mariamme [II], the high priest's daughter, as Antipater's successor. . . .

4. Herod, meanwhile, never relaxed his efforts to compel Pheroras to divorce his wife. But, notwithstanding the abundant cause which he had for his hatred of the creature, he could devise no means of punishing her, until finally, in extreme indignation, he banished both her and his brother from the realm [in 5 B.C.]. Pheroras, accepting this affront with equanimity, departed to his own tetrarchy, swearing that the only limit to his exile should be Herod's death, and that never, so long as his brother lived, would he return to him. Nor, in fact, would he revisit his brother, even during his illness, though urgently pressed to do so; for Herod, believing that he was dying, desired to leave him certain instructions. Herod, however, unexpectedly recovered, and not long after Pheroras himself fell sick; Herod thereupon displayed greater humanity, for he went to him

and affectionately tended him. But he could not cope with the malady, and a few days later Pheroras expired. Notwithstanding the love which Herod had for his brother to his dying day, a report was spread that he had poisoned even him. Nonetheless, he had the corpse conveyed to Jerusalem, gave orders for a solemn national mourning, and honored him with the most imposing funeral. Such was the end to which came one of the murderers of Alexander and Aristobulus.

xxx. 1. But retribution was now, in turn, descending upon the real perpetrator of that crime, Antipater; this retribution arose out of the death of Pheroras. For certain freedmen of the deceased came, in dejection, to the king and informed him that his brother had been carried off by poison; his wife, they said, had served up to him some extraordinary concoction, after eating which he was immediately taken ill. They added that, two days before, her mother and sister had brought from Arabia a woman who was an expert in drugs, to make a love-potion for Pheroras; but instead of this, she had given him a deadly poison at the instigation of Syllæus, who knew her.

2. Beset with all sorts of suspicions, the king put the women-servants and some ladies above that rank to the torture. One victim in her agonies exclaimed, "May God who governs earth and heaven punish the author of our present miseries, Antipater's mother!" Clutching at this clue, the king pushed his search for the facts yet further. The woman then revealed the intimacy of Antipater's mother with Pheroras and the ladies of his family, and their clandestine meetings. She added that Pheroras and Antipater, on their return from the king, would pass the whole night drinking with those women, without allowing a single servant, male or female, to be present. This information was given by one of the ladies of rank.

3. Herod had each of the slave girls separately tortured. All their evidence agreed with that already stated; they added that it was by a mutual arrangement that Antipater had withdrawn to Rome and Pheroras to Peræa; for they were constantly saying to each other,

"After Alexander and Aristobulus, we and our wives will be Herod's next victims. Having slain Mariamme and her offspring, he will spare none, so it will be better to flee as far as possible from the ferocious beast." Antipater, they continued, would often complain to his mother that he was already grey-headed, while his father grew younger every day; he would perhaps be the first to die, before he began to be really king. Even supposing his father ever did die (and when would that be?) his enjoyment of his heritage must be extremely short.

Then there were these hydra-heads, the sons of Aristobulus and Alexander, shooting up. His father had robbed him of his hopes for his children, by nominating as the next heir to the throne not one of his own children, but Herod, the son of Mariamme [II]. In that at least he betrayed his extreme senility, if he supposed that that part of his will would stand; for he, Antipater, would take good care to leave none of the family alive. Never had father so hated his children, yet Herod hated his brother far more; only the other day he had given him [Antipater] a hundred talents to break off all intercourse with Pheroras. And when Pheroras remarked, "Why, what harm were we doing him?" he had replied: "Would to heaven he would rob us of everything and leave us to live in nakedness. But it is impossible to escape so bloodthirsty a beast, who will not even allow us to show affection for anyone. Now we must meet in secret; we shall be able to do so openly if ever we possess the courage and arms of men."

4. To these revelations the tortured women added that Pheroras had had designs of flying with them to Petra. Herod believed all these statements because of the detail of the hundred talents, which he had mentioned to none but Antipater. The first to feel the explosion of his wrath was Doris, Antipater's mother; he stripped her of all the finery which he had bestowed on her and for the second time dismissed her from court. With the ladies of Pheroras's household he made his peace and showed them special attentions after their tortures. But he was scared with fright and flared up at the least suspicion, and many innocent persons were

haled by him to torture, for fear that a single culprit should escape him.

5. His attention was now directed to Antipater the Samaritan, agent to his son Antipater. From him, under torture, he learned that Antipater had procured from Egypt, through Antiphilus, one of his companions, a deadly poison intended for the king; that from Antiphilus it had passed into the hands of Theudion, Antipater's uncle, who had delivered it to Pheroras, since it was he whom Antipater had commissioned to kill Herod while he himself was at Rome and out of the way of suspicion; and that Pheroras had entrusted the poison to his wife. The king sent for her and ordered her instantly to produce what she had received. She went out, as though to fetch it, and then flung herself from the roof, in order to evade conviction and the king's rack. However, by the providence, it seems, of God, whose vengeance was pursuing Antipater, she fell not on her head, but on another part of her body, and was not killed. She was carried to the king, who had restoratives applied, as she was stunned by the fall. He then asked her why she had thrown herself from the roof, and swore that if she told the truth, he would exempt her from all punishment, but if she prevaricated he would tear her body to pieces with tortures and leave not a limb for burial.

6. At this the woman hesitated an instant and then replied: "After all, why should I longer guard these secrets, now that Pheroras is dead? Merely to save Antipater who has been the ruin of us all? Listen to me, O king, and may God hear me too, a witness to the truth of my words who cannot be deceived! At the time when you were sitting weeping beside the dying Pheroras, he called me to him and said, 'Much have I been mistaken, my wife, in my brother's feelings towards me; I hated him who loves me so tenderly; I plotted to kill him who is so overwhelmed with grief for me even before my death. I am but receiving the reward of my impiety. As for you, bring that poison which Antipater left us, and which you are keeping for his destruction, and promptly destroy it under my eyes,

lest I carry away with me an avenging demon even
to the world below.' So I brought it, as he bade me,
and emptied most of it into the fire beneath his eyes,
but reserved a little for myself against the uncertainties
of the future and my terror of you."

7. After this declaration she produced the box containing a mere scrap of the poison. The king then applied torture to the mother and brother of Antiphilus,
who both confessed that Antiphilus had brought the
box from Egypt and asserted that he had procured the
drug from another brother, a doctor in Alexandria. The
ghosts of Alexander and Aristobulus were indeed patrol-
ing the palace from end to end, detecting and disclos-
ing all the mysteries, and dragging to judgment persons who seemed farthest removed from suspicion. Thus,
even Mariamme, the high priest's daughter, was discovered to be privy to the plot; for her brothers, when
put upon the rack, denounced her. The king's punishment for the mother's audacity fell upon her son: her
Herod, whom he had appointed successor to Antipater,
was struck out of the will.

xxxi. 1. Corroborative evidence of Antipater's designs,
the last link in the chain, was now furnished by Bathyl-
lus, his freedman. This man arrived with another noxious drug, composed of the poison of asps and the secre-
tions of other reptiles, in order that Pheroras and his
wife might be armed with this against the king, should
the first poison fail to take effect. A further object of
his visit, subsidiary to the audacious attempt on the
father's life, was the conveyance of letters fabricated
by Antipater to injure his [half-] brothers, Archelaus and
Philip. These sons of the king, now growing lads and
full of manly spirit, were receiving their education in
Rome. Anxious to rid himself of these scions springing
up to dash his hopes, Antipater forged several letters to
their injury in the name of their friends in Rome, while
he prevailed on others by bribery to write that the young
princes were constantly railing at their father, publicly
deploring the fate of Alexander and Aristobulus, and
indignant at their own recall; for their father was now

summoning them back, and it was this fact which caused Antipater the greatest uneasiness.

2. Even before his departure abroad, Antipater, while still in Judæa, used to procure, at a price, the sending of such letters of abuse of his brothers written in Rome, and then, in order to avoid suspicion, would go to his father and make excuses for his brothers, urging that such and such statements were false, while other matters mentioned were mere youthful indiscretions. Now in Rome, having to pay immense sums to the writers of these letters against his brothers, his efforts were directed to confusing the evidence of such outlay. To this end he bought up costly apparel, embroidered carpets, cups of silver and gold, and many other precious objects, in order to conceal under the enormous total of these outgoings the wages paid for the other affair. His returns showed an expenditure of 200 talents. . . .

But now, though even all these petty knaveries were exposed with the larger crime, now when every fresh torture was loudly proclaiming him a parricide, when the letters were revealing him as once more a fratricide, none the less not one of the visitors to Rome told him of the turn of his fortunes in Judæa, although seven months elapsed between his conviction and his return; so intense was the hatred which all bore him. Perhaps, moreover, the lips of those who were minded to speak were sealed by the spirits of his murdered brothers. However that may be, he wrote from Rome to announce the good news of his early return and of the honors paid to him by Cæsar in taking leave of him.

3. The king, impatient to lay hands on the conspirator and fearing that he might be forewarned and on his guard, replied in an equally dissembling letter, couched in affectionate terms and bidding him hasten his return; because if he made speed, Herod added, he would be prepared to relinquish his complaints against his mother, for Antipater was not ignorant of her dismissal from court. He had previously received at Tarentum a letter announcing the death of Pheroras and had displayed the profoundest grief, for which some applauded him, attributing it to the loss of an uncle;

but his emotion, it seems, was due to the failure of the plot. He wept not for Pheroras, but for his accomplice. He was, moreover, already alarmed at the thought of his past proceedings—had the poison been discovered? But now, when he received in Cilicia the above-mentioned letter from his father, he instantly pressed on.

However, as he was entering the harbor of Celenderis, the thought of his mother's disgrace came over him, and even without such prompting his soul had already a premonition of the future. The more far-sighted of his friends advised him not to put himself into his father's clutches until he had clearly ascertained the reasons for his mother's dismissal, as they feared that his arrival might only serve to swell the charges against her. But the less reflective, anxious rather to see their native country than to serve Antipater's interests, urged him to push on and not by procrastinating to afford his father ground for sinister suspicions and his traducers a handle for calumny. "Even supposing," they said, "any intrigue against you is now on foot, it is because of your absence; none would have ventured on such a thing had you been there. It is absurd to let vague suspicions rob you of certain happiness and not to run to your father's arms to receive the kingdom which is tottering on his unaided shoulders." Antipater, under the impulse of his evil genius, followed their advice, and sailing across, landed at the port of Augustus, at Cæsarea.

4. Here he found a solitude, unlooked for, profound, and ominous; all avoided him, none ventured to approach him. For, equally hated though he had always been, this hatred was now at liberty to show itself. Moreover, fear of the king kept many aloof, for every city by now was full of the Antipater scandal, and the only person ignorant how he stood was Antipater himself. No man ever had a more brilliant escort than his when he sailed for Rome, none on return a more ignominious reception. Divining now the disasters which had befallen at home, he still maintained a crafty dissimulation, and though dead with fright at the bottom of his heart, contrived to preserve an imposing exterior.

There was no longer any possibility of flight or retreat from the perils encompassing him. However, he had received no definite tidings of events at the palace—owing to the king's threats against informers—and he still cherished a ray of hope: perhaps nothing had been discovered; perhaps, even if anything had been discovered, he might mend matters by effrontery and guile, his sole means of salvation.

5. Armed, then, with these weapons he entered the palace without his friends, for they had been insolently stopped at the outer gate. At the time there was a visitor within—Varus, the governor of Syria. Antipater proceeded to his father's presence, and seeking courage in audacity, approached as though to kiss him. Herod, with arms extended and head averted, cried out: "That too betrays the parricide: he would embrace me, with such accusations against him! Perdition take thee, most impious wretch, and touch me not until you have cleared yourself of the charges. I offer you a tribunal, and for judge, this timely visitor, Varus. Go and prepare your defense for tomorrow; I leave you that interval for your artifices." Unable through consternation to utter a word in reply, Antipater withdrew, and his mother and his wife came to him and told him in detail of all the evidence against him. Then he collected himself and applied himself to preparing his defense.

xxxii. 1. On the following day the king assembled a council of his relatives and friends, inviting Antipater's friends to attend as well. He himself presided, with Varus, and ordered all the informers to be produced. Among these were some domestics of Antipater's mother, recently arrested in the act of carrying a letter from her to her son in these terms: "As your father has discovered all, do not come near him, unless you have obtained support from Cæsar." When these witnesses had been brought in with the rest, Antipater entered and, falling prostrate at his father's feet, said: "I beseech you, father, do not condemn me in advance, but lend an unprejudiced ear to my defense; for I shall, if you permit, establish my innocence."

2. Herod burst out upon him to be silent and then

addressed Varus: "That you, Varus, and every honest judge will condemn Antipater as an abandoned criminal, I am fully persuaded. What I fear is that *my* fate may also appear hateful to you, and that you may judge me deserving of every calamity for having begotten such sons. And yet you ought rather to pity me for having been the most devoted of fathers to such abominable wretches. My late sons, whom when they were quite young I thought fit to destine for the throne—whom I not only expensively educated in Rome, but introduced to Cæsar's friendship, and made an object of envy to other sovereigns—these I found to be conspirators. They have died, mainly to further Antipater's interests; he was young, he was the heir, and to secure him was the object which I had most at heart. And now this foul monster, gorged with the benefits of my forbearance, has turned his bloated insolence upon me. He thought me too long-lived; my old age oppressed him; he could not endure the idea of becoming king by other means than parricide. Justly indeed has he served me for bringing him back, a castaway from the country, ousting the sons whom a princess bore me and declaring him heir to the throne!

"I admit, Varus, my own infatuation. It was I who exasperated those sons against me by cutting off their just expectations in the interests of Antipater. When did I ever indulge them as I have this scoundrel? To him in my own lifetime I well nigh resigned my power. I nominated him in my will, in the public eye, heir to the throne; I assigned him a private income of fifty talents, apart from liberal contributions from my personal revenues. Recently, when he set sail for Rome, I presented his wiles. Varus, you must be on your guard. I know to Cæsar, alone of all my children, as his father's preserver. What crime did those others commit comparable to that of Antipater? Or what proof was brought against them so convincing as that which establishes this traitor's guilt?

"However, this parricide has presumed to open his mouth, hoping once more to smother the truth under his wiles. Varus, you must be on your guard. I know the creature and foresee the plausible pleading, the

hypocritical lamentations, that are to follow. This is
the man who, in former days when Alexander was alive,
advised me to beware of him and not to trust my life to
all men's hands; this is he who conducted me to my
couch and looked round to see that no assassin was
concealed; this is he who dispensed my hours of slumber, ensured my freedom from care, consoled me in my
sorrow for my victims, and sounded the feelings of his
surviving brothers; this is my buckler, my bodyguard!
When I recall, Varus, his knavery and hypocrisy on each
occasion, I can scarce believe I am alive and marvel
how I escaped so deep a schemer. But since some evil
genius is bent on desolating my house and raising up
against me, one after another, those who are nearest to
my heart, I may weep over my unjust destiny, I may
groan in spirit over my forlorn state, but not one shall
escape who thirsts for my blood, no, not though conviction should extend to all my children."

3. Here his emotion rendered further speech impossible, and he signalled to Nicolaus,* one of his friends,
to state the evidence. But now Antipater, who still lay
prostrate at his father's feet, raised his head and cried
out: "You, father, have made my defense yourself, for
how could I be a parricide—I who, as you admit, have
ever served as your protector? You call my filial piety
imposture and hypocrisy. How could I, cunning in all
else, have been so senseless as not to perceive that, while
it was difficult to conceal from man the concoction of
so atrocious a crime, it was impossible to hide it from the
Judge in heaven, who sees all, who is present everywhere? Was I ignorant of my brothers' fate, whom God
so relentlessly punished for their wicked designs upon
you? And then, what motive could have instigated me
against you? Aspiration to the throne? But I reigned
already! Suspicion of your hatred? But was I not beloved? Had I other reason to fear you? Nay, by preserving you I inspired fear in others. Was it lack of money?
Who had more at his disposal than I? Even had I been

---

* Nicolaus of Damascus, whose *Universal History,* it has already
been noted, was a main source for Josephus.

the most abandoned of men, with the heart of a ferocious beast, must I not have been reclaimed, father, by your benefactions? For, as you have said yourself, you recalled me from exile, you gave me preference over such a number of sons, you proclaimed me king in your own lifetime, and by loading me with other favors made me the envy of all.

"Ah me! that fatal journey! What an opportunity I gave to jealousy, what an ample period to those who were intriguing against me! Yet it was for you, father, and to fight your battles that I took that journey, to prevent Syllæus from treating your old age with contempt. Rome is witness to my filial piety and Cæsar, the lord of the universe, who has often called me 'Philopator.'* Take, father, these letters from him. These are more trustworthy than the calumnies against me here; these are my sole vindication; here are the proofs which I offer of my tender feelings for you. Remember how reluctantly I embarked, knowing the lurking hostility to me within this realm. It was you, father, who involuntarily brought about my ruin, by compelling me to give my envious foes an opportunity for calumny.

"But here I am to meet my accusers; here I am, the 'parricide,' who has traversed sea and land, and nowhere been molested! But I do not ask for your love on the strength of the evidence so far given of my innocence;† for I stand condemned before God and before you, father. But, condemned though I am, I entreat you not to rely on admissions extracted by the torture of others. Let the fire be applied to me! Let the instruments of torment course through my frame nor spare this polluted body! For, if I am a parricide, I ought not to die without being put upon the rack."

These ejaculations, accompanied by moaning and tears, moved all to compassion, including Varus. Herod alone remained dry-eyed, furious and knowing that the evidence was true.

4. Thereupon Nicolaus, as ordered by the king, ad-

---

* "Lover of his father."
† Text doubtful.

dressed the assembly. He began with a full exposure
of Antipater's knavery, dissipating the commiseration
which his speech had aroused. He then launched out into a severe indictment, attributing to him all the crimes
which had been committed throughout the realm, and
in particular the execution of his brothers, demonstrat-
ing that they owed their death to Antipater's calumnies.
He added that he had further designs on the survivors
as presumptive heirs to the throne; "Would one who had
prepared to poison his father have stopped short at his
brothers?" Passing on to the evidence for the poisoning
plot, he brought forward in succession all the information extracted; being roused to indignation on the subject of Pheroras, at the idea of Antipater converting
even him into a fratricide and, by corrupting the king's
nearest of kin, infecting the whole palace with pollution. With many more observations, supported by proofs,
Nicolaus concluded his speech.

5. Varus then called on Antipater for his defense. But
he would say no more than "God is witness of my innocence" and remained prostrate and silent. The governor, thereupon, called for the poison and had it applied to a prisoner under sentence of death, who drank
it and instantly expired. Then, after a private interview
with Herod, Varus drafted his report of the meeting for
Cæsar, and a day later took his departure. The king had
Antipater put in irons and dispatched messengers to the
emperor to inform him of the catastrophe.

6. It was subsequently discovered that Antipater had
also plotted against Salome. For a domestic of Antiphilus arrived from Rome with letters from a maid-ser-
vant of Livia, named Acme; she wrote to the king to
say that she had found among Livia's papers some letters from Salome, which, as his well-wisher, she had
privately transmitted to him. These letters of Salome,
containing the most cruel abuse of the king and the
most scathing condemnation of his conduct, were forgeries of Antipater, who had bribed Acme to send them
to Herod. He was convicted by the letter which the
woman addressed at the same time to him, in these
terms: "As you desired, I have written to your father

171

and forwarded those letters, and feel sure that, when
he has read them, he will not spare his sister. Be good
enough, when all is over, to remember what you promised."

7. When this letter was brought to light, with those
concocted to injure Salome, a suspicion crossed the
king's mind that perhaps the letters incriminating Alexander were also forgeries. He was, moreover, deeply distressed at the thought that he had almost killed his sister also, owing to Antipater's intrigues. He determined,
therefore, to delay no longer to punish him for all his
crimes. But when proceeding to extreme measures against
Antipater, he was arrested by a serious illness. He wrote,
however, to Cæsar on the subject of Acme and the fraud
which had been practiced on Salome; he also called for
his will and modified it. He now named Antipas king,
passing over his eldest sons, Archelaus and Philip, who
had also been the objects of Antipater's calumnies. To
Augustus he bequeathed, besides gifts in kind, one thousand talents; to the empress, the children, friends, and
freedmen of the emperor about five hundred; to the other
members of his own family he assigned large tracts of
territory and considerable sums of money, honoring his
sister Salome with the most magnificent presents of all.
Such were the corrections which Herod made in his
will.

xxxiii. 1. His illness steadily grew worse, aggravated
as were the attacks of disease by age and despondency.
For he was now nearly seventy years old, and his tragic
experiences with his children had so broken his spirit
that even in good health he no longer enjoyed any of
the pleasures of life. His malady was further increased
by the thought that Antipater was still alive; for he had
determined that his execution should be no casual affair,
but seriously undertaken on his recovery.

2. To his other troubles was now added an insurrection of the populace. There were in the capital two rabbis with a reputation as profound experts in the laws
of their country, who consequently enjoyed the highest
esteem of the whole nation; their names were Judas, son
of Sepphoræus, and Matthias, son of Margalus. Their

lectures on the laws were attended by a large youthful audience, and day after day they drew together quite an army of men in their prime. Hearing now that the king was gradually sinking under despondency and disease, these rabbis threw out hints to their friends that this was the fitting moment to avenge God's honor and to pull down those structures which had been erected in defiance of their fathers' laws. It was, in fact, unlawful to place in the Temple either images or busts or any representation whatsoever of a living creature; notwithstanding this, the king had erected over the great gate a golden eagle. This it was which these rabbis now exhorted their disciples to cut down, telling them that, even if the action proved hazardous, it was a noble deed to die for the law of one's country; for the souls of those who came to such an end attained immortality and an eternally abiding sense of felicity. It was only the ignoble, uninitiated in their philosophy, who clung in their ignorance to life and preferred death on a sickbed to that of a hero.

3. While they were discoursing in this strain, a rumor spread that the king was dying; the news caused the young men to throw themselves more boldly into the enterprise. At mid-day, accordingly, when numbers of people were perambulating the Temple, they let themselves down from the roof by stout cords and began chopping off the golden eagle with hatchets. The king's captain, to whom the matter was immediately reported, hastened to the scene with a considerable force, arrested about forty of the young men and conducted them to the king. Herod first asked them whether they had dared to cut down the golden eagle; they admitted it. "Who ordered you to do so?" he continued. "The law of our fathers." "And why so exultant, when you will shortly be put to death?" "Because, after our death, we shall enjoy greater felicity."

4. These proceedings provoked the king to such fury that he forgot his disease and had himself carried to a public assembly, where at great length he denounced the men as sacrilegious persons who, under the pretext of zeal for the law, had some more ambitious aim in

view, and demanded that they should be punished for
impiety. The people, apprehensive of wholesale prose-
cutions, besought him to confine the punishment to the
instigators of the deed and to those who had been arrested in the perpetration of it, and to forgo his anger
against the rest. The king grudgingly consented; those
who had let themselves down from the roof together with
the rabbis he had burned alive; the remainder of those
arrested he handed over to his executioners.

5. From this time onwards Herod's malady began to
spread to his whole body and his sufferings took a variety of forms. He had fever, though not a raging fever, an
intolerable itching of the whole skin, continuous pains
in the intestines, tumors in the feet as in dropsy, in-
flammation of the abdomen, and gangrene of the privy
parts, engendering worms, in addition to asthma, with
great difficulty in breathing, and convulsions in all his
limbs. His condition led diviners to pronounce his mala-
dies a judgment on him for his treatment of the rabbis.
Yet, struggling as he was with such numerous sufferings, he clung to life, hoped for recovery, and devised
one remedy after another. Thus he crossed the Jordan
to take the warm baths at Callirrhœ, the waters of which
descend into the Dead Sea and from their sweetness are
also used for drink. There, the physicians deciding to
raise the temperature of his whole body with hot oil,
he was lowered into a bath full of that liquid, whereupon he fainted and turned up his eyes as though he
were dead. His attendants raising an uproar, their cries
brought him to himself, but now despairing of recovery,
he gave orders to distribute fifty drachmas per head to
the soldiers and considerable sums to their officers and
to his friends.

6. He started on his return journey and reached Jericho in an atrabilious condition, in which, hurling defiance as it were at death itself, he proceeded to devise
an outrageous scheme. Having assembled the distinguished men from every village from one end of Judæa
to the other, he ordered them to be locked into the hippodrome. He then summoned his sister Salome and her
husband Alexas and said: "I know that the Jews will

celebrate my death by a festival; yet I can obtain a vicarious mourning and a magnificent funeral, if you consent to follow my instructions. You know these men here in custody; the moment I expire, have them surrounded by the soldiers and massacred; so shall all Judæa and every household weep for me, whether they will or no."

7. At the moment when he was giving these instructions, he received letters from his ambassadors at Rome, informing him that Acme had been executed by Cæsar's orders and Antipater condemned to death; but, the letter continued, if his father were content with banishing him, he had Cæsar's permission to do so. At this news he for a while recovered his spirits, but later, under the strain of lack of nourishment and a convulsive cough, overpowered by his tortures, he endeavored to anticipate the hour of destiny. He took an apple and called for a knife, as it was his custom to cut up this fruit when eating it, and then, looking round to see that there was no one to prevent him, raised his hand to strike himself. However, his cousin Achiab rushed up, and seizing his hand, arrested the blow.

Instantly there arose loud lamentations throughout the palace, in the belief that the king had passed away. Antipater, quick to catch the sound, took heart again, and radiant with joy, besought his jailers, for a remuneration, to loose him and let him go. The head jailer, however, not only prevented this, but hastened to the king and reported his prisoner's design. Herod, with a shout which might have seemed beyond a sick man's strength, instantly sent his guards and had Antipater executed. He ordered his body to be buried at Hyrcanium. After that he again amended his will, nominating Archelaus, his eldest son and brother of Antipas, heir to the throne, and Antipas tetrarch.

8. Herod survived the execution of his son but five days. He expired [early in 4 B.C.] after a reign of thirty-four years, reckoning from the date when, after putting Antigonus to death, he assumed control of the state; or thirty-seven years, from the date when he was proclaimed king by the Romans. In his life as a whole he

was blessed, if ever man was, by fortune. A commoner, he mounted to a throne, retained it for all those years, and bequeathed it to his own children; in his family life, on the contrary, no man was more unfortunate. Before the army had learned of his decease, Salome left the palace with her husband and released the prisoners whom Herod had ordered to be put to death, telling them that the king had changed his mind and now dismissed them all to their homes.

Not until after their departure did she and her husband announce the news to the soldiers, summoning them and the rest of the people to a public assembly in the amphitheater at Jericho. Here Ptolemy, to whom the king had entrusted his signet-ring, came forward, pronounced a benediction on the deceased king, delivered an exhortation to the people, and read a letter which Herod had left for the troops, in which he earnestly appealed to them to be loyal to his successor. After this letter, he opened and read the codicils. Under these, Philip inherited Trachonitis and the neighboring districts. Antipas, as we have already mentioned, was appointed tetrarch [of Galilee and Peræa], and Archelaus king. The last-named received a charge from Herod to carry his ring to Cæsar, with the documents relating to the administration of the realm, under seal, because he had vested in Cæsar the control of all his dispositions and the ratification of the will. In the remaining particulars the directions of the previous will were to hold good.

9. Archelaus was instantly hailed with acclamations and congratulations; and the troops advancing by companies, with the people, made promises of allegiance on their own part, and invoked upon him the blessing of God. The king's funeral next occupied attention. Archelaus, omitting nothing that could contribute to its magnificence, brought forth all the royal ornaments to accompany the procession in honor of the deceased. The bier was of solid gold, studded with precious stones, and had a covering of purple, embroidered with various colors; on this lay the body enveloped in a purple robe, a diadem encircling the head and surmounted by a

crown of gold, the scepter beside his right hand. Around the bier were Herod's sons and a large group of his relations; these were followed by the guards, the Thracian contingent, Germans and Gauls, all equipped as for war. The remainder of the troops marched in front, armed and in orderly array, led by their commanders and subordinate officers; behind these came five hundred of Herod's servants and freedmen, carrying spices. The body was thus conveyed for a distance of two hundred furlongs to Herodion, where, in accordance with the directions of the deceased, it was interred. So ended Herod's reign.

BOOK II

Judæa Loses Her Independence

i. 1. The necessity under which Archelaus found himself of undertaking a journey to Rome was the signal for fresh disturbances. After keeping seven days' mourning for his father and providing the usual funeral banquet for the populace on a sumptuous scale—a Jewish custom which reduces many to poverty, such entertainment of the people being considered obligatory and its omission an act of impiety—he changed into white raiment and went forth to the Temple, where the people received him with varied acclamations. Speaking from a golden throne on a raised platform he greeted the multitude. He thanked them for the zeal that they had displayed over his father's funeral and for the marks of homage shown to himself, as to a king whose claim to the throne was already confirmed. He would, however, he said, for the present abstain not only from the exercise of the authority, but even from the assumption of the titles, of royalty, until his right to the succession had been ratified by [Augustus] Cæsar, to whose ruling everything had been submitted under the terms of the will. Even when, as he reminded them, the army at Jericho had desired to place the diadem on his head, he had declined it. He would, none the less, make an ample return alike to the soldiers and to the citizens for their devotion and goodwill, as soon as the supreme authorities had definitely declared him king; for it would be his earnest and constant endeavor to treat them better than they had been treated by his father.

2. Delighted at these professions, the multitude at once proceeded to test his intentions by making large demands. One party clamored for a reduction of the property taxes, another for the abolition of the sales taxes, a third for the liberation of the prisoners. To all

these requests, in his desire to ingratiate himself with the people, he readily assented. Then, after offering a sacrifice, he regaled himself with his friends. Towards evening, however, a large number of those who were bent on revolution assembled on the same spot, and now that the public mourning for the king was ended, began a lamentation on their own account, bewailing the fate of those whom Herod had punished for cutting down the golden eagle from the gate of the Temple. This mourning was in no subdued tones: there were piercing shrieks, a dirge directed by a conductor, and lamentations with beating of the breast which resounded throughout the city; all this in honor of the unfortunate men who, they asserted, had in defense of their country's laws and the Temple perished on the pyre. These martyrs ought, they clamored, to be avenged by the punishment of Herod's favorites, and the first step was the deposition of the high priest whom he had appointed, as they had a right to select a man of greater piety and purer morals.

3. Archelaus, exasperated by these proceedings, but in haste to depart, wished to defer retaliation, from fear that, if he provoked the hostility of the people, he would be detained by a general rising. He, accordingly, endeavored to appease the rebels by persuasion, without resort to force, and quietly sent his general to entreat them to desist. This officer on entering the Temple, and before he had even opened his mouth, was driven off by the rioters with a shower of stones; many others whom Archelaus sent in after him to call them to reason were similarly treated. To all remonstrances they replied with anger, and it was evident that, given any accession to their numbers, they had no intention of remaining inactive.

And now the feast of unleavened bread, which the Jews call Passover, came round; it is an occasion for the contribution of a multitude of sacrifices, and a vast crowd streamed in from the country for the ceremony. The promoters of the mourning for the rabbis stood in a body in the Temple, procuring recruits for their faction. This alarmed Archelaus, who, wishing to prevent

the contagion from spreading to the whole crowd, sent
in a tribune in command of a cohort, with orders to
restrain by force the ringleaders of the sedition. Indignant at the appearance of the troops, the whole crowd
pelted them with stones; most of the cohort were killed,
while their commander was wounded and escaped with
difficulty. Then, as if nothing serious had happened, the
rioters returned to their sacrifices. Archelaus, however,
now felt that it would be impossible to restrain the mob
without bloodshed, and let loose upon them his entire
army, the infantry advancing in close order through
the city, the cavalry by way of the plain. The soldiers,
falling unexpectedly upon the various parties busy with
their sacrifices, slew about three thousand of them and
dispersed the remainder among the neighboring hills.
The heralds of Archelaus followed and ordered everyone
to return home; so they all abandoned the festival and
departed.

ii. 1. Archelaus himself with his mother [Malthace]
and his friends, Poplas, Ptolemy, and Nicolaus, now descended to the coast, leaving Philip to take charge of
the realm and to protect his private interests. [Herod's
sister] Salome, with her children, also accompanied him,
as did the nephews and sons-in-law of the late king, ostensibly to support the claims of Archelaus to the succession, but in reality to accuse him of the recent ille-
gal proceedings in the Temple.

2. At Cæsarea the party was met by Sabinus, procurator of Syria, on his way up to Judæa to take charge of
Herod's estate. He was prevented from continuing his
journey by the arrival of Varus,* whose presence Archelaus had, through Ptolemy, urgently solicited. Sabinus,
in deference to Varus, abandoned for the moment his
intention of rushing to the castles and excluding Archelaus from access to his father's treasuries, and promising to take no action until Cæsar had given his decision,
remained at Cæsarea. But as soon as those who had obstructed his designs had left, Varus for Antioch, Arche-

---

* Varus, as governor of the province of Syria, outranked Sabinus, who was the imperial finance officer there.

laus for Rome, he sped to Jerusalem and took possession
of the palace, and then, summoning the governors of
the forts and the controllers of the treasury, endeavored
to search into the accounts and to take possession of the
castles. These officers, however, mindful of the injunctions of Archelaus, continued to guard their respective
trusts, for which they professed to hold themselves responsible to Cæsar, rather than to Archelaus.

3. Meanwhile another claimant to the throne had
set out for Rome, namely, [Archelaus's brother] Antipas,
who maintained that the will in which he had been
named king had greater validity than the codicil. He
had received previous promises of support from Salome
and from many of his relations who had sailed with
Archelaus. He had won over his mother and Ptolemy,
brother of Nicolaus, from whose influence much was
expected, owing to the confidence reposed in him by
Herod, who had honored him above all his friends. But
what Antipas mainly relied on was the brilliant eloquence of his advocate Irenæus; on the strength of this
he refused to listen to those who advised him to give
way to Archelaus, in consideration of his rights of
seniority and the terms of the codicil. At Rome, all the
relations, who detested Archelaus, transferred their support to him [i.e., Antipas]; the object that was upper-
most in the minds of every one of these was autonomy
under the administration of a Roman governor, but in
default of that they preferred to have Antipas for king.

4. They were aided in this design by Sabinus, who,
in dispatches to Cæsar, accused Archelaus and highly
commended Antipas. Salome and her friends now drew
up their indictment and placed it in Cæsar's hands;
Archelaus responded by drafting a summary statement
of his rights and sending in his father's ring and papers
by Ptolemy to the emperor. Cæsar, after reflecting in
private on the allegations of both parties, the extent of
the kingdom, the amount of the revenue, as well as the
number of Herod's children, and after perusing the letters on the subject which he had received from Varus
and Sabinus, summoned a council of leading Romans,
at which for the first time he gave a seat to Caius, the

son of Agrippa and his daughter Julia, whom he had
adopted himself; he then called upon the parties to
speak.

5. Thereupon Antipater, son of Salome, the ablest
orator among the opponents of Archelaus, rose as his
accuser. Archelaus, he stated, although at the moment
ostensibly suing for a crown, had in reality long since
acted as king. He was now merely playing upon the pa-
tient ears of Cæsar, whose sentence upon the subject of
the succession he had not awaited. For, after Herod's
death, had he not suborned persons to place the diadem
on his head, sat in state upon the throne and given
audience as a king, made changes in the ranks of the
army and conferred promotions, assented to all the
favors which the people had claimed from him as
sovereign, and liberated those whom his father had imprisoned for the gravest crimes? And after all this, he
had now come to beg from his lord for the shadow of
royalty, of which he had already appropriated the substance, thus making Cæsar a dispenser not of realities,
but of mere titles! A further charge which Antipater
brought against Archelaus was that even in his mourning for his father he had played the hypocrite, in the
day-time assuming a pose of grief, at night drinking to
riotous excess. In this connection, he added that the
recent outbreak of the populace was attributable to their
indignation at such conduct.

Proceeding to the main contention of his speech, he
laid great stress on the multitude of Jews who had been
massacred around the sanctuary, poor people who had
come for a festival, and while offering their sacrifices,
had themselves been brutally immolated. There had been,
he said, such a pile of corpses in the Temple as would
never have been raised even by the ruthless inroad of a
foreign foe. It was, indeed, because he foresaw this
ferocity of Archelaus that his father had never deigned
to hold out to him even a hope of ascending the throne,
until the day when, more stricken in mind than in body,
and incapable of sound reasoning, he did not even know
whose name he was inscribing in the codicil as that of
his successor; when, moreover, he had no fault to find

with the heir named in the will which he had drafted while he possessed health of body and a mind quite unclouded by affliction. But, he continued, even if greater weight were attached by any to the decision of an invalid, Archelaus had pronounced his own deposition from the kingdom by his outrages upon it. What would he become, once invested with authority by Cæsar, who before receiving it had massacred such multitudes!

6. After dilating at length in this strain, and producing most of the relatives as witnesses to each item in his accusation, Antipater concluded his speech. Nicolaus then rose in defence of Archelaus. He maintained that the slaughter in the Temple had been rendered necessary, because the victims had shown themselves enemies not only of the kingdom, but also of Cæsar, the arbiter of the kingdom. As for the other charges made against Archelaus, he showed that his accusers themselves had advised him to act as he did. The validity of the codicil, he claimed, was proved by this fact above all, that in it Cæsar was constituted surety for the succession; one who was sane enough to cede his authority to the master of the world was surely not mistaken in his selection of an heir. The sagacity shown in his choice of the donor was a guarantee of his sanity in the choice of the recipient.

7. Nicolaus on his side having fully stated his case, Archelaus came forward and fell, in silence, at the knees of Cæsar. The emperor very graciously raised him up, intimating that he thought him worthy to succeed his father, but pronouncing no final decision. After dismissing his council, he passed the day in reflection on what he had heard, considering whether he ought to appoint as successor one of those named in the wills or to divide the dominion among all the children; for the numerous members of this family all seemed in need of support.

iii. 1. But before Cæsar had come to any decision on these matters, Malthace, the mother of Archelaus, was taken ill and died, and dispatches arrived from Varus in Syria concerning the revolt of the Jews. This outbreak had been foreseen by Varus, who, after the sailing of Archelaus, had gone up to Jerusalem to repress its promoters, and as it was evident that the people would not remain quiet, had left in the city one of the three legions from Syria which he had brought with him; he himself then returned to Antioch. It was the arrival of Sabinus which gave the Jews an occasion for insurrection. For this officer endeavored to force the guardians of the citadels to hand them over to him and instituted an exacting search for the royal treasures, relying for this task not only on the soldiers left by Varus, but on a crowd of his own slaves, all of whom he armed and employed as instruments of his avarice. So, on the arrival of Pentecost—thus the Jews call a feast which occurs seven weeks after [Passover] and takes its name from the number of intervening days—it was not the customary ritual so much as indignation which drew the people in crowds to the capital. A countless multitude flocked in from Galilee, from Idumæa, from Jericho, and from Peræa beyond the Jordan; but it was the native population of Judæa itself which, both in numbers and ardor, was pre-eminent. Distributing themselves into three divisions, they formed three camps, one on the north of the Temple, another on the south, adjoining the hippodrome, and the third near the palace, on the west. Thus investing the Romans on all sides, they held them under siege.

2. Sabinus, terrified at their numbers and determination, dispatched messenger after messenger to Varus, begging for his prompt support and assuring him that, if he delayed, the legion would be cut to pieces. He himself mounted to the highest tower in the fortress—called Phasael, after Herod's brother, who was slain by the Parthians—and thence signalled to the legionaries to attack the enemy, for he was in such a panic that he had not even the courage to descend to his own men. The soldiers, obedient to this poltroon, leaped into the Temple and engaged in a stubborn contest with the Jews. So long as they remained unassailed from above, their military experience gave them the advantage over the novices opposed to them; but when a large body of Jews mounted the porticoes and poured their missiles

down upon their heads, many fell, and the Romans found it no easy task either to defend themselves against those attacking them from above or to hold their ground against their other opponents in hand-to-hand fight.

3. Harassed by these two foes, the legionaries set fire to the porticoes, which for massive grandeur and magnificence were wonderful works of art. Of the Jews who occupied them, many, suddenly enveloped, perished in the flames; many leaped down among their enemies and were slain by them; some flung themselves over the precipitous wall in their rear; others, in despair, threw themselves on their own swords to avoid becoming victims of the flames; while any who successfully crept down from the wall and dashed at the Romans fell an easy prey, owing to their dazed condition. Then, their enemies either slain or dispersed in panic, the soldiers fell upon God's treasury, now reft of defenders, and plundered it to the amount of some four hundred talents; of this sum all that was not stolen by them was collected by Sabinus.

4. However, the effect of this loss of buildings and of lives was only to rally the Jews in far greater strength and efficiency against the Romans. Surrounding the palace, they threatened to kill them to a man unless they promptly withdrew; if Sabinus were prepared to retire with his legion, they guaranteed him a safe conduct. The rebels now had with them the bulk of the royal troops which had deserted to their side. The most efficient division of those troops, however, still adhered to the Romans, namely, three thousand Sebastenians under Rufus and Gratus, the latter commanding the royal infantry, the former the cavalry—a pair, either of whom, even without any force under him, was worth an army, owing to their bravery and acumen. So the Jews pressed the siege, making assaults on the fortress, while at the same time they loudly called on Sabinus and his followers to depart and not to stand in the way of men who after such a lapse of time were on the road to recovering their national independence. Sabinus would have been quite content to slink away, but he mistrusted their promises and suspected that their mildness was

a bait to ensnare him; he was, moreover, hoping for succor from Varus and so let the siege drag on.

iv. 1. Meanwhile, the country also, in various districts, was a prey to disorder, and the opportunity induced numbers of persons to aspire to sovereignty. In Idumæa, two thousand of Herod's veterans formed up in arms and took the field against the royal troops. They were opposed by Achiab, the king's cousin, who, avoiding an engagement in the plain, fell back on the strongest positions. At Sepphoris in Galilee, Judas, son of Ezechias, the brigand-chief who in former days infested the country and was subdued by King Herod, raised a considerable body of followers, broke open the royal arsenals, and, having armed his companions, attacked the other aspirants to power.

2. In Peræa, Simon, one of the royal slaves, proud of his tall and handsome figure, assumed the diadem. Perambulating the country with the brigands whom he had collected, he burned down the royal palace at Jericho and many other stately mansions, such incendiarism providing him with an easy opportunity for plunder. Not a house of any respectability would have escaped the flames had not Gratus, the commander of the royal infantry, with the archers of Trachonitis and the finest troops of the Sebastenians, gone out to encounter this rascal. In the ensuing engagement numbers of the Peræans fell. Simon himself, endeavoring to escape up a steep ravine, was intercepted by Gratus, who struck the fugitive from the side a blow on the neck, which severed his head from his body. The palace at Betharamatha, near the Jordan, was likewise burned to the ground by another body of Peræan insurgents.

3. Now, too, a mere shepherd had the temerity to aspire to the throne. He was called Athrongæus, and his sole recommendations to raise such hopes were vigor of body, a soul contemptuous of death, and four brothers resembling himself. To each of these he entrusted an armed band and employed them as generals and satraps for his raids, while he himself, like a king, handled matters of graver moment. It was now that he donned the diadem, but his raiding expeditions throughout the coun-

try with his brothers continued long afterwards. Their principal object was to kill Romans and royalists, but no Jew from whom they had anything to gain escaped if he fell into their hands. On one occasion, they ventured to surround, near Emmaus, an entire Roman company engaged in convoying corn and arms to the legion. Their centurion, Arius, and forty of his bravest men were shot down by the brigands; the remainder, in danger of a like fate, were rescued through the intervention of Gratus with his Sebastenians. After perpetrating throughout the war many such outrages upon compatriot and foreigner alike, three of them [the brothers] were eventually captured, the eldest by Archelaus, the two next by Gratus and Ptolemy; the fourth made terms with Archelaus and surrendered. Such was the end to which they ultimately came; but at the period of which we are speaking, these men were making the whole of Judæa one scene of guerrilla warfare.

v. 1. On receiving the dispatches from Sabinus and his officers, Varus was alarmed for the whole legion and resolved to hasten to its relief. Accordingly, mobilizing the two remaining legions with the four regiments of horse which were attached to them, he marched for Ptolemais, having ordered the auxiliary troops furnished by the kings and chieftains to assemble at that place. On his way through Berytus, his army was further increased by 1500 armed recruits from that city. When the other contingent of allies had joined him at Ptolemais, as well as Aretas the Arab, who, in memory of his hatred of Herod, brought a considerable body of cavalry and infantry, Varus at once sent a detachment of his army into the region of Galilee adjoining Ptolemais, under the command of his friend Gaius; the latter routed all who opposed him, captured and burned the city of Sepphoris and reduced its inhabitants to slavery. Varus himself with the main body pursued his march into the country of Samaria; he spared the city, finding that it had taken no part in the general tumult, and encamped near a village called Arous. This belonged to Ptolemy, and for that reason was sacked by the Arabs, who were infuriated even against the friends of Herod.

Thence he advanced to Sappho, another fortified village, which they likewise sacked, as well as all the neighboring villages that they encountered on their march. The whole district became a scene of fire and blood, and nothing was safe against the ravages of the Arabs. Emmaus, the inhabitants of which had fled, was burned to the ground by the orders of Varus, in revenge for the slaughter of Arius and his men.

2. Proceeding thence to Jerusalem, he had only to show himself at the head of his troops to disperse the Jewish camps. Their occupants fled up country; but the Jews in the city received him and disclaimed all responsibility for the revolt, asserting that they themselves had never stirred, that the festival had compelled them to admit the crowd, and that they had been rather besieged with the Romans than in league with the rebels. Prior to this, Varus had been met outside the city by Joseph, the cousin of Archelaus, with Rufus and Gratus, at the head of the royal army and the Sebastenians, and by the Roman legionaries in their customary equipment; for Sabinus, not venturing to face Varus, had previously left the city for the coast. Varus now detached part of his army to scour the country in search of the authors of the insurrection, many of whom were brought in. Those who appeared to be the less turbulent individuals he imprisoned; the most culpable, in number about two thousand, he crucified.

3. He was informed that in Idumæa ten thousand still held together in arms. Finding that the Arabs were not properly conducting themselves as allies, but were rather making war to gratify their private resentment, and from hatred of Herod, were doing more injury to the country than he had intended, he dismissed them, and with his own legions marched in haste to meet the rebels. They, before any action took place, on the advice of Achiab, surrendered; Varus discharged the rank and file and sent the leaders to Cæsar for trial. Cæsar pardoned all with the exception of certain individuals of royal blood, for their number included some relatives of Herod; these he ordered to be punished for taking up arms against a sovereign who was of their own family.

Having thus restored order in Jerusalem, Varus left as garrison the legion previously quartered there and returned to Antioch.

vi. 1. Meanwhile, Archelaus in Rome had to defend himself in a new suit against certain Jewish deputies, who, before the revolt, had set out with the permission of Varus to plead for the autonomy of their nation. Fifty deputies appeared, but more than eight thousand of the Jews in Rome espoused their cause. Cæsar assembled a council, composed of the Roman magistrates and his friends, in the temple of the Palatine Apollo, a building erected by himself with astonishingly rich ornamentation. The Jewish crowd took up a position with the deputies; opposite them was Archelaus with his friends; the friends of his relatives appeared neither on the one side nor on the other, scorning through hatred and envy to join Archelaus, yet ashamed to let Cæsar see them among his accusers. Another person present was Philip, brother of Archelaus, whom Varus, out of friendliness, had sent off under escort with two objects: primarily to support Archelaus, but also to come in for a share of Herod's estate in case Cæsar should distribute it among all his descendants.

2. The plaintiffs, being given permission to state their case, began by enumerating Herod's enormities. It was not a king, they said, whom they had had to tolerate, but the most cruel tyrant that ever existed. Numerous had been his victims, but the survivors had suffered so much that they envied the fate of the dead. For he had tortured not only the persons of his subjects, but also their cities; and while he crippled the towns in his own dominion, he embellished those of other nations, lavishing the life-blood of Judæa on foreign communities. In place of their ancient prosperity and ancestral laws, he had sunk the nation to poverty and the last degree of iniquity. In short, the miseries which Herod in the course of a few years had inflicted on the Jews surpassed all that their forefathers had suffered during all the time since they left Babylon to return to their country in the reign of Xerxes.

And yet so chastened and habituated to misfortune

had they become [they said], that they had consented to this bitter servitude being made hereditary and had actually chosen the heir themselves! This Archelaus, son of such a tyrant, they had, on his father's decease, promptly acclaimed king; they had joined in his mourning for Herod's death, in his prayers for the prosperity of his own reign. But he, anxious apparently not to be taken for a bastard son of Herod, had ushered in his reign with the massacre of three thousand citizens; that was the grand total of the victims which he had offered to God on behalf of his throne, that was the number of corpses with which he had filled the Temple at a festival! It was, however, but natural that those who had survived such disasters should now at length turn and confront their calamities and desire to face their blows, in accordance with the laws of war. They implored the Romans to take pity on the relics of Judæa and not to fling what remained of it to those who were savagely rending it in pieces, but to unite their country to Syria and to entrust the administration to governors from among themselves. The Jews would then show that, calumniated though they now were as factious and always at war, they knew how to obey equitable rulers. With this petition the Jews brought their accusation to a close. Nicolaus then rose, and after refuting the charges brought against the occupants of the throne, retorted by an accusation of the national character, impatient of all authority and insubordinate towards their sovereigns. The relatives of Archelaus who had gone over to his accusers also came in for a share of his strictures.

3. Cæsar, after hearing both parties, dismissed the assembly. His decision was announced a few days later: he gave half the kingdom to Archelaus, with the title of ethnarch, promising, moreover, to make him king, should he prove his deserts; the other half he divided into two tetrarchies, which he presented to two other sons of Herod, one to Philip, the other to Antipas, who had disputed the throne with Archelaus. Antipas had for his province Peræa and Galilee, with a revenue of two hundred talents. Batanæa, Trachonitis, Auranitis and

certain portions of the domain of Zeno in the neighborhood of Panias, producing a revenue of a hundred talents, were allotted to Philip. The ethnarchy of Archelaus
comprised the whole of Idumæa and Judæa, besides the
district of Samaria, which had a quarter of its tribute
remitted in consideration of its having taken no part in
the insurrection. The cities subjected to Archelaus were
Strato's Tower [Cæsarea], Sebaste, Joppa and Jerusalem;
the Greek towns of Gaza, Gadara, and Hippos were, on
the other hand, detached from his principality and annexed to Syria. The territory given to Archelaus produced a revenue of four hundred talents.

Salome, besides the legacy which the king had left
her in his will, was declared mistress of Jamnia, Azotus
and Phasaelis; Cæsar also made her a present of the
palace of Ascalon, her revenue from all sources amounting to sixty talents; her estates, however, were placed
under the jurisdiction of Archelaus. Each of the other
members of Herod's family received the legacy named
in the will. To the king's two unmarried daughters
Cæsar presented, in addition, 500,000 [drachmas] of silver and gave them in marriage to the sons of Pheroras.
After this division of the estate, he further distributed
among the family Herod's legacy to himself, amounting
to a thousand talents, reserving only some trifling works
of art which he kept in honor of the deceased.

vii. 1. At this time a young man, who, though by
birth a Jew, had been brought up at Sidon at the house
of a Roman freedman, on the strength of a certain
physical resemblance passed himself off as the prince
Alexander, whom Herod had put to death, and came to
Rome in the hope of imposing upon others. He had as
his assistant a compatriot, perfectly acquainted with
the affairs of the realm, acting upon whose instructions
he gave out that the executioners sent to kill him and
Aristobulus had, out of compassion, stolen them away,
substituting in their stead the corpses of individuals
who resembled them. With this tale he completely deceived the Jews of Crete, and being handsomely furnished with supplies, sailed across to Melos, where,
through the extreme plausibility of his story, he col-

lected a much larger sum and even induced his hosts to embark with him for Rome. Landing at Puteoli, he was loaded with presents by the Jewish colony there and was escorted on his way like a king by the friends of his supposed father. The resemblance was so convincing that those who had seen Alexander and known him well swore that this was he. At Rome all Jewry poured forth to see him, and vast crowds thronged the narrow streets through which he was borne; for the crazy Melians went so far as to carry him in a litter and to provide a royal retinue at their own expense.

2. Cæsar, who had an exact recollection of Alexander's features, as he had been arraigned by Herod at his tribunal, divined, even before he had seen the fellow, that the affair was an imposture, based on resemblance; however, to give a chance to a more favorable hope, he sent Celadus, one of those who knew Alexander best, with orders to bring the young man to him. Celadus had no sooner set eyes on him than he detected the points of difference in the face, and noting that his whole person had a coarser and servile appearance, penetrated the whole plot. The audacity of the fellow's statements quite exasperated him. For, when questioned about Aristobulus, he was in the habit of replying that he, too, was alive, but had been purposely left behind in Cyprus as a precaution against treachery, as they were less exposed to assault when separated.

Celadus, therefore, took him aside and said, "Cæsar will reward you by sparing your life, if you will inform him who induced you to play such a trick." Promising Celadus to give the required information, he accompanied him to Cæsar and denounced the Jew who had thus traded upon his resemblance to Alexander; for, as he said, he had in every town received more presents than Alexander ever received in his lifetime. Cæsar laughed at these words and enrolled the pseudo-Alexander, as an able-bodied man, among the oarsmen of his galleys; his inspiring genius he ordered to execution. As for the Melians he considered them sufficiently punished for their folly by their lavish extravagance.

3. Archelaus, on taking possession of his ethnarchy,

did not forget old feuds, but treated not only the Jews but even the Samaritans with great brutality. Both parties sent deputies to Cæsar to denounce him, and in the ninth year of his rule [A.D. 6] he was banished to Vienne, a town in Gaul, and his property was confiscated to the imperial treasury. It is said that before he received his summons from Cæsar he had this dream: he thought he saw nine tall and full-grown ears of corn on which oxen were browsing. He sent for the soothsayers and some Chaldæans and asked them their opinion of its meaning. Various interpretations being given, a certain Simon, of the sect of the Essenes, said that in his view the ears of corn denoted years and the oxen a revolution, because in ploughing they turn over the soil; he would therefore reign for as many years as there were ears of corn and would die after a checkered experience of revolutionary changes. Five days later Archelaus was summoned to his trial.

4. I think mention may also fitly be made of the dream of his wife Glaphyra. Daughter of Archelaus, king of Cappadocia, she had for her first husband Alexander, the brother of Archelaus, of whom we have been speaking, and son of King Herod, who put him to death, as we have already related. After his death she married Juba, king of Libya, on whose decease* she returned home and lived in widowhood with her father. There Archelaus, the ethnarch, saw her and fell so passionately in love with her that he instantly divorced his wife Mariamme and married her. So she came back to Judæa, where, not long after her arrival, she imagined that Alexander stood beside her and said: "Your Libyan marriage might have sufficed you, but not content with that, you now return to my hearth and home, having taken to yourself a third husband, and him, audacious woman, my own brother.† But I will not brook this outrage and shall reclaim you whether you will or no." After relating this dream she survived barely two days.

---

* This is wrong: Juba II is known to have been alive as late as A.D. 23.

† Marriage with a brother's widow (unless she was childless) was forbidden: *Leviticus* 18. 16; 20. 21.

viii. 1. The territory of Archelaus was now reduced to a province, and Coponius, a Roman of the equestrian order, was sent out as procurator, entrusted by Augustus with full powers, including the infliction of capital punishment. Under his administration, a Galilæan named Judas incited his countrymen to revolt, upbraiding them as cowards for consenting to pay tribute to the Romans and tolerating mortal masters, after having God for their lord. This man was a sophist who founded a sect of his own [the Zealots], having nothing in common with the others.

The Jewish Sects

2. Jewish philosophy, in fact, takes three forms. The followers of the first school are called Pharisees, of the second Sadducees, of the third Essenes.

The Essenes have a reputation for cultivating peculiar sanctity. Of Jewish birth, they show a greater attachment to each other than do the other sects. They shun pleasures as a vice and regard temperance and the control of the passions as a special virtue. Marriage they disdain, but they adopt other men's children, while yet pliable and docile, and regard them as their kin and mold them in accordance with their own principles. They do not, indeed, on principle condemn wedlock and the propagation thereby of the race, but they wish to protect themselves against women's wantonness, being persuaded that none of the sex keeps her plighted troth to one man.

3. Riches they despise, and their community of goods is truly admirable; you will not find one among them distinguished by greater opulence than another. They have a law that new members on admission to the sect shall contribute their property to the order, with the result that you will nowhere see either abject poverty or inordinate wealth; the individual's possessions join the common stock, and all, like brothers, enjoy a single patrimony. Oil they consider defiling, and anyone who accidentally comes in contact with it scours his person, for they make a point of keeping a dry skin and of al-

ways being dressed in white. They elect officers to attend to the interests of the community, the special services of each officer being determined by the whole body.

4. They occupy no one city, but settle in large numbers in every town. On the arrival of any of the sect from elsewhere, all the resources of the community are put at their disposal, just as if they were their own, and they enter the houses of men whom they have never seen before as though they were their most intimate friends. Consequently, they carry nothing whatever with them on their journeys, except arms as a protection against brigands. In every city there is one of the order expressly appointed to attend to strangers, who provides them with raiment and other necessaries. In their dress and deportment they resemble children under rigorous discipline. They do not change their garments or shoes until they are torn to shreds or worn threadbare with age. There is no buying or selling among them, but each gives what he has to any in need and receives from him in exchange something useful to himself; they are, moreover, freely permitted to take anything from any of their brothers without making any return.

5. Their piety towards the Deity takes a peculiar form. Before the sun is up they utter no word on mundane matters, but offer to him certain prayers, which have been handed down from their forefathers, as though entreating him to rise. They are then dismissed by their superiors to the various crafts in which they are severally proficient and are strenuously employed, until the fifth hour, when they again assemble in one place, and after girding their loins with linen cloths, bathe their bodies in cold water.

After this purification, they assemble in a private apartment, which none of the uninitiated is permitted to enter; pure now themselves, they repair to the refectory, as to some sacred shrine. When they have taken their seats in silence, the baker serves out the loaves to them in order, and the cook sets before each one plate with a single course. Before meat the priest says a grace, and none may partake until after the prayer.

When breakfast is ended, he pronounces a further grace; thus at the beginning and at the close they do homage to God as the bountiful giver of life. Then laying aside their raiment, as holy vestments, they again betake themselves to their labors until the evening. On their return they sup in like manner, and any guests who may have arrived sit down with them.

No clamor or disturbance ever pollutes their dwelling; they speak in turn, each making way for his neighbor. To persons outside, the silence of those within appears like some awful mystery; it is in fact due to their invariable sobriety and to the limitation of their allotted portions of meat and drink to the demands of nature.

6. In all other matters they do nothing without orders from their superiors; two things only are left to individual discretion, the rendering of assistance and compassion. Members may of their own motion help the deserving, when in need, and supply food to the destitute; but presents to relatives are prohibited, without leave from the managers. Holding righteous indignation in reserve, they are masters of their temper, champions of fidelity, very ministers of peace. Any word of theirs has more force than an oath; swearing they avoid, regarding it as worse than perjury, for they say that one who is not believed without an appeal to God stands condemned already. They display an extraordinary interest in the writings of the ancients, singling out in particular those which make for the welfare of soul and body; with the help of these, and with a view to the treatment of diseases, they make investigations into medicinal roots and the properties of stones.

7. A candidate anxious to join their sect is not immediately admitted. For one year, during which he remains outside the fraternity, they prescribe for him their own rule of life, presenting him with a small hatchet, the loin-cloth already mentioned, and white raiment. Having given proof of his temperance during the probationary period, he is brought into closer touch with the rule and is allowed to share the purer kind of holy water, but is not yet received into the meetings of the

community. For after this exhibition of endurance, his character is tested for two years more, and only then, if found worthy, is he enrolled in the society. But before he may touch the common food, he is made to swear tremendous oaths: first that he will practice piety towards the Deity, next that he will observe justice towards men: that he will wrong none whether of his own mind or under another's orders; that he will forever hate the unjust and fight the battle of the just; that he will forever keep faith with all men, especially with the powers that be, since no ruler attains his office save by the will of God; that, should he himself bear rule, he will never abuse his authority nor, either in dress or by other outward marks of superiority, outshine his subjects. [He swears] to be forever a lover of truth and to expose liars; to keep his hands from stealing and his soul pure from unholy gain; to conceal nothing from the members of the sect and to report none of their secrets to others, even though tortured to death. He swears, moreover, to transmit their rules exactly as he himself received them; to abstain from robbery; and in like manner to carefully preserve the books of the sect and the names of the angels. Such are the oaths by which they bind their proselytes.

8. Those who are convicted of serious crimes they expel from the order, and the ejected individual often comes to a most miserable end. For, being bound by their oaths and usages, he is not at liberty to partake of other men's food, and so falls to eating grass and wastes away and dies of starvation. This has led them in compassion to receive many back in the last stage of exhaustion, deeming that torments which have brought them to the verge of death are a sufficient penalty for their misdoings.

9. They are just and scrupulously careful in their trial of cases, never passing sentence in a court of less than a hundred members; the decision thus reached is irrevocable. After God they hold most in awe the name of the lawgiver [Moses], any blasphemer of whom is punished with death. It is a point of honor with them to obey their elders, and a majority. For instance, if ten

sit together, one will not speak if the nine desire silence. They are careful not to spit into the midst of the company or to the right, and are stricter than all Jews in abstaining from work on the seventh day; for not only do they prepare their food on the day before, to avoid kindling a fire on that one, but they do not venture to remove any vessel or even to go to stool. On other days they dig a trench a foot deep with a mattock—such is the nature of the hatchet which they present to the neophytes—and wrapping their mantle about them, that they may not offend the rays of the Deity, sit above it. They then replace the excavated soil in the trench. For this purpose they select the more retired spots,* and though this discharge of the excrements is a natural function, they make it a rule to wash themselves after it, as if defiled.

10. They are divided, according to the duration of their discipline, into four grades, and so far are the junior members inferior to the seniors, that a senior if but touched by a junior, must take a bath, as after contact with an alien. They live to a great age—most of them to upwards of a century—in consequence, I imagine, of the simplicity and regularity of their mode of life. They make light of danger and triumph over pain by their resolute will; death, if it come with honor, they consider better than immortality. The war with the Romans tried their souls through and through by every variety of test. Racked and twisted, burned and broken, and made to pass through every instrument of torture, in order to induce them to blaspheme the lawgiver or to eat some forbidden thing, they refused to yield to either demand, nor ever once did they cringe to their persecutors or shed a tear. Smiling in their agonies and mildly deriding their tormentors, they cheerfully resigned their souls, confident that they would receive them back again.

11. For it is a fixed belief of theirs that the body is corruptible and its constituent matter impermanent, but that the soul is immortal and imperishable. Ema-

---

* See *Deuteronomy* 23. 12-14.

nating from the finest ether, these souls become en-
tangled, as it were, in the prison-house of the body, to
which they are dragged down by a sort of natural spell;
but when once they are released from the bonds of the
flesh, then, as though liberated from a long servitude,
they rejoice and are borne aloft. Sharing the belief of
the sons of Greece, they maintain that for virtuous souls
there is reserved an abode beyond the ocean, a place
which is not oppressed by rain or snow or heat, but is
refreshed by the ever gentle breath of the west wind
coming in from ocean; while they relegate base souls
to a murky and tempestuous dungeon, big with never-
ending punishments.

The Greeks, I imagine, had the same conception when
they set apart the Isles of the Blessed for their brave
men, whom they call heroes and demigods, and the region of the impious for the souls of the wicked down
in Hades, where, as their mythologists tell, persons such
as Sisyphus, Tantalus, Ixion, and Tityus are undergoing punishment. Their aim was first to establish the
doctrine of the immortality of the soul, and secondly to
promote virtue and to deter from vice; for the good are
made better in their lifetime by the hope of a reward
after death, and the passions of the wicked are restrained
by the fear that, even though they escape detection while
alive, they will undergo never-ending punishment after
their decease. Such are the theological views of the
Essenes concerning the soul, whereby they irresistibly
attract all who have once tasted their philosophy.

12. There are some among them who profess to fore-
tell the future, being versed from their early years in
holy books, various forms of purification and apo-
thegms of prophets; and seldom, if ever, do they err in
their predictions.

13. There is yet another order of Essenes, which,
while at one with the rest in its mode of life, customs,
and regulations, differs from them in its views on marriage. They think that those who decline to marry cut
off the chief function of life, the propagation of the
race, and what is more, that were all to adopt the same
view, the whole race would very quickly die out. They

give their wives, however, a three years' probation, and only marry them after they have by three periods of purification* given proof of fecundity. They have no intercourse with them during pregnancy, thus showing their motive in marrying is not pleasure but the procreation of children. In the bath the women wear a dress, the men a loin-cloth. Such are the usages of this order.

14. Of the two first-named schools, the Pharisees, who are considered the most accurate interpreters of the laws, and hold the position of the leading sect, attribute everything to Fate and to God; they hold that to act rightly or otherwise rests, indeed, for the most part with men, but that in each action Fate co-operates. Every soul, they maintain, is imperishable, but the soul of the good alone passes into another body, while the souls of the wicked suffer eternal punishment.

The Sadducees, the second of the orders, do away with Fate altogether, and remove God beyond, not merely the commission, but the very sight, of evil. They maintain that man has the free choice of good or evil, and that it rests with each man's will whether he follows the one or the other. As for the persistence of the soul after death, penalties in the underworld, and rewards, they will have none of them.

The Pharisees are affectionate to each other and cultivate harmonious relations with the community. The Sadducees, on the contrary, are, even among themselves, rather boorish in their behavior, and in their intercourse with their peers are as rude as to aliens. Such is what I have to say on the Jewish philosophical schools.

Judæa under the Emperor Tiberius

ix. 1. When the ethnarchy of Archelaus was converted into a province, the other princes, Philip and Herod (surnamed Antipas), continued to govern their respective tetrarchies. As for Salome, she at her death [sometime between A.D. 9 and 12] bequeathed her top-

---

* Translator's note: the text can hardly be right.

archy to Julia, the wife of Augustus, together with Jamnia and the palm-groves of Phasaelis.

On the death of Augustus [in A.D. 14], who had directed the state for fifty-seven years, six months and two days, the empire of the Romans passed to Tiberius, son of Julia [by her former husband]. On his accession, Herod [Antipas] and Philip continued to hold their tetrarchies and respectively founded cities: Philip built Cæsarea near the sources of the Jordan, in the district of Paneas, and Julias in lower Gaulanitis; Herod built Tiberias in Galilee and a city which also took the name of Julia, in Peræa.

2. Pilate, being sent by Tiberius as procurator to Judæa [in A.D. 26], introduced into Jerusalem, by night and under cover, the effigies of Cæsar which are called standards. This proceeding, when day broke, aroused immense excitement among the Jews; those on the spot were in consternation, considering their laws to have been trampled under foot, as those laws permit no image to be erected in the city; while the indignation of the townspeople stirred the country-folk, who flocked together in crowds. Hastening after Pilate to Cæsarea, the Jews implored him to remove the standards from Jerusalem and to uphold the laws of their ancestors. When Pilate refused, they fell prostrate around his house and for five whole days and nights remained motionless in that position.

3. On the ensuing day Pilate took his seat on his tribunal in the great stadium, and summoning the multitude, with the apparent intention of answering them, gave the arranged signal to his armed soldiers to surround the Jews. Finding themselves in a ring of troops, three deep, the Jews were struck dumb at this unexpected sight. Pilate, after threatening to cut them down, if they refused to admit Cæsar's images, signaled to the soldiers to draw their swords. Thereupon the Jews, as by concerted action, flung themselves in a body on the ground, extended their necks, and exclaimed that they were ready rather to die than to transgress the law. Overcome with astonishment at such intense religious

zeal, Pilate gave orders for the immediate removal of the standards from Jerusalem.

4. On a later occasion, he provoked a fresh uproar by expending upon the construction of an aqueduct the sacred treasure known as *Corbonas;* the water was brought from a distance of 400 furlongs. Indignant at this proceeding, the populace formed a ring round the tribunal of Pilate, then on a visit to Jerusalem, and besieged him with angry clamor. He, foreseeing the tumult, had interspersed among the crowd a troop of his soldiers, armed but disguised in civilian dress, with orders not to use their swords, but to beat any rioters with cudgels. He now from his tribunal gave the agreed signal. Large numbers of the Jews perished, some from the blows which they received, others trodden to death by their companions in the ensuing flight. Cowed by the fate of the victims, the multitude was reduced to silence.

5. At this time Agrippa, son of the Aristobulus who was put to death by his father Herod, came to Tiberius to accuse Herod [Antipas] the tetrarch. The emperor having declined to countenance the charge, Agrippa remained in Rome, paying court to various notabilities and in particular to Gaius, son of Germanicus, who was still a private citizen. On one occasion when he was entertaining him at dinner, Agrippa, after paying him all kinds of compliments, finally raised his hands to heaven and openly prayed that he might soon see Gaius master of the world, through the decease of Tiberius. This was reported by one of Agrippa's domestics to Tiberius; whereupon the emperor, in indignation, threw Agrippa into prison, where he kept him under rigorous treatment for six months until his own death [in A.D. 37], which closed a reign of twenty-two years, six months and three days. . . .

Josephus in Galilee (A.D. 66)

In the year 66, in the reign of Nero, a revolt began in Jerusalem, stirred up primarily by the Zealots, and it soon took on the scale of a na-

tional effort (with serious repercussions in the large Jewish communities in Syria and North Africa as well). A Zealot, Eleazar son of Simon, eventually obtained supreme command.

xx. 4. Other generals were selected for Idumæa, namely, Jesus son of Sapphas, one of the chief priests, and Eleazar, son of the high priest Neus; and the existing governor of Idumæa, Niger, called the Peræan because he was a native of Peræa beyond Jordan, received instructions to act under the orders of these officers. Nor were the other districts neglected; Joseph, son of Simon, was sent to take command at Jericho, Manasseh to Peræa, John the Essene to the province of Thamna, with Lydda, Joppa and Emmaus also under his charge. John, son of Ananias, was appointed commanding officer of the provinces of Gophna and Acrabetta; Josephus, son of Matthias, was given the two Galilees, with the addition of Gamala, the strongest city in that region.*

5. Each of these generals executed his commission to the best of his zeal or ability. As for Josephus, on his arrival in Galilee, he made it his first care to win the affection of the inhabitants, knowing that this would be of the greatest advantage to him, however he might otherwise fail. He realized that he would conciliate the leaders by associating them with him in his authority, and the people at large, if his orders were in the main given through the medium of their local acquaintances. He therefore selected from the nation seventy persons of mature years and the greatest discretion and appointed them magistrates of the whole of Galilee, and seven individuals in each city to adjudicate upon petty disputes, with instructions to refer more important matters and capital cases to himself and the seventy.

6. Having established these principles for the internal regulation of the various towns, he proceeded to take measures for their security from external attack.

---

* In ch. 7 of the *Life*, however, Josephus says he was sent by "the leading men in Jerusalem . . . to induce the disaffected to lay down their arms and to impress upon them the desirability of reserving these for the picked men of the nation."

Foreseeing that Galilee would bear the brunt of the Romans' opening assault, he fortified the most suitable places, namely, Jotapata, Bersabe, Selame, Caphareccho, Japha, Sigoph, the mount called Itabyrion, Tarichææ, and Tiberias. He further provided with walls the caves in Lower Galilee in the neighborhood of the lake of Gennesareth, and in Upper Galilee the rock known as Acchabaron, Seph, Jamnith, and Mero. In Gaulanitis he fortified Seleucia, Soganæa and Gamala. The inhabitants of Sepphoris alone were authorized by him to erect walls on their own account, because he saw that they were in affluent circumstances, and even without orders, eager for hostilities.* Similarly, John, son of Levi, fortified Gischala at his own expense, on the instruction of Josephus. The other fortresses were all built under the personal superintendence of Josephus, who both assisted in and directed the operations. Moreover, he levied in Galilee an army of upwards of a hundred thousand young men, all of whom he equipped with old arms collected for the purpose.

7. Another task remained. He understood that the Romans owed their invincible strength above all to discipline and military training. If he despaired of providing similar instruction, to be acquired only by long use, he observed that their discipline was due to the number of their officers, and he therefore divided his army on Roman lines and increased the number of his company commanders. He instituted various ranks of soldiers and set over them decurions and centurions, above whom were tribunes, and over these generals in command of more extensive divisions. He taught them the transmission of signals, the trumpet calls for the charge and the retreat, attacks by the wings and enveloping maneuvers, how relief should be sent by the victorious portion to those who were hard pressed and aid extended to any in distress. He expounded all that conduces to fortitude of soul or bodily endurance; but above all he trained them for war by continually dwelling upon

---

* In the *Life*, on the contrary, Sepphoris is described as consistently pro-Roman.

the good order maintained by the Romans and telling them that they would have to fight against men who by their vigor and intrepidity had become masters of well-nigh the whole world. He told them that he should test their military discipline, even before they went into action, by noting whether they abstained from their habitual malpractices—theft, robbery, and rapine—and ceased to defraud their countrymen and to regard as personal profit an injury sustained by their most intimate friends. For, he added, the armies that are most successful in war are those in which every combatant has a clear conscience; whereas those who were depraved at heart would have to contend not only with their adversaries but also with God.

8. Such was the tenor of his unceasing exhortations. He had now mustered an army, ready for action, of sixty thousand infantry and three hundred and fifty cavalry, besides some four thousand five hundred mercenaries, in whom he placed most confidence; he had also a bodyguard of six hundred picked men about his person. These troops, the mercenaries excepted, were maintained without difficulty by the towns. Each town sent out on service only one half of its levy and kept back the remainder to provide them with supplies; thus one party was told off for military, and the other for fatigue duty, and in return for the corn which their comrades sent them, the men under arms assured them protection.

xxi. 1. While Josephus was thus directing affairs in Galilee, there appeared upon the scene an intriguer, a native of Gischala, named John, son of Levi, the most unscrupulous and crafty of all who have ever gained notoriety by such infamous means. Poor at the opening of his career, his penury had for long thwarted his malicious designs. A ready liar and clever in obtaining credit for his lies, he made a merit of deceit and practiced it upon his most intimate friends; while affecting humanity, the prospect of lucre made him the most sanguinary of men; always full of high ambitions, his hopes were fed on the basest of knaveries. For he was a brigand, who at the outset practiced his trade alone, but afterwards found for his daring deeds accomplices, whose numbers, small at first, grew with his success. He was, moreover, careful never to take into partnership any-one likely to fall an easy prey to an assailant, but se-lected good, strapping fellows, with stout hearts and military experience. He ended by mustering a band of four hundred men, for the most part fugitives from the region of Tyre and the villages in that neighbor-hood. With their help he plundered the whole of Galilee and harried the masses, whose minds were already dis-tracted by the impending war.

2. He was already aspiring to the command and had yet higher ambitions, but was checked by impecuniosity. Perceiving that Josephus was delighted at his energy, John first induced him to entrust him with the rebuild-ing of the walls of his native town, an undertaking in which he made a large profit at the expense of the wealthy citizens. He next contrived to play a very crafty trick: with the avowed object of protecting all the Jews of Syria from the use of oil not supplied by their own countrymen, he sought and obtained permission to de-liver it to them at the frontier. He then bought up that commodity, paying Tyrian coin of the value of four Attic drachmas for four amphoræ and proceeded to sell half an amphora at the same price. As Galilee is a spe-cial home of the olive and the crop had been plentiful, John, enjoying a monopoly, by sending large quantities to districts in want of it, amassed an immense sum of money, which he forthwith employed against the man who had brought him his gains. Supposing that if he could get rid of Josephus he would himself become gov-ernor of Galilee, he directed his band of brigands to push their raids more vigorously than ever. In the anarchy thus produced throughout the district, either the gover-nor would go to the rescue, in which case he would find means of laying an ambush and making away with him, or if Josephus neglected to take measures against the brigands, he would calumniate him to his countrymen. Lastly, he had long since been spreading a report that Josephus intended to betray the country to the Romans,

and in numerous similar ways he was scheming to ruin his chief.

3. About this time, some young men of the village of Dabarittha, units of the guard posted in the great plain, laid an ambush for Ptolemy, the overseer of Agrippa and Berenice, and robbed him of all the baggage that he was convoying, including a large number of rich vestments, a quantity of silver goblets and six hundred pieces of gold. Being unable to dispose secretly of such booty, they brought the whole to Josephus, then at Tarichææ. He censured them for this act of violence to servants of the king, and committed the goods to the keeping of Annæus, the most important citizen of Tarichææ, intending to return them to their legitimate owners when an opportunity presented itself.

This action brought him into the greatest peril, for the plunderers, indignant at receiving no portion of the spoil, and divining the intention of Josephus to present the king and queen with the fruits of their labors, ran round the villages by night, denouncing Josephus to all as a traitor. They also created a ferment in the neighboring cities, with the result that at daybreak a hundred thousand men in arms had collected against him. The multitude, assembled in the hippodrome at Tarichææ, made loud and angry demonstrations; some clamored for the stoning of the traitor, others to have him burned alive; the mob was instigated by John, who was seconded by Jesus, son of Sapphas, then chief magistrate of Tiberias.

The friends and bodyguard of Josephus, terrified at the assault of the crowd, all fled with the exception of four; he himself was asleep and awoke only at the moment when his enemies were about to set fire to the house. His four faithful companions urged him to fly; but he, undaunted by the general desertion or by the number of his assailants, rushed out with raiment rent and ashes sprinkled on his head, his hands behind his back and his sword suspended from his neck. At this spectacle his familiar friends, the Tarichæans in particular, were moved to compassion, but the country-folk and those of the neighborhood who regarded him as a nui-

sance railed at him and bade him instantly produce the
public money and confess his treasonable compact; for
they concluded from his demeanor that he would deny
none of the crimes of which they suspected him, and
had only made all this pitiable exhibition of himself in
order to procure their pardon. But in reality, this pose
of humiliation was merely part of a stratagem; with
the design of producing dissension among his indignant
opponents, he promised to make a full confession on the
subject which had roused their ire, and on obtaining
permission to speak, thus addressed them:

"About this money—I had no intention of either sending it to Agrippa or appropriating it myself; far be it
from me ever to reckon as a friend one who is your
foe, or as personal gain anything involving loss to the
community. But as I saw, citizens of Tarichææ, that
your city above all needed to be put in a state of defense
and that it was in lack of funds to construct ramparts;
as, moreover, I feared that the people of Tiberias and
of the other cities had their eyes on these spoils, I decided quietly to keep this money in order to encompass
you with a wall. If this does not meet your approval, I
am prepared to produce what was brought to me and
leave you to plunder it; if, on the contrary, I have con-
sulted your best interests, do not punish your benefactor."

4. At these words the people of Tarichææ applauded,
but those from Tiberias and elsewhere vilified and threatened him; and the two parties let Josephus alone and
fell to quarrelling with each other. He, now relying on
the supporters he had won—the Tarichæans numbered
as many as forty thousand—proceeded to address the
whole multitude more freely. He severely censured them
for their precipitance, promised to fortify Tarichææ with
the funds at his disposal, and undertook to provide
similar protection for the other cities as well. Money,
he added, would be forthcoming, would they but agree
who was the enemy against whom its provision was
necessary, instead of furiously attacking the man who
provided it.

5. Thereupon the majority of the deluded crowd with-

drew, though still highly excited; but two thousand men in arms made a rush upon him. He was too quick for them and succeeded in regaining his lodging, which they beset with menacing cries. Josephus now had recourse to a second ruse. He mounted to the roof, quelled their clamor with a motion of his hand, and said that he had no idea what they wanted, as their confused shouts prevented him from hearing them; he would, however, comply with all their demands, if they would send in a deputation to confer quietly with him. On hearing that, the leaders of the party, with the magistrates, entered the house. He then haled them to the most secluded portion of the building, closed the outer door, and had them scourged till he had flayed them all to the bone. The mob, meanwhile, remained standing round the house, supposing their delegates to be engaged in a prolonged parley. Suddenly Josephus had the door thrown open and the men dismissed, all covered with blood, a spectacle which struck such terror into his menacing foes that they dropped their arms and fled.

6. These proceedings intensified John's malice, and he devised a second plot against Josephus. Feigning sickness, he wrote to Josephus to request his permission to take the hot baths at Tiberias for the good of his health. Thereupon Josephus, whose suspicions of the conspirator were not yet aroused, wrote to his lieutenants in the town to give John hospitality and to provide for his needs. He, after enjoying these benefits for two days, proceeded to carry into effect the object of his visit: by deception or bribery he corrupted the citizens and endeavored to induce them to revolt from Josephus. Hearing of this, Silas, whom Josephus had appointed to guard the town, hastened to inform his chief of the conspiracy. Josephus, on receipt of his letter, set off, and after a rapid night march, reached Tiberias at daybreak.

The whole population came out to meet him except John. He, though suspecting that this visit boded ill for himself, sent one of his acquaintances with a message, pretending to be indisposed and bedridden, and so prevented from paying his respects. But when Josephus had assembled the Tiberians in the stadium and was en-

deavoring to address them on the subject of the news
which he had received, John secretly sent out some soldiers with orders to kill him. The people, seeing these
men drawing their swords, raised a shout; at their cries
Josephus turned round, beheld the blade actually at his
throat, leaped down to the beach—he had been standing,
to harangue the people, on a hillock six cubits high—
and jumping with two of his guards into a boat that was
moored hard by, escaped to the middle of the lake.

7. His soldiers, however, hastily seized their arms and
advanced against the conspirators. Thereupon Josephus,
fearing that the outbreak of civil war might bring ruin
upon the city, all for the misdeeds of a few envious individuals, sent instructions to his men to restrict themselves to providing for their own safety, to kill nobody,
and to call none of the culprits to account. In accordance with these orders they took no further action; but
the inhabitants of the district, on learning of the plot
and the contriver of it, mustered in force to attack John,
who hastily made his escape to Gischala, his native
place.

The Galilæans from one town after another flocked to
Josephus; myriads of men in arms came and protested
that they were there to punish John, the public enemy,
and that they would burn him alive with the city that
harbored him. Josephus thanked them for their goodwill,
but checked their impetuosity, preferring to overcome
his enemies by diplomacy rather than by slaughter. Instead, he obtained from each city a list of names of
those who had joined in John's revolt, this information
being readily given by their fellow-citizens, and then issued a public proclamation that all who within five days
had not abandoned John would have their property
seized and their houses burned to the ground, along
with their families. This threat immediately produced
the desertion of three thousand of his followers, who
came to Josephus and threw down their arms at his
feet; with the remainder, some two thousand Syrian fugitives, John, abandoning open hostilities, was again driv-
en to resort to clandestine plots.

He accordingly now sent secret emissaries to Jeru-

salem to denounce Josephus as growing too great, declaring that he might at any moment appear at the
capital as its tyrant, unless he were checked in time.
The people, who foresaw these calumnies, attached no
importance to them; but their leaders, with some of the
magistrates, from motives of envy, secretly supplied
John with money to enable him to collect mercenaries
and make war on Josephus. They further took it upon
themselves to pass a decree recalling him from his command. As, however, they did not regard this decree as
sufficient, they sent out a force of two thousand five
hundred men with four men of mark, namely, Joesdrus,
son of Nomicus, Ananias, son of Sadok, Simon and
Judas, sons of Jonathan, all very able speakers, with
the object of undermining the popularity of Josephus.
If he were prepared to leave without demur, they were
to allow him an opportunity of rendering an account of
himself; if he insisted on remaining, they were to treat
him as a public enemy.

Friends of Josephus had, meanwhile, sent him word
that troops were on their way to Galilee, but gave no
hint of the reason, as his adversaries had planned their
scheme in secret conclave. Consequently he had taken
no precautions and four cities went over to his opponents as soon as they appeared, namely, Sepphoris,
Gabara, Gischala, and Tiberias. These, however, he soon
reclaimed without recourse to arms, and then by stratagem got the four leaders into his power with the best
of their troops and sent them back to Jerusalem. The
citizens were highly indignant at these individuals, and
would have killed them, as well as their employers, had
they not promptly taken flight.

8. John from this time forth was confined by fear
of Josephus within the walls of Gischala. A few days
later Tiberias again revolted, the inhabitants having appealed to King Agrippa for aid. He did not arrive on
the agreed date, but on that same day, a small body of
Roman cavalry happening to appear, the Tiberians issued a proclamation excluding Josephus from the city.
Their defection was immediately reported to him at
Tarichææ. He had just sent all his soldiers on a forag-

ing excursion; he could neither go out alone to face the rebels nor afford to remain idle, for fear that the king's troops, profiting by his delay, might forestall him in occupying the town; on the following day, moreover, he could take no action owing to the restrictions of the Sabbath.

In this dilemma the idea occurred to him of circumventing the rebels by a ruse. After ordering the gates of Tarichææ to be closed, in order that no hint of his project might reach the city which was the objective of his attack, he collected all the boats which he could find on the lake—there were two hundred and thirty, with no more than four sailors on board each—and with this fleet sailed at full speed for Tiberias. Keeping far enough from the town to prevent the inhabitants from detecting that his ships were unmanned, he let them ride in the offing, while he, with no more than seven of his armed guards, advanced within view of all. On perceiving him from the walls, where they were still heaping invectives upon him, his adversaries, imagining that all the boats were filled with troops, were terrified, threw down their arms and, waving suppliants' olive branches, implored him to spare the city.

9. Josephus severely threatened and reproached them, first for their folly, after taking up arms against Rome, in wasting their strength beforehand upon civil strife and so fulfilling their enemies' fondest wishes; next for their eagerness to make away with their guardian and protector, and their shamelessness in closing their city to him, who had built its walls; he declared himself ready, notwithstanding, to receive deputies who would offer an apology and assist him to secure the town. At once ten citizens, the principal men of Tiberias, came down; these he took on board one of the vessels and conveyed some distance from the land. Next he required fifty more, the most eminent members of the council, to come forward, ostensibly to give him their word as well. And so, always inventing some new pretext, he called up one party after another, presumably to ratify the agreement. As the boats were successively filled, he gave orders to the skippers to sail with all speed to

Tarichææ and to shut the men up in prison. Thus, in the end, he arrested the whole council of six hundred members and some two thousand other citizens, and shipped them off to Tarichææ.

10. Those who were left indicated, with loud cries, a certain Cleitus as the prime mover of the revolt, and urged the governor to vent his wrath upon him. Josephus, being determined to put no one to death, ordered one of his guards, named Levi, to go ashore and cut off Cleitus's hands. The soldier, afraid to venture alone into the midst of a host of enemies, refused to go. Cleitus, thereupon, seeing Josephus on the boat fuming with anger and prepared to leap out himself to chastise him, implored him from the beach to leave him one of his hands. The governor consenting to this, on condition that he cut off the other himself, Cleitus drew his sword with his right hand and severed the left from his body; such was his terror of Josephus.

Thus, with empty ships and seven guards, he captured, on that occasion, an entire population, and once more reduced Tiberias to submission. But a few days later, discovering that the city had revolted again along with Sepphoris, he delivered it over to his soldiers to plunder it. However, he collected all the spoil and restored it to the townsfolk. He followed the same procedure at Sepphoris; for that town also was subdued by him, and he wished to give the inhabitants a lesson by pillaging it, and then by restoring their property to regain their affection. . . .

BOOK III

The Siege of Jotapata (A.D. *67*)

i. 1. The news of the reverses sustained in Judæa filled Nero, as was natural, with secret consternation and alarm, but in public he affected an air of disdain and indignation. "These unfortunate incidents," he said, "were due to remiss generalship rather than to the valor of the enemy;" and the majesty of empire made him think it became him to treat black tidings with lofty contempt and to appear to possess a soul superior to all accidents. His inward perturbation, however, was betrayed by his anxious reflection.

2. He was deliberating into whose hands he should entrust the East in its present commotion, with the double task of punishing the Jewish rebels and of forestalling a revolt of the neighboring nations, which were already catching the contagion. He could find none but Vespasian a match for the emergency and capable of undertaking a campaign on so vast a scale. Vespasian was one who had been a soldier from his youth and grown gray in the service; he had earlier in his career pacified and restored to Roman rule the West when convulsed by the Germans; he had by his military genius added to the Empire Britain, till then almost unknown, and thus afforded Claudius, Nero's [adoptive] father, the honors of a triumph which cost him no personal exertion.

3. Regarding, therefore, this record as of happy augury, seeing in Vespasian a man with the steadiness resulting from years and experience, with sons who would be a sure hostage for his fidelity, and whose ripe manhood would act as the arm of their father's brain. Moved, maybe, also by God, who was already shaping the destinies of empire, Nero sent this general to take command of the armies in Syria; lavishing upon him, at this urgent

214

crisis, such soothing and flattering compliments as are
called for by emergencies of this kind. From Achæa,
where he was in attendance on Nero, Vespasian dispatched his son Titus to Alexandria to call up the fifteenth legion from that city. He himself, after crossing
the Hellespont, proceeded by land to Syria, where he
concentrated the Roman forces and numerous auxiliary
contingents furnished by the kings of the neighboring
districts. . . .

iv. 2. [When Titus brought his army from Alexandria
to Ptolemais,] there he found his father with his two
legions, the most distinguished of all, the fifth and the
tenth, and now united to them the fifteenth which he
had brought himself. These legions were accompanied
by eighteen cohorts; five more cohorts with one squadron of cavalry came to join them from Cæsarea, and
five squadrons of cavalry from Syria. Of the twenty-
three cohorts, ten numbered each a thousand infantry,
the remaining thirteen had each a strength of six hundred infantry and a hundred and twenty cavalry. A
further considerable force of auxiliaries had been mustered by the kings Antiochus, Agrippa, and Soæmus,
each of whom furnished two thousand unmounted bowmen and a thousand cavalry; the Arab Malchus sent
a thousand cavalry and five thousand infantry, mainly
bowmen. Thus the total strength of the forces, horse
and foot, including the contingents of the kings,
amounted to sixty thousand, without counting the servants who followed in vast numbers and may properly
be included in the category of combatants, whose military training they shared; for, taking part in peace time
in all their masters' maneuvers and in war time in their
dangers, they yielded to none but them in skill and
prowess.

v. 1. One cannot but admire the forethought shown
in this particular by the Romans, in making their servant class useful to them not only for the ministrations
of ordinary life but also for war. If one goes on to study
the organization of their army as a whole, it will be
seen that this vast empire of theirs has come to them as
the prize of valor, and not as a gift of fortune. For their

nation does not wait for the outbreak of war to give men their first lesson in arms; they do not sit with folded hands in peace time only to put them in motion in the hour of need. On the contrary, as though they had been born with weapons in hand, they never have a truce from training, never wait for emergencies to arise. Moreover, their peace maneuvers are no less strenuous than veritable warfare; each soldier daily throws all his energy into his drill, as though he were in action. Hence that perfect ease with which they sustain the shock of battle—no confusion breaks their customary formation, no panic paralyzes, no fatigue exhausts them—and as their opponents cannot match these qualities, victory is the invariable and certain consequence. Indeed, it would not be wrong to describe their maneuvers as bloodless combats and their combats as sanguinary maneuvers.

The Romans never lay themselves open to a surprise attack, for, whatever hostile territory they may invade, they engage in no battle until they have fortified their camp. This camp is not erected at random or unevenly; they do not all work at once or in disorderly parties; if the ground is uneven, it is first leveled; a site for the camp is then measured out in the form of a square. For this purpose the army is accompanied by a multitude of workmen with tools for building.

2. The interior of the camp is divided into rows of tents. The exterior circuit presents the appearance of a wall and is furnished with towers at regular intervals; and on the spaces between the towers are placed "quick-firers," catapults, "stone-throwers," and every variety of artillery engines, all ready for use. In this surrounding wall are set four gates, one on each side, spacious enough for beasts of burden to enter without difficulty and wide enough for sallies of troops in emergencies. The camp is intersected by streets symmetrically laid out; in the middle are the tents of the officers, and precisely in the center the headquarters of the commander-in-chief, resembling a small temple. Thus, as it were, an improvised city springs up, with its market-place, its artisan quarter, its seats of judgment, where captains

and taxiarchs adjudicate upon any differences which
may arise. The outer wall and all the buildings within
are completed quicker than thought, so numerous and
skilled are the workmen. In case of need, the camp is
further surrounded by a fosse, four cubits deep and of
equal breadth.

3. Once entrenched, the soldiers take up their quarters in their tents by companies, quietly and in good
order. All their fatigue duties are performed with the
same discipline, the same regard for security: the procuring of wood, food-supplies, and water, as required—
each party has its allotted task. The hour for supper
and breakfast is not left to individual discretion: all
take their meals together. The hours for sleep, sentinel-
duty, and rising, are announced by the sound of the
trumpet; nothing is done without a word of command.
At daybreak the rank and file report themselves to their
respective centurions, the centurions go to salute the
tribunes, the tribunes with all the officers then wait on
the commander-in-chief, and he gives them, according
to custom, the watchword and other orders to be communicated to the lower ranks. The same precision is
maintained on the battle-field: the troops wheel smartly
round in the requisite direction, and whether advancing
to the attack or retreating, all move as a unit at the
word of command.

4. When the camp is to be broken up, the trumpet
sounds a first call; at that none remain idle. Instantly,
at this signal, they strike the tents and make all ready
for departure. The trumpets sound a second call to prepare for the march; at once they pile their baggage on
the mules and other beasts of burden and stand ready
to start, like runners breasting the cord on the race-
course. They then set fire to the encampment, both because they can easily construct another and to prevent
the enemy from ever making use of it. A third time the
trumpets give a similar signal for departure, to hasten
the movements of stragglers, whatever the reason for
their delay, and to ensure that none is out of his place
in the ranks. Then the herald, standing on the right of
the chief officer, inquires three times in their native

tongue whether they are ready for war. Three times they loudly and lustily shout in reply, "We are ready," some even anticipating the question; and, worked up to a kind of martial frenzy, along with the shout they raise their right arms in the air.

5. Then they advance, all marching in silence and in good order, each man keeping his place in the ranks, as if in face of the enemy.

The infantry are armed with cuirass and helmet and carry a sword on either side; that on the left is far the longer of the two, the dagger on the right being no longer than a span. The picked infantry, forming the general's guard, carry a lance and round shield, the regiments of the line a javelin and oblong buckler; the equipment of the latter further includes a saw, a basket, a pick and an axe, not to mention a strap, a bill-hook, a chain and three days' rations, so that an infantry man is almost as heavily laden as a pack-mule.

The cavalry carry a large sword on their right side, a long pike in the hand, a buckler resting obliquely on the horse's flank, and in a quiver slung beside them, three or more darts with broad points and as long as spears; their helmets and cuirasses are the same as those worn by all the infantry. The select cavalry, forming the general's escort, are armed in precisely the same manner as the ordinary troopers. The legion which is to lead the column is always selected by lot.

6. Such is the routine of the Roman army on the march and in camp; such are the various arms which they bear. In battle nothing is done unadvisedly or left to chance: consideration invariably precedes action, and action conforms to the decision reached. Consequently the Romans rarely err, and, if they do make a slip, easily repair their error. They consider, moreover, that a well-concerted plan, even if it ends in failure, is preferable to a happy stroke of fortune, because accidental success is a temptation to improvidence, whereas deliberation, though occasionally followed by misfortunes, teaches the useful lesson how to avoid their recurrence. They further reflect that one who profits by a happy accident can take no credit for it, while disasters

which occur contrary to all calculations leave one at least the consolation that no proper precautions were neglected.

7. By their military exercises the Romans instil into their soldiers fortitude not only of body but also of soul. Fear, too, plays its part in their training, for they have laws which punish with death not merely desertion of the ranks, but even a slight neglect of duty, and their generals are held in even greater awe than the laws. For the high honors with which they reward the brave prevent the offenders whom they punish from regarding themselves as treated cruelly.

This perfect discipline makes the army an ornament of peace time and in war welds the whole into a single body—so compact are their ranks, so alert their movements in wheeling to right or left, so quick their ears for orders, their eyes for signals, their hands to act upon them. Prompt as they consequently ever are in action, none are slower than they in succumbing to suffering, and never have they been known in any predicament to be beaten by numbers, by ruse, by difficulties of ground, or even by fortune; for they have more assurance of victory than of fortune. Where counsel thus precedes active operations, where the leaders' plan of campaign is followed up by so efficient an army, no wonder that the Empire has extended its boundaries on the east to the Euphrates, on the west to the ocean, on the south to the most fertile tracts of Libya, on the north to the Danube and the Rhine. One might say without exaggeration that great as are their possessions, the people that won them are greater still.

8. If I have dwelt at some length on this topic, my intention was not so much to extol the Romans as to console those whom they have vanquished and to deter others who may be tempted to revolt. Perhaps, too, any cultured readers who are unacquainted with the subject may profit by an account of the organization of the Roman army. I will now resume my narrative at the point where I digressed.

vi. 1. Vespasian was detained for some time with his son Titus at Ptolemais, consolidating his forces. Meanwhile Placidus was scouring Galilee and had begun by killing large numbers of those who fell into his hands, these being weak civilians who were exhausted by flight. Afterwards, observing that the combatants always took refuge in the cities which Josephus had fortified, he proceeded to attack the most formidable of them, Jotapata. He expected to have no difficulty in capturing it by a sudden assault, and thus to procure for himself a high reputation with his chiefs and for them a considerable advantage for the future campaign, for, once the strongest town had fallen, terror would induce the rest to surrender.

In this hope, however, he was greatly deceived. Forewarned of his approach, the people of Jotapata awaited his coming outside the town and burst unexpectedly upon the Romans. Being a large body, well prepared for battle and kindled by the thought of the danger threatening their native city, their wives and their children, they quickly routed their opponents and wounded a large number of them. They killed no more than seven, because the Romans retired in good order and, their bodies being completely protected, received only superficial wounds, while their Jewish assailants, lightly equipped and opposed to heavy-armed regulars, kept their distance and did not venture to come to close quarters with them. The Jews on their side had three killed and a few wounded. Placidus, thus finding himself too feeble for an assault on the town, beat a retreat.

2. But Vespasian, impatient to invade Galilee himself, now set out from Ptolemais, after drawing up his army for the march in the customary Roman order. The auxiliary light-armed troops and archers were sent in advance, to repel any sudden incursions of the enemy and to explore suspected woodland suited for the concealment of ambuscades. Next came a contingent of heavy-armed Roman soldiers, infantry and cavalry. They were followed by a detachment composed of ten men from each century, carrying their own kit and the necessary instruments for marking out the camp; after these came the pioneers to straighten sinuosities on the route, to level the rough places and to cut down obstructing

woods, in order to spare the army the fatigues of a
toilsome march. Behind these Vespasian posted his personal equipage and that of his lieutenants, with a strong
mounted escort to protect them. He himself rode behind
with the pick of the infantry and cavalry and his guard
of lancers.

Then came the cavalry units of the legions (for to
each legion are attached a hundred and twenty horse).
These were followed by the mules carrying the siege
towers and the other machines. Then came the legates,
the prefects of the cohorts and the tribunes, with an
escort of picked troops. Next the ensigns surrounding
the eagle, which in the Roman army precedes every legion, because it is the king and the bravest of all the
birds: it is regarded by them as the symbol of empire,
and whoever may be their adversaries, an omen of
victory. These sacred emblems were followed by the
trumpeters, and behind them came the solid column,
marching six abreast. A centurion, according to custom,
accompanied them to superintend the order of the ranks.
Behind the infantry the servants attached to each legion followed in a body, conducting the mules and other
beasts of burden which carried the soldiers' kit. At the
end of the column came the crowd of mercenaries, and
last of all for security a rearguard composed of light
and heavy infantry and a considerable body of cavalry.

3. Proceeding with his army in this order, Vespasian
reached the frontiers of Galilee. Here he established his
camp and restrained the ardor of his soldiers, who were
burning for the fray, being content to parade his forces
before the enemy, with a view to intimidating them and
giving time for reconsideration, if they wished, before
an engagement, to desert their friends. At the same
time he made preparations for besieging the strongholds.
The general's appearance on the scene in fact aroused
in many regret for their revolt, and in all alarm. The
troops under the command of Josephus, who were camping beside a town called Garis, not far from Sepphoris,
discovering that the war was upon them, and that they
might at any moment be attacked by the Romans, dispersed and fled, not only before any engagement, but

before they had even seen their foes. Josephus was left with a few companions; he saw that he had not sufficient forces to await the enemy, that the Jews were crestfallen, and that the majority of them, if they could gain the enemy's confidence, would gladly capitulate. Already he had fears for the ultimate issue of the war; for the moment he decided to remove as far as possible from the risk of a conflict. Accordingly, with the remnant of his troops, he took refuge in Tiberias.

vii. 1. Vespasian's first objective was the city of Gabara, which he carried at the first assault, finding it deprived of effective combatants. Entering the city he slew all males who were of age, the Romans showing no mercy to old or young, so bitter was their hatred of the nation and their memory of the affront which had been done to Cestius.* Not content with setting fire to the city, Vespasian burned all the villages and country towns in the neighborhood; some he found completely deserted, in the others he reduced the inhabitants to slavery.

2. The arrival of Josephus filled the city which he had chosen as his refuge with alarm, for the people of Tiberias felt that he would never have fled, had he not abandoned all hope of success in the contest. In this they correctly interpreted his opinion, for he foresaw the final catastrophe for which the fortunes of the Jews were heading, and recognized that their only hope of salvation lay in submission. As for himself, although he might look for pardon from the Romans, he would have preferred to suffer a thousand deaths rather than betray his country and disgracefully abandon the command which had been entrusted to him, in order to seek his fortune among those whom he had been commissioned to fight. He decided therefore to write to the authorities at Jerusalem an exact statement of the position of affairs, neither exaggerating the strength of the enemy, which might subsequently lead to his being taunted with cowardice, nor underrating it, for fear of encouraging

* The reference is to the rout of an army under Cestius Gallus at Jerusalem in November 66, narrated in II xviii 9-xix 9 (but not included in the present volume).

them to hold out when possibly inclined to repent. If the magistrates intended to negotiate, they were asked to reply to that effect without delay; if they decided to continue the war, they should send him a force capable of coping with the Romans. Having written a letter to this effect, he sent it by express messengers to Jerusalem.

3. Vespasian was impatient to make an end of Jotapata, having heard that it was the refuge to which most of the enemy had retired, and that it was, moreover, their strong base. He accordingly sent a body of infantry and cavalry in advance to level the road leading to it, a stony mountain track, difficult for infantry and quite impracticable for mounted troops. In four days their task was completed and a broad highway opened for the army. On the fifth, which was the twenty-first of the month Artemisius [June 8, 67], Josephus hurriedly left Tiberias and entered Jotapata, his arrival raising the dejected spirits of the Jews. A deserter brought to Vespasian the welcome intelligence of the general's movement, and urged him to hasten to attack the city, because its fall, could he but secure Josephus, would amount to the capture of all Judæa. Vespasian caught at this information as a godsend, regarding it as by God's providential ordering that the man who was reputed to be the most sagacious of his enemies had thus deliberately entered a prison; he instantly dispatched Placidus and the decurion Æbutius, a man of marked energy and ability, with a thousand horse, with orders to invest the town and prevent Josephus from escaping secretly.

4. Vespasian followed them the next day with all his army, and marching until evening, arrived before Jotapata. Leading his troops up to the north side of the city he encamped on a hill seven furlongs distant from it, seeking a position as conspicuous as possible to the enemy in order to intimidate them. In fact the spectacle had such an instantaneous effect on the Jews that none ventured outside the walls. The Romans, after their full day's march, were not prepared to make an immediate attack, but they surrounded the city with a double cordon of infantry, and posted outside these a third line of cavalry, blocking all means of exit. This maneuver,

cutting off hope of escape, stimulated the Jews to deeds of gallantry; for nothing in war so rouses the martial spirit as necessity.

5. Next day an attack was made. At first those of the Jews who were encamped opposite the Romans outside the walls merely held their ground against the enemy; but when Vespasian brought up his archers, slingers, and all his other marksmen in full force and gave orders to shoot down these opponents, while he himself with the infantry pushed up the slope at the point where the wall offered little difficulty, Josephus, alarmed for the fate of the town, made a sally with the whole multitude of the Jews. Falling in a body upon the Romans they drove them from the ramparts and performed many signal feats of prowess and daring. However, they suffered as much loss as they inflicted, for if the Jews were emboldened by despair, the Romans were no less roused by shame. On the one side were skilled experience and strength, the other had recklessness for its armor and passion for its leader. The battle lasted all day, and night alone parted the combatants. Of the Romans very many were wounded and thirteen killed. The Jewish casualties were seventeen killed and six hundred wounded.

6. On the following day, when the Romans returned to the attack, the Jews made a fresh sally and offered a much more stubborn resistance, from the confidence inspired by their unexpectedly successful resistance on the previous day. But the Romans on their side proved more resolute opponents, being inflamed to fury by shame and regarding a lack of instant victory as tantamount to defeat. So for five days the Romans incessantly renewed their assaults and the garrison of Jotapata their sallies and their yet more stubborn defense from the ramparts, the Jews undaunted by their enemy's strength, the Romans undeterred by the difficulties which their objective presented.

7. The town of Jotapata is almost entirely built on precipitous cliffs, being surrounded on three sides by ravines so deep that sight fails in the attempt to fathom the abyss. On the north side alone, where the town has

straggled sideways up a descending spur of the mountains, is it accessible. But Josephus, when he fortified the city, had enclosed this·quarter, too, within his wall, in order to prevent the enemy from occupying the ridge which commanded it. Concealed by other mountains surrounding it, the town was quite invisible until one came right up to it. Such was the strong position of Jotapata.

8. Vespasian, pitting his strength against the nature of the ground and the determination of the Jews, resolved to press the siege more vigorously; he accordingly summoned his principal officers to deliberate with him on the plan of attack. It was decided to erect earthworks against the accessible portion of the wall, whereupon the whole army was sent out to procure the necessary materials. The mountain forests surrounding the town were stripped, and besides timber, enormous masses of stones were collected. Then one party of soldiers spread screens of hurdles over palisades, as a cover from missiles from above, and thus protected, constructed the earthworks, suffering little or no injury from their assailants on the ramparts, while others pulled to pieces the adjacent mounds and kept their comrades constantly supplied with earth. With this triple division of labor not a man was idle. The Jews, meanwhile, launched from the walls great boulders upon the enemy's shelters with all sorts of projectiles, the crash of which, even when they failed to penetrate, was so loud and terrific as to impede the workers.

9. Vespasian now had his artillery engines—numbering in all one hundred and sixty—brought into position round the spot and gave orders to fire upon the defenders on the wall. In one tremendous volley the catapults sent lances hurtling through the air, the stone-projectors discharged blocks of the weight of a talent, firebrands flew, and there was a hail of arrows, with the effect not only of driving the Jews from the ramparts, but of rendering untenable all the space behind them which came within range of the missiles. For the artillery fire was reinforced by a simultaneous volley from a host of Arab archers, javelin-men, and slingers. Though checked in their defense of the ramparts, the

Jews did not remain inactive. Parties of them sallied out
in guerrilla fashion, stripped off the enemy's shelters and
assailed the workmen thus exposed, and wherever the
latter fell back, they demolished the earthworks and set
fire to the palisades and hurdles. At length Vespasian,
on tracing the cause of this injury to the separation of
the earthworks (as the intervals afforded the Jews a
loophole for attack) united the various shelters and
simultaneously closed up his troops, with the result that
further Jewish incursions were repressed.

10. The embankment was now rising and almost on
a level with the battlements when Josephus, thinking it
shameful if he could not devise some counter-measures
to save the town, summoned masons and directed them
to increase the height of the wall. On their protesting
that building was impossible under such a hail of missiles, he invented the following protection for them.
Palisades were, by his orders, fixed to the wall, and over
these were spread hides of oxen that had just been
flayed, to catch in their folds the stones hurled by the
engines, while the other projectiles would glance off
their surface and their moisture would extinguish the
flaming brands. Under this screen the builders, working
in security day and night, raised the wall to a height of
twenty cubits, erected numerous towers, and crowned
the whole with a stout parapet. At this spectacle the Romans, who imagined themselves already masters of the
town, were greatly disheartened; the ingenuity of Josephus and the perseverance of the inhabitants astounded
them.

11. Vespasian was no less provoked both at the clever-
ness of this stratagem and at the audacity of the people of Jotapata, for emboldened by their new fortification, they recommenced their sallies against the Romans.
Every day parties of them came into conflict with the
besiegers, employing all the ruses of guerrilla warfare,
pillaging whatever fell in their way and setting fire to
the rest of the Roman works. This continued until Vespasian, ordering his troops to cease fighting, resolved
to resort to a blockade and to starve the city into surrender. The defenders, he reckoned, would either be re-

duced by their privations to sue for mercy or, if they remained obdurate to the last, would perish of hunger. Moreover, if it came to a battle, he counted on obtaining a far easier victory if, after an interval, he renewed his attack upon exhausted opponents. He accordingly gave orders to keep a strict guard on all the exits from the city.

12. The besieged had abundance of grain and of all other necessaries, salt excepted, but they lacked water because, there being no springs within the town, the inhabitants were dependent on rain-water; but in this region rain rarely, if ever, falls in summer, which was precisely the season at which they were besieged. The mere idea of thirst filled them with dire despondency, and already they were chafing, as though water had entirely failed. For Josephus, seeing the abundance of the city's other supplies and the courageous spirit of its defenders, and desirous to prolong the siege beyond the expectation of the Romans, had from the first put them on water rations. This control system appeared to them harder than actual want; the constraint of their liberty only increased their craving and they became as limp as though they had already reached the last extremity of thirst. The Romans were not ignorant of their plight: from the slopes above they could see over the wall the Jews flocking to one place and having their water doled out to them, and directing their catapults upon the spot, killed numbers of them.

13. Vespasian expected that the water in the cisterns would ere long be exhausted and the city reduced to capitulate. To crush this hope, Josephus had a number of dripping garments hung round the battlements, with the result that the whole wall was suddenly seen streaming with water. The Romans were filled with dismay and consternation at the spectacle of all this water being wasted as a jest by those who they supposed had not even enough to drink. The general himself, despairing of reducing the place by famine, reverted to armed measures and force. That was just what the Jews desired, for having given up all hope for themselves and

the city, they preferred death in battle to perishing of hunger and thirst.

14. After this stratagem, Josephus devised yet another to procure himself supplies in abundance. There was, leading down to the ravine on the west side, a gully so difficult to traverse that it had been neglected by the enemy's outposts; by this route Josephus succeeded in sending letters, by some of his men, to Jews outside the city with whom he wished to communicate, and receiving replies from them. By the same means he stocked the town with all necessaries when its supplies began to fail. The messengers sent out had general orders to creep past the sentries on all fours and to wear fleeces on their backs, in order that, if they were seen at night, they might be taken for dogs. However, the guards eventually detected the ruse and blocked the gully.

15. Josephus, now recognizing that the city could not long hold out and that his own life would be endangered if he remained there, took counsel with the principal citizens about the means of flight. The people discovered his intention and crowded round him, imploring him not to abandon them, as they depended on him alone. If he remained, they urged, he would be their one hope of the town being saved, as everyone, because he was with them, would put his heart into the struggle; were capture in store for them, even then he would be their one consolation. Moreover, it would be unworthy of him to fly from his foes, to desert his friends, to leap, in the storm, from the vessel on which he had embarked in a calm. For his departure would wreck the town, as none would have the heart to resist the enemy any longer, when he whose presence would have given them courage was gone.

16. Josephus, suppressing any allusion to his own safety, assured them that it was in their own interests that he had contemplated departure; for his presence in the town could not materially assist them if they were saved, and if they were taken what end would be served by his perishing with them? Were he, on the contrary, once clear of the siege, he could from outside render them the greatest service, for he would promptly mus-

ter the Galilæans from the country and, by creating a diversion elsewhere, draw off the Romans from their city. He failed to see how his presence at their side could assist them in present circumstances, or have any other effect except to spur the Romans to press the siege more vigorously than ever, as they attached so much importance to his capture; whereas, if they heard that he had fled, they would considerably relax the ferocity of their attack. Unmoved, however, by these words, the multitude only clung to him more ardently: children, old men, women with infants in their arms, all threw themselves weeping before him; they embraced and held him by his feet, they implored him with sobs to stay and share their fortune. All this they did, I cannot but think, not because they grudged him his chance of safety, but because they thought of their own; for with Josephus on the spot, they were convinced that no disaster could befall them.

17. Josephus suspected that this insistence would not go beyond supplication if he yielded, but meant that watch would be kept upon him if he opposed their wishes. Moreover, his determination to leave them was greatly shaken by compassion for their distress. He therefore decided to remain, and making the universal despair of the city into a weapon for himself, "Now is the time," he exclaimed, "to begin the combat, when all hope of deliverance is past. Fine is it to sacrifice life for renown and by some glorious exploit to ensure, in falling, the memory of posterity!" Suiting his action to his words, he sallied out with his bravest warriors, dispersed the guards, and penetrating to the Romans' camp, tore up the tents of skin under which they were sheltered on the embankment, and set fire to the works. This he repeated the next day, and the day after that, and for a series of days and nights indefatigably continued the fight.

18. The Romans suffered from these sallies, for they were ashamed to fly before Jews, and when they put the latter to flight the weight of their arms impeded them in the pursuit, while the Jews always did some mischief before the enemy could retaliate, and then took

refuge in the town. In view of this, Vespasian ordered
his legionaries to shun these attacks and not to be drawn
into an engagement with men who were bent on death.
"Nothing," he said, "is more redoubtable than despair,
and their impetuosity, deprived of an objective, will be
extinguished, like fire for lack of fuel. Besides, it becomes even Romans to think of safety as well as victory, since they make war not from necessity, but to increase their empire." Thenceforth he relied mainly on
his Arab archers and the Syrian slingers and stone-
throwers to repel the Jewish assaults; the greater part
of his artillery was also constantly in action. Severely
handled by the engines, the Jews gave way, but once
past the reach of their adversaries' long-range projectiles
they flung themselves furiously on the Romans and
fought desperately, prodigal of life and limb, one party
after another relieving their exhausted comrades.

19. The length of the siege and the sallies of the
enemy made Vespasian feel that the position was re-
versed and himself the besieged; so, now that the earthworks were approaching the ramparts, he decided to
bring up the "ram." This is an immense beam, like the
mast of a ship, reinforced at its extremity with a mass
of iron in the form of a ram's head, whence the machine takes its name. It is suspended at its middle point
by ropes, like the beam of a balance, to another beam
which is supported at either end by posts fixed in the
ground. A large body of men first draw the ram backward and then, all pushing together with all their weight,
heave it forward so that it batters the wall with the
projecting iron. And there is no tower so strong, no wall
so thick, as, even though it sustain the initial impact, to
withstand the repeated assaults of this engine.

Such was the expedient to which the Roman general
had recourse, being impatient to carry the city by storm,
as the long blockade, coupled with the activity of the
Jews, was proving injurious. The Romans now brought
forward the catapults and the rest of their artillery within range of the Jews on the ramparts who were endeavoring to beat them off, and put these engines into action;
the archers and slingers simultaneously advanced. While

the fire of these troops would not permit any to venture
on the ramparts, another party brought up the ram, protected by a long line of hurdles, over which was a covering of skin for the greater security of themselves and of
their engine. At the first blow the wall was shaken and
a piercing cry arose from the interior of the town as
though it had already been taken.

20. Josephus, seeing that under the repeated blows
constantly directed upon the same spot the wall was on
the verge of collapsing, devised a method of paralyzing
for a while the force of the machine. He directed that
sacks filled with chaff should be let down by ropes at
the place which the ram was seen continually to be battering, with the object of deflecting the head and dead-
ening the force of the blow by the soft cushion which
received it. This seriously retarded the Romans, for
wherever they turned their engine, those above retorted
by opposing their sacks beneath the strokes, and so the
wall suffered no injury from the impact until the Romans invented a counter-device of long poles to the ends
of which were attached scythes, with which they cut
the cords supporting the sacks. The engine having thus
recovered its efficacy, and the newly built wall already
showing signs of giving way, Josephus and his comrades,
as a last resort, had recourse to fire. Snatching up all
the dry wood which they could find, they rushed out
from three quarters of the town and set fire to the engines, wicker shelters, and props of the enemy's earthworks. The Romans did little to save them, stupefied
by their opponents' audacity and outstripped by the
flames in their efforts to rescue them; for fed by dry
tinder, with the addition of bitumen, pitch, and sulphur,
the fire flew in all directions quicker than thought, and
works which had cost the Romans such severe labor
were consumed in a single hour.

21. On this occasion one Jew who made his mark
deserves record and remembrance; his name was Eleazar, son of Sameas, a native of Saba in Galilee. Lifting
an enormous stone, he hurled it from the wall at the
ram with such force that he broke off its head; then, leaping down, he carried off his trophy from the midst of

the enemy and bore it with perfect composure to the foot
of the ramparts. Now become a target for all his foes,
and receiving their hits in his defenseless body, he was
pierced by five arrows. But without a thought for these,
he scaled the wall and there stood, conspicuous to all
the admirers of his bravery; then, writhing under his
wounds, he fell headlong with the ram's head in his
hands. Next to him, those who most distinguished themselves were two brothers, Netiras and Philip, also Galilæans, from the village of Ruma; dashing out against
the lines of the tenth legion, they charged the Romans
with such impetuosity and force that they broke their
ranks and put to flight all whom they encountered.

22. Following in the wake of these men, Josephus and
the rest of the people, with firebrands in their hands,
again sallied out and set fire to the machines, shelters
and earthworks of the fifth legion and of the tenth,
which had been routed; the other legions hastily buried
their machinery and all combustible materials. Towards
evening the Romans re-erected the ram and brought it
up to the spot where the wall had been weakened by its
previous blows. At this moment, one of the defenders
of the ramparts hit Vespasian with an arrow in the sole
of the foot. The wound was slight, the distance having
broken the force of the missile, but the incident created
a vast commotion among the Romans. The sight of blood
alarmed those immediately surrounding Vespasian; the
news at once spread through the whole army, and most
of the soldiers, abandoning the siege, came running towards their general in consternation and terror. The
first on the spot was Titus, with grave fears for his father, so that the troops were doubly agitated, both by
their affection for their chief and by the sight of his
son's anguish. However, Vespasian found little difficulty
in allaying both the fears of his son and the tumult of
the army. Mastering his pain, he hastened to show himself to all who had trembled for his life, and so roused
them to fight the Jews more fiercely than ever. Each
wished to be the first to brave danger in avenging his
general, and with shouts of mutual encouragement, they
rushed for the ramparts.

23. Josephus and his men, though falling one upon another under the hail of missiles from the catapults and stone-projectors, still were not driven from the battlements, but with fire, iron, and stones continued to assail the soldiers who, under cover of their wicker shelters, were propelling the ram. However, their efforts had little or no effect, and they were incessantly falling, because the enemy saw them without being seen; for, with the glare of their own lights all round them, they formed as conspicuous a mark for the enemy as in broad daylight, while they found difficulty in avoiding the projectiles from the engines which they could not see in the distance. Thus the missiles from the "quick-firers" and catapults came with such force as to strike down whole files, and the whizzing stones hurled by the engine carried away the battlements and broke off the angles of the towers. Indeed, there is no body of troops, however strong, that the force and mass of these stones cannot lay low to the last rank.

Some incidents of that night will give an idea of the power of this engine. One of the men standing on the wall beside Josephus had his head carried away by a stone, and his skull was shot, as from a sling, to a distance of three furlongs; a woman with child was struck on the belly just as she was leaving her house at daybreak, and the babe in her womb was flung half a furlong away—so mighty was the force of these stone-projectors. More alarming even than the engines was their whirring drone, more frightful than the missiles the crash. Then there was the thud of the dead falling one after another from the wall. Fearful shrieks from the women within the town mingled with the moans of the dying victims without. The whole surrounding area in front of the fighting line ran with blood, and the piles of corpses formed a path to the summit of the wall. The echo from the mountains around added to the horrible din; in short, nothing that can terrify ear or eye was wanting on that dreadful night. Multitudes of the defenders of Jotapata fell in valiant fight, multitudes were wounded, and not till towards the hour of the morning watch did the wall, after incessant battering, succumb to the machines. The besieged, however, blocking the breach with their persons and their weapons, threw up a makeshift defense before the Romans could lay the gangways for the escalade.

24. Vespasian, having allowed his troops a brief respite after the fatigues of the night, reassembled them soon after daybreak for the final assault. His object was to draw off the defenders from the breach. With this intention, he ordered the bravest of his cavalry to dismount and marshalled them in three divisions* opposite the ruined portions of the wall; protected by armor from head to foot and with lances couched, they were to be the first to enter the town the moment the gangways were laid; behind these he placed the flower of the infantry. (The rest of the cavalry were deployed all along the mountainside facing the ramparts, to prevent the escape of a single fugitive when the town was taken.) Further in the rear he posted the archers in a semicircle, with directions to have their arrows ready to shoot, along with the slingers and the artillery, under similar orders. Other parties were then told off to bring up ladders and plant them against the wall where it was still intact, in order that some of the besieged, in the attempt to repel them, might be induced to abandon the defense of the breach, and the remainder, overwhelmed by a hail of missiles, be forced to give way.

25. Josephus, penetrating this design, entrusted the protection of the intact portions of the wall to the fatigued and older men, expecting that there they would come to no harm; but he placed at the breach the most vigorous of his men, and at the head of each group six men, drawn by lot, among whom he himself drew for his place to bear the brunt of the battle. He instructed his men, when the legions raised their war-cry, to stop their ears, so as not to be frightened; when the volley of missiles came, to crouch down and cover their bodies with their bucklers, and to fall back for a while, until the archers had emptied their quivers; but, the instant the gangways were laid, to spring on to them themselves

* Translator's note: Or "three deep."

and confront the enemy by means of his own instruments. "Let each man fight," he continued, "not as the savior of his native place, but as its avenger, as though it were lost already. Let him picture to himself the butchery of the old men, the fate of the children and women at the hands of the foe, momentarily impending. Let the anticipation of these threatened calamities arouse his concentrated fury, and let him vent it upon the would-be perpetrators."

26. Such was the disposition of his two divisions. But when the crowd of non-combatant townsfolk, women and children, beheld the city encircled by a triple cordon of troops—for the Romans had not shifted for the battle any of the guards which they had posted at the outset—when they saw, moreover, at the foot of the ruined walls the enemy sword in hand, and above them the mountainside gleaming with arms and higher still the arrows of the Arab archers pointed at the town, they shrieked aloud, a last shriek, as it were, at their capture, as though the catastrophe were no longer imminent but already upon them. Josephus, fearing that the wailing of the women might unman the combatants, had them shut up in their houses, ordering them with threats to hold their peace. He then took up his allotted position at the breach, and regardless of the ladders which were being brought up elsewhere, breathlessly awaited the hail of arrows.

27. And now the trumpeters of all the legions simultaneously sounded, the troops raised a terrific shout, and at a given signal arrows poured from all quarters, intercepting the light. Mindful of the injunctions of Josephus, his comrades screened their ears from the shout and their bodies from the volleys; and as the planks were laid, they dashed out across them, before those who had laid them could set foot on them. In the ensuing hand-to-hand fight with their mounting enemy, they displayed all manner of feats of strength and gallantry, endeavoring in the depth of calamity to prove themselves not inferior to men who, without the same interests at stake, were so courageous. None relaxed his struggle with a Roman until he had killed him or per-

ished. But whereas the Jews, now becoming exhausted by the incessant combat, had none to replace their foremost champions, in the Roman ranks the exhausted men were relieved by fresh troops, and when one party was driven back another instantly took its place. The assailants cheered each other on, and side linked to side, with their bucklers protecting them above, they formed an invulnerable column, which with its united mass, like one solid body, pushed the Jews before them and was even now mounting the ramparts.

28. In this critical situation, Josephus, taking counsel from necessity—ready as she is in invention when stimulated by despair—ordered boiling oil to be poured upon this roof of close-locked shields. His men had it ready, and at once from all quarters deluged the Romans with large quantities, flinging after it the vessels, still scalding hot. This broke their formation; the Romans, burning and in excruciating agony, rolled headlong from the ramparts. For the oil instantaneously penetrated beneath their armor from head to foot, spreading over the whole surface of their bodies and devouring the flesh with the fierceness of a flame, this liquid being from its nature quick in absorbing heat, and from its fatty properties, slow in cooling. Encumbered with their cuirasses and their helmets, the victims had no escape from the scalding fluid; leaping and writhing in anguish, they dropped from the scaling-bridges. Those who turned to fly were blocked by their comrades pressing forward to the assault and became an easy mark for Jewish assailants in their rear.

29. But, in the midst of these trials, the Romans showed no lack of fortitude, nor yet the Jews of resourcefulness. The former, though they saw their comrades in tortures from the drenching oil, none the less rushed on against those who poured it, each cursing the man in front of him for impeding the charge. The Jews, on their side, invented a second ruse to trip their assailants, by pouring over the gangway-planks boiled fenugreek, on which the Romans slipped and stumbled backward. Whether attempting to retreat or to advance, not a man could remain erect. Some collapsed on their

backs on the gangways and were crushed under foot; many fell off on to the earthworks, where they were pierced by the arrows of the Jews; for in consequence of this prostration of the Romans, the defenders, relieved from hand-to-hand fighting, showed good marksmanship. After severe losses sustained in this assault, the troops, towards evening, were called off by the general. The Romans had many dead and more wounded. The defenders of Jotapata lost only six dead, but upwards of three hundred wounded were brought back to the town. This combat took place on the twentieth of the month Dæsius [July 8, 67]. . . .

[*A brief digression now describes the Roman capture of the neighboring town of Japhia and of the Samaritans on Mount Gerizim, and of the massacres which followed.*]

33. Meanwhile the defenders of Jotapata were still holding out and beyond all expectation bearing up under their miseries, when on the forty-seventh day of the siege the earthworks of the Romans overtopped the wall. That same day a deserter reported to Vespasian the reduced numbers and strength of the defense, and that, worn out with perpetual watching and continuous fighting, they would be unable longer to resist a vigorous assault and might be taken by stratagem, if the attempt were made. He stated that about the last watch of the night—an hour when they expected some respite from their sufferings and when jaded men easily succumb to morning slumber—the sentinels used to drop asleep; and that was the hour when he advised the Romans to attack. Vespasian, knowing the Jews' loyalty to each other and their indifference to chastisement, regarded the deserter with suspicion. For on a former occasion a man of Jotapata who had been taken prisoner had held out under every variety of torture, and without betraying to the enemy a word about the state of the town, even under the ordeal of fire, was finally crucified, meeting death with a smile. However, the probability of his account lent credit to the traitor; and so, thinking that the

man might be speaking the truth, and that, even if
his story were a trap, no serious risk would be run by
acting upon it, Vespasian ordered him into custody and
made ready his army for the capture of the city.

34. At the hour named they advanced in silence to
the walls. The first to mount them was Titus, with one
of the tribunes, Domitius Sabinus, followed by a few
men of the fifteenth legion. They cut down the sentries
and entered the city. Behind them came Sextus Cal-
varius, a tribune, and Placidus with the troops under
their command. The citadel had actually been taken,
the enemy was ranging through the heart of the town,
and it was now broad daylight, before the vanquished inhabitants were aware of the capture. Most of them were
worn out with fatigue and asleep, and if any awoke, a
thick mist, which happened at the time to envelop the
city, obscured their vision. At length, when the whole
army had poured in, they started up, but only to realize
their calamity; the blade at their throat brought home to
them that Jotapata was taken.

The Romans, remembering what they had borne during the siege, showed no quarter or pity for any, but
thrust the people down the steep slope from the citadel
in a general massacre. Even those still able to fight here
found themselves deprived of the means of defense by
the difficulties of the ground; crushed in the narrow alleys and slipping down the declivity, they were engulfed
in the wave of carnage that streamed from the citadel.
The situation even drove many of Josephus's picked men
to suicide; seeing themselves powerless to kill a single
Roman, they could at least forestall death at Roman
hands, and retiring in a body to the outskirts of the
town, they there put an end to themselves.

35. Those soldiers of the guard who, the moment it
was known that the town was taken, had succeeded in
escaping, took refuge in one of the northern towers,
where for some time they held their own; but, being
surrounded by large numbers of the enemy, they at
length surrendered and cheerfully extended their throats
to their assailants. The Romans might have boasted that
this last phase of the siege had cost them no loss of

life, had not one of them, the centurion Antonius, fallen
when the town was captured. He was killed by treachery.
One of the many fugitives who had taken refuge in the
caverns besought Antonius to extend his hand to him,
as a pledge of protection and to assist him to rise; the
centurion incautiously complied, whereupon the Jew
from below instantly stabbed him with his spear beneath the groin, and killed him on the spot.

36. On that day the Romans massacred all who
showed themselves; on the ensuing days they searched
the hiding-places and wreaked their vengeance on those
who had sought refuge in subterranean vaults and caverns, sparing none, whatever their age, save infants and
women. The prisoners thus collected were twelve hundred; the total number of the dead, whether killed in the
final assault or in the previous combats, was computed
at forty thousand. Vespasian ordered the city to be
razed and had all its forts burned to the ground. Thus
was Jotapata taken in the thirteenth year of the principate of Nero, on the new moon of Panemus [July 20].

viii. 1. A search for Josephus was then instituted
by the Romans, to satisfy both their own resentment
and the keen desire of their general, who considered
that the issue of the war depended largely on his capture. So the bodies of the slain and the men in hiding
were closely examined. But Josephus, when the city was
on the point of being taken, aided by some divine providence, had succeeded in stealing away from the midst
of the enemy and plunged into a deep pit, giving access
on one side to a broad cavern, invisible to those above.
There he found forty persons of distinction in hiding,
with a supply of provisions sufficient to last for a considerable time. During the day he lay hid, as the enemy
were in occupation of every quarter of the town, but at
night he would come up and look for some loophole for
escape, and reconnoiter the sentries; but finding every
spot guarded on his account and no means of eluding
detection, he descended again into the cave. So for two
days he continued in hiding. On the third, his secret
was betrayed by a woman of the party, who was captured; whereupon Vespasian at once eagerly sent two

tribunes, Paulinus and Gallicanus, with orders to offer Josephus security and to urge him to come up.

2. On reaching the spot they pressed him to do so and pledged themselves for his safety, but failed to persuade him. His suspicions were based not on the humane character of the envoys, but on the consciousness of all he had done and the feeling that he must suffer proportionately. The presentiment that he was being summoned to punishment persisted, until Vespasian sent a third messenger, the tribune Nicanor, an old acquaintance and friend of Josephus. He, on his arrival, dwelt on the innate generosity of the Romans to those whom they had once subdued, assuring him that his valor made him an object rather of admiration than of hatred to the commanding officers, and that the general was anxious to bring him up from his retreat, not for punishment—that he could inflict though he refused to come forth—but from a desire to save a brave man. He added that Vespasian, had he intended to entrap him, would never have sent him one of his friends, thus using the fairest of virtues, friendship, as a cloak for the foulest of crimes, perfidy; nor would he himself have consented to come in order to deceive a friend.

3. While Josephus was still hesitating, even after Nicanor's assurances, the soldiers in their rage attempted to set fire to the cave, but were restrained by their commander, who was anxious to take the Jewish general alive. But as Nicanor was urgently pressing his proposals and Josephus overheard the threats of the hostile crowd, suddenly there came back into his mind those nightly dreams, in which God had foretold to him the impending fate of the Jews and the destinies of the Roman sovereigns. He was an interpreter of dreams and skilled in divining the meaning of ambiguous utterances of the Deity; a priest himself and of priestly descent, he was not ignorant of the prophecies in the sacred books. At that hour, he was inspired to read their meaning, and recalling the dreadful images of his recent dreams, he offered up a silent prayer to God. "Since it pleases Thee," so it ran, "who didst create the Jewish nation, to break Thy work, since fortune has wholly passed to the Ro-

mans, and since Thou hast made choice of my spirit to announce the things that are to come, I willingly surrender to the Romans and consent to live; but I take Thee to witness that I go, not as a traitor, but as Thy minister."

4. With these words he was about to surrender to Nicanor. But when the Jews who shared his retreat understood that Josephus was yielding to entreaty, they came round him in a body, crying out, "Ah! well might the laws of our fathers groan aloud and God Himself hide His face for grief—God who implanted in Jewish breasts souls that scorn death! Is life so dear to you, Josephus, that you can endure to see the light in slavery? How soon have you forgotten yourself! How many have you persuaded to die for liberty! False, then, was that reputation for bravery, false that fame for sagacity, if you can hope for pardon from those whom you have fought so bitterly, or, supposing that they grant it, can deign to accept your life at their hands. Nay, if the fortune of the Romans has cast over you some strange forgetfulness of yourself, the care of our country's honor devolves on *us*. We will lend you a right hand and a sword. If you meet death willingly, you will have died as general of the Jews; if unwillingly, as a traitor." With these words they pointed their swords at him and threatened to kill him if he surrendered to the Romans.

5. Josephus, fearing an assault, and holding that it would be a betrayal of God's commands, should he die before delivering his message, proceeded, in this emergency, to reason philosophically with them.

"Why, comrades," said he, "this thirst for our own blood? Why set asunder such fond companions as soul and body? One says that I am changed: well, the Romans know the truth about that. Another says, 'It is honorable to die in war': yes, but according to the law of war, that is to say by the hand of the conqueror. Were I now flinching from the sword of the Romans, I should assuredly deserve to perish by my own sword and my own hand; but if they are moved to spare an enemy, how much stronger reason have we to spare ourselves? It would surely be folly to inflict on ourselves treatment which we seek to avoid by our quarrel with them. 'It is honorable to die for liberty,' says another: I concur, but on condition that one dies fighting, by the hands of those who would rob us of it. But now they are neither coming to fight us nor to take our lives. It is equally cowardly not to wish to die when one ought to do so, and to wish to die when one ought not. What is it we fear that prevents us from surrendering to the Romans? Is it not death? And shall we then inflict upon ourselves certain death, to avoid an uncertain death, which we fear, at the hands of our foes? 'No, it is slavery we fear,' I shall be told. Much liberty we enjoy at present! 'It is noble to destroy oneself,' another will say. Not so, I retort, but most ignoble; in my opinion there could be no more arrant coward than the pilot who, for fear of a tempest, deliberately sinks his ship before the storm.

"No, suicide is alike repugnant to that nature which all creatures share, and an act of impiety towards God who created us. Among the animals there is not one that deliberately seeks death or kills itself; so firmly rooted in all is nature's law—the will to live. That is why we account as enemies those who would openly take our lives and punish as assassins those who clandestinely attempt to do so. And God—think you not that He is indignant when man treats His gift with scorn? For it is from Him that we have received our being, and it is to Him that we should leave the decision to take it away. All of us, it is true, have mortal bodies, composed of perishable matter, but the soul lives for ever, immortal; it is a portion of the Deity housed in our bodies. If, then, one who makes away with or misapplies a deposit entrusted to him by a fellow-man is reckoned a perjured villain, how can he who casts out from his own body the deposit which God has placed there hope to elude Him whom he has thus wronged? It is considered right to punish a fugitive slave, even though the master he leaves be a scoundrel; and shall we fly from the best of masters, from God Himself, and not be deemed impious?

"Know you not that they who depart this life in accordance with the law of nature and repay the loan that they received from God, when He who lent is pleased to reclaim it, win eternal renown; that their houses and families are secure; that their souls, remaining spotless and obedient, are allotted the most holy place in heaven, whence, in the revolution of the ages, they return to find in chaste bodies a new habitation? But as for those who have laid mad hands upon themselves, the darker regions of the nether world receive their souls, and God, their father, visits upon their posterity the outrageous acts of the parents. That is why this crime, so hateful to God, is punished also by the sagest of legislators. With us it is ordained that the body of a suicide should be exposed unburied until sunset, although it is thought right to bury even our enemies slain in war. In other nations the law requires that a suicide's right hand, with which he made war on himself, should be cut off, holding that as the body was unnaturally severed from the soul, so the hand should be severed from the body.

"We shall do well then, comrades, to listen to reason and not to add to our human calamities the crime of impiety towards our creator. If our lives are offered us, let us live. There is nothing dishonorable in accepting this offer from those who have had so many proofs of our valor; if they think fit to kill us, death at the hands of our conquerors is honorable. But, for my part, I shall never pass over to the enemy's ranks, to prove a traitor to myself; I should indeed then be far more senseless than deserters who go over to the enemy for safety, whereas I should be going to destruction—my own destruction. I pray, however, that the Romans may prove faithless; if, after pledging their word, they put me to death, I shall die content, for I shall carry with me the consolation, better than a victory, that their triumph has been sullied by perjury."

6. By these and many similar arguments Josephus sought to deter his companions from suicide. But desperation stopped their ears, for they had long since devoted themselves to death. They were, therefore, in-

furiated at him, and ran at him from this side and that,
sword in hand, upbraiding him as a coward, each one
seeming on the point of striking him. But he, addressing one by name, fixing his general's eye of command
upon another, clasping the hand of a third, shaming
a fourth by entreaty, and torn by all manner of emotions at this critical moment, succeeded in warding off
from his throat the blades of all, turning like a wild
beast surrounded by the hunters to face his successive
assailants. Even in his extremity, they still held their
general in reverence; their hands were powerless, their
swords glanced aside, and many, in the act of thrusting
at him, spontaneously dropped their weapons.

7. But, in his straits, his resource did not forsake
him. Trusting to God's protection, he put his life to the
hazard, and said: "Since we are resolved to die, come,
let us leave the lot to decide the order in which we are
to kill ourselves; let him who draws the first lot fall by
the hand of him who comes next; fortune will thus take
her course through the whole number, and we shall be
spared from taking our lives with our own hands. For
it would be unjust that, when the rest were gone, any
should repent and escape." This proposal inspired confidence; his advice was taken, and he drew lots with
the rest. Each man thus selected presented his throat to
his neighbor, in the assurance that his general was
forthwith to share his fate; for sweeter to them than
life was the thought of death with Josephus. He, however (should one say by fortune or by the providence of
God?), was left alone with one other; and anxious
neither to be condemned by the lot nor, should he be
left to the last, to stain his hand with the blood of a
fellow-countryman, he persuaded this man also, under
a pledge, to remain alive.

8. Having thus survived both the war with the Romans and that with his own friends, Josephus was
brought by Nicanor into Vespasian's presence. The Romans all flocked to see him, and from the multitude
crowding around the general arose a hubbub of dis-
cordant voices—some exulting at his capture, some
threatening, some pushing forward to obtain a nearer

view. The more distant spectators clamored for the punishment of their enemy, but those close beside him recalled his exploits and marveled at such a reversal of fortune. Of the officers there was not one who, whatever his past resentment, did not then relent at the sight of him. Titus in particular was specially touched by the fortitude of Josephus under misfortunes and by pity for his youth. As he recalled the combatant of yesterday and saw him now a prisoner in his enemy's hands, he was led to reflect on the power of fortune, the quick vicissitudes of war, and the general instability of human affairs. So he brought over many Romans at the time to share his compassion for Josephus, and his pleading with his father was the main influence in saving the prisoner's life. Vespasian, however, ordered him to be guarded with every precaution, intending shortly to send him to Nero.

9. On hearing this, Josephus expressed a desire for a private interview with him. Vespasian having ordered all to withdraw except his son Titus and two of his friends, the prisoner thus addressed him: "You imagine, Vespasian, that in the person of Josephus you have taken a mere captive; but I come to you as a messenger of greater destinies. Had I not been sent on this errand by God, I knew the law of the Jews and how it becomes a general to die. To Nero do you send me? Why then? Think you that [Nero and] those who before your accession succeed him will continue? You will be Cæsar, Vespasian, you will be emperor, you and your son here. Bind me then yet more securely in chains and keep me for yourself; for you, Cæsar, are master not of me only, but of land and sea and the whole human race. For myself, I ask to be punished by stricter custody, if I have dared to trifle with the words of God."

To this speech Vespasian, at the moment, seemed to attach little credit, supposing it to be a trick of Josephus to save his life. Gradually, however, he was led to believe it, for God was already rousing in him thoughts of empire, and by other tokens foreshadowing the throne. He found, moreover, that Josephus had proved a veracious prophet in other matters. For one of the two

245

friends in attendance at the private interview remarked: "If these words are not a nonsensical invention of the prisoner to avert the storm which he has raised, I am surprised that Josephus neither predicted the fall of Jotapata to its inhabitants nor his own captivity." To this Josephus replied that he had foretold to the people of Jotapata that their city would be captured after forty-seven days and that he himself would be taken alive by the Romans. Vespasian, having privately questioned the prisoners on these statements and found them true, then began to credit those concerning himself. While he did not release Josephus from his custody or chains, he presented him with raiment and other precious gifts, and continued to treat him with kindness and solicitude, being warmly supported by Titus in these courtesies.

BOOK V

The Siege of Jerusalem (A.D. 70)

i. 6. . . . . . Titus, having assembled part of his forces at headquarters and sent orders to the rest to join him at Jerusalem, was now on the march from Cæsarea. He had the three legions, which under his father had previously ravaged Judæa, and the twelfth, which under Cestius had once been defeated; this legion, bearing a general reputation for valor, now with the recollection of what it had suffered, advanced with the greater alacrity for revenge. Of these he directed the fifth to join him by the Emmaus route and the tenth to ascend by way of Jericho while he himself set out with the others, being further attended by the contingents from the allied kings in greatly increased strength, and by a considerable body of Syrian auxiliaries.

The gaps in the four legions caused by the drafts which Vespasian had sent with Mucianus to Italy were filled by the new troops brought up by Titus, for two thousand picked men from the armies at Alexandria and three thousand guards from the Euphrates accompanied him. With these was the most tried of all his friends for loyalty and sagacity, Tiberius Alexander, hitherto in charge of Egypt in the interests of Titus and his father, and now deemed worthy to take command of these armies because he had been the first to welcome the dynasty just arising, and with splendid faith had attached himself to its fortunes while they were still uncertain. Pre-eminent moreover, through years and experience, as a counselor in the exigencies of war, he now accompanied Titus.*

---

* Nero had been assassinated in the previous year and was succeeded on the throne, following a short civil war, by Titus' father Vespasian. Tiberius Julius Alexander, scion of a wealthy Jewish family in Egypt (and nephew of Philo), was then prefect of Egypt, having earlier been procurator of Judæa.

ii. 1. As Titus advanced into enemy territory, his vanguard consisted of the contingents of the kings with the whole body of auxiliaries. Next to these were the pioneers and camp-measurers, then the officers' baggage-train; behind the troops protecting them came the commander-in-chief, escorted by the lancers and other picked troops, and followed by the legionary cavalry. These were succeeded by the engines, and these by the tribunes and prefects of cohorts with a picked escort; after them and surrounding the eagle came the ensigns preceded by their trumpeters, and behind them the solid column, six abreast. The servants attached to each legion followed in a body, preceded by the baggage-train. Last of all came the mercenaries with a rear guard to keep watch on them.

Leading his army forward in this orderly array, according to Roman usage, Titus advanced through Samaria to Gophna, previously captured by his father and now garrisoned. After resting here one night he set forward at dawn, and at the end of a full day's march encamped in the valley which is called by the Jews in their native tongue "Valley of Thorns," close to a village named Gabath Saul, which means "Saul's Hill," at a distance of about thirty furlongs from Jerusalem. From here, with some six hundred picked horsemen, he rode forward to reconnoiter the city's strength and to test the mettle of the Jews, whether on seeing him they would be terrified into surrender before any actual conflict; for he had learned, as indeed was the fact, that the people were longing for peace, but were overawed by the insurgents and brigands and remained quiet merely from inability to resist.

2. So long as he rode straight along the high road leading directly to the wall, no one appeared outside the gates; but when he diverged from the route and led his troop of horse in an oblique line towards the tower Psephinus, the Jews suddenly dashed out in immense numbers at a spot called "the Women's Towers," through the gate facing Helena's monuments, broke through the cavalry, and placing themselves in front of those who were still galloping along the road, pre-

vented them from joining their comrades who had left it, thus cutting Titus off with a handful of men.

For him to proceed was impossible, because the ground outside the ramparts was all cut up by trenches for gardening purposes and intersected by cross walls and numerous fences; while to rejoin his own men was, he saw, impracticable owing to the intervening masses of the enemy and the retirement of his comrades on the highway, most of whom, unaware of the prince's peril and believing that he too had turned simultaneously, were in full retreat. Perceiving that his safety depended solely on his personal prowess, he turned his horse's head, and shouting to his companions to follow, dashed into the enemy's midst, struggling to cut his way through to his own party. Then, more than ever, might the reflection arise that the hazards of war and the perils of princes are under God's care; for of all that hail of arrows discharged at Titus, who wore neither helmet nor cuirass—for he had gone forward, as I said, not to fight, but to reconnoiter—not one touched his person, but, as if his assailants purposely missed their mark, all whizzed harmlessly by. He, meanwhile, with his sword constantly dispersing those on his flank and prostrating multitudes who withstood him to the face, rode his horse over his fallen foes.

At Cæsar's intrepidity the Jews shouted and cheered each other on against him, but wherever he turned his horse there was flight and a general stampede. His comrades, in danger, closed up to him, riddled in rear and flank; for each man's one hope of escape lay in pushing through with Titus before he was cut off. Two, in fact, further behind, thus fell: one with his horse was surrounded and speared, the other who dismounted was killed and his steed led off to the city; with the remainder Titus safely reached the camp. The Jews thus successful in their first onset were elated with inconsiderate hopes, and this transient turn of fortune afforded them high confidence as to the future.

3. Cæsar, being joined during the night by the legion from Emmaus, next day broke up his camp and advanced to Scopus, as the place is called, from which was

obtained the first view of the city and the grand pile of the temple gleaming afar; whence the spot, a low prominence adjoining the northern quarter of the city, is appropriately named Scopus. Here, at a distance of seven furlongs from the city, Titus ordered one combined camp to be formed for two of the legions, and the fifth to be stationed three furlongs in their rear; considering that men worn out with the fatigue of a night's march deserved to be screened from molestation while throwing up their entrenchments. Scarcely had they begun operations when the tenth legion also arrived, having come by way of Jericho, where a party of soldiers had been posted to guard the pass formerly taken by Vespasian. These troops had orders to encamp at a distance of six furlongs from Jerusalem at the mount called the Mount of Olives, which lies over against the city on the east, being separated from it by a deep intervening ravine called Kedron.

4. And now for the first time the mutual dissension of the factions within the town, hitherto incessantly at strife, was checked by the war from without suddenly bursting in full force upon them. The rival parties, beholding with dismay the Romans forming three several encampments, started a sorry alliance and began to ask each other what they were waiting for, or what possessed them to let themselves be choked by the erection of three fortifications. The enemy unmolested was building himself a rival city, while they sat behind their ramparts, like spectators of excellent and expedient operations, with hands and weapons idle!

"Is then," they exclaimed, "our valor to be displayed only against ourselves, while the Romans, through our party strife, make a bloodless conquest of the city?" Stimulating each other with such language and uniting forces, they seized their weapons, dashed out suddenly against the tenth legion, and racing across the ravine with a terrific shout, fell upon the enemy while engaged upon his fortifications. The latter to facilitate their work were in scattered groups and to this end had laid aside most of their arms; for they imagined that the Jews would never venture upon a sally, or that if moved

to do so, their energies would be dissipated by their dissensions. They were therefore taken by surprise and
thrown into disorder.

Abandoning their work, some instantly retreated, while
many rushing for their arms were struck down before
they could round upon the foe. The Jews meanwhile
were continually being reinforced by others who were
encouraged by the success of the first party, and with
fortune favoring them seemed both to themselves and
to the enemy far in excess of their actual numbers.
Moreover, men habituated to discipline and proficient in
fighting in ordered ranks and by word of command,
when suddenly confronted with disorderly warfare, are
peculiarly liable to be thrown into confusion. Hence on
this occasion too, the Romans, being taken unawares,
gave way to repeated assaults. Whenever, indeed, any
were overtaken and turned upon the foe, they checked
the Jewish rush and wounded many who in the ardor of
pursuit were off their guard; but as more and more
Jews sallied out from the town, the disorder of the
Romans increased, until they were finally routed from
the camp.

Indeed, in all probability, the entire legion would then
have been in jeopardy, had not Titus, hearing of their
position, instantly come to their aid. Roundly chiding
their cowardice, he rallied the fugitives and then falling
upon the Jews in flank with his band of picked followers, slew many, wounded more, routed the whole body
and drove them headlong down into the ravine. They
suffered severely on the declivity, but having reached
the farther bank turned to face the Romans and, with
the brook between them, renewed the combat. So the
battle raged till noon; and then shortly after midday,
Titus, to check further sallies, deployed the reinforcements brought by himself, together with the auxiliary
cohorts, and dismissed the remainder of the legion to
the ridge to resume their fortification.

5. The Jews, however, mistook this move for flight,
and seeing the watchman whom they had posted on the
ramparts signaling by shaking his robe, another crowd,
perfectly fresh, sprang forth with such impetuosity that

their rush was comparable to that of the most savage of
beasts. In fact not one of the opposing line awaited their
charge, but, as if struck [by a bolt] from an engine, they
broke their ranks and turned and fled up the mountain
side, leaving Titus, with a few followers, half way up
the slope. The friends who out of regard for the commander-in-chief stood their ground indifferent to danger
all earnestly entreated him to retire before these Jews
who courted death, and not to risk his life for men who
ought to have remained to protect him. He should consider what he owed to fortune, and not act the part
of a common soldier, lord as he was alike of the war
and of the world; he on whom all depended ought not
to face so imminent a risk. These advisers Titus appeared not even to hear, but withstanding the Jews who
were rushing at him up the hill, confronted, struck and
slew them as they pressed upon him, and then falling
upon the masses thrust them backward down the slope.
Yet, terrified though they were at his intrepidity and
strength, they did not even then retreat to the city, but
inclining to either side to avoid him continued their pursuit of those who were flying up the hill; whereupon he
attacked them again in flank, and strove to check the
rush.

Meanwhile, the troops who were fortifying the camp
above, on seeing their comrades below in flight, were
themselves once more seized with such consternation
and alarm that the whole legion scattered; for they
imagined that the Jewish charge was irresistible and
that Titus himself had been routed, because the rest
would never, they thought, have fled while he held his
ground. Like men beset by panic, they sped in all directions, until some, catching sight of their general in
the thickest of the fight and greatly alarmed on his
account, with shouts announced his danger to the whole
legion. Shame rallied them, and upbraiding one another
with a worse guilt than flight in their desertion of Cæsar,
they put forth their utmost energies against the Jews,
and having once made them give ground, proceeded to
thrust them off the slope into the valley. The Jews retired, fighting step by step, but the Romans, having the

advantage of position, finally drove them all into the ravine. Titus, still pressing upon his immediate opponents, now sent the legion back to resume their fortifications, while he, with his former band, withstood and held the enemy at bay. Thus if, without a syllable added in flattery or withheld from envy, the truth must be told, Cæsar personally twice rescued the entire legion when in jeopardy, and enabled them to intrench themselves in their camp unmolested.

iii. 1. During a temporary lull in the war without the walls, faction renewed its hostilities within. When the day of unleavened bread came round on the fourteenth of the [Macedonian] month Xanthicus, the reputed anniversary of the Jews' first liberation from Egypt, Eleazar and his men partly opened the gates [of the Temple] and admitted citizens desiring to worship within the building. But John, making the festival a cloak for his treacherous designs, armed with concealed weapons the less conspicuous of his followers, most of whom were unpurified, and by his earnest endeavors got them stealthily passed into the Temple to take prior possession of it. Once within, they cast off their garments and were suddenly revealed as armed men.

The purlieus of the sanctuary were instantly a scene of the utmost disorder and confusion, the people who had no connection with the party strife regarding this as an indiscriminate attack upon all; the Zealots, as directed against themselves alone. The latter, however, neglecting any longer to guard the gates and not waiting to come to close quarters with the intruders, leaped down from the battlements and took refuge in the temple vaults; while the visitors from the city, cowering beside the altar and huddled together around the sanctuary, were trampled under foot and mercilessly struck with clubs and swords. Many peaceable citizens from enmity and personal spite were slain by their adversaries as partisans of the opposite faction, and any who in the past had offended one of the conspirators, being now recognized as a Zealot, was led off to punishment. But while the innocent were thus brutally treated, the intruders granted a truce to the criminals and let them go when they emerged from the vaults. Being now in possession of the inner court of the Temple and all the stores which it contained, they could bid defiance to Simon. The sedition, hitherto of a tripartite character, was thus again reduced to two factions.

2. Titus, now deciding to abandon Scopus and encamp nearer the city, posted a picked body of horse and foot of such strength as he deemed sufficient to check the enemy's sallies, and gave orders to his main army to level the intervening ground right up to the walls. Every fence and palisade with which the inhabitants had enclosed their gardens and plantations having accordingly been swept away, and every fruit tree within the area felled, the cavities and gullies on the route were filled up, the protuberant rocks demolished with tools of iron, and the whole intervening space from Scopus to Herod's monuments, adjoining the spot called the Serpents' Pool, was thus reduced to a dead level.

3. During this period the Jews contrived the following stratagem to trick the Romans. The more daring of the insurgents, issuing forth from the so-called Women's Towers, as though they had been ejected by the partisans of peace and were in terror of being attacked by the Romans, kept close together cowering in a bunch. Meanwhile their comrades, lining the walls so as to be taken for the populace, shouted "Peace," begged for protection, and invited the Romans to enter, promising to open the gates; these cries they accompanied by showers of stones aimed at their own men, as if to drive them from the gates. The latter made a feint of forcing an entry and petitioning those within, and constantly rushing towards the Romans and again retreating showed signs of extreme agitation.

Their ruse did not fail to impose on the rank and file: imagining that they had one party at their mercy, to be punished at will, and hoping that the other would throw open the city, they were on the point of proceeding to action. Titus, on the contrary, viewed this surprising invitation with suspicion. For having only the day before, through Josephus, invited them to terms, he had met with no reasonable response; he therefore now ordered

his men to remain where they were. However, some who
were stationed in the forefront of the works had, without awaiting orders, seized their arms and rushed towards the gates. The pretended outcasts at first retired
before them, but as soon as the Romans came between
the gateway towers, they darted out and surrounded and
attacked them in rear; while those on the wall showered
upon them a volley of stones and every species of missile, killing many and wounding most. For it was no
easy matter to escape from the wall with the enemy
pressing them behind; moreover, shame at their error
and dread of their officers impelled them to persevere
in their blunder. Consequently, it was only after a prolonged combat with spears and after receiving many
wounds from the Jews—inflicting, to be sure, no fewer
in return—that they eventually repelled their encircling
enemy. Even when they retired, the Jews still followed
and kept them under fire as far as the tomb of Helena.

4. Then, with vulgar abuse of their good fortune,
they jeered at the Romans for being deluded by a ruse
and brandishing their bucklers danced and shouted for
joy. The soldiers, for their part, were met by threats
from their officers and a furious Cæsar. "These Jews,"
he protested, "with desperation for their only leader, do
everything with forethought and circumspection: their
stratagems and ambuscades are carefully planned, and
their schemes are further favored by fortune because of
their obedience and their mutual loyalty and confidence;
while Romans who, through orderly discipline and obedience to command, have ever found even fortune their
slave, are now brought to grief by conduct the very opposite, are defeated through their intemperate pugnacity,
and—direst disgrace of all—while fighting without a
leader under the eyes of Cæsar! Deeply indeed may the
laws of the service mourn, deeply too my father when
he hears of this rebuff; seeing that he, though grown
gray in warfare, never met with a like disaster, while
those laws invariably punish with death the very slightest breach of discipline, whereas now they have beheld
a whole corps quit the ranks! However, these rash adven-

turers shall learn forthwith that, among Romans, even a victory without orders given is held dishonorable."

From such determined language to his officers it was clear that Titus intended to put the law into force against all. The offenders, accordingly, gave themselves up for lost, expecting in a moment to meet their merited death; but the legions, flocking round Titus, made intercession for their fellow-soldiers, imploring him, in consideration of the obedience of them all, to forgive the recklessness of a few, and assuring him that these would retrieve their present error by future meritorious deeds.

5. To these entreaties, backed by considerations of expediency, Cæsar yielded; for he held that while in the case of an individual punishment should actually be carried into execution, where numbers were concerned it should not go beyond reproof. He was therefore reconciled to the soldiers, after strictly admonishing them to be wiser in future, while he privately reflected how best to avenge himself on the Jews for their stratagem. In four days all the intervening ground up to the walls was leveled; and Titus, now anxious to secure a safe passage for the baggage and camp-followers, drew up the flower of his forces facing the northern and western portions of the wall, in lines seven deep: the infantry in front, the cavalry behind; each of these arms in three ranks, the archers forming a seventh line in the middle. The sallies of the Jews being held in check by this formidable array, the beasts of burden belonging to the three legions with their train of followers passed securely on. Titus himself encamped about two furlongs from the ramparts, at the angle opposite the tower called Psephinus, where the circuit of the wall bends back from the north to the west. The other division of the army entrenched itself opposite the tower named Hippicus, likewise at a distance of two furlongs from the city. The tenth legion kept its position on the Mount of Olives.

The City of Jerusalem and the Temple

iv. 1. The city was fortified by three walls, except where it was enclosed by impassable ravines, a single rampart there sufficing. It was built, in portions facing each other, on two hills separated by a central valley, in which the tiers of houses ended.

Of these hills, that on which the upper city lay was far higher and had a straighter ridge than the other; consequently, owing to its strength it was called by King David—the father of Solomon the first builder of the Temple—the Stronghold, but we called it the Upper Agora. The second hill, which bore the name of Acra and supported the lower city, was a hog's back. Opposite this was a third hill, by nature lower than Acra, and once divided from it by another broad ravine. Afterwards, however, the Hasmonæans, during the period of their reign, both filled up the ravine, with the object of uniting the city to the Temple, and also reduced the elevation of Acra by levelling its summit, in order that it might not block the view of the Temple. The Valley of the Cheesemakers, as the ravine was called, which, as we said, divides the hill of the upper city from that of the lower, extends down to Siloam; for so we called that fountain of sweet and abundant water. On the exterior the two hills on which the city stood were encompassed by deep ravines, and the precipitous cliffs on either side of it rendered the town nowhere accessible.

2. Of the three walls, the most ancient, owing to the surrounding ravines and the hill above them on which it was reared, was well-nigh impregnable. But, besides the advantage of its position, it was also strongly built, David and Solomon and their successors on the throne having taken pride in the work. Beginning on the north at the tower called Hippicus, it extended to the Xystus, and then joining the council-chamber terminated at the western portico of the Temple. Beginning at the same point in the other direction, westward, it descended past the place called Bethso to the Gate of the Essenes, then

turned southwards above the fountain of Siloam; thence it again inclined to the east towards Solomon's pool, and after passing a spot which they call Ophel, finally joined the eastern portico of the Temple.

The second wall started from the gate in the first wall which they called Gennath, and, enclosing only the northern district of the town, went up as far as Antonia.

The third began at the tower Hippicus, whence it stretched northwards to the tower Psephinus, and then descending opposite the monuments of Helena (queen of Adiabene and daughter of King Izates), and proceeding past the royal caverns, it bent round a corner tower over against the so-called Fuller's Tomb and joining the ancient rampart terminated at the valley called Kedron. This wall was built by Agrippa to enclose the later additions to the city, which were quite unprotected; for the town, overflowing with inhabitants, had gradually crept beyond the ramparts. Indeed, the population, uniting to the hill the district north of the Temple, had encroached so far that even a fourth hill was surrounded with houses. This hill, which is called Bezetha, lay opposite Antonia, but was cut off from it by a deep fosse, dug on purpose to sever the foundations of Antonia from the hill and so to render them at once less easy of access and more elevated, the depth of the trench materially increasing the height of the towers. The recently built quarter was called in the vernacular Bezetha, which might be translated into Greek as New Town.

Seeing then the residents of this district in need of defense, Agrippa, the father and namesake of the present king, began the above-mentioned wall; but, fearing that Claudius Cæsar might suspect from the vast scale of the structure that he had designs of revolution and revolt, he desisted after merely laying the foundations. Indeed the city would have been impregnable, had the wall been continued as it began; for it was constructed of stones twenty cubits long and ten broad, so closely joined that they could scarcely have been undermined with tools of iron or shaken by engines. The wall itself was ten cubits broad, and it would doubtless have attained a greater height than it did, had not the ambition of its founder been frustrated. Subsequently, although hurriedly erected by the Jews, it rose to a height of twenty cubits, besides having battlements of two cubits and bulwarks of three cubits high, bringing the total altitude up to twenty-five cubits.

3. Above the wall, however, rose towers, twenty cubits broad and twenty high, square and solid as the wall itself, and in the joining and beauty of the stones in no wise inferior to a temple. Over this solid masonry, twenty cubits in altitude, were magnificent apartments, and above these, upper chambers and cisterns to receive the rain-water, each tower having broad spiral staircases. Of such towers the third wall had ninety, disposed at intervals of two hundred cubits; the line of the middle wall was broken by fourteen towers, that of the old wall by sixty. The whole circumference of the city was thirty-three furlongs [or about 3.8 miles]. But wonderful as was the third wall throughout, still more so was the tower Psephinus, which rose at its north-west angle and opposite to which Titus encamped. For, being seventy cubits high, it afforded from sunrise a prospect embracing both Arabia and the utmost limits of Hebrew territory as far as the sea; it was of octagonal form.

Over against this was the tower Hippicus, and close to it two others, all built by King Herod into the old wall, and for magnitude, beauty and strength without their equal in the world. For, apart from his innate magnanimity and his pride in the city, the king sought, in the super-excellence of these works, to gratify his private feelings; dedicating them to the memory of three persons to whom he was most fondly attached, and after whom he named these towers—brother, friend, and wife. The last, as we have previously related, he had for love's sake actually slain; the others he had lost in war, after valiant fight.

Now Hippicus, called after his friend, was quadrangular, its length and breadth being each twenty-five cubits, and to the height of thirty cubits it was solid throughout. But above this solid and compact mass of masonry was a reservoir, twenty cubits deep, to receive the rain-water, and over this a double-roofed chamber, twenty-five cubits high, with roofs of diverse colors. This again was crowned by turrets two cubits, and battlements three cubits high, so that the total altitude amounted to eighty cubits.

The second tower, which he named Phasael after his brother, was of equal length and breadth, forty cubits each; forty cubits was also the height of its solid base. Above and around this ran a cloister, ten cubits high, protected by parapets and bulwarks. Over this and rising from the center of the cloister was built another tower, apportioned into sumptuous apartments, including a bath, in order that nothing might be wanting to impart to this tower the appearance of a palace. Its summit was crowned with battlements and turrets, and its total height was about ninety cubits. In form it resembled the tower of Pharos that emits its beacon light to navigators approaching Alexandria, but in circumference it was much larger. It had now become the seat of Simon's tyranny.

The third tower, Mariamme—for such was the queen's name—was solid to a height of but twenty cubits, its breadth being also twenty cubits and its length the same. But its upper residential quarters were far more luxurious and ornate than those of the other towers, the king considering it appropriate that the one named after a woman should so far surpass in decoration those called after men, as they outdid the woman's tower in strength. The total height of this last was fifty-five cubits.

4. But while such were the proportions of these three towers, they seemed far larger owing to their site. For the old wall in which they stood was itself built on a lofty hill, and above the hill rose as it were a crest thirty cubits higher still; on this the towers stood and thus gained immensely in elevation. Marvellous, too, were the dimensions of the stones; for these were not composed of ordinary blocks or boulders such as men might carry, but were cut out of white marble. The length of each block was twenty cubits, the breadth ten, and the depth five, and so nicely were they joined to one another that each tower seemed like one natural

rock, that had later been polished by the hands of craftsmen into shape and angles; so wholly imperceptible was the fitting of the joints.

Adjoining and on the inner side of these towers, which lay to the north of it, was the king's palace, baffling all description: indeed, in extravagance and equipment no building surpassed it. It was completely enclosed within a wall thirty cubits high, broken at equal distances by ornamental towers, and contained immense banqueting-halls and bed-chambers for a hundred guests. The interior fittings are indescribable—the variety of the stones (for species rare in every other country were here collected in abundance), ceilings wonderful both for the length of the beams and the splendor of their surface decoration, the host of apartments with their infinite varieties of design, all amply furnished, while most of the objects in each of them were of silver or gold. All around were many circular cloisters, leading one into another, the columns in each being different, and their open courts all of greensward. There were groves of various trees intersected by long walks, which were bordered by deep canals, and ponds everywhere studded with bronze figures, through which the water was discharged; and around the streams were numerous cots for tame pigeons. However, it is impossible adequately to delineate the palace, and the memory of it is harrowing, recalling as it does the ravages of the brigands' fire. For it was not the Romans who burned it to the ground, but this was done, as we have said already, by conspirators within the walls at the opening of the revolt. The conflagration beginning at Antonia passed to the palace, and spread to the roofs of the three towers.

v. 1. Though the Temple, as I said, was seated on a strong hill, the level area on its summit originally barely sufficed for shrine and altar, the ground around it being precipitous and steep. But King Solomon, the actual founder of the Temple, having walled up the eastern side, a single portico was reared on this made ground; on its other sides the sanctuary remained exposed. In course of ages, however, through the constant additions of the

people to the embankment, the hill-top by this process
of levelling up was widened. They further broke down
the north wall and thus took in an area as large as the
whole temple enclosure subsequently occupied. Then,
after having enclosed the hill from its base with a wall
on three sides, and accomplished a task greater than
they could ever have hoped to achieve—a task upon
which long ages were spent by them as well as all their
sacred treasures, though replenished by the tributes offered to God from every quarter of the world—they
built around the original block the upper courts and the
lower temple enclosure. The latter, where its foundations were lowest, they built up from a depth of three
hundred cubits; at some spots this figure was exceeded.
The whole depth of the foundations was, however, not
apparent; for they filled up a considerable part of the
ravines, wishing to level the narrow alleys of the town.
Blocks of stone were used in the building measuring
forty cubits; for lavish funds and popular enthusiasm
led to incredible enterprises, and a task seemingly in-
terminable was through perseverance and in time actually achieved.

2. Nor was the superstructure unworthy of such foundations. The porticoes, all in double rows, were supported by columns five and twenty cubits high—each a
single block of the purest white marble—and ceiled with
panels of cedar. The natural magnificence of these columns, their excellent polish and fine adjustment presented a striking spectacle, without any adventitious embellishment of painting or sculpture. The porticoes were
thirty cubits broad, and the complete circuit of them,
embracing the tower of Antonia, measured six furlongs.
The open court was from end to end variegated with
paving of all manner of stones.

Proceeding across this towards the second court of
the Temple, one found it surrounded by a stone balustrade, three cubits high and of exquisite workmanship;
in this at regular intervals stood slabs giving warning,
some in Greek, others in Latin characters, of the law
of purification, to wit that no foreigner was permitted
to enter the holy place, for so the second enclosure of

the Temple was called. It was approached from the first by fourteen steps; the area above was quadrangular, and screened by a wall of its own. The exterior height of this, actually forty cubits, was disguised by the steps, the interior altitude was but five and twenty; for the floor being built on a higher level, the whole was not visible from within, a portion being concealed by the hill.

Beyond the fourteen steps there was a space of ten cubits between them and the wall, forming a level terrace. From this again other flights of five steps led up to the gates. Of these there were eight on the north and south, four on either side, and two on the east—necessarily; since in this quarter a special place of worship was walled off for the women, rendering a second gate requisite; this approach opened opposite to the first. On the other sides there was one gate on the south and one on the north giving access to the women's court; for women were not permitted to enter by the others nor yet to pass by way of their own gate beyond the partition wall. This court was, however, thrown open for worship to all Jewish women alike, whether natives of the country or visitors from abroad. The west end of the building had no gate, the wall there being unbroken. The porticoes between the gates, on the inner side of the wall in front of the treasury chambers, were supported by exceedingly beautiful and lofty columns; these porticoes were single, but except in point of size, in no way inferior to those in the lower court.

3. Of the gates, nine were completely overlaid with gold and silver, as were also their door-posts and lintels; but one, that outside the sanctuary, was of Corinthian bronze, and far exceeded in value those plated with silver and set in gold. Each gateway had two doors, and each door was thirty cubits in height and fifteen in breadth. Beyond and within the entrances, however, the portals expanded, embracing on either side turret-like chambers measuring thirty cubits in breadth and length, and over forty cubits in height, each supported by two columns, twelve cubits in circumference. The dimensions of the other gates were all alike, but the one be-

yond the Corinthian gate, opening from the women's court on the east, opposite the gate of the sanctuary, was far larger, having an altitude of fifty cubits, with doors of forty, and richer decoration, being overlaid with massive plates of silver and gold. The nine gates were thus plated by Alexander the father of Tiberius [Julius Alexander]. Fifteen steps led up from the women's compartment to the greater gate, these steps being shallower than the five at each of the other gates.

4. The sacred edifice itself, the holy Temple, in the central position, was approached by a flight of twelve steps. The façade was of equal height and breadth, each being a hundred cubits; but the building behind was narrower by forty cubits, for in front it had, as it were, shoulders extending twenty cubits on either side. The first gate was seventy cubits high and twenty-five broad and had no doors, displaying unexcluded the void expanse of heaven; the entire face was covered with gold, and through it the first edifice was visible to a spectator without, in all its grandeur, and the surroundings of the inner gate, all gleaming with gold, fell beneath his eye. But, whereas the sanctuary within consisted of two separate chambers, the first building alone stood exposed to view, from top to bottom, towering to a height of ninety cubits, its length being fifty and its breadth twenty.

The gate opening into the building was, as I said, completely overlaid with gold, as was the whole wall around it. It had, moreover, above it those golden vines from which depended grape-clusters as tall as a man, and it had golden doors fifty-five cubits high and sixteen broad. Before these hung a veil of equal length, of Babylonian tapestry, with embroidery of blue and fine linen, of scarlet also and purple, wrought with marvellous skill. Nor was this mixture of materials without its mystic meaning: it typified the universe. For the scarlet seemed emblematical of fire, the fine linen of the earth, the blue of the air, and the purple of the sea; the comparison in two cases being suggested by their color, and in that of the fine linen and purple by their origin, as the one is produced by the earth and the other by the sea. On this tapestry was portrayed a panorama of the heavens, the signs of the zodiac excepted.

5. Passing within, one ·found oneself in the ground-floor of the sanctuary. This was sixty cubits in height, the same in length, and twenty cubits in breadth. But the sixty cubits of its length were again divided. The first portion, partitioned off at forty cubits, contained within it three most wonderful works of art, universally renowned: a lampstand, a table, and an altar of incense. The seven lamps (such being the number of the branches from the lampstand) represented the planets; the loaves on the table, twelve in number, the circle of the zodiac and the year; while the altar of incense, by the thirteen fragrant spices from sea and from land, both desert and inhabited, with which it was replenished, signified that all things are of God and for God.

The innermost recess measured twenty cubits, and was screened in like manner from the outer portion by a veil. In this stood nothing whatever: unapproachable, inviolable, invisible to all, it was called the Holy of Holies.

Around the sides of the lower part of the sanctuary were numerous chambers, in three stories, communicating with one another; these were approached by entrances from either side of the gateway. The upper part of the building had no similar chambers, being proportionately narrower, but rose forty cubits higher in a severer style than the lower story. These forty cubits, added to the sixty of the ground-floor, amount to a total altitude of a hundred cubits.

6. The exterior of the building wanted nothing that could astound either mind or eye. For, being covered on all sides with massive plates of gold, the sun was no sooner up than it radiated so fiery a flash that persons straining to look at it were compelled to avert their eyes, as from the solar rays. To approaching strangers it appeared from a distance like a snow-clad mountain; for all that was not overlaid with gold was of purest white. From its summit protruded sharp golden spikes to prevent birds from settling upon and polluting the roof.

Some of the stones in the building were forty-five cubits in length, five in height and six in breadth.

In front of it stood the altar, fifteen cubits high, and with a breadth and length extending alike to fifty cubits, in shape a square with horn-like projections at the corners, and approached from the south by a gently sloping acclivity. No iron was used in its construction, nor did iron ever touch it.

Surrounding both the sanctuary and the altar was a low stone parapet, fair and graceful, about a cubit high, which separated the laity outside from the priests.

Persons afflicted with gonorrhea or leprosy were excluded from the city altogether; the Temple was closed to women during their menstruation, and even when free from impurity they were not permitted to pass the boundary which we have mentioned above. Men not thoroughly clean were barred from admission to the inner court, from which even priests were excluded when undergoing purification.

7. All who were of priestly lineage but were prevented from officiating by some physical defect were admitted within the parapet, along with those free from any imperfection, and received the portions which were their birthright, but wore ordinary dress; none but the officiating priest was clad in the holy vestments. The priests who were without blemish went up to the altar and the sanctuary clothed in fine linen, scrupulously abstaining from strong drink through reverence for the ritual, lest they should be guilty of any transgression in their ministrations.

The high priest accompanied them, not on all occasions, but on the seventh days and new moons, and on any national festival or annual assemblage of all the people. When ministering, he wore breeches which covered his thighs up to the loins, an under vest of linen, and over that a blue robe reaching to the feet, full and tasselled; and from the tassels hung golden bells and pomegranates alternately, the bells symbolizing thunder and the pomegranates lightning. The embroidered sash which attached this robe to the breast consisted of five bands of variegated colors: gold, purple, scarlet, fine linen, and blue; with which, as we have said, the veils in the sanctuary were also interwoven. Of the same mixture of materials, with gold preponderating, was the high priest's ephod. In form like an ordinary cuirass, it was fastened by two golden brooches, set with very large and beautiful sardonyxes, on which were engraved the names of those after whom the tribes of the nation were called. Attached to the other side were twelve more stones, in four rows of three each: sardius, topaz, emerald; carbuncle, jasper, sapphire; agate, amethyst, jacinth; onyx, beryl, chrysolite; on each of which, again, was engraved the name of one of the heads of the tribes. His head was covered by a tiara of fine linen wreathed with blue, encircling which was another crown, of gold, whereon were embossed the sacred letters, to wit, four vowels [YHVH]. These robes were not worn by the high priest in general, when he assumed plainer attire, but only when he penetrated to the innermost sanctuary; this he entered alone once in the year, on the day on which it was the universal custom to keep fast to God. Of the city and the Temple, and of the customs and laws relating to the latter, we shall speak more minutely hereafter;* for on these topics much yet remains to be told.

8. The tower of Antonia lay at the angle where two porticoes, the western and the northern, of the first court of the Temple met; it was built upon a rock fifty cubits high and on all sides precipitous. It was the work of King Herod and a crowning exhibition of the innate grandeur of his genius; for, to begin with, the rock was covered from its base upwards with smooth flagstones, both for ornament and in order that anyone attempting to ascend or descend it might slip off. Next, in front of the actual edifice, there was a wall three cubits high; and behind this the tower of Antonia rose in majesty to an altitude of forty cubits. The interior resembled a palace in its spaciousness and appointments, being divided into apartments of every description and for every purpose, including cloisters, baths, and broad court-

---

* The references here and in the next section (and frequently in the *Antiquities*) are to a projected work which was never published and presumably not completed.

yards for the accommodation of troops; so that from its possession of all conveniences it seemed a town, from its magnificence a palace.

The general appearance of the whole was that of a tower with other towers at each of the four corners; three of these turrets were fifty cubits high, while that at the southeast angle rose to seventy cubits, and so commanded a view of the whole area of the Temple. At the point where it impinged upon the porticoes of the Temple, there were stairs leading down to both of them, by which the guards descended; for a Roman cohort was permanently quartered there, and at the festivals took up positions in arms around the porticoes to watch the people and repress any insurrectionary movement. For if the Temple lay as a fortress over the city, Antonia dominated the Temple, and the occupants of that post were the guards of all three; the upper town had its own fortress—Herod's palace. The hill Bezetha was, as I said, cut off from Antonia; the highest of all the hills, it was encroached on by part of the new town and formed on the north the only obstruction to the view of the Temple. As I propose hereafter to give a fuller and more circumstantial description of the Temple and the walls, these remarks shall for the present suffice.

The Narrative of the Siege Resumed

vi. 1. The strength of the combatants and insurgents within the city was as follows. Simon had an army, exclusive of the Idumæans, of ten thousand men; over these were fifty officers, Simon himself being commander-in-chief. His Idumæan contingent numbered five thousand and had ten chiefs, among whom James, son of Sosas, and Simon, son of Cathlas, ranked highest. John, at the time when he seized the temple, had an army of six thousand men, commanded by twenty officers; but now the Zealots also had joined him, having abandoned their quarrel, to the number of two thousand four hundred, led by Eleazar, their former chief, and Simon, son of Arinus.

These two factions, being, as we said, at war with

each other, the citizens were their common prize, and those of the people who discountenanced their iniquities became the prey of both. Simon occupied the upper town, the great wall as far as the Kedron, and a portion of the old wall, from the point where it bent eastward at Siloam to its descent to the court-house of Monobazus, king of Adiabene beyond the Euphrates; he held also the fountain and part of the Acra, that is to say, the lower town, as far as the palace of Helena, the mother of Monobazus. John held the Temple with much of the environs, Ophel and the valley called Kedron. The region between them they reduced to ashes and left as the arena of their mutual conflicts, for not even when the Romans were encamped beneath the walls, did the civil strife slacken within. The brief return to comparative sanity when they made their first sally was followed by a relapse, and the parties divided and fell to fighting once more, doing all that their besiegers could have desired. Certainly, they suffered nothing worse at the hands of the Romans than what they inflicted upon each other, nor after her experience of them did the city meet with any novel calamity; on the contrary, her more cruel disaster preceded her fall, and the relief which her captors brought her outweighed the loss. For I maintain that it was the sedition that subdued the city, and the Romans the sedition, a foe far more stubborn than her walls; and that all the tragedy of it may properly be ascribed to her own people, all the justice to the Romans. But let everyone follow his own opinion whither the facts may lead him.

2. Such being the situation within the walls, Titus, with some picked cavalry, made a tour of inspection without, to select a spot against which to direct his attack. Baffled at all other points, the ravines rendering access impossible, while beyond them the first wall seemed too solid for his engines, he decided to make the assault opposite the tomb of John [Hyrcanus] the high priest; for here the first line of ramparts was on lower ground, and the second was disconnected with it, the builders having neglected to fortify the sparsely populated portions of the new town, while there was an

easy approach to the third wall, through which his intention was to capture the upper town and so, by way of Antonia, the Temple.

In the meantime, while Titus was riding round the city, one of his friends, named Nicanor, having approached too near with Josephus, was wounded by an arrow in the left shoulder while endeavoring to parley with those on the wall, to whom he was not unknown, on the subject of peace. Cæsar, apprised by this incident of their animosity, since they would not refrain from assaulting even those who approached them for their welfare, was stimulated to undertake the siege. He at once gave the legions permission to lay waste the suburbs and issued orders to collect timber and erect earthworks. Forming his army into three divisions for these operations, he placed the javelin-men and archers in the intervals between the embankments, and in front of them the quick-firers [or scorpions], catapults, and stone-projectors [ballistæ], to check any sallies of the enemy against the works and any attempts from the ramparts to impede them. So the trees were felled and the suburbs rapidly stripped; but while the timber was being collected for the earthworks and the whole army busily engaged in the work, the Jews on their side were not inactive. The people who were victims of rapine and massacre now began to take heart, hoping to gain some respite while their oppressors were occupied with the external foe and to have their revenge on the culprits, should the Romans prove victorious.

3. But John, though his followers were impatient for an encounter with the enemy outside, from fear of Simon did not stir. Simon, however, being nearer the besiegers, was not inactive, but posted his artillery upon the ramparts, both the engines which they had formerly taken from Cestius, and those captured when they overpowered the garrison of Antonia [in A.D. 66]. The possession of these, however, was for most of them useless owing to inexperience; but some few, instructed by the deserters, made a blundering use of them. They also assailed the builders with stones and arrows from the wall, and dashing out by companies engaged them in

close combat. The workmen were protected from the missiles by hurdles stretched over palisades, and from the enemy's sallies by the artillery.

Wonderfully constructed as were the engines of all the legions, those of the tenth were supreme. Their quick-firers were more powerful and their stone-projectors larger, enabling them to repel not only the sallying parties but also those on the ramparts. The rocks which they hurled weighed a talent and had a range of two furlongs or more; and their impact, not only to those who first met it but even to those considerably in rear, was irresistible.

The Jews, however, at the first were on their guard against the stone, for, being white, its approach was intimated not only to the ear by the whiz, but also to the eye by its brilliance. Watchmen were accordingly posted by them on the towers, who gave warning whenever the engine was fired and the stone in transit, by shouting in their native tongue, "Sonny's coming;" whereupon those in the line of fire promptly made way and lay down, owing to which precautions the stone passed harmlessly through and fell in their rear. To frustrate this it occurred to the Romans to blacken it; when, as it was no longer equally discernible beforehand, they hit their mark and destroyed many with a single shot. Yet, though under this galling fire, the Jews did not suffer the Romans to raise their earthworks unmolested, but by every resource of ingenuity and daring strove, night and day, to thwart them.

4. The works being completed, the engineers measured the distance to the wall with lead and line, which they cast from the embankments—the only practicable method for men under fire from above—and finding that the battering-rams could reach it, they brought them up. Titus then, after posting his artillery nearer the walls, to prevent the defenders from obstructing the rams, gave the order to strike. Suddenly, from three different quarters, a terrific din echoed round the city, a cry went up from the citizens within, and the rebels themselves were seized with a like alarm. Seeing themselves exposed to a common danger, both parties now bethought them

of a common defense. The rival factions shouted across to each other that they were doing all they could to assist the enemy, when they ought, even if God denied them lasting concord, for the present at least to postpone their mutual strife and unite against the Romans; whereupon Simon proclaimed that all were at liberty to pass from the Temple to the wall, and John, though mistrusting him, gave his permission. The parties, consigning their hatred and private quarrels to oblivion, thus became one body, and lining the ramparts, they hurled from them showers of firebrands at the machines and kept those who were impelling the battering-engines under incessant fire. The more venturesome, dashing out in bands, tore up the hurdles protecting the machines, and falling upon the gunners, seldom through skill but generally through intrepidity, got the better of them.

Titus, however, invariably came in person to the relief of those who were hard pressed, and posting his horsemen and archers on either side of the engines, kept the incendiaries at bay, beat back assailants from the towers, and brought the battering-rams into action. For all that, the wall did not succumb to the blows, save that the ram of the fifteenth legion dislodged the corner of a tower. But the wall itself was unimpaired, for it was not involved in immediate danger along with the tower, which projected far out and so could not easily bring down with it any of the main rampart.

5. The Jews, having desisted from their sallies for a while and watched their opportunity when the Romans had dispersed about the works and their several encampments, in the belief that from exhaustion and terror their enemy had retired, suddenly all dashed out together through a concealed gate near the Hippicus tower, carrying firebrands to burn the works and determined to push their attack right up to the Roman entrenchments. At their shouts the legionaries near the spot instantly mustered and those further off came dashing up. But Jewish daring outstripped Roman discipline, and having routed those who first encountered them, they pressed on against the assembling troops.

A fierce conflict ensued around the engines, one side

striving to set them alight, the other to prevent them; confused shouts arose from both and many of the foremost fighters fell. Jewish desperation, however, was proving superior, already the fire was gaining hold upon the works, and the whole would probably have perished in the flames, along with the engines, had not the picked troops from Alexandria in the main stood firm, displaying a gallantry which exceeded their own reputation (for indeed they surpassed on that occasion regiments of greater renown), until Cæsar, bringing up the most stalwart of his cavalry, charged the enemy. A dozen of the foremost he slew with his own hand. Terrified at their fate the remainder gave way; he followed, drove them all into the town, and rescued the works from the flames.

One incident in this engagement was the capture of a Jewish prisoner, whom Titus ordered to crucifixion before the walls, in the hope that the spectacle might lead the rest to surrender in dismay. Moreover, after the retreat, John, the chieftain of the Idumæans, while talking before the wall to an acquaintance in the ranks, was pierced in the breast by an arrow from an Arab's bow and killed on the spot. This loss occasioned profound grief to the Idumæans and sorrow to the Jewish insurgents; for he was distinguished alike for gallantry and sound judgment.

vii. 1. On the ensuing night the Romans themselves were thrown into baseless alarm. For Titus had given command for the construction of three towers, fifty cubits high, to be erected on the respective embankments, in order that from them he might repel the defenders of the ramparts; and one of these accidentally fell in the middle of the night. The crash was tremendous, and the terrified troops, supposing that the enemy were upon them, all rushed to arms. Alarm and confusion pervaded the legions. None being able to say what had happened, they scattered far and wide in their perplexity, and sighting no enemy became scared of one another, and each hurriedly asked his neighbor the password, as though the Jews had invaded their camps. In fact they behaved like men beset by panic fright, until Titus, having learned what had happened, gave orders to make it generally known; and thus, though with difficulty, was the alarm allayed.

2. The Jews, stubbornly though they held out against everything else, suffered severely from these towers; for from them they became targets for the lighter artillery, the javelin-men, archers, and stone-throwers. Being so high up, these assailants were out of range, while there was no means of mastering the towers, their weight rendering it difficult to overturn them and their casing of iron impossible to set them on fire. If, on the other hand, they withdrew out of range of missiles, they could no longer check the impact of the rams, whose incessant battering was gradually taking effect.

And now at length the wall began to succumb to Victor (so the Jews themselves called the largest of the Roman engines, from its victory over all obstacles). They had long been exhausted with fighting and watching on night duty at a distance from the city; moreover, through indolence and their invariably misguided judgment, they decided that to defend this wall was superfluous, as two others remained behind it. Most of them, accordingly, turned slack and retired; and when the Romans mounted the breach which Victor had made, all deserted their posts and fled back to the second wall. Those who had scaled the ramparts now opened the gates and admitted the whole army. The Romans having thus on the fifteenth day [of the siege], being the seventh of the [Macedonian] month Artemisius, become masters of the first wall, razed a large part of it along with the northern quarter of the city, previously destroyed by Cestius.

3. Titus now shifted his camp within the first wall to the site called "Camp of the Assyrians," occupying all the ground between it and the Kedron, but keeping far enough back to be out of bowshot from the second wall, which he forthwith proceeded to attack. The Jews, dividing their forces, maintained a stubborn defense from the ramparts—John's division fighting from Antonia, from the north portico of the Temple, and in front of the tomb of King Alexander [Jannæus]; while Simon's troops occupied the approach alongside the tomb of

John [Hyrcanus], the high priest, and manned the wall as far as the gate through which water was conveyed to the Hippicus tower. Often they would dash out from the gates and fight hand to hand, and though driven back on to the walls and defeated in these close combats through lack of the Romans' military skill they had the advantage of them in the battles from the ramparts. Experience combined with strength was the Romans' mainstay; daring, fostered by fear, along with their innate fortitude under calamities, sustained the Jews. Moreover, they still cherished hopes of salvation, as did the Romans of speedy victory.

Neither army felt fatigue: assaults, battles at the wall, sallies by companies continued incessantly throughout the day, and no form of warfare was omitted. Beginning at dawn, night scarcely brought them respite—its hours were sleepless for both and more terrible than day, one party dreading every moment the capture of the wall, the other a Jewish invasion of their camps. Both armies thus passed the night under arms and at the first break of day were ready for battle.

Among the Jews there was rivalry who should be foremost in the fray and so win favor with his officers. Simon in particular was regarded with reverence and awe, and such was the esteem in which he was held by all under his command, that each was quite prepared to take his very own life had he given the order. With the Romans, on the other hand, the incentives to valor were their habit of victory and inexperience of defeat, their continuous campaigns and perpetual training, the magnitude of their empire, and above all Titus, ever and everywhere present beside all. For cowardice when Cæsar was with them and sharing the contest seemed monstrous, while the man who fought bravely had as witness of his valor one who would also reward it; nay, it was gain already to be known to Cæsar as courageous.

Hence, many in their enthusiasm displayed greater valor than their strength warranted. Thus, when in the course of these days the Jews were arrayed in stout force outside the walls, and both armies were as yet engaged in distant combat with javelins, a certain trooper, Longinus, leapt out of the Roman lines and dashed into the midst of the Jewish phalanx. Breaking their ranks by his charge, he slew two of their bravest, piercing one in front as he advanced to meet him, and transfixing the other through the side, as he turned to flee, with the spear which he drew from his comrade's body; he then escaped unscathed to his own lines from the midst of the enemy. His valor gained him distinction, and led many to emulate his gallantry. The Jews, for their part, regardless of suffering, thought only of the injury which they could inflict, and death seemed to them a trivial matter if it involved the fall of one of the enemy. Titus, on the other hand, cared as much for his soldiers' safety as for success; and pronouncing inconsiderate impetuosity to be mere desperation, and valor only deserving of the name when coupled with forethought and a regard for the actor's security, he ordered his troops to prove their manhood without running personal risks.

4. He now brought up the battering-ram against the central tower of the north wall, where a certain Jewish cheat, named Castor, lay in ambush with ten others of like character, the rest having been routed by the archers. Here for some time they remained motionless, crouching beneath the parapet, but when the tower began to rock they rose up, and Castor, stretching out his hands in suppliant pose, called upon Cæsar and in piteous tones implored him to have mercy on them. Titus, in the simplicity of his heart, believed him, and hoping that the Jews were at length repenting, stopped the battering of the ram, forbade the archers to shoot at the suppliants, and directed Castor to state what he wanted. The latter replying that he desired to come down under pledge of protection, Titus said that he congratulated him on his sound judgment, and would congratulate the city, if all were now of the same mind, and gladly offer them security. But while five of Castor's ten companions joined in this feigned supplication, the rest cried out that they would never be slaves of the Romans, so long as they might die free men.

During this protracted dispute, the assault was suspended, and Castor sent word to Simon to take his time in deliberating on the necessary measures, as he could fool the Roman command for a long while yet. While dispatching this message he was to all appearance urging his recalcitrant comrades to accept the proffered pledge. They, on the other hand, in seeming indignation, brandished their naked swords above the breastworks and, striking their own breast-plates, fell down as though slain. Titus and his staff, amazed at the men's intrepidity, and unable from below to see exactly what had happened, admired their courage and commiserated their fate.

Meanwhile, Castor was struck close to the nose with an arrow, which missile he instantly drew out and showed to Titus, complaining of being unfairly treated. Cæsar sternly rebuked the archer and commissioned Josephus, who was at his side, to offer his hand to Castor. Josephus, however, not only declined to go himself, convinced that these suppliants meant no good, but restrained those of his friends who were anxious to step forward. However, Æneas, one of the deserters, volunteered to go; and Castor calling out for someone to take the money which he was bringing with him, Æneas ran forward the more eagerly with robes extended to receive it. Castor thereupon picked up a boulder and hurled it at him; it missed Æneas who managed to avoid it, but wounded another soldier who had come up.

Cæsar, now that his eyes were opened to the trick, decided that in warfare compassion was mischievous—severe measures affording less scope for artifice—and, indignant at this mockery, put the battering-ram more vigorously into action. When the tower began to give way, Castor and his friends set fire to it, and, leaping through the flames into the vault beneath, again impressed the Romans, who imagined that they had plunged into the fire, with a sense of their courage.

viii. 1. At this spot, on the fifth day after the capture of the first wall, Cæsar stormed the second; and, as the Jews had fled from it, he made his entry with a thousand legionaries and his own picked troops, in that district of the new town where lay the wool-shops, the braziers' smithies and the clothes market, and where the narrow alleys descended obliquely to the ramparts. Now, had he either at once broken down more of the wall or, by right of war, followed up his entry by sacking what he had captured, no loss, I imagine, would have attended his triumph. But, in fact, because he hoped to shame the Jews by his reluctance to injure when in a position to do so, he omitted to widen the breach to facilitate a retreat, never supposing that after such treatment they would plot against their benefactor. Accordingly, on entering, he would not allow his troops to kill any persons caught or to fire the houses; to the factions he offered a free exit from the city to fight, if such was their desire, without detriment to the people, while to the people he promised restoration of their property. For his paramount object was to preserve the city for himself and the Temple for the city.

The people indeed had long been ready to act on his advice, but the militants mistook his humanity for weakness and regarded these overtures as due to his inability to capture the rest of the town. Threatening, therefore, to kill any of the townsfolk who should mention surrender, and butchering all who let fall a word about peace, they attacked the Roman division that had entered. Some confronted them in the streets, some assailed them from the houses, while others, rushing outside the wall by the upper gates, caused such commotion among the sentries on the ramparts that they leaped down from the towers and made off to their camp. There were cries from those within, surrounded by a ring of enemies, and from those without, alarmed for their intercepted comrades.

The Jews, constantly growing in numbers and greatly at an advantage through their knowledge of the streets, wounded multitudes of the enemy and with their charges thrust them before them. The Romans, on their side, mainly through sheer necessity continued to resist, as it was impossible for all to retire at once through the narrow breach; and the entire invading force would probably have been annihilated, had not Titus come to their relief. Posting his archers at the ends of the streets and taking up a position himself where the throng was thickest, he, with showers of arrows, kept the enemy at bay, assisted by Domitius Sabinus, a man who proved his gallantry in this as in other engagements. So Cæsar stood his ground, incessantly shooting his arrows and stemming the advance of the Jews, until all his soldiers had retired.

2. Thus, after gaining possession of the second wall, were the Romans ejected. Within the city the spirits of the war party, elated at their success, rose high; since they imagined that the Romans would never again venture into the city, or that, if they did, they themselves would prove invincible. For God was blinding their minds because of their transgressions; and they perceived neither how the forces still left to the Romans far outnumbered those which had been expelled, nor yet the stealthy approach of famine. For it was still possible to feed upon the public miseries and to drink of the city's life-blood; but honest men had long since felt the pinch of want, and many were already failing for lack of necessaries.

The factions, however, regarded the destruction of the people as a relief to themselves; for they held that only those should be preserved who were enemies to peace and determined to devote their lives to resisting the Romans, and rejoiced at the wasting away of masses of their opponents who were only an encumbrance. Such were their feelings towards those within; while, having blocked and walled up the breach with their own bodies, they were holding up the Romans who were again attempting to break through. For three days they maintained a stubborn defense and held their ground, but on the fourth, unable to withstand a gallant assault of Titus, they were compelled to fall back to their former refuge. Titus, once more master of the wall, immediately razed the whole of the northern portion, and placing garrisons in the towers in the southern quarter, laid his plans for an attack on the third wall.

ix. 1. He now decided to suspend the siege for a while and to afford the factions an interval for reflection, to see if the demolition of the second wall or haply dread

279

of famine might lead to any surrender, as the fruits of
their rapine could not long suffice them; and he turned
the period of inaction to good account. For the appointed day having arrived for the distribution of the
soldiers' pay, he ordered his officers to parade the forces
and count out the money to each man in full view of
the enemy. So the troops, as was their custom, drew
forth their arms from the cases in which till now they
had been covered and advanced clad in mail, the cavalry
leading their horses which were richly caparisoned.

The area in front of the city gleamed far and wide
with silver and gold, and nothing was more gratifying
to the Romans, or more awe-inspiring to the enemy,
than that spectacle. For the whole of the old wall and
the north side of the temple were thronged with spectators, the houses across the wall were to be seen packed
with craning heads, and there was not a spot visible in
the city which was not covered by the crowd. Even the
hardiest were struck with dire dismay at the sight of
this assemblage of all the forces, the beauty of their
armor and the admirable order of the men; and I cannot but think that the rebels would have been converted
by that vision, had not the enormity of their crimes
against the people made them despair of obtaining pardon from the Romans. But, death being the punishment
in store for them if they desisted, they thought it far
better to die in battle. Fate, moreover, was prevailing to
involve both innocent and guilty, city and sedition, in a
common ruin.

2. In four days the several Roman legions had all
received their pay. On the fifth, no overtures for peace
having come from the Jews, Titus formed the legions
into two divisions and began raising earthworks opposite Antonia and John's monument respectively; his design being to carry the upper town at the latter point,
and the Temple by way of Antonia, for unless the Temple
were secured, to hold even the town would be precarious.
The erection of two banks at each of these two quarters
was accordingly begun, one being assigned to each legion. Those at work alongside the monument were impeded by sallies of the Idumæans and the troops of

Simon; those before Antonia suffered obstruction from John's followers and the Zealots. Their adversaries, moreover, were successful, not only with hand-missiles, owing to superiority of position, but also with their engines, which they had now learned to use, daily practice having gradually fostered their skill; and they possessed three hundred quick-firers and forty stone-projectors, by means of which they seriously retarded the erection of the Roman earthworks.

Titus, conscious that the preservation or destruction of the city vitally affected himself, while pressing the siege did not omit to urge the Jews to reconsider their policy. Blending active operations with advice, and aware that speech is often more effectual than arms, he not only personally exhorted them to seek salvation by the surrender of the city, already practically taken, but also delegated Josephus to parley with them in their native tongue, thinking that possibly they might yield to the expostulation of a fellow-countryman.

3. Josephus, accordingly, went round the wall, and endeavoring to keep out of range of missiles and yet within ear-shot, repeatedly implored them to spare themselves and the people, to spare their country and their temple, and not to display towards them greater indifference than was shown by aliens. The Romans, he urged, though without a share in them, yet reverenced the holy places of their enemies, and had thus far restrained their hands from them, whereas men who had been brought up in them, and were they preserved would alone enjoy them, were bent on their destruction. Indeed, they beheld their stoutest walls prostrate and but one remaining, weaker than those which had fallen; they knew that the might of the Romans was irresistible and that to serve them was no new experience for themselves.

Be it granted that it was noble to fight for freedom, they should have done so at first; but after having once succumbed and submitted for so long, to seek then to shake off the yoke was the part of men madly courting death, not of lovers of liberty. To scorn meaner masters might, indeed, be legitimate, but not those to whom the universe was subject. For what was there that had escaped the Romans, save maybe some spot useless through heat or cold? Fortune, indeed, had from all quarters passed over to them, and God, who went the round of the nations bringing to each in turn the rod of empire, now rested over Italy.

There was, in fact, an established law, as supreme among brutes as among men: "Yield to the stronger" and "The mastery is for those pre-eminent in arms." That was why their forefathers, men who in soul and body, aye, and in resources to boot, were by far their superiors, had yielded to the Romans—a thing intolerable to them, had they not known that God was on the Roman side.

As for them, on what did they rely in thus holding out, when the main part of the city was already captured, and when those within it, though their walls still stood, were in a plight even worse than capture? Assuredly, the Romans were not ignorant of the famine raging in the city, which was now consuming the populace, and would ere long consume the combatants as well. For, even were the Romans to desist from the siege and not fall upon the city with drawn swords, yet they had at their doors a war with which none could contend, gaining strength every hour, unless indeed they could take arms and fight against famine itself, and alone of all men, master even its pangs.

They would do well, he added, to repent ere irretrievable disaster befell them and to incline to salutary counsels while they had the opportunity; for the Romans would bear them no malice for the past, unless they persisted in their contumacy to the end. They were naturally lenient in victory, and would put above vindictiveness considerations of expediency, which did not consist in having on their hands either a depopulated city or a devastated country. That was why, even at this late hour, Cæsar desired to grant them terms, whereas, if he took the city by storm, he would not spare a man of them, especially after the rejection of offers made to them when in extremities. That the third wall would be quickly carried was vouched for by the fall of those already captured; and even were that defense impregnable, the famine would fight for the Romans against them.

4. Josephus, during this exhortation, was derided by many from the ramparts, by many execrated, and by some assailed with missiles. Failing to move them by this direct advice, he passed to reminiscences of their nation's history.

"Ah, miserable wretches," he cried, "unmindful of your own true allies, would you make war on the Romans with arms and might of hand? What other foe have we conquered thus, and when did God, who created, fail to avenge the Jews if they were wronged? Will you not turn your eyes and mark what place is that whence you issue to battle and reflect how mighty an Ally you have outraged? Will you not recall your fathers' superhuman exploits and what enemies this holy place has quelled for us in days of old? For myself, I shudder at recounting the works of God to unworthy ears; yet listen, that you may learn that you are warring not against the Romans only, but also against God.

"Nechaos, also called Pharaoh, the reigning king of Egypt, came down with a prodigious host and carried off Sarah, a princess and the mother of our race. What action, then, did her husband Abraham, our forefather, take? Did he avenge himself on the ravisher with the sword? He had, to be sure, three hundred and eighteen officers under him, each in command of a boundless army. Or did he not rather count these as nothing, if unaided by God, and uplifting pure hands towards this spot which you have now polluted, enlist the invincible Ally on his side? And was not the queen, after one night's absence, sent back immaculate to her lord, while the Egyptian, in awe of the spot that you have stained with the blood of your countrymen and trembling at his visions of the night, fled, bestowing silver and gold upon those Hebrews beloved of God?

"Need I speak of the migration of our fathers to Egypt? Oppressed and in subjection to foreign monarchs for four hundred years, yet, though they might have defended themselves by resort to arms and violence, did they not commit themselves to God? Who has not heard tell of Egypt overrun with all manner of beasts and wasted with every disease, of the barren land, the failing Nile, the ten successive plagues, and how in consequence our fathers were sent forth under escort without bloodshed, without risk, God conducting them as the future guardians of his shrine?

"Or again did not Philistia and the image Dagon rue the rape of our sacred ark by the Syrians? Did not the whole nation of those raiders rue the deed, ulcerated in their secret parts and excreting their entrails along with their food, until with the hands which stole it they restored it, to the sound of cymbals and timbrels, and with all manner of expiations propitiating the sanctuary? God's leadership it was that brought our fathers this triumph, because, without resort to hand or weapon, they committed the issue to His decision.

"When Sennacherib, king of Assyria, with all Asia following in his train, encamped around this city, was it by human hands he fell? Were not those hands at rest from arms and raised in prayer, while God's angel, in one night, destroyed that countless host? And when the Assyrian arose next morning, did he not find 185,000 corpses, and with the remainder flee from the Hebrews who were neither armed nor pursuing?

"You know, moreover, of the bondage in Babylon, where our people passed seventy years in exile and never reared their heads for liberty, until Cyrus granted it in gratitude to God. Yes, it was through him that they were sent forth and re-established the temple-worship of their Ally. In short, there is no instance of our forefathers having triumphed by arms or failed of success without them when they committed their cause to God; if they sat still they conquered, as it pleased their Judge; if they fought they were invariably defeated.

"Thus, when the king of Babylon besieged this city, our king Zedekiah having, contrary to the prophetic warnings of Jeremiah, given him battle, was himself taken prisoner and saw the town and the Temple leveled to the ground. Yet, how much more moderate was that monarch than your leaders, and his subjects than you!

For, though Jeremiah loudly proclaimed that they were hateful to God for their transgressions against Him, and would be taken captive unless they surrendered the city, neither the king nor the people put him to death. But you—to pass over those scenes within, for it would be beyond me adequately to portray your enormities—you, I say, assail with abuse and missiles me who exhort you to save yourselves, exasperated at being reminded of your sins and intolerant of any mention of those crimes which you actually perpetrate every day.

"Or again, when our ancestors went forth in arms against Antiochus, surnamed Epiphanes, who was blockading this city and had grossly outraged the Deity, they were cut to pieces in the battle, the town was plundered by the enemy and the sanctuary for three years and six months lay desolate.

"Why need I mention more? But, pray, who enlisted the Romans against our country? Was it not the impiety of its inhabitants? Whence did our servitude arise? Was it not from party strife among our forefathers, when the madness of Aristobulus and Hyrcanus and their mutual dissensions brought Pompey against the city, and God subjected to the Romans those who were unworthy of liberty? Yes, after a three months' siege they surrendered, though innocent of such offenses as yours against the sanctuary and against the laws, and possessing far ampler resources for war.

"Or know we not the fate of Antigonus, son of Aristobulus, in whose reign God again smote the people for their offenses by the capture of this city; when Herod, son of Antipater, brought up Sossius, and Sossius a Roman army, by whom they were for six months invested and besieged, until in retribution for their sins they were captured and the city was sacked by the enemy?

"Thus invariably have arms been refused to our nation, and warfare has been the sure signal for defeat. For it is, I suppose, the duty of the occupants of holy ground to leave everything to the arbitrament of God and to scorn the aid of human hands, can they but conciliate the Arbiter above. But as for you, what have you done that is blessed by the lawgiver? What deed that he has cursed have you left undone? How much more impious are you than those who have been defeated in the past! Secret sins—I mean thefts, treacheries, adulteries—are not beneath your disdain, while in rapine and murder you vie with each other in opening up new and unheard of paths of vice; aye, and the Temple has become the receptacle for all, and native hands have polluted those divine precincts, which even Romans reverenced from afar, forgoing many customs of their own in deference to your law.

"And after all this do you expect Him, thus outraged, to be your ally? Righteous suppliants are ye, forsooth, and pure the hands with which you appeal to your protector! With such, I ween, our king besought aid against the Assyrian, when God in one night laid low that mighty host! And so like are the deeds of the Romans to those of the Assyrian, that you may look for a like vengeance yourselves! Did not he accept money from our king on condition that he would not sack the city, and then come down, in violation of his oaths, to burn the sanctuary; whereas the Romans are but demanding the customary tribute, which our fathers paid to theirs? Once they obtain this, they neither sack the city, nor touch the holy things, but grant you everything else: the freedom of your families, the enjoyment of your possessions and the protection of your sacred laws.

"It is surely madness to expect God to show the same treatment to the just as to the unjust. Moreover, He knows how, at need, to inflict instant vengeance, as when He broke the Assyrians on the very first night when they encamped hard by. So that had He judged our generation worthy of freedom or the Romans of punishment, He would, as He did the Assyrians, have instantly visited them—when Pompey intermeddled with the nation, when after him Sossius came up, when Vespasian ravaged Galilee, and lastly now, when Titus was approaching the city. And yet [Pompey] the Great and Sossius, far from sustaining any injury, took the city by storm; Vespasian from his war against us mounted to a throne; while as for Titus, the very springs flow more copiously for him which had erstwhile dried up

for you. For before his coming, as you know, Siloam
and all the springs outside the town were failing, insomuch that water was sold by the jug; whereas now they
flow so freely for your enemies as to suffice not only
for themselves and their beasts but even for gardens.
This miracle, moreover, has been experienced ere now
on the fall of the city, when the Babylonian whom I
mentioned marched against it and captured and burned
both the city and the sanctuary, although the Jews of
that day were guilty, I imagine, of no such rank impiety as yours. My belief, therefore, is that the Deity has
fled from the holy places and taken His stand on the
side of those with whom you are now at war.

"Nay, an honorable man will fly from a wanton house
and abhor its inmates, and can you persuade yourselves
that God still remains with His household in their iniquity—God who sees every secret thing and hears what
is buried in silence? And what is there veiled in silence
or secrecy among you? Nay, what has not been exposed
even to your foes? For you parade your enormities and
daily contend who shall be the worst, making an exhibition of vice as though it were virtue.

"Yet a way of salvation is still left you, if you will,
and the Deity is easily reconciled to such as confess
and repent. Oh! iron-hearted men, fling away your
weapons, take compassion on your country even now
tottering to its fall, turn round and behold the beauty
of what you are betraying—what a city! what a temple!
what countless nations' gifts! Against these would any
man direct the flames? Is there any who wishes that
these should be no more? What could be more worthy
of preservation than these—ye relentless creatures, more
insensible than stone! Yet if you look not on these with
the eyes of genuine affection, at least have pity on your
families, and let each set before his eyes his children,
wife, and parents, ere long to be the victims either of
famine or of war. I know that I have a mother, a wife,
a not ignoble family, and an ancient and illustrious
house involved in these perils; and maybe you think
that it is on their account that my advice is offered.
Slay them, take my blood as the price of your own

salvation! I too am prepared to die, if my death will lead to your learning wisdom."

x. 1. Yet, though Josephus with tears thus loudly appealed to them, the insurgents neither yielded nor deemed it safe to alter their course. The people, however, were incited to desert; and selling for a trifling sum, some their whole property, others their most valuable treasures, they would swallow the gold coins to prevent discovery by the brigands, and then, escaping to the Romans, on discharging their bowels, have ample supplies for their needs. For Titus dismissed the majority into the country, whithersoever they would; a fact which induced still more to desert, as they would be relieved from the misery within and yet not be enslaved by the Romans. The partisans of John and Simon, however, kept a sharper look-out for the egress of these refugees than for the ingress of Romans, and whoever afforded but a shadow of suspicion was instantly slaughtered.

2. To the well-to-do, however, to remain in the city was equally fatal; for under pretext of desertion individuals were put to death for the sake of their property. The recklessness of the insurgents kept pace with the famine, and both horrors daily burst out in more furious flame. For, as corn was nowhere to be seen, they would rush in and search the houses, and then if they found any they belabored the inmates as having denied the possession of it; if they found none they tortured them for more carefully concealing it. The personal appearance of the wretches was an index whether they had it or not: those still in good condition were presumed to be well off for food, while those already emaciated were passed over, as it seemed senseless to kill persons so soon to die of starvation. Many clandestinely bartered their possessions for a single measure—of wheat, if they were rich, of barley, if they were poor; then shutting themselves up in the most remote recesses of their houses, some in the extremity of hunger devoured the grain unground, others so baked it as necessity and fear dictated. Nowhere was any table laid; they snatched the food half-cooked from the fire and tore it in pieces.

3. Pitiful was the fare and lamentable the spectacle,

the stronger taking more than their share, the weak whimpering. Famine, indeed, overpowers all the emotions, but of nothing is it so destructive as of shame; what at other times would claim respect is then treated with contempt. Thus, wives would snatch the food from husbands, children from fathers, and—most pitiable sight of all—mothers from the very mouths of their infants, and while their dearest ones were pining in their arms they scrupled not to rob them of the life-giving drops. Nor, though thus feeding, did they escape detection—everywhere the rebels hovered even over these wretches' prey. For, whenever they saw a house shut up, this was a signal that the inmates were taking food, and forthwith bursting open the doors they leaped in, and forcing the morsels almost out of their very jaws, brought them up again. Old men were beaten, clutching their victuals, and women were dragged by the hair, concealing what was in their hands. There was no compassion for hoary hairs or infancy: children were actually lifted up with the fragments to which they clung and dashed to the ground. To those who had anticipated their raid and already swallowed their expected spoil they were yet more brutal, as defrauded of their due. Horrible were the methods of torture which they devised in their search for food, blocking with pulse the passages in their poor victims' frames and driving sharp stakes up their bodies; and one would shudder at the mere recital of the pangs to which they were subjected to make them confess to the possession of a single loaf or to reveal the hiding-place of a handful of barley-meal.

Yet their tormentors were not famished: their cruelty would have been less, had it had the excuse of necessity; they were but practicing their recklessness and providing supplies for themselves against the days to come. Again, if any under cover of night had crept out to the Roman outposts to gather wild herbs and grass, they would go to meet them and, at the moment when these imagined themselves clear of the enemy, snatch from them what they had procured; and oft though their victims implored them, invoking even the awful name of God, to return them a portion of what they had at their own peril obtained, not a morsel was given them. They might congratulate themselves if, when robbed, they were not killed as well.

4. Such was the treatment to which the lower classes were subjected by the thugs; the men of rank and wealth, on the other hand, were brought up to the tyrants. Of them some were falsely accused of conspiracy and executed, as were others on the charge of betraying the city to the Romans; but the readiest expedient was to suborn an informer to state that they had decided to desert. One who had been fleeced by Simon was passed on to John, and he who had been plundered by John was taken over by Simon; they pledged each other in turn in the burghers' blood and shared the carcases of their unfortunate victims. As rivals for power they were divided, but in their crimes united; for the one who gave his comrade no share in the proceeds of the miseries of others was ranked a scurvy villain, and he who received no share was aggrieved at his exclusion from the barbarity, as though defrauded of some good thing.

5. To narrate their enormities in detail is impossible; but, to put it briefly, no other city ever endured such miseries, nor since the world began has there been a generation more prolific in crime. Indeed they ended by actually disparaging the Hebrew race, in order to appear less impious in so treating aliens, and owned themselves, what indeed they were, slaves, the dregs of society and the bastard scum of the nation. It was they who overthrew the city, and compelled the reluctant Romans to register so melancholy a triumph, and all but attracted to the Temple the tardy flames. Verily, when from the upper town they beheld it burning, they neither grieved nor shed a tear, though in the Roman ranks these signs of emotion were detected. But this we shall describe hereafter in its place, with a full exposition of the facts.

xi. 1. Meanwhile the earthworks of Titus were progressing, notwithstanding the galling fire from the ramparts to which his men were exposed. The general, moreover, sent a detachment of horse with orders to lie in wait for any who issued from the town into the ravines in quest of food. These included some of the combatants, no longer satisfied with their plunder, but the majority were citizens of the poorer class, who were deterred from deserting by fear for their families; for they could neither hope to elude the rebels if they attempted to escape with their wives and children, nor endure to leave them to be butchered by the brigands on their behalf. Famine, however, emboldened them to undertake these excursions, and it but remained for them if they escaped unobserved from the town to be taken prisoners by the enemy. When caught, they were driven to resist, and after a conflict it seemed too late to sue for mercy. They were accordingly scourged and subjected to torture of every description, before being killed, and then crucified opposite the walls.

Titus indeed commiserated their fate, five hundred or sometimes more being captured daily; on the other hand, he recognized the risk of dismissing prisoners of war, and that the custody of such numbers would amount to the imprisonment of their custodians; but his main reason for not stopping the crucifixions was the hope that the spectacle might perhaps induce the Jews to surrender, for fear that continued resistance would involve them in a similar fate. The soldiers out of rage and hatred amused themselves by nailing their prisoners in different postures; and so great was their number, that space could not be found for the crosses nor crosses for the bodies.

2. The insurgents, however, far from relenting at these sufferings, deluded the remainder by inventing a contrary motive for them. Dragging the relatives of the deserters to the wall, together with any citizens who were anxious to accept the offer of terms, they showed them what was the fate of those who sought refuge with the Romans, asserting that the arrested victims were not captives, but suppliants. This, until the truth became known, kept back many who were eager to desert; some, however, instantly fled, as to certain punishment, regarding death at the enemy's hands as rest in compari-

son with starvation. But Titus now gave orders to cut
off the hands of several of the prisoners, that they
might not be mistaken for deserters and that their
calamity might add credit to their statements, and then
sent them in to Simon and John, exhorting them now at
least to pause, and not compel him to destroy the city,
but by repentance at the eleventh hour to gain their own
lives, their magnificent city, and a temple unshared by
others. At the same time he went round the embankments, urging on the workmen, as if intending shortly
to follow up his threats by action.

To this message the Jews retorted by heaping abuse
from the ramparts upon Cæsar himself, and his father,
crying out that they scorned death, which they honorably
preferred to slavery; that they would do Romans every
injury in their power while they had breath in their
bodies; that men so soon, as he himself said, to perish,
were unconcerned for their native place, and that the
world was a better temple for God than this one. But,
they added, it would yet be saved by Him who dwelt
therein, and while they had Him for their ally they
would deride all menaces unsupported by action; for the
issue rested with God. Such, with invectives interspersed,
were their exclamations. . . .

4. Though the Romans had begun their earthworks
on the twelfth of the month Artemisius, they were
scarcely completed on the twenty-ninth, after seventeen
days of continuous toil. For the four embankments were
immense. Of the first two, that at Antonia was thrown
up by the fifth legion over against the middle of the
pool called Struthion, the other by the twelfth legion
about twenty cubits away. The tenth legion, at a considerable distance from these, was employed in the
northern region and over against the pool termed Amyg-
dalon; while, thirty cubits from them, the fifteenth were
at work opposite the high priest's monument.

But while the engines were now being brought up,
John from within had undermined the ground from Antonia right up to the earthworks, supporting the tunnels
with props, and thus leaving the Roman works suspended; having then introduced timber besmeared with

pitch and bitumen he set the whole mass alight. The props being consumed, the mine collapsed in a heap, and with a tremendous crash the earthworks fell in. At first dense volumes of smoke arose with clouds of dust, the fire being smothered by the debris, but as the materials which crushed it were eaten away, a vivid flame now burst forth. The Romans were in consternation at this sudden catastrophe and dispirited by the enemy's ingenuity; moreover, coming at the moment when they imagined victory within their grasp, the casualty damped their hopes of ultimate success. It seemed useless to fight the flames, when even if they were extinguished their earthworks were overwhelmed.

5. Two days later Simon's party launched a further attack on the other earthworks, for the Romans had there brought up the rams and were already battering the wall. A certain Gephthæus, of Garis, a town in Galilee, and Magassarus, a soldier of the king and henchman of Mariamme, along with the son of a certain Nabatæus from Adiabene, called from his misfortune by the name of Ceagiras, signifying "lame," snatched up torches and rushed forth against the engines. No bolder men than these three sallied from the town throughout this war or inspired greater terror; for, as though racing for friendly ranks and not into a mass of enemies, they neither slackened nor turned aside, but, plunging through the midst of the foe, set light to the machines. Assailed by shots and sword-thrusts from every quarter, nothing could move them from the field of danger until the fire had caught hold of the engines.

The flames now towering aloft, the Romans came rushing from their encampments to the rescue; while the Jews obstructed them from the ramparts and, utterly regardless of their own lives, struggled hand to hand with those who were endeavoring to extinguish the conflagration. On the one side were the Romans striving to drag the battering-engines out of the fire, their wicker shelters all ablaze; on the other, the Jews holding on to them through the flames, clutching the red-hot iron and refusing to relinquish the rams. From these the fire spread to the earthworks, outstripping the defenders.

Thereupon the Romans, enveloped in flames and despairing of the preservation of the works, beat a retreat
to their camps; while the Jews, hotly pursuing, their
numbers continually augmented by fresh reinforcements
from the city, and flushed with success, pressed on with
uncontrolled impetuosity right up to the entrenchments,
and finally grappled with the sentries.

There is a line of troops, relieved from time to time,
who are stationed in front of every camp and come under a severe Roman law that he who quits his post under
any pretext whatsoever dies. These men, preferring an
heroic death to capital punishment, stood firm; and seeing the straits of their comrades many of the fugitives
for very shame returned. Posting the "quick-firers" along
the camp-wall, they kept at bay the masses who, without a thought for safety or personal defense, were surg-
ing up from the town; for the Jews grappled with any
whom they met, and all unguardedly flinging themselves
bodily upon the spear-points, struck at their antagonists.
But their superiority lay less in deeds than in daring,
and the Romans yielded rather to intrepidity than to injuries received.

6. But now Titus appeared from Antonia, whither he
had gone to inspect a site for fresh earthworks. Severely
reprimanding his troops for having, while mastering the
enemy's fortifications, thus jeopardized their own and
put themselves in the position of the besieged, by letting
loose the Jews upon them from their prison house, he
then with his picked force, himself at their head, got
round and took the enemy in flank. But though attacked
in front as well, they turned and resolutely withstood
him. In the medley of the fight, blinded by the dust and
deafened by the din, neither side could any longer distinguish friend from foe. The Jews still held out, though
now less through prowess than from despair of salvation, while the Romans were braced by a regard for
glory, for the honor of their arms, and for Cæsar foremost in danger; insomuch that I imagine that in the
excess of their fury they would have ended by wiping
out the entire Jewish host, had not their enemy, anticipating the turn of the battle, retreated into the city.

The Romans, however, with their earthworks demolished, were in deep dejection, having lost in one hour the fruit of their long labor, and many despaired of ever carrying the town by the ordinary appliances.

xii. 1. Titus now held a consultation with his officers. The more sanguine were of opinion that he should bring up his entire force and essay to carry the wall by storm; for hitherto separate sections only had been engaged with the Jews, whereas under a mass attack the Jews would be powerless to resist their onset, as they would be overwhelmed by the hail of missiles. Of the more cautious, some were for reconstructing the earthworks; others advised that they should dispense with these and resort to a blockade, merely guarding against the egress of the besieged and the introduction of supplies, and that, leaving the city to the famine, they should avoid direct conflict with the foe; for there was no contending with desperate men whose prayer was to fall by the sword, and for whom, if that was denied them, a harder fate was in store.

To Titus, however, to remain totally inactive with so large a force appeared undignified, while to contend with men who would soon destroy each other seemed superfluous. At the same time he pointed out the extreme difficulty of throwing up earthworks, owing to lack of materials, and the even greater difficulty of guarding against sallies; for to encompass the city with troops would, owing to its extent and the obstacles presented by the ground, be no easy matter, and would moreover expose them to the risk of enemy attacks. They might guard the obvious outlets, but the Jews from necessity and their knowledge of the locality would contrive secret routes; and, should supplies be furtively smuggled in, the siege would be still further protracted. He feared, moreover, that the glory of success would be diminished by the delay; for though time could accomplish everything, yet rapidity was essential to renown. If, however, they wished to combine speed and security, they must throw a wall round the whole city. Only thus could every exit be blocked, and the Jews would then either in utter despair of salvation surrender the city, or, wasted by famine, fall an easy prey; for he himself would not remain altogether inactive, but would once more turn his attention to the earthworks when he had an enfeebled foe to obstruct him. And if anyone considered this a great and arduous operation, let him reflect that it ill became Romans to undertake a trivial task, and that without toil nothing great could lightly be achieved by any man.

2. Having by these arguments convinced his officers, Titus ordered them to distribute the task among the forces. The troops thereupon were seized with a sort of preternatural enthusiasm, and the circuit of the wall being respectively apportioned, not only the legions, but their component companies vied with one another: the soldier studied to please his decurion, the decurion the centurion, and he the tribune, while the emulation of the tribunes extended to the staff-officers, and in the rivalry between the officers Cæsar himself was umpire; for he went round himself frequently every day and inspected the work. . . .

The [Roman] wall was thirty-nine furlongs in length and had attached to its outer side thirteen forts, whose united circumferences amounted to ten furlongs. The whole was built in three days; such rapidity, over a work that might well have occupied months, being well-nigh incredible. Having enclosed the city within this wall and posted garrisons in the forts, Titus went round himself during the first watch of the night and inspected everything; the second watch he entrusted to [Tiberius Julius] Alexander; for the third the commanders of the legions drew lots. The sentries, too, had their allotted hours of rest and all night long patrolled the intervals between the forts.

3. For the Jews, along with all egress, every hope of escape was now cut off; and the famine, enlarging its maw, devoured the people by households and families. The roofs were thronged with women and babes completely exhausted, the alleys with the corpses of the aged; children and youths, with swollen figures, roamed like phantoms through the market-places and collapsed wherever their doom overtook them. As for burying their

relatives, the sick had not the strength, while those with vigor still left were deterred both by the multitude of the dead and by the uncertainty of their own fate. Many fell dead while burying others, and many went forth to their tombs ere fate was upon them. And amidst these calamities there was neither lamentation nor wailing: famine stifled the emotions, and with dry eyes and grinning mouths these slowly dying victims looked on those who had gone to their rest before them.

The city, wrapped in profound silence and night laden with death, was in the grip of a yet fiercer foe—the brigands. For, breaking into habitations that were now mere charnel-houses, they rifled the dead, and stripping the coverings from the bodies, departed with shouts of laughter. They tried the points of their swords on the corpses and ran them through some of the prostrate but still living wretches, to test the temper of the blade, but any who implored them to lend them their hand and sword they disdainfully left to the mercy of the famine. And each victim expired with his eyes fixed on the Temple and averted from the rebels whom he left alive. The latter at the outset ordered the bodies to be buried at the public expense, finding the stench intolerable; afterwards, when incapable of continuing this, they flung them from the ramparts into the ravines.

4. When Titus, going his rounds, beheld these valleys choked with dead and the thick matter oozing from under the clammy carcases, he groaned and, raising his hands to heaven, called God to witness that this was not his doing. Such was the situation within the city. Meanwhile the Romans, relieved from further sallies of the rebels (for now even these felt the grip of despondency and famine) were in the highest spirits, with abundant supplies of corn and other necessaries from Syria and the adjoining provinces; and many of them would approach the ramparts and, displaying masses of victuals, inflame by their superabundance the pangs of the enemy's hunger.

The rebels still remaining unmoved by these sufferings, Titus, commiserating the remnants of the people and anxious at least to rescue the survivors, recom-

menced the erection of earthworks, though timber was
now procured with difficulty; for, all the trees round the
city having been felled for the previous works, the
troops had to collect fresh material from a distance of
ninety furlongs. The new mounds were raised only opposite Antonia, in four sections, and were much larger
than the former embankments. Cæsar, meanwhile, making the round of the legions and expediting operations,
plainly showed the brigands that they were now in his
hands. In them alone, however, all remorse for evils was
extinct; and divorcing soul from body they treated both
as aliens. For neither could suffering tame their souls
nor anguish affect their bodies, seeing that they continued, like dogs, to maul the very carcase of the people and to pack the prisons with the feeble.

xiii. 1. Simon indeed did not suffer even Matthias,
to whom he owed his possession of the city, to go un-
tortured to his death. This Matthias was the son of
Bœthus, claimed high priestly ancestry, and had won the
special confidence and esteem of the people. At the time
when the multitude were being maltreated by the Zealots,
to whom John had now attached himself, he had persuaded the citizens to admit Simon as an ally, without
making any previous stipulation with him or anticipating foul play on his part. But when Simon had once entered and become master of the town, he considered the
very man who had advocated his cause an enemy, equally with the rest, as having done so from pure simplicity.
And now he had him brought up, accused him of siding
with the Romans, and without even granting him an opportunity of defense, condemned him to death, along
with three of his sons; the fourth having already fled to
Titus. Moreover, when Matthias entreated that he might
be slain before his children, begging this favor in return for his having opened the gates to him, Simon
ordered that he should be slain last. He was, accordingly, butchered over the bodies of his sons, who had been
slaughtered before his eyes, after having been led out
in view of the Romans; for such were the instructions
given by Simon to Ananus, son of Bagadates, the most
truculent of his satellites, with the ironical remark,

"Let him see whether his friends to whom he intended to desert will assist him." He moreover refused burial to the bodies.

After these a priest named Ananias, son of Masbalus, a person of distinction, and Aristeus, the secretary of the council, a native of Emmaus, and along with them fifteen eminent men from among the people were executed. They further detained the father of Josephus in prison, issued a proclamation forbidding any throughout the city to confabulate or congregate in one spot —for fear of treason—and put to death without inquiry persons taking part in joint lamentation.

2. A spectator of these scenes, Judas, son of Judas, one of Simon's lieutenants and entrusted by him with the custody of a tower, partly perhaps out of compassion for the victims thus cruelly slain, but mainly thinking of his own safety, called together ten of the men under him on whom he could most rely and said: "How long are we to tolerate these crimes? Or what prospect have we of escaping by keeping faith with this villain? Is not the famine already upon us, the Roman army all but in the town, and Simon treacherous even to his benefactors? Have we not reason to fear that he will soon punish us, while a Roman pledge can be trusted? Come, let us surrender the ramparts and save ourselves and the city! Simon will suffer no great hardship if, despairing of his life, he is brought sooner to justice."

The ten assenting to these proposals, early next morning he dispatched the rest of the men under his command in various directions, to prevent any discovery of the plot, and about the third hour called to the Romans from the tower. Of the latter some disdained him, others were incredulous, while the majority shrank from interfering, certain of taking the city ere long without running any risks. However, while Titus was preparing to advance to the wall with a body of troops, Simon, receiving timely intelligence, forestalled him by promptly occupying the tower, arrested and slew the men in full view of the Romans, and after mutilating their bodies flung them over the ramparts.

3. Meanwhile, Josephus while going his rounds—for he was unremitting in his exhortations—was struck on the head with a stone and instantly dropped insensible. The Jews made a rush for the body, and he would have been dragged into the city, had not Cæsar promptly sent out a rescue party. During the ensuing conflict Josephus was borne away, little conscious of what was passing; while the rebels, supposing that they had killed the man for whose blood they thirsted most, shouted with delight. The rumor spreading to the town, the residue of the populace were deeply dejected, believing that he who gave them courage to desert had really perished. The mother of Josephus, hearing in prison that her son was dead, remarked to her warders, "Ever since Jotapata I was sure of it; indeed I had no joy of him in his lifetime;" but in private lamentation to her handmaidens she said, "This, then, is the fruit that I reap of my blessed child-bearing that I am to be denied the burial of the son by whom I hoped to have been buried."

Happily, however, neither the distress which this false report occasioned her nor the solace which it brought to the brigands was of long duration; for Josephus, quickly recovering from the blow, came forward, and shouting to his foes that he would ere long be avenged on them for his wound, renewed his exhortations to the citizens to accept his assurances. The sight of him animated the people and filled the rebels with dismay.

4. As for the deserters, some, having no alternative, hastily leaped from the ramparts; others, starting out with stones, as for a skirmish, then fled to the Romans. Hither, however, a harsher fate pursued them than that of their comrades within; and they found satiety in the Roman camp more rapidly fatal than the famine which they had left at home. For they arrived swollen from hunger, like persons afflicted with dropsy, and then, overcharging at a gulp their empty stomachs, burst asunder; though some had learned by experience to restrain their appetites and little by little administered nourishment to bodies unused to the load.

But even those who thus escaped were overtaken later by another catastrophe. For one of the refugees in the

Syrian ranks was discovered picking gold coins from
his excrements. These pieces, as we have said, they had
swallowed before their departure, because they were all
searched by the rebels and gold was so abundant in the
town that they could purchase for twelve Attic drachmas coin formerly worth five-and-twenty. This artifice
being, however, detected in one instance, a rumor ran
through the camps that the deserters had come full of
gold, whereupon the Arab rabble with the Syrians proceeded to cut open the suppliants and search their intestines. No more cruel calamity, in my opinion, befell
the Jews than this; actually in one night no less than
two thousand were ripped up.

5. On learning of this outrage Titus very nearly ordered his horse to surround the culprits and shoot them
down, being only checked by the multitude of persons
implicated, those who would have to be punished far
outnumbering their victims. Summoning, however, the
commanders both of the auxiliaries and of the legions
(for some of his own soldiers also were involved in the
charge) and addressing both groups, he said that he was
indignant that soldiers in his service should be guilty
of such acts for the sake of uncertain lucre, and did not
blush for their own arms, made of silver and gold. To
the Arabs and Syrians he expressed his wrath, first at
the idea that in a foreign war they should give unre-
strained license to their passions, and next that they
should induce Romans to lend their name to their own
murderous brutality and hatred of the Jews, seeing that
some of the very legionaries now shared their infamy.
These foreigners he threatened with death, should any
be found daring to repeat the crime; the legionaries
he directed to search for suspected offenders and to bring
them up to him.

But avarice, it seems, defies all punishment, and a dire
love of gain is ingrained in human nature, no other passion being so headstrong as greed. Though, in truth, in
other circumstances these passions observe some bounds
and submit to deterrents, here God and no other had
condemned His whole people and was turning every
avenue of salvation to their destruction. Thus what

Cæsar had prohibited with threats men still ventured furtively to practice upon the deserters. Advancing to meet the fugitives before the troops had caught sight of them, these barbarians would massacre them, and then, looking round to see that no Roman eye was upon them, rip them up and extract the filthy lucre from their bowels. In a few only was it found; the bare hope of finding it caused the wanton destruction of most. This calamity in fact drove many of the deserters back.

6. John, when the plunder from the people failed him, had recourse to sacrilege, melting down many of the temple-offerings and many of the vessels required for public worship, bowls and salvers and tables; nor did he abstain from the vessels for pure wine sent by Augustus and his consort. For the Roman sovereigns ever honored and added embellishment to the temple, whereas this Jew now pulled down even the donations of foreigners, remarking to his companions that they should not scruple to employ divine things on the Divinity's behalf, and that those who fought for the temple should be supported by it. He accordingly drew every drop of the sacred wine and of the oil, which the priests kept for pouring upon the burned offerings and which stood in the inner temple, and distributed these to his horde, who without horror anointed themselves and drank therefrom. Nor can I here refrain from uttering what my emotion bids me say. I believe that, had the Romans delayed to punish these reprobates, either the earth would have opened and swallowed up the city, or it would have been swept away by a flood, or have tasted anew the thunderbolts of the land of Sodom. For it produced a generation far more godless than the victims of those visitations, seeing that these men's frenzy involved the whole people in their ruin.

7. But why need I severally recount the calamities? Why, indeed, when Mannæus, son of Lazarus, who sought refuge in those days with Titus, reported that there were carried out through a single gate, which had been entrusted to him, 115,880 corpses, between the fourteenth of the month Xanthicus [May 1], on which the general encamped before their walls, and the new moon of

302

Panemus [July 20]? All these were of the poorer class; nor had he undertaken this charge himself, but being responsible for the payment of public funds he was bound to keep count. The remainder were buried by their relatives, burial consisting merely in bringing them forth and casting them out of the town. This refugee was followed by many eminent citizens, who reported that the corpses of the lower classes thrown out through the gates amounted in all to 600,000; of the rest it was impossible to discover the number. They added that, when strength failed them to carry out the poor, they piled the bodies in the largest mansions and shut them up; also that a measure of corn had been sold for a talent, and that later when it was no longer possible to gather herbs, the city being all walled in, some were reduced to such straits that they searched the sewers for old cow dung and ate the offal therefrom, and what once would have disgusted them to look at had now become food. The tale of these horrors aroused the compassion of the Romans; yet the rebels who witnessed them relented not, but endured to go even to these extremes. For they were blinded by Fate, which, alike for the city and for themselves, was now imminent.

BOOK VI

The Capture of Jerusalem

i. 1. The sufferings of Jerusalem thus daily grew worse, the fury of the rebels being intensified by the calamities in which they were involved, and the famine now extending its ravages from the people to themselves. The piles of corpses throughout the city, presenting a horrible spectacle and emitting a pestilential stench, were moreover an impediment to the combatants in their sallies; for, like men inured to countless carnage on the battlefield, they were compelled on the march to trample over the bodies. Yet, they set foot on them without a shudder, without pity, without a thought of any evil omen to themselves from this outrage to the departed. With hands imbrued with the blood of their countrymen they rushed forth to war with the foreigner, upbraiding the Deity (so I cannot but think) for His tardiness in punishing them; for it was no hope of victory but despair of escape which now nerved them to the battle. The Romans, meanwhile, though sorely harassed in the collection of timber, had completed their earthworks in one and twenty days, having, as already stated, cleared the whole district around the town to a distance of ninety furlongs.

Pitiful too was the aspect of the country, sites formerly beautified with trees and parks now reduced to an utter desert and stripped bare of timber; and no stranger who had seen the old Judæa and the entrancingly beautiful suburbs of her capital, and now beheld her present desolation, could have refrained from tears or suppressed a sigh at the greatness of the change. For the war had ruined all the marks of beauty, and no one who knew it of old, coming suddenly upon it, would have recognized the place, but, though beside it, he would have looked for the city.

2. The completion of the earthworks proved, to the Romans no less than to the Jews, a source of apprehension. For, while the .latter thought that, should they fail to burn these also, the city would be taken, the Romans feared that they would never take it, should these embankments too be destroyed. For there was a dearth of materials, and the soldiers' bodies were now sinking beneath their toils, and their minds under a succession of reverses. Indeed, the calamities of the city caused more despondency to the Romans than to the citizens, for they found their opponents in no wise chastened by their severe misfortunes, while their own hopes were continually dashed, their earthworks mastered by the enemy's stratagems, their engines by the solidity of the walls, their close combat by the daring of their antagonists. But worst of all was the discovery that the Jews possessed a fortitude of soul that could surmount faction, famine, war, and such a host of calamities. They fancied the impetuosity of these men to be irresistible and their cheerfulness in distress invincible; for what would they not endure if favored by fortune, who were impelled to valor by disasters? For these reasons, then, the Romans strengthened yet more their guard upon the earthworks.

3. John and his party within Antonia, on the other hand, while taking precautions for the future, in the event of the demolition of the wall, also made an attack on the works before the rams were brought up. In this enterprise, however, they did not succeed, but having advanced with torches, returned with ardent hopes grown cold, ere they had approached the earthworks. For, to begin with, there seemed to be no unanimity in their design. They dashed out in small parties, at intervals, hesitatingly and in alarm, in short not like Jews: the characteristics of the nation—daring, impetuosity, the simultaneous charge, the refusal to retreat even when worsted—were all lacking. But while their own advance was abnormally spiritless, they found the Romans drawn up in stouter array than usual, with their bodies and armor so completely screening the earthworks as to leave no loophole for firebrands from any quarter what-

ever, and each man's heart braced to die rather than quit his post. For not only would all their hopes be cut off, should these works also be burned up, but the soldiers felt it a dire disgrace that craft should invariably triumph over valor, desperation over arms, numbers over experience, and Jews over Romans.

The artillery, moreover, rendered assistance, reaching the sallying parties with their missiles; each enemy who fell obstructed the man in his rear, and the risk of advancing damped their ardor. Of those who did penetrate past the reach of these projectiles, some sped back, before coming to close quarters, dismayed by the admirable order and serried ranks of their antagonists, others only when pricked by the points of the javelins. Finally, reviling each other for cowardice, they all retired, their object unattained. This attack took place on the new moon of the month Panemus.

On the retreat of the Jews, the Romans brought up the siege-engines, being assailed from Antonia with rocks, fire, iron, and every species of missile with which necessity supplied the Jews, who, notwithstanding their confident reliance on their ramparts and their contempt of the engines, yet strove to prevent the Romans from bringing them up. The latter, surmising that the anxiety of the Jews to save Antonia from assault arose from some weakness in the wall and hoping that the foundations were rotten, redoubled their efforts. Nevertheless it resisted the battering; but the Romans, under an incessant fire and undeterred by the perils to which they were exposed from above, brought the siege-engines effectively into action. As, however, they were at a disadvantage and crushed by the boulders, another party, locking their bucklers over their bodies, with hands and crowbars started undermining the foundations and by perseverance succeeded in dislodging four stones. Night suspended the labors of both combatants, but in the course of it the wall, whose shaking by the rams was followed by the collapse of the mine, at the point where John in his designs on the former earthworks had dug beneath it, suddenly fell to the ground.

4. The effect of this incident on the spirits of both

belligerents was surprising. For the Jews, who might reasonably have been disheartened by it, were, in consequence of their being prepared for this catastrophe and having taken precautions to meet it, quite confident, as Antonia still remained; whereas the unlooked-for joy of the Romans at the downfall was extinguished by the appearance of a second wall which John and his party had built within. True, the assault of this one looked easier than that of the first, as the ascent would be facilitated by the debris; they also imagined the wall itself to be far weaker than that of Antonia and that, being a temporary structure, it would be rapidly destroyed. Still, none ventured to mount; for manifest destruction awaited the first assailants.

5. Titus, believing that the ardor of troops in warfare is best roused by hope and encouraging words, and that exhortations and promises often induce forgetfulness of danger and sometimes even contempt of death, called his stalwarts together and put to the proof the mettle of his men.

"Fellow-soldiers," he said, "to deliver an oration inciting to enterprises involving no risk is to cast a direct slur on the persons addressed, while it assuredly convicts him who delivers it of unmanliness. Exhortation, in my opinion, is needed only for hazardous affairs, since in other circumstances men may be expected to act of their own accord. That the scaling of this wall is arduous I, therefore, myself grant you at the outset; but that to contend with difficulties best becomes those who aspire to heroism, that it is glorious to die with renown, and that the gallantry of those who lead the way will not go unrewarded—on those points I would now dwell. In the first place, then, let that be an incentive to you that to some might perhaps be a deterrent— I mean the long-suffering of the Jews and their fortitude in adversity. For shameful were it that Romans, soldiers of mine, men who in peace are trained for war, and in war are accustomed to conquer, should be outdone, either in strength or courage, by Jews, and that when final victory is in sight and we are enjoying the co-operation of God. For our reverses are but the outcome of the Jews' desperation, while their sufferings are increased by your valiant exploits and the constant co-operation of the Deity. For faction, famine, siege, the fall of ramparts without impact of engines—what can these things mean but that God is wroth with them and extending His aid to us? Surely, then, to allow ourselves not merely to be surpassed by inferiors but to betray a divine Ally would be beneath our dignity.

"It would indeed be disgraceful that Jews, to whom defeat brings no serious discredit since they have learned to be slaves, should, in order to end their servitude, scorn death and constantly charge into our midst, not from any hope of victory, but for the sheer display of bravery; and yet that you, masters of well-nigh every land and sea, to whom not to conquer is disgrace, should never once venture into the enemy's ranks, but should wait for famine and fortune to bring them down, sitting idle with weapons such as these, and that though at a little hazard you have it in your power to achieve everything. Yes, Antonia once mounted, and the city is ours; for, even if—and I do not expect it—any further battle awaits us with those within, your position over their heads commanding the very air your enemies breathe would ensure a complete and speedy victory.

"I refrain on this occasion from an encomium on the warrior's death and the immortality reserved for those who fall in the frenzy of battle, but for any who think otherwise the worst I could wish is that they may die in peace of disease, soul and body alike condemned to the tomb. For what brave man knows not that souls released from the flesh by the sword on the battlefield are hospitably welcomed by that purest of elements, the ether, and placed among the stars, and that as good genii and benignant heroes they manifest their presence to their posterity; while souls which pine away in bodies wasted by disease, however pure they may be from stain or pollution, are obliterated in subterranean night and pass into profound oblivion, their life, their bodies, aye and their memory, brought simultaneously to a close? But if men are doomed to an inevitable end and the sword is a gentler minister there-

of than any disease, surely it were ignoble to deny to
the public service what we must surrender to fate.

"Thus far I have spoken on the assumption that any
who may attempt this feat must necessarily perish. Yet
the valiant may come safe through even the most hazardous of enterprises. For in the first place, the ruined wall
will be easy to mount; again, all that has been built up
will be easy to overthrow, do you but summon courage
for the task, with growing numbers stimulating and
supporting one another, and your determination will
soon break the enemy's spirit. Peradventure you may
find the exploit bloodless, if you but begin; for, though
they will in all probability endeavor to thwart your
ascent, yet if unperceived you once force a way through,
their resistance may well break down, though but a
handful of you elude them. As for him who leads the
assault, I should blush were I not to make him an enviable man in the award of honors; and while the sur-
vivor shall command those who are now his equals, the
blessed meed of valor shall follow the fallen to the
grave.". . .

ii. 1. Titus now ordered the troops that were with
him to raze the foundations of Antonia and to prepare
an easy ascent for the whole army. Then, having learned
that on that day—it was the seventeenth of Panemus
[Tammuz]—the so-called continual sacrifice had for lack
of lambs ceased to be offered to God and that the people were in consequence terribly despondent, he put
Josephus forward with instructions to repeat to John
the same message as before, namely, that if he was ob-
sessed by a criminal passion for battle, he was at liberty to come out with as many as he chose and fight, without involving the city and the sanctuary in his own
ruin; but that he should no longer pollute the Holy
Place nor sin against God; and that he had his permission to perform the interrupted sacrifices with the help
of such Jews as he might select.

Josephus, standing so that his words might reach
the ears not only of John but also of the multitude, delivered Cæsar's message in Hebrew, with earnest appeals to them to spare their country, to disperse the

flames that were already licking the sanctuary, and to restore to God the expiatory sacrifices. His words were received by the people in dejection and silence; but the tyrant, after many invectives and imprecations upon Josephus, ended by saying that he could never fear capture, since the city was God's.

At this Josephus cried aloud: "Pure indeed have you kept it for God! The Holy Place too remains undefiled! Your looked-for Ally has suffered no impiety from you and still receives His customary sacrifices! Most impious wretch, should anyone deprive you of your daily food, you would consider him an enemy; and do you hope to have God, whom you have bereft of His everlasting worship, for your Ally in this war? And do you impute your sins to the Romans, who, to this day, are concerned for our laws and are trying to force you to restore to God those sacrifices which *you* have interrupted? Who would not bewail and lament for the city at this amazing inversion, when aliens and enemies rectify your impiety, while you, a Jew, nurtured in her laws, treat them more harshly even than your foes?

"Yet, be sure, John, it is no disgrace to repent of misdeeds, even at the last; and if you desire to save your country, you have a noble example set before you in Jehoiachin, king of the Jews. He, when of old his conduct had brought the Babylonian's army upon him, of his own free will left the city before it was taken, and with his family endured voluntary captivity, rather than deliver up these holy places to the enemy and see the house of God in flames. Therefore is he celebrated in sacred story by all Jews, and memory, in a stream that runs down the ages ever fresh, passes him on to posterity immortal. A noble example, John, even were it dangerous to follow; but I can warrant you even pardon from the Romans. Remember, too, that I who exhort you am your countryman, that I who make this promise am a Jew; and it is right that you should consider who is your counselor and whence he comes. For never may I live to become so abject a captive as to abjure my race or to forget the traditions of my forefathers!

"Once again are you indignant and shout your abuse

310

at me; and indeed I deserve even harsher treatment for offering advice in fate's despite and for struggling to save those whom God has condemned. Who knows not the records of the ancient prophets and that oracle which threatens this poor city and is even now coming true? For they foretold that it would then be taken whensoever one should begin to slaughter his own countrymen. And is not the city, aye and the whole Temple, filled with your corpses? God it is then, God Himself, who with the Romans is bringing the fire to purge His Temple and exterminating a city so laden with pollutions."

2. At these words, spoken with lamentation and tears, Josephus' voice broke down with sobs. Even the Romans pitied him in his emotion and admired his resolution; but John and his followers were only the more exasperated against the Romans, being eager to get Josephus also into their power. Many, however, of the upper class were moved by the speech. Some of these, indeed, intimidated by the rebels' guards, remained where they were, though convinced that they themselves and the city were both doomed to destruction; but there were others who, watching their opportunity for escaping in safety, made off to the Romans. Among these were the chief priests Joseph and Jesus, and certain sons of chief priests; namely three sons of Ishmæl who was beheaded in Cyrene, four of Matthias, and one son of another Matthias. The last had escaped after the death of his father, who was slain with three of his sons by Simon, son of Gioras, as related above. Many others also of the aristocracy went over with the chief priests. Cæsar both received them with all other courtesy, and recognizing that they would find life distasteful amidst foreign customs, dispatched them to Gophna, advising them to remain there for the present, and promising to restore every man's property, so soon as he had leisure after the war. They accordingly retired, gladly and in perfect security, to the small town assigned; but when nothing more was seen of them, the rebels again circulated a report that the deserters had been slaughtered by the Romans, with the evident intention of deterring

the rest from attempting to escape. The ruse, as before, was successful for a while, terror checking desertions.

3. Subsequently, however, Titus recalled these men from Gophna and ordered them to go round the ramparts with Josephus and let the people see them; whereupon great numbers fled to the Romans. Grouped together and standing before the Roman lines, the refugees, with lamentation and tears, implored the rebels, as their best course, to admit the Romans freely to the city and to save the fatherland; or, failing that, at all events to withdraw from the Temple and to preserve the sacred edifice for them, since the Romans would never venture, except under the direst necessity, to set fire to the holy places.

These appeals only excited fiercer opposition, and retorting by heaping abuse upon the deserters, they ranged their quick-firers, catapults, and *ballistæ* above the holy gates, so that the surrounding temple-court from the multitude of dead resembled a common burial-ground and the Temple itself a fortress. Into those hallowed and inviolable precincts they rushed in arms, their hands yet hot with the blood of their countrymen; and to such lengths of crime did they proceed, that the indignation which the Jews might naturally have displayed had the Romans inflicted such wanton outrages upon them was now manifested by the Romans against the Jews, for profaning their own sacred places. Of the soldiers, indeed, there was not one who did not regard the Temple with awe and reverence and pray that the brigands might relent ere it met with irretrievable calamity.

4. Titus, yet more deeply distressed, again upbraided John and his friends. "Was it not you," he said, "most abominable wretches, who placed this balustrade before your sanctuary? Was it not you that ranged along it those slabs, engraved in Greek characters and in our own, proclaiming that none may pass the barrier? And did we not permit you to put to death any who passed it, even were he a Roman? Why then, you miscreants, do you now actually trample corpses underfoot within it? Why do you defile your temple with the blood of for-

eigner and native? I call the gods of my fathers to witness and any deity that once watched over this place—
for now I believe that there is none—I call my army, the
Jews within my lines, and you yourselves to witness that
it is not I who force you to pollute these precincts. Exchange the arena of conflict for another and not a Roman shall approach or insult your holy places; nay, I
will preserve the Temple for you, even against your will."

5. This message from Cæsar being transmitted through
Josephus, the brigands and their tyrant, attributing his
exhortations rather to cowardice than goodwill, treated
them with contempt. Titus, thereupon, seeing that these
men had neither compassion for themselves nor regard
for the Temple, once more reluctantly resumed hostilities.
It was impossible to bring up his whole force against
them owing to the confined nature of the ground; he
therefore selected thirty of the best men from each century, entrusted every thousand to a tribune, and ap-
pointing Cerealius commander-in-chief, gave orders to
attack the guards about the ninth hour of the night.
He was himself in arms and prepared to descend with
them, but was restrained by his friends on account of
the gravity of the risk and the observations of the officers, who remarked that he would achieve more by sitting still in Antonia as director of the contest of his
troops than by going down and exposing himself in the
forefront; for under the eyes of Cæsar all would play
the man. To this persuasion Cæsar yielded, telling his
men that his sole reason for remaining behind was that
he might judge of their gallantry, so that none of the
brave might go unnoticed and unrewarded nor any of
an opposite character escape the penalty, but that he,
who had power both to punish and to reward, might be
a spectator and witness of all. At the hour mentioned he
dispatched them upon their enterprise, while he himself
advanced to a spot from which he could see all below,
and from Antonia anxiously awaited the issue.

6. The force thus dispatched did not, however, find
the guards asleep, as they had hoped, but, the latter
springing up with a shout, they were instantly involved
in a close struggle; and at the cry of the sentries their

comrades dashed out in a dense body from within. The
Romans met the charge of the front ranks, while those
behind fell foul of their own party, and many treated
their friends as foes. For recognition by the voice was
rendered impossible for any by the confused din on
either side, as was ocular recognition by the darkness of
the night; moreover, some were so blinded by passion
and others by fear as to strike indiscriminately all who
fell in their way. The Romans, who interlocked their
shields and charged by companies, suffered less from
such ignorance; each man, too, recollected the watchword. But the Jews, constantly scattering and alike attacking and retreating at random, were frequently taken
by each other for enemies: each man in the darkness
receiving a returning comrade as if he were an advancing Roman. Indeed more were wounded by their own
friends than by the foe, until, with the dawn of day,
the battle thenceforward was discernible to the eye and,
parting into their respective lines, they could employ
their missiles and maintain their defense in good order.

Nor did either side give way or relax its efforts. The
Romans, as under the eye of Cæsar, vied man with man
and company with company, each believing that that
day would lead to his promotion, if he but fought with
gallantry. The Jews had as arbiter of their own daring
deeds their fear for themselves and for the Temple, and
the looming presence of the tyrant, encouraging some,
rousing others by the lash and by menaces into action.
The contest was perforce for the most part stationary,
the maneuvers to and fro being limited to a narrow
space and quickly over; for neither side had room for
flight or pursuit. And at every incident of the fight an
appropriate roar went up from Antonia; were their comrades gaining, they shouted to them to be of good cheer,
were they falling back, to stand fast. It was like a battle on the stage, for nothing throughout the engagement
escaped the eyes of Titus or of those around him. At
length, after an action which opened at the ninth hour
of the night, they broke off about the fifth hour of the
day, neither side having seriously repelled their adversaries from the very spot on which the conflict began,

and victory remaining undecided in this drawn battle. Of the Romans many distinguished themselves; the Jewish heroes were, of the ,party of Simon, Judas son of Mareotes, and Simon son of Hosaias; of the Idumæans, James and Simon, the latter the son of Acatelas, the former of Sosas; of John's contingent, Gephthæus and Alexas; of the Zealots, Simon son of Ari.

7. Meanwhile, the rest of the Roman army, having in seven days overthrown the foundations of Antonia, had prepared a broad ascent to the Temple. The legions now approaching the first wall began to raise embankments: one facing the northwest angle of the inner temple, a second over against the northern hall which stood between the two gates, and two more; one opposite the western portico of the outer court of the Temple, the other outside opposite the northern portico. The works, however, did not advance without causing the troops great fatigue and hardship, the timber being conveyed from a distance of a hundred furlongs. They also suffered occasionally from stratagems owing to their overwhelming superiority, being themselves less on their guard, while they found the Jews through their present despair of escape more daring than before.

Thus, some of the cavalry, whenever they went out to collect wood or fodder, used to take the bridles off their horses and turn them loose to graze while they were foraging; and these the Jews, sallying out in companies, carried off. This happening repeatedly, Cæsar, correctly believing that these raids were due rather to the negligence of his own men than to the courage of the Jews, determined by an act of unusual severity to make the rest more attentive to the care of their horses. He accordingly ordered off one of the troopers who had lost his horse to capital punishment, and by that fearful example preserved the steeds of the others; for they no longer let them graze, but went forth on their errands clinging to them as though man and beast were by nature inseparable. The assault on the Temple and the erection of the earthworks thus occupied the energies of the Romans.

8. The day after the ascent of the legions, many

of the rebels, who with plunder now failing them were
hard pressed by famine, joined forces and attacked the
Roman sentries on the Mount of Olives at about the
eleventh hour of the day; expecting firstly to find them
off their guard, and secondly to catch them while taking refreshment, and thus easily to break through. The
Romans, however, forewarned of their approach, promptly rushed from the neighboring forts to the spot and
checked their forcible efforts to scale or to cut their
way through the camp wall. A sharp contest ensued, in
which many gallant feats were performed on either side;
the Romans displaying military skill combined with
strength, the Jews reckless impetuosity and unbridled
rage. Shame commanded the one party, necessity the
other; for to let loose the Jews, now caught as it were
in a net, seemed to the Romans most disgraceful, while
their enemy's one hope of safety lay in forcing their
way through the wall.

Among other incidents, a trooper from one of the cohorts, named Pedanius—when the Jews were at last
repulsed and being driven down into the ravine—urging his horse at top speed along their flank, snatched
up one of the flying foe, a youth of sturdy frame and
in full armor, grasping him by the ankle; so far did he
stoop from his horse when at the gallop, and such mus-
cular strength of arm and body, along with consummate
horsemanship, did he display. Carrying off his captive
like some precious treasure, he came with his prize to
Cæsar. Titus expressed his admiration of the captor's
strength, ordered his captive to punishment for his assault on the wall, and then devoted his attention to the
struggle for the Temple and the acceleration of the earthworks.

9. Meanwhile the Jews, sorely suffering from their
encounters, as the war slowly yet steadily rose to a
climax and crept towards the sanctuary, cut away, as
from a mortifying body, the limbs already affected, to
arrest further ravages of the disease. In other words, they
set fire to that portion of the north-west portico which
was connected with Antonia, and afterwards hacked
away some twenty cubits, their own hands thus begin-

ning the conflagration of the holy places. Two days later, on the twenty-fourth of the month above mentioned, the Romans set light to the adjoining portico; and when the flames had spread to a distance of fifty cubits, it was again the Jews who cut away the roof, and with no reverence whatever for these works of art severed the connection thereby formed with Antonia. For that reason, though they might have prevented the building from being set alight, instead when the fire attacked it they remained motionless and merely measured the extent of its ravages by their own convenience. Thus conflicts around the Temple raged incessantly, and fights between small parties sallying out upon each other were continuous.

10. In the course of these days a Jew, named Jonathan, a man of mean stature and despicable appearance, undistinguished by birth or otherwise, coming forward opposite the tomb of the high priest John [Hyrcanus], and addressing the Romans in much opprobrious language, challenged the best of them to single combat. Of those in the adverse ranks at this point, the majority regarded him with contempt, some probably with apprehension, while others were influenced by the not unreasonable reflection that it was wise to avoid a conflict with one who courted death; being aware that men who despaired of their lives had not only ungovernable passions but also the ready compassion of the Deity, and that to risk life in an encounter with persons, whom to defeat were no great exploit, while to be beaten would involve ignominy as well as danger, would be an act, not of bravery, but of recklessness.

For long no antagonist came forward and the Jew continued to rail at them as cowards—for the fellow was supremely conceited and contemptuous of the Romans —until a trooper from one of the squadrons, named Pudens, disgusted at his language and arrogance, perhaps also thoughtlessly presuming on his puny stature, leaped forward, and was otherwise gaining on his adversary in the encounter, when he was betrayed by fortune, for he fell; whereupon Jonathan sprang upon him and dispatched him. Then, trampling on the corpse,

317

brandishing his bloody sword, and with his left hand
waving his buckler, he shouted lustily to the army,
glorying over his prostrate foe and jeering at his Roman spectators until, in the midst of his dancing and
buffoonery, Priscus, a centurion, bent his bow and trans-
fixed him with an arrow, calling forth from Jews and
Romans simultaneous cries of a contrary nature. The
victim, writhing in agony, fell upon the body of his
foe, illustrating how swift in war is the nemesis that
overtakes irrational success. . . .

iv. 2. . . . The troops were by now setting fire to the
gates, and the silver melting all around quickly admitted
the flames to the woodwork, whence they spread in dense
volumes and caught hold of the porticoes. The Jews,
seeing the fire encircling them, were deprived of all
energy of body and mind; in utter consternation none
attempted to ward off or extinguish the flames. Paralyzed, they stood and looked on. Yet, though dismayed by
the ravage being wrought, they learned no lesson with
regard to what was left, but as if the very sanctuary
were now ablaze, only whetted their fury against the
Romans. So throughout that day and the ensuing night
the fire prevailed; for they could only set light to portions of the porticoes, and not to the whole range at
once.

3. On the following day Titus, after giving orders to
a division of his army to extinguish the fire and make
a road to the gates to facilitate the ascent of the legions, called together his generals. Six of his chief staff-
officers were assembled, namely Tiberius Alexander, the
prefect of all the forces; Sextus Cerealius, Larcius Lepi-
dus, and Titus Phrygius, the respective commanders of
the fifth, tenth, and fifteenth legions; Fronto Haterius,
prefect of the two legions from Alexandria; and Marcus
Antonius Julianus, procurator of Judæa; and the procurators and tribunes being next collected, Titus brought
forward for debate the subject of the Temple.

Some were of opinion that the law of war should be
enforced, since the Jews would never cease from rebellion while the Temple remained as the focus for con-
course from every quarter. Others advised that if the

Jews abandoned it and placed no weapons whatever upon it, it should be saved, but that if they mounted it for purposes of warfare, it should be burned; as it would then be no longer a temple, but a fortress, and thenceforward the impiety would be chargeable not to the Romans, but to those who forced them to take such measures. Titus, however, declared that even were the Jews to mount it and fight therefrom, he would not wreak vengeance on inanimate objects instead of men, nor under any circumstances burn down so magnificent a work; for the loss would affect the Romans, inasmuch as it would be an ornament to the empire if it stood. Fortified by this pronouncement, Fronto, Alexander, and Cerealius now came over to his view. He then dissolved the council, and directing the officers to allow the other troops an interval of repose, that he might find them reinvigorated in action, he gave orders to the picked men from the cohorts to open a road through the ruins and extinguish the fire.

4. Throughout that day, fatigue and consternation crushed the energies of the Jews; but on the following day, with recruited strength and renewed courage, they sallied out through the eastern gate upon the guards of the outer court of the Temple, at about the second hour. The Romans stubbornly met their charge, and forming a screen in front with their shields like a wall, closed up their ranks; it was evident, however, that they could not long hold together, being no match for the number and fury of their assailants. Cæsar, who was watching the scene from Antonia, anticipating the breaking of the line, now brought up his picked cavalry to their assistance. The Jews could not withstand their onset: the fall of the foremost led to a general retreat. Yet whenever the Romans retired [the Jews] returned to the attack, only to fall back once more when their opponents wheeled round; until, about the fifth hour of the day, the Jews were overpowered and shut up in the inner court of the Temple.

5. Titus then withdrew to Antonia, determined on the following day, at dawn, to attack with his whole force, and invest the Temple. That building, however,

God indeed long since had sentenced to the flames; but now in the revolution of the years had arrived the fated day: the tenth of the month Lous [Ab], the day on which of old it had been burned by the king of Babylon. The flames, however, owed their origin and cause to God's own people, for, on the withdrawal of Titus, the insurgents, after a brief respite, again attacked the Romans, and an engagement ensued between the guards of the sanctuary and the troops who were endeavoring to extinguish the fire in the inner court; the latter routing the Jews and pursuing them right up to the sanctuary. At this moment, one of the soldiers, awaiting no orders and with no horror of so dread a deed, but moved by some supernatural impulse, snatched a brand from the burning timber and, hoisted up by one of his comrades, flung the fiery missile through a low golden door, which gave access on the north side to the chambers surrounding the sanctuary. As the flame shot up, a cry, as poignant as the tragedy, arose from the Jews, who flocked to the rescue, lost to all thought of self-preservation, all husbanding of strength, now that the object of all their past vigilance was vanishing.

6. Titus was resting in his tent after the engagement, when a messenger rushed in with the tidings. Starting up just as he was, he ran to the Temple to arrest the conflagration; behind him followed his whole staff of generals, while in their train came the excited legionaries, and there was all the hubbub and confusion attending the disorderly movement of so large a force. Cæsar, both by voice and hand, signalled to the combatants to extinguish the fire; but they neither heard his shouts, drowned in the louder din which filled their ears, nor heeded his beckoning hand, distracted as they were by the fight or their fury. The impetuosity of the legionaries, when they joined the fray, neither exhortation nor threat could restrain; passion was for all the only leader. Crushed together about the entrances, many were trampled down by their companions; many, stumbling on the still hot and smoldering ruins of the porticoes, suffered the fate of the vanquished. As they drew nearer to the sanctuary they pretended not even

to hear Cæsar's orders and shouted to those in front of them to throw in the firebrands. The insurgents, for their part, were now powerless to help; and on all sides was carnage and flight. Most of the slain were civilians, weak and unarmed people, each butchered where he was caught. Around the altar a pile of corpses was accumulating; down the steps of the sanctuary flowed a stream of blood, and the bodies of the victims killed above went sliding to the bottom.

7. Cæsar, finding himself unable to restrain the impetuosity of his frenzied soldiers, and the fire gaining the mastery, passed with his generals within the building and beheld the holy place of the sanctuary and all that it contained—things far exceeding the reports current among foreigners and not inferior to their proud reputation among ourselves. As the flames had nowhere yet penetrated to the interior, but were consuming the chambers surrounding the temple, Titus, correctly assuming that the structure might still be saved, rushed out and by personal appeals endeavored to induce the soldiers to quench the fire; while he directed Liberalius, a centurion of his bodyguard of lancers, to restrain, by resort to clubs, any who disobeyed orders. But their respect for Cæsar and their fear of the officer who was endeavoring to check them were overpowered by their rage, their hatred of the Jews, and a lust for battle more unruly still. Most of them were further stimulated by the hope of plunder, believing that the interior was full of money and actually seeing that all the surroundings were made of gold. However, the end was precipitated by one of those who had entered the building, and who, when Cæsar rushed out to restrain the troops, thrust a firebrand, in the darkness, into the hinges of the gate. At once a flame shot up from the interior, Cæsar and his generals withdrew, and there was none left to prevent those outside from kindling a blaze. Thus, against Cæsar's wishes, was the Temple set on fire.

8. Deeply as one must mourn for the most marvellous edifice which we have ever seen or heard of, whether we consider its structure, its magnitude, the richness of its every detail, or the reputation of its holy places, yet

may we draw very great consolation from the thought
that there is no escape from Fate, for works of art and
places any more than for living beings. And one may
well marvel at the exactness of the cycle of Destiny; for,
as I said, she waited until the very month and the very
day on which in bygone times the Temple had been
burned by the Babylonians. From its first foundation by
King Solomon up to its present destruction, which took
place in the second year of Vespasian's reign, the total
period amounts to one thousand one hundred and thirty
years seven months and fifteen days; from its rebuilding by Haggai in the second year of the reign of Cyrus
until its fall under Vespasian, six hundred and thirty-
nine years and forty-five days.

v. 1. While the Temple blazed, the victors plundered
everything that fell in their way and slaughtered wholesale all who were caught. No pity was shown for age,
no reverence for rank. Children and greybeards, laity
and priests alike were massacred; every class was pursued and encompassed in the grasp of war, whether
suppliants for mercy or offering resistance. The roar of
the flames streaming far and wide mingled with the
groans of the falling victims; and owing to the height
of the hill and the mass of the burning pile, one would
have thought that the whole city was ablaze. And then
the din—nothing more deafening or appalling could be
conceived than that. There were the war-cries of the
Roman legions sweeping onward in mass, the howls of
the rebels encircled by fire and sword, the rush of the
people who, cut off above, fled panic-stricken only to
fall into the arms of the foe, and their shrieks as they
met their fate. With the cries on the hill were blended
those of the multitude in the city below; and now many
who were emaciated and tongue-tied from starvation,
when they beheld the sanctuary on fire, gathered strength
once more for lamentations and wailing. Peræa and the
surrounding mountains contributed their echoes, deepen-
ing the din. But yet more awful than the uproar were
the sufferings. You would indeed have thought that the
temple-hill was boiling over from its base, being everywhere one mass of flame, but yet that the stream of

blood was more copious than the flames and the slain more numerous than the slayers. For the ground was nowhere visible through the corpses, but the soldiers had to clamber over heaps of bodies in pursuit of the fugitives. The brigand crowd succeeded in pushing through the Romans and with difficulty forcing their way into the outer court of the Temple, and thence to the city; while what was left of the populace took refuge on the outer portico. Of the priests some, at the first, tore up the spikes from the sanctuary, with their leaden sockets, and hurled them at the Romans, but afterwards, finding their efforts unavailing and the flames breaking out against them, they retired to the wall, which was eight cubits broad, and there remained. Two persons of distinction, however, having the choice of saving their lives by going over to the Romans or of holding out and sharing the fortune of the rest, plunged into the fire and were consumed with the temple, namely Meirus, son of Belgas, and Josephus, son of Dalæus.

2. The Romans, thinking it useless, now that the Temple was on fire, to spare the surrounding buildings, set them all alight, both the remnants of the porticoes and the gates, excepting two, one on the east and the other on the south; these also they subsequently razed to the ground. They further burned the treasury-chambers, in which lay vast sums of money, vast piles of raiment, and other valuables; for this, in short, was the general repository of Jewish wealth, to which the rich had consigned the contents of their dismantled houses. They then proceeded to the one remaining portico of the outer court, on which the poor women and children of the populace and a mixed multitude had taken refuge, numbering six thousand. And before Cæsar had come to any decision or given any orders to the officers concerning these people, the soldiers, carried away by rage, set fire to the portico from below; with the result that some were killed plunging out of the flames, others perished amidst them, and out of all that multitude not a soul escaped. They owed their destruction to a false prophet, who had on that day proclaimed to the people in the city that God commanded them to go up to the Temple

court, to receive there the tokens of their deliverance. Numerous prophets, indeed, were at this period suborned by the tyrants to delude the people, by bidding them await help from God, in order that desertions might be checked and that those who were above fear and precaution might be encouraged by hope. In adversity man is quickly persuaded; but when the deceiver actually pictures release from prevailing horrors, then the sufferer wholly abandons himself to expectation.

3. Thus it was that the wretched people were deluded at that time by charlatans and pretended messengers of the Deity; while they neither heeded nor believed in the manifest portents that foretold the coming desolation, but as if thunderstruck and bereft of eyes and mind, disregarded the plain warnings of God. So it was when a star, resembling a sword, stood over the city, and a comet, which continued for a year. So again when, before the revolt and the commotion that led to war, at the time when the people were assembling for the feast of unleavened bread, on the eighth of the month Xanthicus, at the ninth hour of the night, so brilliant a light shone round the altar and the sanctuary that it seemed to be broad daylight; and this continued for half an hour. By the inexperienced this was regarded as a good omen, but by the sacred scribes it was at once interpreted in accordance with after events.

At that same feast a cow that had been brought by someone for sacrifice gave birth to a lamb in the midst of the court of the Temple. Moreover, the eastern gate of the inner court—it was of brass and very massive, and when closed towards evening could scarcely be moved by twenty men; fastened with iron-bound bars, it had bolts which were sunk to a great depth into a threshold consisting of a solid block of stone—this gate was observed at the sixth hour of the night to have opened of its own accord. The watchmen of the Temple ran and reported the matter to the captain, and he came up and with difficulty succeeded in shutting it. This again to the uninitiated seemed the best of omens, as they supposed that God had opened to them the gate of blessings; but the learned understood that the security of the Temple was dissolving of its own accord and that the opening of the gate meant a present to the enemy, interpreting the portent in their own minds as indicative of coming desolation.

Again, not many days after the festival, on the twenty-first of the month Artemisium, there appeared a miraculous phenomenon, passing belief. Indeed, what I am about to relate would, I imagine, have been deemed a fable, were it not for the narratives of eyewitnesses and for the subsequent calamities which deserved to be so signalized. For, before sunset throughout all parts of the country, chariots were seen in the air and armed battalions hurtling through the clouds and encompassing the cities. Moreover, at the feast which is called Pentecost, the priests on entering the inner court of the Temple by night, as their custom was in the discharge of their ministrations, reported that they were conscious, first of a commotion and a din, and after that of a voice as of a host, "We are departing hence."

But a further portent was even more alarming. Four years before the war, when the city was enjoying profound peace and prosperity, there came to the feast at which it is the custom of all Jews to erect tabernacles to God, one Jesus, son of Ananias, a rude peasant, who, standing in the Temple, suddenly began to cry out, "A voice from the east, a voice from the west, a voice from the four winds; a voice against Jerusalem and the sanctuary, a voice against the bridegroom and the bride, a voice against all the people." Day and night he went about all the alleys with this cry on his lips. Some of the leading citizens, incensed at these ill-omened words, arrested the fellow and severely chastised him. But he, without a word on his own behalf or for the private ear of those who smote him, only continued his cries as before. Thereupon, the magistrates, supposing, as was indeed the case, that the man was under some supernatural impulse, brought him before the Roman governor. There, although flayed to the bone with scourges, he neither sued for mercy nor shed a tear, but merely introducing the most mournful of variations into his ejaculation, responded to each stroke with, "Woe to Jerusalem!" When Albinus, the governor, asked him who and whence he was and why he uttered these cries, he answered him never a word, but unceasingly reiterated his dirge over the city, until Albinus pronounced him a maniac and let him go.

During the whole period up to the outbreak of war he neither approached nor was seen talking to any of the citizens, but daily, like a prayer that he had conned, repeated his lament, "Woe to Jerusalem!" He neither cursed any of those who beat him from day to day, nor blessed those who offered him food: to all men that melancholy presage was his one reply. His cries were loudest at the festivals. So for seven years and five months he continued his wail, his voice never flagging nor his strength exhausted, until in the siege, having seen his presage verified, he found his rest. For, while going his round and shouting in piercing tones from the wall, "Woe once more to the city and to the people and to the temple," as he added a last word, "and woe to me also," a stone hurled from the *ballista* struck and killed him on the spot. So with those ominous words still upon his lips he passed away.

4. Reflecting on these things one will find that God has a care for men, and by all kinds of premonitory signs shows His people the way of salvation, while they owe their destruction to folly and calamities of their own choosing. Thus the Jews, after the demolition of Antonia, reduced the Temple to a square, although they had it recorded in their oracles that the city and the sanctuary would be taken when the Temple should become four-square. But what more than all else incited them to the war was an ambiguous oracle, likewise found in their sacred scriptures, to the effect that at that time one from their country would become ruler of the world. This they understood to mean someone of their own race, and many of their wise men went astray in their interpretation of it. The oracle, however, in reality signified the sovereignty of Vespasian, who was proclaimed emperor on Jewish soil. For all that, it is impossible for men to escape their fate, even though they foresee it. Some of these portents, then, the

Jews interpreted to please themselves, others they treated
with contempt, until the ruin of their country and their
own destruction convicted them of their folly.

vi. 1. The Romans, now that the rebels had fled
to the city, and the sanctuary itself and all around it
were in flames, carried their standards into the Temple
court, and setting them up opposite the eastern gate,
there sacrificed to them, and with rousing acclamations hailed Titus as imperator. So glutted with plunder
were the troops, one and all, that throughout Syria the
standard of gold was depreciated to half its former
value.

Among the priests still holding out on the wall of
the sanctuary a lad, who was parched with thirst, confessed his condition to the Roman guards and besought
them to pledge him security. Taking pity on his youth
and distress, they promised him protection; whereupon
he came down and drank, and then, after filling with
water a vessel which he had brought with him, raced
back to his comrades above. The guards all failing to
catch him and cursing his perfidy, he replied that he
had broken no covenant; for the accepted pledge did not
bind him to remain with them, but merely permitted
him to descend and procure water. Both these actions
he had done, and therefore considered that he had been
true to his word. Such cunning, especially in so young
a boy, astonished the Romans whom he had outwitted;
however, on the fifth day, the priests, now famishing,
came down, and being conducted by the guards to Titus,
implored him to spare their lives. But he told them that
the time for pardon had for them gone by, that the one
thing for whose sake he might with propriety have
spared them was gone, and that it behoved priests to
perish with their temple, and so ordered them to
execution.

2. The tyrants and their followers, beaten on all
sides in the war and surrounded by a wall preventing
any possibility of escape, now invited Titus to a parley.
Anxious, with his innate humanity, at all events to
save the town, and instigated by his friends, who supposed that the brigands had at length been brought to

reason, Titus took up a position on the west of the outer court of the Temple; there being at this point gates opening above the Xystus and a bridge which connected the upper city with the Temple and now parted the tyrants from Cæsar. The multitude stood in crowds on either side: the Jews around Simon and John, excited by hopes of pardon, the Romans beside Cæsar eagerly waiting to hear their claim. Titus, after charging his troops to keep a check on their rage and their missiles, and stationing an interpreter beside him, proceeded, in token of his conquest, to address them first.

"Well, sirs, are you at length sated with your country's woes—you who, without bestowing a thought on our strength or your own weakness, have through inconsiderate fury and madness lost your people, your city, and your Temple, and are yourselves justly doomed to perish—you who from the first, ever since Pompey reduced you by force, never ceased from revolution and have now ended by declaring open war upon the Romans? Did you rely on numbers? Nay, a mere fraction of the Roman soldiery has proved your match. On the fidelity of allies? Pray, what nation beyond the limits of our empire would prefer Jews to Romans? On physical strength, perhaps? Yet you are aware that the Germans are our slaves. On the solidity of your walls? But what wall could be a greater obstacle than the ocean, encompassed by which the Britons yet do homage to the Roman arms? On the determination of spirit and the astuteness of your generals? Yet you knew that even Carthaginians were defeated.

"No, assuredly you were incited against the Romans by Roman humanity. To begin with, we allowed you to occupy this land and set over you kings of your own blood; then we maintained the laws of your forefathers and permitted you, not only among yourselves but also in your dealings with others, to live as you willed. Above all, we permitted you to exact tribute for God and to collect offerings, without either admonishing or hindering those who brought them—only that you might grow richer at our expense and make preparations with our money to attack us! And then, enjoying such privileges, you turned your superabundance against the donors, and like untameable reptiles spat your venom upon those who caressed you.

"You held, be it granted, Nero's indolence in contempt, and, like fractures or ruptures, remained for a time malignantly quiescent, only to show your true character on the outbreak of a more serious malady, when you let your ambitions soar unbounded to shameless expectations. My father came into the country, not to punish you for events under Cestius, but to admonish you. Had he come to extirpate the nation, his duty surely was to hasten to the root of your strength and to sack this city forthwith; whereas he proceeded to ravage Galilee and the surrounding district, thus affording you time for repentance. But by you his humanity was taken for weakness, and upon our clemency you nursed your audacity. On Nero's decease, you acted like the basest scoundrels. Emboldened by our intestine troubles, when I and my father had departed for Egypt, you abused your opportunities by preparing for hostilities, and were not ashamed to harass those, now made emperors, whose humanity as generals you had experienced.

"Thus, when the empire found refuge in us, when throughout its length was universal tranquillity and foreign nations were sending embassies of congratulation, once again the Jews were in arms. There were embassies from you to your friends beyond the Euphrates fostering revolt; fortifications being built up anew; seditions, contentions of tyrants, and civil war—the only things befitting men so base. I came to this city, the bearer of gloomy injunctions from my reluctant father. The news that the townsfolk were disposed to peace rejoiced my heart. As for you, before hostilities began I urged you to pause; for a long while after you had begun them I spared you: I gave pledges of protection to deserters, I kept faith with them when they fled to me. Many were the prisoners whom I compassionated, forbidding their oppressors to torture them; with reluctance I brought up my engines against your walls; my soldiers, thirsting for your blood, I invariably restrained;

after every victory, as if defeated myself, I invited you to
peace. On approaching the Temple, again in deliberate
forgetfulness of the laws of war, I besought you to spare
your own shrines and to preserve the temple for yourselves, offering you unmolested egress and assurance
of safety, or, if you so wished, an opportunity for battle
on some other arena. All offers you scorned and with
your own hands set fire to the Temple.

"And after all this, most abominable wretches, do
you now invite me to a parley? What have you to save
comparable to what is lost? What protection do you
think you deserve after losing your temple? Nay, even
now you stand in arms, and at the last extremity, do
not so much as pretend to be suppliants. Miserable men,
on what do you rely? Is not your folk dead, your temple
gone, your city at my mercy? Are not your very lives in
my hands? And do you yet deem it glorious bravery to
die in the last ditch? I, however, will not emulate your
frenzy. Throw down your arms, surrender your persons,
and I grant you your lives, like a lenient master of a
household punishing the incorrigible and preserving the
rest for myself."

3. To this they replied that they could not accept a
pledge from him, having sworn never to do so; but they
asked permission to pass through his line of circumval-
lation with their wives and children, undertaking to retire
to the desert and to leave the city to him. Thereupon
Titus, indignant that men in the position of captives
should proffer proposals to him as victors, ordered proclamation to be made to them neither to desert nor to
hope for terms any longer, for he would spare none;
but to fight with all their might and save themselves as
best they could, because all his actions henceforth would
be governed by the laws of war. He then gave his
troops permission to burn and sack the city. For that
day they refrained; but on the next they set fire to the
archives, the Acra, the council-chamber, and the region
called Ophlas, the flames spreading as far as the palace
of Queen Helena, which was in the center of the Acra.
The streets also were burned and the houses, packed with
the bodies of the victims of the famine. . . .

330

[*The Romans now prepare for the final onslaught, on the upper town.*]

viii. 3. During those same days, one of the priests named Jesus, son of Thebuthi, after obtaining a sworn pledge of protection from Cæsar, on condition of his delivering up some of the sacred treasures, came out and handed over from the wall of the sanctuary two lamp-stands similar to those deposited in the sanctuary, along with tables, bowls, and platters, all of solid gold and very massive. He further delivered up the veils, the high priests' vestments, including the precious stones, and many other articles used in public worship. Further-more, the treasurer of the temple, by name Phineas, being taken prisoner, disclosed the tunics and girdles worn by the priests, an abundance of purple and scarlet kept for necessary repairs to the veil of the temple, along with a mass of cinnamon and cassia and a mul-titude of other spices, which they mixed and burned daily as incense to God. Many other treasures also were delivered up by him, with numerous sacred ornaments; those services procuring for him, although a prisoner of war, the pardon accorded to the refugees.

4. The earthworks having now been completed after eighteen days' labor, on the seventh of the month Gor-piæus the Romans brought up the engines. Of the rebels, some, already despairing of the city, retired from the ramparts to the Acra, others slunk down into the mines; many, however, posting themselves along the wall, attempted to repel those who were bringing up the siege-engines. But these too the Romans over-powered by numbers and force, but above all, by the high spirits in which they faced men already dispirited and unnerved. And when a portion of the wall broke down and some of the towers succumbed to the battering of the rams, the defenders at once took flight, and even the tyrants were seized with a needlessly serious alarm. For before the enemy had surmounted the breach they were paralyzed and on the verge of flight; and those men, erstwhile so haughty and proud of their impious crimes, might then be seen abject and trembling—a

331

transformation that, even in such villains, was pitiable. They were indeed eager to make a dash for the wall enclosing them, repel the guards, cut their way through and escape; but when they could nowhere see their old faithful henchmen—for these had fled whithersoever the crisis suggested—and when men came running up with tidings, some that the whole western wall was overthrown, others that the Romans had broken through and were even now at hand in search of them, while yet others, whose eyes were bewildered by fright, declared that they could actually see the enemy from the towers, they fell upon their faces, bemoaning their own infatuation, and as though their sinews had been cut from under them, were impotent to fly.

Here may we signally discern at once the power of God over unholy men and the fortune of the Romans. For the tyrants stripped themselves of their security and descended of their own accord from those towers, whereon they could never have been overcome by force, and famine alone could have subdued them; while the Romans, after all the toil expended over weaker walls, mastered by the gift of fortune those that were impregnable to their artillery. For the three towers, which we have described above, would have defied every engine of war.

5. Having then abandoned these, or rather been driven down from them by God, they found immediate refuge in the ravine below Siloam; but afterwards, having recovered a little from their panic, they rushed upon the adjoining section of the barrier. Their courage, however, proving unequal to the occasion (for their strength was now broken alike by terror and misfortune), they were repulsed by the guards and dispersing hither and thither slunk down into the mines.

The Romans, now masters of the walls, planted their standards on the towers, and with clapping of hands and jubilation raised a pæan in honor of their victory. They had found the end of the war a much lighter task than the beginning; indeed, they could hardly believe that they had surmounted the last wall without bloodshed, and seeing none to oppose them, were truly perplexed. Pouring into the alleys, sword in hand, they massacred indiscriminately all whom they met, and burned the houses with all who had taken refuge within. Often in the course of their raids, on entering the houses for loot, they would find whole families dead and the rooms filled with the victims of the famine, and then, shuddering at the sight, retire empty-handed. Yet, while they pitied those who had thus perished, they had no similar feelings for the living, but running everyone through who fell in their way, they choked the alleys with corpses and deluged the whole city with blood, insomuch that many of the fires were extinguished by the gory stream.

Towards evening they ceased slaughtering, but when night fell the fire gained the mastery, and the dawn of the eighth day of the month Gorpiæus [about September 26th] broke upon Jerusalem in flames—a city that had suffered such calamities during the siege that, had she from her foundation enjoyed an equal share of blessings, she would have been thought unquestionably enviable; a city undeserving, moreover, of these great misfortunes on any other ground, save that she produced a generation such as that which caused her overthrow.

ix. 1. Titus, on entering the town, was amazed at its strength, but chiefly at the towers, which the tyrants, in their infatuation, had abandoned. Indeed, when he beheld their solid lofty mass, the magnitude of each block and the accuracy of the joinings, and marked how great was their breadth, how vast their height, "God indeed," he exclaimed, "has been with us in the war. God it was who brought down the Jews from these strongholds; for what power have human hands or engines against these towers?" He made many similar observations to his friends at that time, when he also liberated all prisoners of the tyrants who were found in the forts. And when, at a later period, he demolished the rest of the city and razed the walls, he left these towers as a memorial of his attendant fortune, to whose co-operation he owed his conquest of defenses which defied assault.

2. Since the soldiers were now growing weary of

slaughter, though numerous survivors still came to light, Cæsar issued orders to kill only those who were found in arms and offered resistance and to make prisoners of the rest. The troops, in addition to those specified in their instructions, slew the old and feeble, while those in the prime of life and serviceable they drove together into the Temple and shut them up in the court of the women. Cæsar appointed one of his freedmen as their guard, and his friend Fronto to adjudicate upon the lot appropriate to each. Fronto put to death all the seditious and brigands, information being given by them against each other; he selected the tallest and most handsome of the youth and reserved them for the triumph; of the rest, those over seventeen years of age he sent in chains to the mines in Egypt, while multitudes were presented by Titus to the various provinces, to be destroyed in the theaters by the sword or by wild beasts; those under seventeen were sold. During the days spent by Fronto over this scrutiny, eleven thousand of the prisoners perished from starvation, partly owing to their jailers' hatred, who denied them food, partly through their own refusal of it when offered; moreover, for so vast a multitude even corn failed.

3. The total number of prisoners taken throughout the entire war amounted to ninety-seven thousand, and of those who perished during the siege, from first to last, to one million one hundred thousand. Of these the greater number were of Jewish blood, but not natives of the place; for, having assembled from every part of the country for the feast of unleavened bread, they found themselves suddenly enveloped in the war, with the result that this over-crowding produced first pestilence, and later the added and more rapid scourge of famine. That the city could contain so many is clear from the count taken under Cestius. For he, being anxious to convince Nero, who held the nation in contempt, of the city's strength, instructed the chief priests, if by any means possible, to take a census of the population. Accordingly, on the occasion of the feast called Passover, at which they sacrifice from the ninth to the eleventh hour, and a little fraternity, as it were, gathers round

each sacrifice, of not fewer than ten persons (feasting alone not being permitted), while the companies often include as many as twenty, the victims were counted and amounted to two hundred and fifty-five thousand six hundred; allowing an average of ten diners to each victim, we obtain a total of two million seven hundred thousand, all pure and holy. For those afflicted with leprosy or gonorrhea, or menstruous women, or persons otherwise defiled were not permitted to partake of this sacrifice, nor yet any foreigners present for worship, (4) and a large number of these assemble from abroad.

But now the whole nation had been shut up by fate as in a prison, and the city when war encompassed it was packed with inhabitants. The victims thus outnumbered those of any previous visitation, human or divine. For when all who showed themselves had been either slain or made prisoners by the Romans, the victors instituted a search for those in the mines, and tearing up the ground, slew all whom they met. Here too were found upwards of two thousand dead, of whom some had been destroyed by their own, and some by one another's hands, but the greater number by famine. So horrible was the stench from the bodies which met the intruders, that many instantly withdrew, but others penetrated further through avarice, trampling over heaps of corpses; for many precious objects were found in these passages, and lucre legalized every expedient. Many also of the tyrants' prisoners were brought up; for even at the last they did not abandon their cruelty.

God, however, visited both with fit retribution; for John, perishing of hunger with his brethren in the mines, implored from the Romans that protection which he had so often spurned, and Simon, after a long struggle with necessity, to be related hereafter, surrendered; the latter was reserved for execution at the triumph, while John was sentenced to perpetual imprisonment. The Romans now set fire to the outlying quarters of the town and razed the walls to the ground.

x. 1. Thus was Jerusalem taken in the second year of the reign of Vespasian on the eighth of the month Gorpiæus. Captured on five previous occasions, it was now for the second time devastated. Asochæus, king of Egypt, and after him Antiochus [Epiphanes], then Pompey, and subsequently Sossius in league with Herod took the city but preserved it. But before their days the king of Babylon had subdued it and laid it waste, fourteen hundred and sixty-eight years and six months after its foundation. Its original founder was a Canaanite chief, called in the native tongue "Righteous King" [Melchizedek]; for such indeed he was. In virtue thereof he was the first to officiate as priest of God, and being the first to build the Temple, gave the city, previously called Solyma, the name of Jerusalem. The Canaanite population was expelled by David, the king of the Jews, who established his own people there; and four hundred and seventy-seven years and six months after his time it was razed to the ground by the Babylonians. The period from King David, its first Jewish sovereign, to its destruction by Titus was one thousand one hundred and seventy-nine years; and from its first foundation until its final overthrow, two thousand one hundred and seventy-seven. Howbeit, neither its antiquity, nor its ample wealth, nor its people spread over the whole habitable world, nor yet the great glory of its religious rites, could aught avail to avert its ruin. Thus ended the siege of Jerusalem.

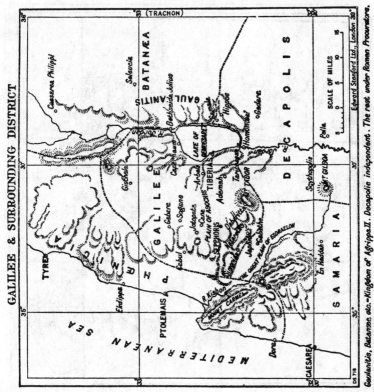

GALILEE & SURROUNDING DISTRICT

Gaulanitis, Batanæa etc.=Kingdom of Agrippa II. Decapolis independent. The rest under Roman Procurators.

Edward Stanford Ltd., London 39°

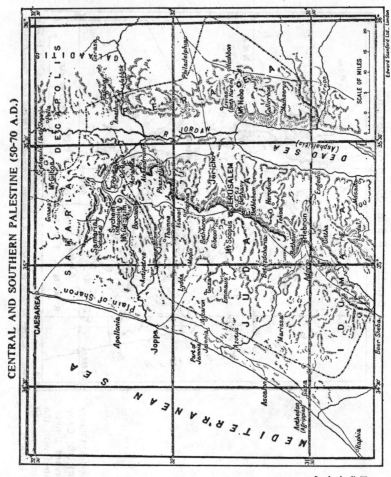

CENTRAL AND SOUTHERN PALESTINE (50-70 A.D.)

Hugh R. Trevor-Roper, general editor of *The Great Histories Series,* is the distinguished Regius Professor of Modern History at Oxford University. He is probably most well known to American readers for his book *The Last Days of Hitler,* which is a classic in the field of modern German history and was the result of official investigations carried out by Professor Trevor-Roper at the behest of British Intelligence in an attempt to unshroud the mystery surrounding the dictator's fate. The book has already been translated into twenty foreign languages. Professor Trevor-Roper is a specialist in sixteenth- and seventeenth-century history and has published several other notable works: *Archbishop Laud, Men and Events.* He has contributed numerous articles on political and historical subjects to the journals and is familiar to American readers of *The New York Times Magazine* and *Horizon.*

Moses I. Finley received his M.A. and Ph.D. from Columbia University and has held research and teaching posts in several American universities. In 1955 he settled in England, and is presently a Fellow of Jesus College and Reader in Ancient Social and Economic History, University of Cambridge. He has written *Studies in Land and Credit in Ancient Athens, The World of Odysseus,* and *The Ancient Greeks* and has edited *The Greek Historians* and *Slavery in Classical Antiquity.* He has contributed numerous articles and reviews to learned journals, as well as to the *New York Review of Books* and *Horizon.*

339

Index

A

Aaron, 50, 56
Abednego see Azariah
Abel, 32-33
Abilmathadachos, 67
Abraham, 39, 42, 48, 55, 283
Acatelas, 315
Achiab, 175, 186, 188
Acme, 171, 175
Ada, 33
Adam, 30-32, 34, 36
Adoreus, 89
Against Apion (Josephus), vii, viii, x, xix, xxxii, xxxiii, 13-22
Agrippa (son of Aristobulus), 156, 202, 207-208
Agrippa II (King of Galilee), 3, 6, 8, 9, 22, 211, 215, 258
Albinus, 326
Alexander (brother of Archelaus), 191-193
Alexander the Great, xi, xiii, xxiii
Alexander (son of Aristobulus), 88, 89, 91, 92, 102, 119, 135, 137-139, 141-143, 145-148, 150-156, 157-158, 161-163, 169, 172
Alexandra, 92
Alexandreion, 88, 89, 90
Alexandria, xiv
Alexas, 128, 159, 174, 315
Aliturus, xiv
Amathus, 89
Amram, 39, 40, 42
Ananias, 203
Ananias (peasant), 325
Ananias (son of Sadok), 211
Annæus, 207
Anthedon, 89
"Antigone," 121
Antigonus, 88, 94, 101, 103, 104, 105, 107, 109-115, 117-119, 121-123, 175, 285
Antioch, 92, 102

Antiochus Epiphanes, xi, xv, 19, 74, 82, 116, 215, 285, 336
Antipas, 172, 175, 181, 190
Antipater, xiii, 82, 91-96, 98, 99, 102, 108, 109, 135, 137-139, 141-142, 146, 150-152, 156-168, 171-172, 175, 182-183, 285
Antiphilus, 163
Antiquities (Justus), x
Antiquities of the Romans (Dionysius), xxi
Antonius, 239
Antony, Marc, xii, 84, 88, 89, 90, 92, 99, 102, 103, 109, 110, 111, 114, 116, 117, 120, 122, 126-129, 136
Apamea, 87, 98
Apollonia, 89
Arabia, xi
Arabs, 108
Aramaic (language), xiv, xv
Archelaus, 137, 139, 146-151, 153, 154, 157-158, 164, 172, 176, 178-184, 187, 189-194, 200
Arethusa, 88
Ari, 315
Arinus, 268
Arioches, 63, 64
Aristeus, 299
Aristobulus II, xiii, 84, 119, 135, 137, 141, 143, 146, 150-153, 156, 157-158, 161-162, 164, 191, 202, 285
Arius, 187-188
Armenians, 37
Artabazes, 122
Artaxerxes I, 20
Ascalon, 92
Aschans, 61-62
Asia Minor, xiv
Asochæus, 336
Assyrian Empire, 81
Astyages, 70
Athenion, 124
Athrongæus, 186
Atratinus, 109

341

343

345